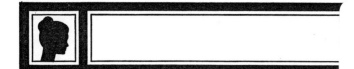

MW01153941

# MENTAL JOGGING

# MENTAL JOGGING

365 Games to Enjoy, to Stimulate the Imagination,
to Increase Ability to Solve Problems and Puzzles

## REID J. DAITZMAN

RICHARD MAREK PUBLISHERS
NEW YORK

Designed by Iris Bass

**Library of Congress Cataloging in Publication Data**

Daitzman, Reid J
    Mental jogging.

    1. Psychological recreations. 2. Word games.
I. Title.
GV1507.P9D33        128'.2        79-16602
ISBN 0-399-90053-5

Printed in the United States of America

# CONTENTS

# INTRODUCTION

MENTAL JOGGING consists of 365 exercises (one for each day) to stimulate creative problem solving of ordinary life events, objects, and experiences. There are no "right" or "wrong" answers. No special expertise in logic, mathematics, science, or art is necessary to do well on the Mental Jogging exercises. The only criterion for success will be your willingness to produce novel and "strange" associations. The items are obvious, difficult, challenging—but fun. Many of the "answers" will evolve over a day, a week, or longer. Be sure to carry a pen or pencil and scratch paper with you at all times. Mental Jogging is addictive. Share and compare your answers with friends. Completing a Mental Jogging item will be as exhilarating as completing a swift 3-mile run. In fact, the best analogy to Mental Jogging is physical jogging.

Mental Jogging is as important as physical jogging. Both the mind and the body must be constantly stimulated for maximum performance. The benefits of physical jogging are well known, and include improved cardiovascular output, lower blood pressure, less frequent illness, increased stamina, and an increased sense of well-being. Likewise, the Mental Jogging exercises are structured to stimulate creative problem solving and to generate novel and unique solutions to ordinary problems. You will be less "bogged-down" at work and at home with solutions that don't feel right. You may be able to break out of a rut by challenging prior solutions and coming up with more viable alternatives.

Included with the Mental Jogging exercises are "warm-up" mental calisthenics. As in physical jogging, a short period prior to the more intense workout is crucial for maximum performance. These mental calisthenics should precede the Mental Jogging exercise.

In physical jogging, it would be impossible to run a marathon after only a 2-week practice and conditioning. Likewise, it would be extremely difficult to generate 40 to 50 responses for each Mental Jogging exercise the first time around. Thus, at first you should be extremely satisfied if you generate the number indicated (e.g., 6, 7, 8, or 9). Later you will find yourself exceeding this minimum number quite effortlessly and perhaps generating 50 to 60 responses per Mental Jogging exercise. (Some of the contributors generated as many as 80 "answers" per item!) Again, the analogy is from physical jogging. Those first few miles at the beginning of training were difficult, whereas the same few miles after running for a few months are now effortless and extremely enjoyable, i.e., the "runner's high."

In fact, a wonderful way to stimulate the production of novel and unique solutions to the Mental Jogging exercises is to first clear your mind through running. Try a Mental Jogging exercise before and after a light workout. Notice the difference between the two mental states. You will probably be more open, less structured, and innovative in your thinking after the physical jogging.

It is important to remember that the Mental Jogging exercises have no "right" or "wrong" answers. Any answer, no matter how "way-out" and "crazy," is a correct answer. Actually, the purpose of Mental Jogging is for you to be able to get to those "crazy" answers that you would not ordinarily think of. For example, take the Mental Jogging exercise ". . . ways to make a phone stop ringing." Typical answers may include: "answer it," "don't answer it," "don't pay your phone bill," "cut the cord," "turn the volume control to off," "blow up the utility company," "remove the bell," "go deaf," "live on an island without electricity," "hook the bell to a light," etc. The first few answers are rather straightforward and are part of our experience. However, the last few answers are "way-out." Try this exercise with a friend and see how many of these answers or other answers are generated.

You may also want to brainstorm with a group of friends and jointly generate answers. As you proceed through Mental Jogging you will become more aware, sensitive, and perceptive of objects and relationships around you. You will become an inventor in the true sense of the word.

Very little is known about the psychology of creative activities. Most scientists conceive a creative situation to be one that combines realistic thinking and imagination. Mental Jogging offers structured exercises that combine many of the characteristics of both problem solving and fantasy. The Mental Jogging exercises resemble fantasy because they call upon the reorganization of past experiences as well as present needs. However, the "solutions" are far from pure fantasy in that they are under voluntary control. The processes of combining both realistic thinking, imagination, and fantasy vary widely among individuals. Certain groups of people engage in occupations that others consider highly creative. However, many of us have jobs and routines that do not allow the full expression of our creative powers. From the time we were children, we have been told "what do do," "how to do it," and "whe to do it." Each of us has passed through fairly set developmental stages in which both intellectual and social expectations were rigidly enforced by society and friends. Hence, we proceeded through our education, first job, and social relationships without thinking about the "why" involved in our decisions. Consequentially, most of us have learned quite adaptively to be "uncreative." We may feel we are stuck in dead-end jobs, supervised by a boss who doesn't know as much as we do, and given tasks to perform that are rather narrow and ill-defined.

Mental Jogging is designed to give you an opportunity to become more sensitive, aware, and alive to objects and relationships around you. As you explore your own answers and share them with others, you will, in turn, learn more about yourself. The fascinating aspect of Mental Jogging is that answers will change as you grow older. Children may have answers to the Mental Jogging exercises that are quite different from those of adults, though both may be equally "right." Many children have not had the opportunity to be controlled by definite patterns, rules, and habits, as much as older folks. The tensions between conformity and spontaneity have not as yet developed. In most organizations, institutions, and even families, emphasis is often placed on the proper forms and techniques, rather than on expressing one's own emotions, perceptions, and ideas. Students acquire conformist modes of expression rather than develop free and spontaneous ones. They have learned that in order to be successful, conformity and dependence are reinforced. Likewise, it is often difficult to both satisfy one's creative potential and to rise within an organization.

It may be difficult, but not impossible! The practice of Mental Jogging will make you a more creative problem solver within your organization. Any business problem may be approached with the same spontaneity of expression as your completion of the Mental Jogging exercises. Take, for example, the problem of ". . . why Factory X is not producing the same quality materials as Factory Y, although the two plants are 'similar' in every respect." Some typical solutions may involve: "personnel," "working conditions," "fringe benefits," "work-break spacing," "poor record-keeping," "unionism," "equipment failure," "sabotage," etc. Can you think of 6 other reasons?

Regular practice increases skill and maximizes performance. Since there are 365 Mental Jogging exercises, you may want to complete one exercise per day, preferably after one warm-up calisthenic or physical jogging. Your productivity will increase dramatically if you practice regularly.

Typical "answers" are included with each Mental Jogging exercise. These answers should be used only as a guide. The answers were generated in response to an advertisement in the Mensa Bulletin. Mensa is an international organization of individuals who place in the upper 2 percent of the population mentally, as measured by standardized tests of intelligence. Some answers were also generated by high school students in New Jersey and Connecticut. A list of those contributors follows the exercises.

8

Your total score depends upon the number of responses generated for any one Mental Jogging exercise. The exercises in this book ask variously for a minimum of 6, 7, 8, or 9 responses. The minimum number of responses (6, 7, 8, or 9, depending upon the exercise) receive 1 point each. You then receive bonuses of 2, 3, 4, or 5 points for every response beyond the minimum. Thus in the exercise "seven or more reasons why blind people ski," you would receive 7 points if you listed 7 reasons, 6 points for 6 reasons, 5 points for 5 reasons, and so on. If you generated 8 to this exercise, you would receive 2 bonus points. Bonus points are awarded for 7, 8, 9, or 10 or more answers, depending upon the exercise. Likewise Super Bonus responses, Extra Super Bonus responses, and Genius responses are worth 3, 4, and 5 points respectively. *In order to simplify your computation of the total score, refer to the Scoring Key on page 11.*

I would be interested in hearing from those *individuals* who score a total of 25,000 points for the 365 Mental Jogging exercises. (These individuals will be listed as Mental Jogging Marathoners in possible future editions of this book.) Finally, if you would like to be considered as a Contributor to Mental Jogging II, forward your name and a self-addressed stamped envelope to me at the address below. You will be sent a list of 20 new Mental Jogging exercises to be completed and possibly included in Mental Jogging II.

A list of Mental Jogging Resources is included in the back of the book. These resources summarize just a tiny amount of the massive scientific literature on creativity. Most college libraries have the cited journals. Leaf through a few. It is stimulating to read how scientists have gone about the business of measuring creativity and outlining those variables that will maximize the expression of creativity.

Welcome to Mental Jogging.

Reid J. Daitzman
1425 Bedford Street, Suite 1A
Stamford, Conn. 06905

# HOW TO CALCULATE YOUR SCORE

1. For each answer up to the number requested, give yourself 1 point.
2. For every bonus answer up to 25, give yourself 2 points each.
3. For answers 26 to 30, give yourself 3 points each.
4. For answers 31 to 50, give yourself 4 points each.
5. For answers 51 to 55 or more, give yourself 5 points each.

## WHAT THE TOTAL SCORE MEANS

|  | six or more | seven or more | eight or more | nine or more |
|---|---|---|---|---|
| Ok, but try harder! | 1–6 | 1–7 | 1–8 | 1–9 |
| Good work! | 8–22 | 9–23 | 10–24 | 11–25 |
| Excellent! You have untapped potential | 24–44 | 25–43 | 26–42 | 27–41 |
| Truly creative | 47–75 | 46–74 | 45–73 | 44–72 |
| Inventor, artist | 79–139 | 78–138 | 77–137 | 76–136 |
| Marathoner, magician | 144+ | 143+ | 142+ | 141+ |

One-half of eight is zero

"So easy it seemed
Once found,
Which yet unfound most would have
Thought impossible."

John Milton

# EXERCISES

# JANUARY

### Mental Calisthenic #1

Sit in a comfortable position, take three deep breaths, and exhale very slowly from your nostrils. Close your eyes and imagine the color RED, then ORANGE, YELLOW, GREEN, BLUE, VIOLET. Arrange the colors alphabetically, from left to right, in your mind. Make them disappear one at a time. Open your eyes. Proceed with a Mental Jogging exercise.

## 1. Six or more ways to avoid spilling coffee while driving

| Response | Score |
|---|---|
| 1. _____ | 1 |
| 2. _____ | 1 |
| 3. _____ | 1 |
| 4. _____ | 1 |
| 5. _____ | 1 |
| 6. _____ | 1 |

| Bonus Responses | |
|---|---|
| 7. _____ | 2 |
| 8. _____ | 2 |
| 9. _____ | 2 |
| 10. _____ | 2 |
| 11. _____ | 2 |
| 12. _____ | 2 |
| 13. _____ | 2 |
| 14. _____ | 2 |
| 15. _____ | 2 |
| 16. _____ | 2 |

Total ☐

## 2. Six or more ways to avoid lightning and thunder

| Response | Score |
|---|---|
| 1. _____ | 1 |
| 2. _____ | 1 |
| 3. _____ | 1 |
| 4. _____ | 1 |
| 5. _____ | 1 |
| 6. _____ | 1 |

| Bonus Responses | |
|---|---|
| 7. _____ | 2 |
| 8. _____ | 2 |
| 9. _____ | 2 |
| 10. _____ | 2 |
| 11. _____ | 2 |
| 12. _____ | 2 |
| 13. _____ | 2 |
| 14. _____ | 2 |
| 15. _____ | 2 |
| 16. _____ | 2 |

Total ☐

## 3. Eight or more things to do in a dark room

| Response | Score |
|---|---|
| 1. _____ | 1 |
| 2. _____ | 1 |
| 3. _____ | 1 |
| 4. _____ | 1 |
| 5. _____ | 1 |
| 6. _____ | 1 |
| 7. _____ | 1 |
| 8. _____ | 1 |
| **Bonus Responses** | |
| 9. _____ | 2 |
| 10. _____ | 2 |
| 11. _____ | 2 |
| 12. _____ | 2 |
| 13. _____ | 2 |
| 14. _____ | 2 |
| 15. _____ | 2 |
| 16. _____ | 2 |

Total ☐

## 4. Six or more things you'd say to the president of the United States

| Response | Score |
|---|---|
| 1. _____ | 1 |
| 2. _____ | 1 |
| 3. _____ | 1 |
| 4. _____ | 1 |
| 5. _____ | 1 |
| 6. _____ | 1 |
| **Bonus Responses** | |
| 7. _____ | 2 |
| 8. _____ | 2 |
| 9. _____ | 2 |
| 10. _____ | 2 |
| 11. _____ | 2 |
| 12. _____ | 2 |
| 13. _____ | 2 |
| 14. _____ | 2 |
| 15. _____ | 2 |
| 16. _____ | 2 |

Total ☐

## 5. Eight or more things you've never said to your brother or sister

| Response | Score |
|---|---|
| 1. _____ | 1 |
| 2. _____ | 1 |
| 3. _____ | 1 |
| 4. _____ | 1 |
| 5. _____ | 1 |
| 6. _____ | 1 |
| 7. _____ | 1 |
| 8. _____ | 1 |
| **Bonus Responses** | |
| 9. _____ | 2 |
| 10. _____ | 2 |
| 11. _____ | 2 |
| 12. _____ | 2 |
| 13. _____ | 2 |
| 14. _____ | 2 |
| 15. _____ | 2 |
| 16. _____ | 2 |

Total ☐

## 6. Six or more things not to say to an Eskimo

| Response | Score |
|---|---|
| 1. _____ | 1 |
| 2. _____ | 1 |
| 3. _____ | 1 |
| 4. _____ | 1 |
| 5. _____ | 1 |
| 6. _____ | 1 |
| **Bonus Responses** | |
| 7. _____ | 2 |
| 8. _____ | 2 |
| 9. _____ | 2 |
| 10. _____ | 2 |
| 11. _____ | 2 |
| 12. _____ | 2 |
| 13. _____ | 2 |
| 14. _____ | 2 |
| 15. _____ | 2 |
| 16. _____ | 2 |

Total ☐

## 7. Six or more ways to tell if someone is a vampire

| Response | Score |
|---|---|
| 1. _____ | 1 |
| 2. _____ | 1 |
| 3. _____ | 1 |
| 4. _____ | 1 |
| 5. _____ | 1 |
| 6. _____ | 1 |

Bonus Responses

| | |
|---|---|
| 7. _____ | 2 |
| 8. _____ | 2 |
| 9. _____ | 2 |
| 10. _____ | 2 |
| 11. _____ | 2 |
| 12. _____ | 2 |
| 13. _____ | 2 |
| 14. _____ | 2 |
| 15. _____ | 2 |
| 16. _____ | 2 |

Total ☐

## 8. Eight or more things to look for from the plane window while flying

| Response | Score |
|---|---|
| 1. _____ | 1 |
| 2. _____ | 1 |
| 3. _____ | 1 |
| 4. _____ | 1 |
| 5. _____ | 1 |
| 6. _____ | 1 |
| 7. _____ | 1 |
| 8. _____ | 1 |

Bonus Responses

| | |
|---|---|
| 9. _____ | 2 |
| 10. _____ | 2 |
| 11. _____ | 2 |
| 12. _____ | 2 |
| 13. _____ | 2 |
| 14. _____ | 2 |
| 15. _____ | 2 |
| 16. _____ | 2 |

Total ☐

## 9. Seven or more ways to provoke a ghost

| Response | Score |
|---|---|
| 1. _____ | 1 |
| 2. _____ | 1 |
| 3. _____ | 1 |
| 4. _____ | 1 |
| 5. _____ | 1 |
| 6. _____ | 1 |
| 7. _____ | 1 |

Bonus Responses

| | |
|---|---|
| 8. _____ | 2 |
| 9. _____ | 2 |
| 10. _____ | 2 |
| 11. _____ | 2 |
| 12. _____ | 2 |
| 13. _____ | 2 |
| 14. _____ | 2 |
| 15. _____ | 2 |
| 16. _____ | 2 |

Total ☐

## 10. Six or more ways to prevent shivering on a cold day

| Response | Score |
|---|---|
| 1. _____ | 1 |
| 2. _____ | 1 |
| 3. _____ | 1 |
| 4. _____ | 1 |
| 5. _____ | 1 |
| 6. _____ | 1 |

Bonus Responses

| | |
|---|---|
| 7. _____ | 2 |
| 8. _____ | 2 |
| 9. _____ | 2 |
| 10. _____ | 2 |
| 11. _____ | 2 |
| 12. _____ | 2 |
| 13. _____ | 2 |
| 14. _____ | 2 |
| 15. _____ | 2 |
| 16. _____ | 2 |

Total ☐

## 11. Seven or more ways to make sunlight

| Response | Score |
|---|---|
| 1. _____ | 1 |
| 2. _____ | 1 |
| 3. _____ | 1 |
| 4. _____ | 1 |
| 5. _____ | 1 |
| 6. _____ | 1 |
| 7. _____ | 1 |

**Bonus Responses**

| | |
|---|---|
| 8. _____ | 2 |
| 9. _____ | 2 |
| 10. _____ | 2 |
| 11. _____ | 2 |
| 12. _____ | 2 |
| 13. _____ | 2 |
| 14. _____ | 2 |
| 15. _____ | 2 |
| 16. _____ | 2 |

Total ☐

## 12. Seven or more non-dietary uses of ice cream

| Response | Score |
|---|---|
| 1. _____ | 1 |
| 2. _____ | 1 |
| 3. _____ | 1 |
| 4. _____ | 1 |
| 5. _____ | 1 |
| 6. _____ | 1 |
| 7. _____ | 1 |

**Bonus Responses**

| | |
|---|---|
| 8. _____ | 2 |
| 9. _____ | 2 |
| 10. _____ | 2 |
| 11. _____ | 2 |
| 12. _____ | 2 |
| 13. _____ | 2 |
| 14. _____ | 2 |
| 15. _____ | 2 |
| 16. _____ | 2 |

Total ☐

## 13. Six or more ways to count to ten

| Response | Score |
|---|---|
| 1. _____ | 1 |
| 2. _____ | 1 |
| 3. _____ | 1 |
| 4. _____ | 1 |
| 5. _____ | 1 |
| 6. _____ | 1 |

**Bonus Responses**

| | |
|---|---|
| 7. _____ | 2 |
| 8. _____ | 2 |
| 9. _____ | 2 |
| 10. _____ | 2 |
| 11. _____ | 2 |
| 12. _____ | 2 |
| 13. _____ | 2 |
| 14. _____ | 2 |
| 15. _____ | 2 |
| 16. _____ | 2 |

Total ☐

## 14. Six or more ways to remember your dreams

| Response | Score |
|---|---|
| 1. _____ | 1 |
| 2. _____ | 1 |
| 3. _____ | 1 |
| 4. _____ | 1 |
| 5. _____ | 1 |
| 6. _____ | 1 |

**Bonus Responses**

| | |
|---|---|
| 7. _____ | 2 |
| 8. _____ | 2 |
| 9. _____ | 2 |
| 10. _____ | 2 |
| 11. _____ | 2 |
| 12. _____ | 2 |
| 13. _____ | 2 |
| 14. _____ | 2 |
| 15. _____ | 2 |
| 16. _____ | 2 |

Total ☐

## 15. Six or more ways to look at the stars

| Response | Score |
|---|---|
| 1. _____ | 1 |
| 2. _____ | 1 |
| 3. _____ | 1 |
| 4. _____ | 1 |
| 5. _____ | 1 |
| 6. _____ | 1 |

**Bonus Responses**

| | |
|---|---|
| 7. _____ | 2 |
| 8. _____ | 2 |
| 9. _____ | 2 |
| 10. _____ | 2 |
| 11. _____ | 2 |
| 12. _____ | 2 |
| 13. _____ | 2 |
| 14. _____ | 2 |
| 15. _____ | 2 |
| 16. _____ | 2 |

Total ☐

## 16. Seven or more uses of beach sand

| Response | Score |
|---|---|
| 1. _____ | 1 |
| 2. _____ | 1 |
| 3. _____ | 1 |
| 4. _____ | 1 |
| 5. _____ | 1 |
| 6. _____ | 1 |
| 7. _____ | 1 |

**Bonus Responses**

| | |
|---|---|
| 8. _____ | 2 |
| 9. _____ | 2 |
| 10. _____ | 2 |
| 11. _____ | 2 |
| 12. _____ | 2 |
| 13. _____ | 2 |
| 14. _____ | 2 |
| 15. _____ | 2 |
| 16. _____ | 2 |

Total ☐

## 17. Eight or more reasons why you shouldn't drop out of school

| Response | Score |
|---|---|
| 1. _____ | 1 |
| 2. _____ | 1 |
| 3. _____ | 1 |
| 4. _____ | 1 |
| 5. _____ | 1 |
| 6. _____ | 1 |
| 7. _____ | 1 |
| 8. _____ | 1 |

**Bonus Responses**

| | |
|---|---|
| 9. _____ | 2 |
| 10. _____ | 2 |
| 11. _____ | 2 |
| 12. _____ | 2 |
| 13. _____ | 2 |
| 14. _____ | 2 |
| 15. _____ | 2 |
| 16. _____ | 2 |

Total ☐

## 18. Six or more ways to avoid long lines at checkout counters

| Response | Score |
|---|---|
| 1. _____ | 1 |
| 2. _____ | 1 |
| 3. _____ | 1 |
| 4. _____ | 1 |
| 5. _____ | 1 |
| 6. _____ | 1 |

**Bonus Responses**

| | |
|---|---|
| 7. _____ | 2 |
| 8. _____ | 2 |
| 9. _____ | 2 |
| 10. _____ | 2 |
| 11. _____ | 2 |
| 12. _____ | 2 |
| 13. _____ | 2 |
| 14. _____ | 2 |
| 15. _____ | 2 |
| 16. _____ | 2 |

Total ☐

## 19. Six or more non-uses of sunglasses

| Response | Score |
|---|---|
| 1. _____ | 1 |
| 2. _____ | 1 |
| 3. _____ | 1 |
| 4. _____ | 1 |
| 5. _____ | 1 |
| 6. _____ | 1 |

**Bonus Responses**

| | |
|---|---|
| 7. _____ | 2 |
| 8. _____ | 2 |
| 9. _____ | 2 |
| 10. _____ | 2 |
| 11. _____ | 2 |
| 12. _____ | 2 |
| 13. _____ | 2 |
| 14. _____ | 2 |
| 15. _____ | 2 |
| 16. _____ | 2 |

Total ☐

## 20. Nine or more ways to tell time without a watch

| Response | Score |
|---|---|
| 1. _____ | 1 |
| 2. _____ | 1 |
| 3. _____ | 1 |
| 4. _____ | 1 |
| 5. _____ | 1 |
| 6. _____ | 1 |
| 7. _____ | 1 |
| 8. _____ | 1 |
| 9. _____ | 1 |

**Bonus Responses**

| | |
|---|---|
| 10. _____ | 2 |
| 11. _____ | 2 |
| 12. _____ | 2 |
| 13. _____ | 2 |
| 14. _____ | 2 |
| 15. _____ | 2 |
| 16. _____ | 2 |

Total ☐

## 21. Eight or more ways to appreciate opera

| Response | Score |
|---|---|
| 1. _____ | 1 |
| 2. _____ | 1 |
| 3. _____ | 1 |
| 4. _____ | 1 |
| 5. _____ | 1 |
| 6. _____ | 1 |
| 7. _____ | 1 |
| 8. _____ | 1 |

**Bonus Responses**

| | |
|---|---|
| 9. _____ | 2 |
| 10. _____ | 2 |
| 11. _____ | 2 |
| 12. _____ | 2 |
| 13. _____ | 2 |
| 14. _____ | 2 |
| 15. _____ | 2 |
| 16. _____ | 2 |

Total ☐

## 22. Six or more uses of the jet stream

| Response | Score |
|---|---|
| 1. _____ | 1 |
| 2. _____ | 1 |
| 3. _____ | 1 |
| 4. _____ | 1 |
| 5. _____ | 1 |
| 6. _____ | 1 |

**Bonus Responses**

| | |
|---|---|
| 7. _____ | 2 |
| 8. _____ | 2 |
| 9. _____ | 2 |
| 10. _____ | 2 |
| 11. _____ | 2 |
| 12. _____ | 2 |
| 13. _____ | 2 |
| 14. _____ | 2 |
| 15. _____ | 2 |
| 16. _____ | 2 |

Total ☐

## 23. Six or more things never to say to a bald-headed man

| Response | Score |
|---|---|
| 1. _____ | 1 |
| 2. _____ | 1 |
| 3. _____ | 1 |
| 4. _____ | 1 |
| 5. _____ | 1 |
| 6. _____ | 1 |

Bonus Responses

| | |
|---|---|
| 7. _____ | 2 |
| 8. _____ | 2 |
| 9. _____ | 2 |
| 10. _____ | 2 |
| 11. _____ | 2 |
| 12. _____ | 2 |
| 13. _____ | 2 |
| 14. _____ | 2 |
| 15. _____ | 2 |
| 16. _____ | 2 |

Total ☐

## 24. Six or more ways to play bridge without a full deck

| Response | Score |
|---|---|
| 1. _____ | 1 |
| 2. _____ | 1 |
| 3. _____ | 1 |
| 4. _____ | 1 |
| 5. _____ | 1 |
| 6. _____ | 1 |

Bonus Responses

| | |
|---|---|
| 7. _____ | 2 |
| 8. _____ | 2 |
| 9. _____ | 2 |
| 10. _____ | 2 |
| 11. _____ | 2 |
| 12. _____ | 2 |
| 13. _____ | 2 |
| 14. _____ | 2 |
| 15. _____ | 2 |
| 16. _____ | 2 |

Total ☐

## 25. Eight or more reasons for not exploring Mars

| Response | Score |
|---|---|
| 1. _____ | 1 |
| 2. _____ | 1 |
| 3. _____ | 1 |
| 4. _____ | 1 |
| 5. _____ | 1 |
| 6. _____ | 1 |
| 7. _____ | 1 |
| 8. _____ | 1 |

Bonus Responses

| | |
|---|---|
| 9. _____ | 2 |
| 10. _____ | 2 |
| 11. _____ | 2 |
| 12. _____ | 2 |
| 13. _____ | 2 |
| 14. _____ | 2 |
| 15. _____ | 2 |
| 16. _____ | 2 |

Total ☐

## 26. Seven or more ways to fell a tree without an ax

| Response | Score |
|---|---|
| 1. _____ | 1 |
| 2. _____ | 1 |
| 3. _____ | 1 |
| 4. _____ | 1 |
| 5. _____ | 1 |
| 6. _____ | 1 |
| 7. _____ | 1 |

Bonus Responses

| | |
|---|---|
| 8. _____ | 2 |
| 9. _____ | 2 |
| 10. _____ | 2 |
| 11. _____ | 2 |
| 12. _____ | 2 |
| 13. _____ | 2 |
| 14. _____ | 2 |
| 15. _____ | 2 |
| 16. _____ | 2 |

Total ☐

## 27. Six or more ways to plow a field without a tractor

| Response | Score |
|---|---|
| 1. _____ | 1 |
| 2. _____ | 1 |
| 3. _____ | 1 |
| 4. _____ | 1 |
| 5. _____ | 1 |
| 6. _____ | 1 |

**Bonus Responses**

| Response | Score |
|---|---|
| 7. _____ | 2 |
| 8. _____ | 2 |
| 9. _____ | 2 |
| 10. _____ | 2 |
| 11. _____ | 2 |
| 12. _____ | 2 |
| 13. _____ | 2 |
| 14. _____ | 2 |
| 15. _____ | 2 |
| 16. _____ | 2 |

Total ☐

## 28. Seven or more ways to make a phone stop ringing

| Response | Score |
|---|---|
| 1. _____ | 1 |
| 2. _____ | 1 |
| 3. _____ | 1 |
| 4. _____ | 1 |
| 5. _____ | 1 |
| 6. _____ | 1 |
| 7. _____ | 1 |

**Bonus Responses**

| Response | Score |
|---|---|
| 8. _____ | 2 |
| 9. _____ | 2 |
| 10. _____ | 2 |
| 11. _____ | 2 |
| 12. _____ | 2 |
| 13. _____ | 2 |
| 14. _____ | 2 |
| 15. _____ | 2 |
| 16. _____ | 2 |

Total ☐

## 29. Eight or more ways to show love

| Response | Score |
|---|---|
| 1. _____ | 1 |
| 2. _____ | 1 |
| 3. _____ | 1 |
| 4. _____ | 1 |
| 5. _____ | 1 |
| 6. _____ | 1 |
| 7. _____ | 1 |
| 8. _____ | 1 |

**Bonus Responses**

| Response | Score |
|---|---|
| 9. _____ | 2 |
| 10. _____ | 2 |
| 11. _____ | 2 |
| 12. _____ | 2 |
| 13. _____ | 2 |
| 14. _____ | 2 |
| 15. _____ | 2 |
| 16. _____ | 2 |

Total ☐

## 30. Eight or more uses of red ribbon

| Response | Score |
|---|---|
| 1. _____ | 1 |
| 2. _____ | 1 |
| 3. _____ | 1 |
| 4. _____ | 1 |
| 5. _____ | 1 |
| 6. _____ | 1 |
| 7. _____ | 1 |
| 8. _____ | 1 |

**Bonus Responses**

| Response | Score |
|---|---|
| 9. _____ | 2 |
| 10. _____ | 2 |
| 11. _____ | 2 |
| 12. _____ | 2 |
| 13. _____ | 2 |
| 14. _____ | 2 |
| 15. _____ | 2 |
| 16. _____ | 2 |

Total ☐

## 31. Seven or more ways to get from New Orleans to Paris

| Response | Score |
|---|---|
| 1. _____ | 1 |
| 2. _____ | 1 |
| 3. _____ | 1 |
| 4. _____ | 1 |
| 5. _____ | 1 |
| 6. _____ | 1 |
| 7. _____ | 1 |

Bonus Responses

| | |
|---|---|
| 8. _____ | 2 |
| 9. _____ | 2 |
| 10. _____ | 2 |
| 11. _____ | 2 |
| 12. _____ | 2 |
| 13. _____ | 2 |
| 14. _____ | 2 |
| 15. _____ | 2 |
| 16. _____ | 2 |

Total ☐

# CONTRIBUTORS' SAMPLE RESPONSES

## 1. Six or more ways to avoid spilling coffee while driving

1. Drink tea.
2. Hold your cup out the sun roof.
3. Get a cup with a lid.
4. Freeze it and eat it like ice cream.
5. Drive slowly and avoid potholes.
6. Have a cup holder molded to your dashboard.
7. Drink it through a baby bottle.
8. Bring coffee candy.
9. Put the cup in a gyroscopically stabilized cup holder (electronically controlled, plugs into cigarette lighter).
10. Drink it before it has a chance to spill.
11. Dump it into a large container.
12. Avoid having it in a moving car in the first place.
13. Mount the cup on a gyroscopically controlled gimbal.
14. Give it to someone with a steady hand.
15. Don't allow the car to move until you drink to a safely low level.
16. Have coffee in a sealed container—do not attempt to drink.
17. Drink beer.
18. Drink soda.
19. Drive slowly.
20. Drive smoothly.
21. Choose a car with an automatic gearbox.
22. Find a straight road.
23. Find a smooth road.
24. Drink from a baby's cup.
25. Drink through a straw.
26. Put the coffee in a vaporizer.
27. Put a little liquid in a large container.
28. Install a dispensing device on car roof or door.
29. Fix a tube directly down your throat.
30. Avoid jerky arm movements.
31. Lower mouth to coffee, not vice versa.
32. Put some sponge rubber in the coffee.
33. Steer with one hand.
34. Steer with your knees.
35. Steer with your feet.
36. Drink only in traffic jams.
37. Drink only when stopped at a red light.
38. Drink the whole lot in one gulp.
39. Let go of the wheel and hope nothing is on a collision course.
40. Freeze coffee into cubes.
41. Leave in its powdered form; do not add water.
42. Leave as coffee beans.
43. Add gelatine and leave to cool.
44. Drive only golf balls (single handed).
45. Put coffee on the grass while driving your golf ball.
46. Drive a steam roller in preference to a car.
47. Drive only a flock of sheep.
48. Avoid drinking coffee whilst driving.
49. Spill coffee whilst stationary.
50. Buy a better car.
51. Hire a chauffeur.
52. Fill the cup half full.
53. Clutch the coffee up tightly between your thighs.
54. Drink coffee intravenously.
55. Stop car.

## 2. Six or more ways to avoid lightning and thunder

1. Move to a desert.
2. Lock yourself in the bathroom without windows.
3. Hide under the bed.
4. Pull down the shades and turn the stereo on extremely loud.
5. Marry a weather-person.
6. Become a weather-person.
7. Build an underground shelter and sit in it.
8. Close your eyes and ears.
9. Move to where the sky is sunny and clear.
10. Fly above the clouds in a plane.
11. Kill Thor.
12. Go in the house.
13. Turn off *Young Frankenstein.*
14. Stay in the basement on a dry floor.
15. Pray (especially if you're working up in a tree at the moment).
16. Stay in the lowest place possible if in the open.
17. Don't stand under trees.
18. Put earplugs in your ears (so you don't hear the thunder).
19. Don't stand in a puddle.
20. Hide in a closet.
21. Wear heavy rubber boots.
22. Sit in a car and don't touch metallic objects.
23. Live in an airplane that remains constantly above thunderclouds.
24. Move to Antarctica.
25. Move to the North Pole.
26. Never venture out of your windowless, soundproof room.
27. Surgically sever your auditory and optical nerves.
28. Kill yourself.
29. Take a rocket to a point above the earth's atmosphere.
30. Live underground.
31. Bury your head firmly under a pillow whenever you see rain.
32. Have yourself hypnotized to lose the ability to perceive lightning and thunder.
33. Live where they are rare, the moon, for example.
34. Get weather forecasts and fly away if storms are forecast.
35. Go to sleep.
36. Go down a coal mine.
37. Erect massive lightning conductor.
38. Meditate.
39. Put on a radio and stay indoors.
40. Live in a submarine.
41. Go to the moon.
42. Lock yourself in a soundproof closet.
43. Be blind and deaf.
44. Call it a different name.
45. Have a warning system.

## 3. Eight or more things to do in a dark room

1. Fulfill your sexual fantasies.
2. Get high.
3. Listen to rock groups like Styx and Kansas.
4. Sleep.
5. Have a deep, meaningful talk with your lover *after* fulfilling your sexual fantasies.
6. Have a séance.
7. Get dressed and see if you match at all.
8. Pretend you're blind.
9. Pretend you are an unborn baby in a womb.
10. Cuddle up with your lover.
11. Read Braille.
12. Kiss.
13. Play blindman's buff.
14. Develop film.
15. See a movie.
16. Tell ghost stories.
17. Be afraid.
18. Think.
19. Listen to music.
20. Pretend it's light.
21. Picture something in your mind and ask someone else to guess what it is.
22. Tell things about yourself and philosophize about life.
23. Describe objects and have someone else guess what they are (like riddles).
24. Tell jokes.
25. Crawl around the room and get the feel of what it's like without seeing it.
26. Rub your eyes and watch the flashes and bursts of light.
27. Think about the mysteries of life.
28. Pray.
29. Think about what you'll do once you get out of the dark room.
30. Think about ways to make light in the room.
31. Pretend you're floating in space, far away from the world and alone.
32. Make out with a girl.
33. Make out with a guy.
34. Watch television.
35. Have a quiet discussion.
36. Have a candlelight dinner.
37. Repair the electrical wiring.
38. Meditate.
39. Look out the window.
40. Wonder why the lights went out.
41. Complain about the irresponsible power company.
42. Light a match.
43. Light a candle.
44. Turn on the lights.
45. Do nothing.
46. Try (unsuccessfully) to read a book.
47. Recite poetry.
48. Make a telephone call.
49. Water plants.
50. Pace back and forth.
51. Urinate.
52. Pack a suitcase.
53. Teach a person with sight what it's like to be blind.
54. Masturbate.
55. Get dressed so when someone asks, "What did you do? Get dressed in the dark?" you can answer yes.
56. Get laid.
57. Make love.
58. Yoga.
59. Converse.
60. Drink.
61. Practice uses of other senses than sight.
62. Hold an encounter group.
63. Do 5BX exercises.
64. Turn the lights on and make love.
65. Open the shades.
66. Count potatoes.
67. Knit.
68. Play the piano.

69. Jump on a pogo stick.
70. Relax.
71. Study the stars.
72. Eat.

## 4. Six or more things you'd say to the President of the United States

1. "Have a peanut."
2. Maybe you should repaint the house.
3. "Hi!"
4. "Your daughter is failing 'You and the Government.'"
5. "The worse you do in office, the better Rich Little's act becomes."
6. "How's your brother?"
7. "Does your wife have breast cancer yet?"
8. "Is Amy home?"
9. "Want to have a domestic affair?"
10. "Why do they call your mother Miss Lillian?"
11. "Howdy."
12. "Haven't I seen you somewhere before?"
13. "You look taller on television."
14. "Would you like to buy Girl Scout cookies?"
15. "Do you use Scope?"
16. "Oh my god, I'm talking to the president!"
17. "Can I have your autograph?"
18. "You go to the movies just like regular people?"
19. "What's the scoop?"
20. "Why are you so stupid as to take the job of president?"
21. "What were your SAT scores?"
22. "I think foreign affairs should be handled more firmly."
23. "You should think more creatively, watch *Star Trek*, read science fiction and fantasy novels, and take this test."
24. "You're a dull president."
25. "You're not a good speaker; you should speak so that you sound a little more confident in yourself."
26. "Good morning, Mr. President."
27. "Good afternoon, Mr. President."
28. "Good evening, Mr. President."
29. "How's your re-election campaign taking shape?"
30. "Need a bright young engineer on your staff?"
31. "I really enjoyed the White House tour I took recently."
32. "Do you think an economic recession is around the corner, as some experts predict?"
33. "What do you think of Richard Nixon?"
34. "If you had it all to do over again, what would you do differently?"
35. "How's the family?"
36. "Welcome to Pennsylvania"(or wherever we are)."
37. "Tell me about your famous lusting after women."
38. "Feel like blowing some dope?"
39. "Who are all the creepy guys hanging around?"
40. "Watch out for would-be assassins."
41. "I like your bulletproof car."
42. "What would you tell a young man aspiring to be president?"
43. "Do you think we'll ever have a woman president?"
44. "Think the National Health Insurance plan has a chance?"
45. "How's William Miller working out at the Fed?"
46. "What do you think of Woodward and Bernstein?"
47. "What are you doing to cure urban blight?"
48. "Put your house in order."
49. "Please pass the butter."
50. "There's a soup stain on your tie."
51. "Can you give me directions to Baltimore?"
52. "How's your sister?"
53. "Wanna get a six-pack and ride around?"

## 5. Eight or more things you've never said to your brother or sister

1. "What do you think of the president's foreign policy?"
2. "How was your trip to Alaska?"
3. "Get me a banana."
4. "I've got VD."
5. "Have fun on your moon-shot!"
6. "$A^2 + B^2 = C^2$."
7. "You can use my stereo anytime you want to."
8. "I love you."
9. "Saw my arm off please."
10. "Please hand me that piano."
11. "Could you move that tree?"
12. "You sing terrific."
13. "I wish you would lose some weight."
14. "Do you know the Pythagorean theorem?"
15. "I love to type."
16. "Ish Kabibble."
17. "I hate candy."
18. "You're so green."
19. "You're healthy looking."
20. "You're the least obnoxious, most easy-to-get-along-with person I know."
21. "Come here and bother me."
22. "I hate you."
23. "You need a shave" (to my sister).
24. "You look sexy" (to both).
25. Curses.
26. The word "accrue."
27. "The speed of light is 2.998 x $10^8$ meters/sec."
28. "Can I borrow $10,000?"
29. "You're the smartest person I ever met."
30. "How does nuclear fusion work?"
31. "You have all the feelings of Mr. Spock."
32. "Eat me."
33. "'How do I love thee? Let me count the ways.'"
34. "Short people don't deserve to live."
35. "Bald is beautiful."
36. "I think you're illegitimate."
37. "*Cogito ergo sum* is false."
38. "I don't still resent our childhood."
39. "I am better than you."
40. "You are better than I."
41. "Sure—I'll give you the money."
42. "Please saw my legs off."
43. "Have you got change for a piaster?"
44. "Paint it blue."
45. "No, thanks, I've already got one."
46. "I always knew I could turn to you."
47. "Do you live here, too?"
48. "Give me your purse or I'll shoot."
49. "Let's make love."
50. "Hi, Mum."
51. "Hi, Dad."

## 6. Six or more things not to say to an Eskimo

1. "I hate snow!"
2. "Huskies are repulsive!"
3. "Igloos are tacky."
4. "Your nose is cold."
5. "The killing of whales is immoral."
6. "Want to go swimming?"
7. "Oh, I'm sorry—I gave your parka to the guys from the Salvation Army."
8. "What's this swimming around in my soup?"
9. "Something in here smells like dead fish."
10. "Mind if I build a fire here in the middle of the floor?"
11. "Some of my best friends are Eskimos."
12. "Do all Eskimos lead such boring lives?"
13. "I guess you have to live in those simple houses because of the weather."
14. "Don't you have any coats that make you look thin?"
15. "Which way is north?"
16. "You look like a neanderthal."
17. "Why don't you go south for the winter?"
18. "I live in the tropics."
19. "Your sled just broke and the dogs ran away."
20. "You are a wasteful person."
21. "Go for a long walk on a short ice-floe."
22. "Your way of life is stupid."
23. "Go build a bonfire in your igloo."
24. "This is Antarctica."
25. "The walruses have migrated south."
26. "Cold enough for you?"
27. "Anyone who eats blubber must be fucked up."
28. "What do you do when you feel like playing pinball?"
29. "I hope the Alaska pipeline breaks open."
30. "I hear the polar ice caps are melting."
31. "Can I sleep with your wife?"
32. "Ever hear of Seward's Folly?"
33. "Stick 'em up!"
34. "You've never had it so good."
35. "Buy my refrigerator."
36. "Would you like to buy some mosquito netting?"
37. "You rub me the wrong way."
38. "Your sled is going to the dogs."
39. "Ever play volleyball in the nude?"
40. "Your house is on fire."
41. "I think it'll be a warm day today."
42. "You know that joke about the Eskimo?"

## 7. Six or more ways to tell if someone is a vampire

1. Notice if his lunch clots.
2. If his teeth have red stains on them.
3. Bring him out into the sunshine and see if his skin burns.

4. Wear a V-neck dress and watch his reaction.
5. Take him to church.
6. Ask him to volunteer at the Red Cross Blood Bank and watch his reaction.
7. Ask him to say "Good evening."
8. Look at him in a mirror.
9. Feed him a pizza with garlic and hot cross buns for dessert.
10. Ask him to make a donation to the blood bank.
11. If he wears dark suits and has piercing eyes.
12. See if he avoids churches.
13. Is he absent when a bat is present?
14. They lurk around blood banks.
15. Black brings out the best in them.
16. Their mouths are constantly open.
17. They're night people.
18. Instead of ordering a gallon of milk, they order a pint of blood.
19. They use the phrase "A man's home is his castle" quite a bit.
20. He's always hanging around (especially by his feet).
21. He has long, sharp canine teeth.
22. He can't stand sunlight.
23. You can't see his shadow (he doesn't cast one).
24. He wears a black ring.
25. He teaches an Advanced Placement course in history.
26. He's afraid of a cross.
27. He sings songs like "You're So Vein."
28. He has relatives in Transylvania.
29. He often goes batty by turning into one.
30. He goes sailing in blood vessels.
31. He gives nasty hickies.
32. He likes long nights.
33. He's not killed by things that would kill someone else.
34. He draws excessively from his blood bank.
35. Ask him.
36. See if he looks like Bela Lugosi.
37. Find out if he likes to suck blood.
38. Look for strange changes during a full moon.
39. See if he keeps a black cape in his closet.
40. Look for bite marks on the necks of people around him.
41. See if he has the full-moon days circled on his calendar.
42. Cut your finger.
43. Cut his finger.
44. Put him in a cage at the zoo marked "Vampire" and see if he thrives.
45. Feeds only on blood.
46. See if he talks like Bela Lugosi.
47. Find out if he sleeps in a coffin.
48. Determine if he has bats in his belfry.
49. Check his blood type, see if it's mixed.

---

**8. Eight or more things to look for from the plane window while flying**

1. Smoke coming from the engines.
2. White puffy cloud formations.
3. Heaven.
4. Flying saucers.
5. Parachutes.
6. Sky divers.
7. People on the wing.
8. The people on the other side of the aisle (reflections in window).
9. Your house.
10. Your street.
11. The Rockies.
12. Big cities.
13. Your car in the airport parking lot.
14. McDonald's golden arches.
15. Birds.
16. Biplanes flying upside down.
17. Two MIG-25s engaging in an aerial dogfight.
18. The dog!
19. Superman.
20. Underdog.
21. The Bat Helicopter (Batman and Robin's of course!).
22. The invisible Wonder Woman plane.
23. Flying carpets.
24. Hang-gliders.
25. The Bermuda Triangle.
26. Your reflection.
27. Pillows.
28. Matzoh ball soup.
29. The Wicked Witch of the North.
30. Patchwork.
31. Ants.
32. Droplets on the window.
33. Fog.
34. A lighted city.
35. Look at the sky, especially the color.
36. Look at the city below, particularly at night.
37. The stars.
38. The moon.
39. The elevators on the wing of the plane.
40. Identify land masses and bodies of water.
41. St. Elmo's fire.
42. Lightning.
43. Flying fish. Maybe.
44. Soviet fighter planes.
45. The trails (exhausts) from other planes.
46. Boats and ships in the ocean.
47. Sunrise.
48. To check whether it's night or day.
49. To see if you're over land or water.
50. To get ideas for your model train set.
51. UFOs.
52. Other planes.
53. The setting sun.
54. The Mississippi.
55. The Grand Canyon.
56. New York City.
57. The St. Louis Arch.
58. The Mohave Desert.
59. The Isle of Capri.
60. The North Pole.
61. Sugarloaf Mountain.
62. The River Thames.
63. The ruins of Machu Picchu.
64. The Seven Wonders of the World.
65. Inspiration.
66. Nuts and bolts from the engine.
67. Fire in the engines.
68. Wings.
69. A wing walker.
70. The blinking light on the end of the wing.
71. Enemy submarines.

---

**9. Seven or more ways to provoke a ghost**

1. Be obnoxious to his great-grandchildren.
2. Bulldoze his grave.
3. Be very loud and offensive in his old house.
4. Call the Duke University parapsychology team.
5. Say nasty things about him in his presence.
6. Marry his widow.
7. Put an apartment complex over the graveyard.
8. Steal his sheets.
9. Steal his chains.
10. Sing Christmas carols.
11. Tell the ghost you're not afraid of him (like Casper).
12. Be a disbeliever.
13. Yell "Holy Ghost!"
14. Tell the ghost he can't walk through walls.
15. Ignore the ghost.
16. Tell the ghost you're writing a book on ghosts, and he'll get a percentage of the profit.
17. Dream, as in *Fiddler on the Roof.*
18. Tell him he doesn't scare you.
19. Spill coffee on his sheet.
20. Tell him you don't believe in him.
21. Ask him if he had ghost toasties and evaporated milk for breakfast.
22. Keep running through him.
23. Laugh at him.
24. Somehow prevent him from keeping his favorite haunts (destroy his haunted house, etc.).
25. Tell him to drop dead.
26. Tell him his sheet is dirty.
27. Tell him his chains are rusty.
28. Tell him he's very friendly.
29. Tell him he's a deadbeat.
30. Tell him he should go out in the sun more often, that he looks very pale.
31. Tell him it's no use trying to fool you, that you can see right through him.
32. Say "boo."
33. Throw a bucket of water on him.
34. Claim there are no such things as ghosts.
35. Hit him with a baseball bat.
36. Stick your tongue out at him.
37. Throw darts at him.
38. Tell him you never liked him when he was alive.
39. Play with a Ouija board.
40. Tickle him.
41. Turn the light off.
42. Don't feed him.
43. Tell him he's not dead.
44. Spray him with spray paint.
45. Take him to an art gallery.
46. Tell him he's Irish.
47. Tell him to join the statistics department.
48. Call him a sissy.
49. Tell him he could have saved $300 on his new Chevrolet at "Z-Frank."
50. Accuse him of cheating at Monopoly.
51. Refuse to play the Bach Fugue and Toccata on the pipe organ in your parlor.

---

**10. Six or more ways to prevent shivering on a cold day**

1. Steal an Eskimo's parka.
2. Build a bonfire in your living room.
3. Think warm thoughts.
4. Don't get out of bed.
5. Wear long johns.
6. Get on the first plane to Hawaii.

7. Take a warm bath (or a hot one) with a friend.
8. Wear bulky sweaters.
9. Think warm.
10. Drink hot chocolate.
11. Nail your mouth shut.
12. Pull out all your teeth.
13. Sit by a fire.
14. Hug someone close to you.
15. Wear very dark clothing and expose as much area to the sun as possible.
16. Wear a lot of layers of clothes.
17. Put hot water bottles under your clothes.
18. Build a fire.
19. Stay in a warm house.
20. Keep moving (run a lot).
21. Don't go outside.
22. Snuggle up to someone warm.
23. Wear electrically heated underwear.
24. Build a heated Plexiglas bubble and travel in that instead of walking around.
25. Move to Southern California where "cold days" don't cause shivering.
26. Drink mulled wine.
27. Jog.
28. Eat a lot of stew.
29. Vodka in coffee.
30. Bedsocks.
31. Take a sauna.
32. Make love fast.
33. Cut nerve.
34. Give hot water enema.
35. Stay in the sauna.
36. Huddle for warmth with a Yugoslavian.
37. Drink a bottle of brandy.
38. Wrap yourself in a buffalo hide.

## 11. Seven or more ways to make sunlight

1. Harness a star.
2. Put a zillion candles (lit) in a circle.
3. Get a humongous amount of yellow helium balloons and put light bulbs in them.
4. Make your own sun out of all those neato chemicals.
5. Drop a scrim onstage, light it with the amber lights from the color bar, and put a small white follow spot in the upper right-hand corner of the scrim (a touch of the reds from the color bar can be added for a dawn/dusk effect).
6. Pull up the shades.
7. Get a bunch of fireflies and have them all light their light-thingies at the same time.

8. Smile.
9. Drink Florida orange juice.
10. Have the gods carry the sun across the sky.
11. Gather all the stars in the sky and put them together.
12. Ask the north wind to blow away the clouds.
13. Go to Florida.
14. Explode a hydrogen bomb.
15. Annihilate matter with antimatter.
16. Slowly feed matter into a black hole.
17. Reverse the photosynthetic process of plants so that the products of the reaction are recombined into sunlight.
18. Gather all the elements that are found in the sun together, put them in a vacuum tube, add energy, and make them glow like sunlight.
19. Blow up the world.
20. Focus telekinetic energy on a point in space to make it glow.
21. Invoke God to make sunlight.
22. Go to a hobby shop and buy your own "Make Your Own Sunlight" kit.
23. Add two parts "essence of sun" with one part moondust and light with a match.
24. Build a nuclear reactor with windows exposing the plasma chamber.
25. Fly out into outer space and drag a star back with you where you want the sunlight to be.
26. First make the universe filled with dust; then have gravitational attraction bring it into a gigantic churning mass; then make it explode into zillions of stars and planets, including the sun.
27. Consult your nearest magician.
28. Consult your nearest theologian.
29. Consult your nearest physicist.
30. Fly above the clouds.
31. Fly to the equator.
32. Use a sunray lamp.
33. The way they do it in the Sunlight Soap factory.
34. Open a jar of Sunpat peanut butter.
35. Bore holes in the earth so sun can come through at night.
36. Erect more mirrors.
37. Polish the surface of the moon.
38. Blow clouds away.
39. Make love.
40. Vaporize egg yolks.

41. Start a fusion reactor in the family room.
42. Convert any handy hydrogen to energy.
43. Crawl out from under your rock.
44. Here—take a hit of this!
45. Buy a star and set it on fire.
46. Make somebody feel good.

## 12. Seven or more non-dietary uses of ice cream

1. To stick an igloo together.
2. Pile about a ton of it in your driveway (all different flavors) and watch it melt.
3. To use as ice packs for sprained ankles and stuff.
4. To use as money.
5. As a new art medium, like snow sculpting.
6. As a facial.
7. As a deodorant (except chocolate chip).
8. To soothe tonsillitis.
9. Let a gallon of raspberry-ripple run down the sides of your living room table as a conversation piece.
10. As a muscle toner—swimming in it would be arduous, therefore muscle-building.
11. And speaking of muscles, how about as weights in the Olympics?
12. To get fat.
13. As decoration.
14. To provide a job for people (example: Good Humor).
15. To fill up your freezer.
16. To give someone something to hold.
17. To give out at birthday parties.
18. Put it on burns.
19. Put it on bee-stings.
20. Use it to make cavities in your teeth.
21. Put some on a sidewalk to attract ants so you can kill them with bug spray.
22. Stick your feet in it on a hot day.
23. Build landscapes in soft ice-cream.
24. Use it to prove it causes cancer in rats and should be taken off the market.
25. Make an impenetrable moat around a castle.
26. As a cooling system in space ships.
27. Use it to mess up the house of someone you don't like.
28. Use it to build an igloo.
29. Put it into a pie and mash it into someone's face.
30. Use it as a bartering tool to

get desired information from a child.
31. Smear it on yourself to cool off on a hot summer's day.
32. Use a scoop as a snowball.
33. Feed it to the cat.
34. Use as samples for training food analysts.
35. Lubricate a slide with it.
36. Put it on your head if you have a headache.
37. Local anaesthetic.
38. For resale at a profit.
39. Reduce the swelling in a sprained ankle.
40. Build an ice-cream man.
41. Use it to chill a six-pack.
42. Lubricate the runners of your sled.
43. Balloon ballast.
44. Bookends (but only for a little while).
45. Paint your house with it.
46. Use it to draw ants and flies.

## 13. Six or more ways to count to ten

1. By ones.
2. By twos.
3. In Arabic.
4. Standing on your head.
5. Singing in the shower.
6. By fives.
7. On your way to work in the morning.
8. Hanging from a tree limb upside down.
9. In fractions.
10. 1, 2, 3, 4, 5, 6, 7, 8, 10, 9.
11. With your eyes closed.
12. While patting your head and rubbing your tummy.
13. In a Turkish bath, in Turkish (or whatever you call it).
14. Upside down, eating crackers.
15. On your fingers.
16. By starting at negative infinity and adding one to it, then adding one to that number, and so on until ten is reached.
17. Backwards.
18. In Spanish.
19. By tens.
20. With Roman numerals.
21. In base 20.
22. In base 100.
23. On an abacus.
24. On a calculator.
25. The usual way.
26. In Russian.
27. In German.
28. In base 4.
29. Standing on your head.
30. In sign language.
31. With illustrated placards.
32. With a computer.
33. On your toes.
34. In binary arithmetic.
35. Backwards from 20.

36. By even numbers.
37. Vault two five-bar gates.
38. Find two one-armed people and use their fingers.
39. Singing songs ("Ten Green Bottles," "One Man Went to Mow").
40. Count steps.
41. Forwards.
42. In Chinese.

---

## 14. Six or more ways to remember your dreams

1. Have someone sit in the room with you and listen to the things you say while dreaming.
2. Go to a dream-center and have them record your dreams electronically.
3. Stay awake.
4. Put a little tiny tape recorder inside your brain to record them.
5. Have a team of dream analysts shrunken down to microscopic sizes and implanted in your dream center to record them.
6. Daydream—you always remember your daydreams.
7. Drink a "remember dreams" potion.
8. Let someone in the dream tell you.
9. Sleep until you wake up naturally, then try to recall them.
10. Go over all your dreams as soon as you wake up and record them somehow.
11. Look at your friends and think of situations or problems you've had because sometimes they remind you of a dream you've had.
12. Remember dreams that are about dreams you had previously, but forgot.
13. Use a mnemonic device.
14. Write them down the instant you wake up.
15. Tell them to your spouse the instant you wake up.
16. With a smile.
17. Recite it into a tape recorder.
18. Act it out.
19. Have yourself hypnotized to remember all dreams.
20. Monitor your REMs.
21. Visit your psychiatrist.
22. Put an x-ray plate under pillow while dreaming.
23. Learn to write them down while you sleep.
24. With trepidation.
25. If you've had this one before, remember the first one.

26. Only have one a year but have it every night.

---

## 15. Six or more ways to look at the stars

1. Lying on your back in a sailboat.
2. Hanging upside down from an apple tree.
3. Laying on a waterbed looking out through a skylight with a friend.
4. Look at photographs.
5. Driving with the sunroof open.
6. Lying on your back on a golf course.
7. Sitting on the edge of a canyon out west.
8. Staring out your bedroom window.
9. On the French Riviera.
10. Through a red helium balloon—they turn purple.
11. While floating in a heated, kidney-shaped swimming pool, stark naked, surrounded by exotic trees and flowers with twinkle lights hidden in them, while soft music plays and you sip strawberry daiquiris.
12. From atop the World Trade Center.
13. From the moon.
14. In soup.
15. Read the Hollywood magazines.
16. With binoculars.
17. Standing up with your head back.
18. With a friend.
19. Hit yourself over the head with a bat.
20. From a spaceship.
21. With a spectroscope.
22. From another end of the galaxy.
23. Look at them as being holes in a black sky with a light behind it.
24. Look at them as being in constellations individually.
25. Look at them from underneath a domed glass roof while lying in bed.
26. With the unaided eye.
27. Through a reflecting telescope.
28. Through a refracting telescope.
29. Through two properly held magnifying glasses.
30. Through a Coke bottle.
31. Through tinted glasses.
32. Through your normal eyeglasses.
33. Sitting on a chair outside.
34. Sitting on a chair inside.
35. Get hit hard on the head.

36. Go to a Hollywood theater on opening night.
37. Look at the American flag.
38. Look in an encyclopedia under "Milky Way."
39. Look on the arithmetic test of a bright elementary school student.
40. With awe.
41. By TV camera on the roof.
42. As sources of power.
43. As goals for aspiring U.S. Army officers.
44. *Per ardua ad astra* (motto of British RAF).
45. Look into water.
46. With a map of Hollywood.
47. From a mountain top.
48. At the All-Star Game.
49. From Skylab.

---

## 16. Seven or more uses of beach sand

1. To fill a gourd and use as a door stop.
2. To melt into flexible glass and mold into diverse shapes.
3. To put in a rock garden.
4. To dye and put in glass bottles as decorations.
5. To make a small-scale tornado for a movie like *The Wizard of Oz*.
6. To keep people from slipping on ice.
7. To bury people with.
8. As instant dandruff.
9. To sell to tourists.
10. To get in your hair.
11. To count.
12. To fill up space.
13. To enable jewelers to sell pearls.
14. To make deserts.
15. To make sandpaper.
16. As an abrasive in washing.
17. As an abrasive in grinding.
18. For filling the bottoms of flower pots.
19. For showing the result of the weathering of rocks.
20. For filling sand boxes.
21. For filling sand bags.
22. For lying on.
23. For building sand castles.
24. For walking on.
25. For the bottom of a fish tank.
26. For losing things in.
27. Filling up weights for lifting.
28. For making counterweights in pulley systems.
29. For making sand paintings.
30. To draw in (or on).
31. Sleep on it.
32. Make an hourglass.
33. Sandblast your old sparkplugs.
34. Prevent crimping of welded pipes.

35. Make love on it.
36. Make an optometrist's glasses-frame heater.
37. With other ingredients, make your own glass.
38. Make a mud pie.
39. Kick it in the face of a 98-pound weakling.
40. Throw on the carpet of someone you don't like.
41. Use it to remove the white lining of a fluorescent tube when making a solar collection.
42. Use it for added traction in the winter by sprinkling it under your car wheels.
43. Use it as ballast in a ship.
44. Make concrete.
45. Holiday for inland sand.
46. As scouring powder for picnic utensils.
47. As site for sports functions.
48. As absorbent for bullets at rifle range.
49. To fill boxers' punch bags.
50. To improve the soil of clay gardens.
51. To grow plants in.
52. Teeth grit in soups and stews.
53. Stuff up engines.
54. Add to sandwiches.
55. Land troops for an invasion.
56. Get it kicked in your face by a bully.

---

## 17. Eight or more reasons why you shouldn't drop out of school

1. You won't have any structured way to spend your days.
2. What would you do while your friends were in school?
3. You won't be able to get into college.
4. No structured way of enriching your mind.
5. Cutting off opportunities in the future.
6. Denying an essential part of your emotional maturation.
7. To make jobs for teachers.
8. To make use of school buildings.
9. To teach teachers something.
10. You meet a lot of people.
11. You learn about people and how to live socially.
12. You do crazy things with friends.
13. Plays.
14. It would probably hurt your grade point average.
15. Keeps you busy.
16. It's probably less monotonous than working.
17. You're introduced to things that you may find are

interesting but never would have looked at them yourself.
18. Widens your horizons.
19. You'll upset your parents.
20. You'll get a more menial, less interesting job.
21. You'll be ostracized by respectable members of your age group.
22. You'll get bored.
23. You won't know important things they teach in school.
24. You'll miss out on the school's social activities.
25. You'll miss out on the school's athletic activities.
26. You'll miss out on the school's cultural activities.
27. Dropouts often turn to drug addiction.
28. The discipline you learn in school is good for a person.
29. It may lower your self-esteem.
30. There may be a gem of knowledge coming your way tomorrow.
31. Schools feel hurt.
32. It's illegal if you are below age.
33. Because "out of school" hurts if it falls on your toe.
34. To build a strong economy.
35. The fall could kill you.
36. You might have to get a job.
37. You'd probably lose your scholarship.
38. Where else can you goof off under the guise of work?
39. You could no longer be class clown.
40. You can't be valedictorian anywhere else.

---

## 18. Six or more ways to avoid long lines at checkout counters

1. Shop early to avoid crowds.
2. Be loud and offensive in the back of the line and people might move to another line or move faster to get away from you.
3. Buy the store and designate a separate checkout counter for yourself.
4. Bribe the cashier to close the counter until you get there.
5. Scream "Fire!"
6. Know the owner.
7. Leave the money on the counter and then leave.
8. Stand in the express line.
9. Call up the supermarket from a pay phone and tell them there's a bomb planted and set to go off in fifteen minutes. After everyone clears out, be the first back in front of the line.

10. Tell everyone there's a big accident outside and three people were killed. When everyone runs outside to see, quickly step to the front of the line.
11. Only shop at off hours.
12. Only shop in out-of-the-way stores.
13. Have your items delivered to your home.
14. Walk to the head of the line, ask the second person in line to do you a favor and pay for this item, and give him exact change. (This works nine out of ten times—I do it myself!)
15. Hire someone to shop for you.
16. Don't *DO* any shopping in the first place. (Grow your own food, make your own clothes, etc.)
17. Shop by mail-order.
18. You make an appointment with the checkout when you enter the store.
19. Increase number of checkouts.
20. Computer scanning of those waiting and calculation of the optimum line to join.
21. Larger price labels.
22. Give prizes for "quick through-put" to encourage cooperation between shopper and checkout operator.
23. Give shoppers a discount if they operate the checkout to learn how it looks from the other side.
24. Only use round dollar figures.
25. Sell only very few items.
26. Make the checkout counters portable.
27. Offer price incentives to shop during slack hours.
28. Only allow few people into shop.
29. Shop in unpopular stores.
30. Shop in unpopular stores.
31. Check yourself out at a closed register.
32. Tell everybody in line that there's a man giving away $20 bills at the back of the store.

---

## 19. Six or more non-uses of sunglasses

1. Put them on your dog.
2. Buy a bunch of different-colored pairs and hang them in front of your window, as a mobile, to catch the light.
3. Hang them on your rearview mirror.
4. Use them as a wishbone.
5. As a tunnel for ants.
6. As a rollercoaster for ants.

7. To break.
8. To give to a creature with six eyes.
9. To lose.
10. To give to a creature with 500 eyes.
11. To use in the rain.
12. To hold your hair out of your eyes.
13. To act as a mirror (only the reflective type) to fix your hair, etc.
14. To look cool.
15. To disguise yourself.
16. Because they look stylish.
17. To keep light out of your eyes when burning things with a magnifying glass.
18. To put on a stuffed animal so it looks cute.
19. For a costume you might be wearing.
20. Dig holes in concrete.
21. Lift heavy objects.
22. Fix radios.
23. Assemble ovens.
24. Print posters.
25. Support television sets.
26. Remove sparkplugs.
27. Compose symphonies.
28. Build houses.
29. Transport bananas.
30. Write obituaries.
31. Erect tents.
32. Drill brass.
33. Illuminate city streets.
34. Probe the human psyche.
35. Invent chocolate pudding.
36. Protect yourself from the freezing cold.
37. Communicate with relatives in Russia.
38. Fuel your car.
39. Knit sweaters.
40. Turn a screw.
41. Fire an employee.
42. Get an "A" on a test.
43. Lay a carpet.
44. Train lions.
45. Remove the trash.
46. Make ball bearings.
47. Cook dinner.
48. Prevent deafness.
49. Perform brain surgery.

---

## 20. Nine or more ways to tell time without a watch

1. Guess.
2. Train your stomach to signal time.
3. Use a sundial.
4. Listen for the hourly "bongs" of the church clock.
5. Look at the position of the sun.
6. Look at the clock on the wall.
7. Start early in the morning and count the minutes.

8. Memorize the actions of different animals at different times and then watch the animals.
9. Make a pendulum with a weight and string.
10. Trust bio clock.
11. Know what time one gets tired.
12. Know what time the chicken crows.
13. Observe change in seasons.
14. The advancement of the culture (example: cave men).
15. Know what time the sun peers over the mountain tops.
16. Notice what time your hair gets dirty.
17. The type of food McDonald's sells.
18. By the position of the stars around the Pole Star (every quarter turn equals 6 hours).
19. With an hour glass (the big sand points to the five and the little sand points to the twelve).
20. By measuring the flow of water from a spring.
21. By looking directly at the sun and estimating its position.
22. Using a slowly burning candle marked off at equal measures.
23. Keeping count of pulse beats of the heart.
24. By the vibration of a quartz crystal when an electric current passes through it.
25. By the moon (moon dial or direct observation, looking at the moon and estimating its position).
26. By the actions and habits of plants.
27. By the amount of growth of a plant or animal.
28. Call the telephone operator.
29. Listen for the beep on the radio.
30. See what shows are on TV and check to see what time they're on.
31. Ask a passerby.
32. Listen for the chimes of Big Ben.
33. Observe when the children leave school.
34. Use your inborn sense of time.
35. At night, make a lot of noise; some neighbor will shout, "Hey, bud, keep down that racket; it's two in the morning!"
36. Challenge someone to a duel at one o'clock sharp and see when he shows up.
37. Use large margin of error in telling time.
38. Wait for the mailman to pass by.

39. Wait for somebody to tell you you're late and ask them "how late?"
40. Town crier.
41. Factory whistle.

---

### 21. Eight or more ways to appreciate opera

1. With no clothes on.
2. On your head with popcorn in your ears.
3. Drunk or stoned.
4. It can't be enjoyed.
5. Facing the wall instead of the stage.
6. Wearing skis while having a barbecue.
7. In your bathtub listening to your stereo.
8. On your head doing yoga.
9. Lying down in a dark room.
10. In your car.
11. By participating in one.
12. Reading the music.
13. By listening to auditions for one.
14. While you're asleep.
15. While you're studying.
16. While you're eating.
17. By taking music appreciation courses.
18. By learning the language it's sung in.
19. Travelling to hear it in its country of origin.
20. Paying to have it performed where you live (if you're far from the metropolitan areas and their companies).
21. By learning the story that is being told before seeing the opera itself.
22. Over the radio.
23. On public television.
24. By sponsoring it.
25. By putting on a tuxedo and taking the evening off.
26. At the Met.
27. Listen to Bev Sills.
28. Alone.
29. With an expert.
30. Have good seats.
31. Bring a friend that enjoys it.
32. Go by yourself if you do not want to be disturbed.
33. Have dinner out first.
34. Go on an empty stomach.
35. Be deaf and read lips.
36. Go to more operas.
37. Go to a baseball game.
38. Get to know Beverly Sills personally.
39. Fake it!
40. Appreciate the subject as a true art form.
41. Study the subject.

---

### 22. Six or more uses of the jet stream

1. Put a herring in it and see if it flies.
2. To cram it.
3. Who cares?
4. There aren't any.
5. To fly jets in.
6. Make cars go faster.
7. To chop down trees without using an axe.
8. To chop down axes without using a tree.
9. Controls the weather.
10. Disperses pollution.
11. Speeds planes up.
12. Slows planes down.
13. Widens the effects of radioactive weapons.
14. One-way lighter-than-air travel.
15. Source of energy for extremely tall windmills.
16. Observable influence on the surface's weather.
17. Area for hypobaric (low pressure)-hypothermic (low temperature) testing of construction materials.
18. Method of transporting biochemical warfare agents to our adversaries without their being detected (just turn them loose up there . . .).
19. Transportation of low-priority messages via paper airplane.
20. Float huge lighter-than-air advertising balloons over key consumer areas.
21. Freeze-dry coffee.
22. Weather forecast.
23. Ballooning.
24. Migration.
25. Navigation.
26. Fuel conservation.
27. For more warm air.
28. To bring more precipitation to the area.
29. Getting someplace on time.
30. To send air-o-grams.
31. Sky diving.
32. Just to know it's there.
33. To cool off hot tamales.

---

### 23. Six or more things never to say to a bald-headed man

1. "Hey, baldy!"
2. "Hi ya, one ball."
3. "Anyone have some wax?"
4. "Where's your rug?"
5. "Put on a hat—the reflection is blinding me."
6. "Are you like that all over your body?"
7. "Can I feel your head?"
8. "Do you shellac it?"
9. "Who does your hair?"
10. "Hey, Kojak."
11. "This is where we part."
12. "I really loathe bald men."
13. "You look like a bad imitation of Yul Brynner."
14. "I hate men."
15. "Goo-goo, Gaa-gaa."
16. "Has being bald adversely affected your love life?"
17. "Would you pose for a statue of Buddha?"
18. "Oh, are you a Hare Krishna?"
19. "Is that natural or do you shave your head?"
20. "Did your toupee blow away?"
21. "How did you achieve that wonderful sheen?"
22. "Bald men excite me; bald women, too."
23. "You ought to wear a hat always!"
24. "I never knew that you could have liver spots on your head."
25. "Are you related to the Coneheads?"
26. "Is everything else dead up there?"
27. "Can I run my fingers over your skull?"
28. "That must come in handy at night riding a bicycle; you don't need reflectors."
29. "Are you a mutant?"
30. "Are you asked a lot of offensive questions about your grotesque head?"
31. "That reminds me . . . care for a game of pool?"
32. "I can SEE myself! Do you use Joy?"
33. "They say syphilis causes hair loss."
34. "Have you been exposed to radiation recently?"
35. "What kind of shampoo did you formerly use?"
36. "I've always hated Yul Brynner."
37. "Would you mind covering your head while I'm putting?"
38. "Don't worry about it . . . nobody *notices* that you're bald. . . ."
39. "At least you've still got eyebrows."
40. "I've been accused of having a receding hairline. From your experience, would you say that's true?"
41. "Have you considered painting racing stripes on it?"
42. "Can you still stand on your head?"
43. "I know a great hair stylist."
44. "Did you know that eleven times more bald men commit suicide than men with hair?"
45. "Would you care to model for my candlemaking class?"
46. "I thought albinos had pink eyes, too."
47. "Good Lord! Mr. Clean!"
48. "Here's Chrome Dome!"
49. "Hi, Curly."
50. "Bed too short?"
51. "Bald-headed men are lousy lovers."
52. "Buy a wig."
53. "Want to go bowling?"
54. "Don't forget to get a trim."
55. "Do you get colds easily?"
56. "You're causing a bad reflection."
57. "Can I touch your head?"
58. "Boy, you sure do need a haircut!"
59. "Every time you walk into a room it sure brightens up."
60. "Mind if I use your shiny head to fix my hair?"
61. "You need Head & Shoulders."
62. "Would you like my comb?"

---

### 24. Six or more ways to play bridge without a full deck

1. Worst hand wins.
2. Don't play.
3. Intoxicated.
4. Draw fake cards.
5. Who cares?
6. Play it mentally (have a non-player give each player a list of cards which he or she will have).
7. Play three-handed (if you're missing just one).
8. Play under the table.
9. Hold the cards in your toes.
10. Drink a bottle of scotch.
11. Buy another deck.
12. Make extras from file cards and then cover the backs of the remaining "real" cards with file cards, too.
13. Tear all the cards in half and make up a full deck of 52 halves. (So what if all the suits aren't right? Just correct the ones you have to, right on the torn half. That deck is ruined, anyway.)
14. Go to a psychiatrist until he convinces you that you *are* playing with a full deck.
15. Program a computer to play on a TV screen, so you'll never need cards again.
16. Arbitrarily assign four

players thirteen cards each (from a random list) and play from memory.
17. Play with dumb opponents.
18. Cheat.
19. Fast shuffle.
20. In the dark.
21. Change the rules.
22. Play with blind opponents.
23. Play with a bunch of retarded people.
24. Play only half a game.
25. Can't play.
26. Play sick so your partner will do all the work.
27. Throw all the cards on the table and accuse the other people of stealing some of the cards.
28. Play by yourself.
29. Pretend you can't count.
30. Spill your red wine on your opponent's dress; when she goes to clean it, take some of her cards.

---

## 25. Eight or more reasons for not exploring Mars

1. Martians.
2. You have to wear snowshoes.
3. There's no McDonald's for Sunday morning breakfast.
4. There's no Holiday Inn.
5. The Martians might not like it.
6. It's been done.
7. We waste natural resources.
8. Men might die.
9. Solve earthly problems first.
10. Dangerous biological organisms might be brought to earth.
11. Jupiter might get mad.
12. We might be ticklish.
13. If man were meant to explore Mars he would have had antennae.
14. It's too far away.
15. It's too cold.
16. The atmosphere is too thin.
17. None of our visiting satellites have found anything worth looking into further.
18. It'll cost too much.
19. Other civilized races in the galaxy may not like it.
20. It could never become habitable for the unprotected human being.
21. Brave men and women would lose their lives trying to explore it.
22. We don't have the technology to do it successfully.
23. Doing so could spur another

unwelcome space and arms race.
24. No rocket.
25. Scared of heights.
26. Afraid of the unknown.
27. Didn't like *My Favorite Martian.*
28. Don't like funny-looking people.
29. Don't like people who can't talk my language.
30. Hate green things.
31. Don't like craters.
32. Martians might mug you.
33. No bathrooms.
34. It takes too long to get there.
35. Mars might smell funny.
36. People on earth would be watching you—*all the time.*
37. No bars!
38. All you do is float around.
39. You couldn't talk to anyone if you saw them.

---

## 26. Seven or more ways to fell a tree without an ax

1. Blow it down.
2. Blow it up.
3. Using shrubbery.
4. Climb to the top and shake it until it snaps.
5. Flash-freeze it until it explodes.
6. Trip it.
7. Drill holes in it, place carpenter ants in the holes, and wait until it gets eaten through.
8. Cut it down with a helicopter.
9. With pruning shears.
10. Have someone else cut it down.
11. Call the axe a wrench and cut down the tree with a wrench.
12. Run into it headfirst.
13. Get a whole flock of woodpeckers.
14. Bury bones under it and let the dogs dig it out.
15. Give it to my brother—he'll ruin anything.
16. Blow on it.
17. Cast a spell.
18. Let loose a horde of gypsy moths.
19. Sandpaper the bottom.
20. Trained beavers.
21. Butter knife (for the very patient).
22. Cut a ring around its base so it dies, and you can push it over (for the very, *very* patient).
23. Divert a stream and erode it away (for the ridiculously patient).

24. Repeatedly ram it with an old car until it breaks (the tree, not the car).
25. Build a roof over it and cut it off from light and water until it dies.
26. Dig up its roots.
27. Saw it down.
28. Pull it down.
29. Dig it out.
30. Burn it down.
31. Burn it up.
32. Plant termites in it.
33. Raise woodpeckers.
34. Let it stay up.
35. Get ten people on one or two branches and it will fall.
36. "Talk" it down.
37. Take out large bites with your teeth.
38. Push it over with a tractor.
39. Find one that has already fallen.
40. Hit it with a 90-foot wall of water.
41. Use a large pocket knife and whittle it down.

---

## 27. Six or more ways to plow a field without a tractor

1. With a car.
2. With an ox pulling the plow.
3. Make your wife pull the plow.
4. Using a sword.
5. Buy some slaves.
6. Use a horse.
7. Fingernails.
8. Toes.
9. Toothpicks.
10. Violin bow.
11. Psychic powers.
12. With a hoe.
13. With a spoon.
14. Use a car with a trailer hitch to drag the farm equipment.
15. Use a jackhammer (only in New England . . .).
16. Use a machine gun.
17. Dig with your fingers.
18. Tell your neighbors that one of your ancestors buried a chestful of coins somewhere in your fields, and whoever finds it can keep half. Then take a two-week vacation.
19. With mules.
20. With water buffalo.
21. With a truck.
22. By hand.
23. Use a bicycle.
24. Scissors.
25. Tweezers.
26. Use a motorcycle.
27. Use a very large comb.
28. Use an atom bomb.
29. Hire wetbacks.

30. Get up early and dig till late afternoon.
31. Hold a gold-digging contest in the field.

---

## 28. Seven or more ways to make a phone stop ringing

1. Yell at it.
2. Shoot it.
3. Don't answer it.
4. Have it connected to a self-destruct mechanism so that if it rings more than five times it blows up.
5. Make someone else answer it.
6. Get a phone for outgoing calls only.
7. Cut down all the telephone poles.
8. Bomb the phone company.
9. Get a phone-answering machine.
10. Throw water on it and make it short-circuit.
11. Leave it off the hook.
12. Keep the phone in a vacuum so you can't hear it ring.
13. Ignore it.
14. Rip the phone off the wall (or wherever) and drive your car over it.
15. Without actually answering the phone, lift the attachment on which the receiver rests and drop it.
16. Blow it up.
17. Tell it to stop ringing.
18. Take it off the hook.
19. Answer it.
20. Make the phone company take it out.
21. Pull the wire out of the wall.
22. Disassemble the phone.
23. Put cloth between the bell and the clapper.
24. Substitute a buzzer for the bell (it'll buzz instead of ring, but you didn't say it couldn't do *something*).
25. Put it underwater.
26. Bury it.
27. Don't pay your bill.
28. Cut the wire.
29. Swear at it.
30. Remove the bell.
31. Dial your own number.
32. Put cotton in your ears.
33. Leave the house.
34. Put it under a pillow.
35. Throw something at it.
36. Disconnect the phone.
37. Place in a pail of water.
38. Toss it outside.
39. Pretend it's not ringing.
40. Smash it to bits.

## 29. Eight or more ways to show love

1. Fondle him/her.
2. Take him/her out to dinner.
3. Give him/her candy.
4. Do strange things to his/her body with the presidential seal.
5. Do favors for him/her.
6. Cook dinner for him/her.
7. Open doors for him/her.
8. A hug.
9. Give him/her money.
10. Write love letters.
11. Sharing.
12. Make love.
13. Buy presents for each other.
14. Kiss each other.
15. Mold each other.
16. Call long distance.
17. Visit unexpectedly.
18. Marry.
19. Do things together.
20. Think of each other always, even when you're apart.
21. Write letters when you're apart.
22. Say "I love you" from the bottom of your heart.
23. Let your partner see it in your eyes.
24. Sacrifice something dear to you for him/her, either voluntarily or out of necessity.
25. Live together.
26. Refrain from making love when you know it's not time yet.
27. Know when you shouldn't live together.
28. Be quiet when you know that nothing you can say will mean as much as just being there.
29. Hold hands.
30. Send flowers unexpectedly.
31. Remember your anniversary.
32. In the dark.
33. With a boy/girl.
34. Physically.
35. Go on an ocean cruise.
36. In the moonlight.
37. With your husband/wife/lover.
38. Send love cards.
39. Smooch.
40. Squeeze.
41. Throw your arms around someone and kiss their entire face.
42. Make love in a kinky way.
43. A nice pat on the back.
44. A genteel blow in one's ear.
45. A sweet smile.
46. Forgiving his/her mistakes.

## 30. Eight or more uses of red ribbon

1. Tie someone up with it.
2. Wear it for a tie.
3. Make a bow out of it.
4. Use it to make a mummy.
5. Use it for wallpaper.
6. Go into the bikini business.
7. Use it as a bloodied gauze in a first-aid course.
8. Make a wig out of it.
9. To tie around a Christmas present.
10. To strangle someone.
11. To tie hair back.
12. To go fishing (use it as a line).
13. To make a net.
14. To lash some sticks together for no reason at all.
15. To make a headband.
16. To suspend a plastic sculpture of an ape from the ceiling.
17. As a bookmark.
18. As mock-up ropes for bondage aficionados.
19. To tie tomatoes to their stakes.
20. As part of a spell to get rid of colds (I'm not kidding; I've actually read of people doing this).
21. To cover a light bulb in an effort to achieve unusual lighting.
22. As bumpers on an air table.
23. As Christmas tree ornaments.
24. As an alternate means of writing "Helter Skelter" in red if blood is lacking.
25. As a tourniquet.
26. As a mnemonic device (tie it around your finger).
27. As identification ("Your contact will be wearing a red ribbon around his neck, Tanya").
28. To perform an experiment about stomach juices (swallow it and pull it up two hours later).
29. To be the finish line in a race.
30. To sell to raise money to buy drugs.
31. To use as a scarf on a small stuffed animal.
32. To wrap packets of money with.
33. Tie up party favors.
34. To stretch across streets so cars will skid as they go by.
35. To keep as a pet ribbon if they are permitted in your apartment building.
36. To make a shadow that looks like a snake on the wall.
37. As a gag.
38. To put out a candle.
39. To commit suicide (stuff plugs into your mouth and nose).
40. To infuriate a very small bull.
41. To use as lips on a cloth doll.
42. To patch a sock.
43. To make fringes for a mod pocketbook.
44. To tease a kitten.
45. To make tassels for your go-go dancing outfit.
46. To test for color blindness.
47. Shred it and dump it in water to color for ice cubes.
48. To replace the hair on a Raggedy Ann doll.
49. Make a fake thermometer.
50. Make business graphs and charts.
51. Dye it yellow, and tie it on an old oak tree.
52. Wrap presents.
53. Make Christmas presents.
54. Tie it around yourself, and present yourself to a loved one.
55. Hang it outside your window, so you can see wind direction.
56. Use it as a blindfold.
57. Hang curtains with it.
58. Lace up *red* shoes with it (wouldn't want to clash).
59. Find white and blue ribbon to go with it, and make yourself a flag.
60. Type with it.
61. Make a barber pole.
62. Make dollhouse curtains.
63. Wrap it around your head and pretend you're a Shriner.
64. Trail marker.
65. Danger signal.
66. Prize marker.
67. Tail of a kite.
68. Streamers.
69. Boundary marker.
70. Put on your dog.

## 31. Seven or more ways to get from New Orleans to Paris

1. By banana boat.
2. Hitchhike.
3. Stow away on a boat or plane.
4. Stuff yourself inside a bottle, throw yourself into the Mississippi, and hope you float to France.
5. Do not pass Go, do not collect $200.
6. Take a slow boat from China.
7. Date a wealthy French man/woman.
8. Board the *Delta Queen* and go with the currents.
9. Do your best impersonation of "God Walks on $H_2O$."
10. Travel the fifty states. There is a Paris on the mainland.
11. Be one of the signers of the Louisiana Purchase.
12. By raft, then you can write a book like Thor Heyerdahl.
13. By submarine (yellow).
14. Up, up, and away (by balloon).
15. Psychic energy (teleport).
16. By transport or beam (*The Enterprise*).
17. Fall asleep in Louisiana and dream of being in Paris.
18. Reincarnation (it's rather slow but who cares when you have eternity?).
19. Ride a trained whale.
20. Riverboat up the Mississippi to St. Lawrence Seaway, out through Canada and across the Atlantic.
21. Fly New Orleans–Atlanta–New York–Paris (or any other route *ad nauseam*).
22. Dirigible direct.
23. Sailboat down around South America, through the Straits of Magellan, and across the Pacific.
24. Train down through Central America to the Panama Canal, and ocean liner across the Pacific.
25. Kayak down through the Gulf and across the Atlantic.
26. Bicycle to Baltimore, and pedalboat out the Chesapeake Bay and across the Atlantic.
27. Amphibious vehicle across land, rivers, open country, and ocean, heedless of damage to private property.
28. Scuba dive.
29. Hitch a ride with trained dolphins.
30. U.F.O.
31. Horseback.
32. Mule train.
33. Follow the stars.
34. Swim.
35. Fly.
36. Mail yourself in a large box marked "Fragile."
37. Join the Olympics and pray they go to Europe this year.
38. Win the Pillsbury Bake-off.
39. Beg.
40. Let someone take you.
41. Go around the world, then to the right.

# FEBRUARY

### Mental Calisthenic #2

Sit in a comfortable position in an area free of distractions and noises. Take three deep breaths and exhale through your nostrils. Close your eyes and imagine a BLACK SQUARE, BLACK TRIANGLE, BLACK CIRCLE, BLACK OVAL, and BLACK RECTANGLE. Repeat the exercise, this time make the shapes another color, of your choice. Arrange the BLACK shapes alphabetically, from left to right. Make them disappear one at a time. Open your eyes. Proceed with a Mental Jogging exercise.

**32. Eight or more things you could do if you weren't watching television**

| Response | Score |
|---|---|
| 1. | 1 |
| 2. | 1 |
| 3. | 1 |
| 4. | 1 |
| 5. | 1 |
| 6. | 1 |
| 7. | 1 |
| 8. | 1 |

Bonus Responses

| Response | Score |
|---|---|
| 9. | 2 |
| 10. | 2 |
| 11. | 2 |
| 12. | 2 |
| 13. | 2 |
| 14. | 2 |
| 15. | 2 |
| 16. | 2 |
| Total | |

**33. Six or more things to do if you're in the water without a lifejacket and you can't swim**

| Response | Score |
|---|---|
| 1. | 1 |
| 2. | 1 |
| 3. | 1 |
| 4. | 1 |
| 5. | 1 |
| 6. | 1 |

Bonus Responses

| Response | Score |
|---|---|
| 7. | 2 |
| 8. | 2 |
| 9. | 2 |
| 10. | 2 |
| 11. | 2 |
| 12. | 2 |
| 13. | 2 |
| 14. | 2 |
| 15. | 2 |
| 16. | 2 |
| Total | |

## 34. Seven or more bets you should never make at a horse race

| Response | Score |
|---|---|
| 1. | 1 |
| 2. | 1 |
| 3. | 1 |
| 4. | 1 |
| 5. | 1 |
| 6. | 1 |
| 7. | 1 |

**Bonus Responses**

| | |
|---|---|
| 8. | 2 |
| 9. | 2 |
| 10. | 2 |
| 11. | 2 |
| 12. | 2 |
| 13. | 2 |
| 14. | 2 |
| 15. | 2 |
| 16. | 2 |

Total ☐

## 35. Seven or more reasons why gold costs more than lead

| Response | Score |
|---|---|
| 1. | 1 |
| 2. | 1 |
| 3. | 1 |
| 4. | 1 |
| 5. | 1 |
| 6. | 1 |
| 7. | 1 |

**Bonus Responses**

| | |
|---|---|
| 8. | 2 |
| 9. | 2 |
| 10. | 2 |
| 11. | 2 |
| 12. | 2 |
| 13. | 2 |
| 14. | 2 |
| 15. | 2 |
| 16. | 2 |

Total ☐

## 36. Seven or more things to avoid while playing backgammon

| Response | Score |
|---|---|
| 1. | 1 |
| 2. | 1 |
| 3. | 1 |
| 4. | 1 |
| 5. | 1 |
| 6. | 1 |
| 7. | 1 |

**Bonus Responses**

| | |
|---|---|
| 8. | 2 |
| 9. | 2 |
| 10. | 2 |
| 11. | 2 |
| 12. | 2 |
| 13. | 2 |
| 14. | 2 |
| 15. | 2 |
| 16. | 2 |

Total ☐

## 37. Six or more ways to win big at roulette

| Response | Score |
|---|---|
| 1. | 1 |
| 2. | 1 |
| 3. | 1 |
| 4. | 1 |
| 5. | 1 |
| 6. | 1 |

**Bonus Responses**

| | |
|---|---|
| 7. | 2 |
| 8. | 2 |
| 9. | 2 |
| 10. | 2 |
| 11. | 2 |
| 12. | 2 |
| 13. | 2 |
| 14. | 2 |
| 15. | 2 |
| 16. | 2 |

Total ☐

## 38. Six or more reasons not to join a fraternity or sorority

| Response | Score |
|---|---|
| 1. _____ | 1 |
| 2. _____ | 1 |
| 3. _____ | 1 |
| 4. _____ | 1 |
| 5. _____ | 1 |
| 6. _____ | 1 |

Bonus Responses

| | |
|---|---|
| 7. _____ | 2 |
| 8. _____ | 2 |
| 9. _____ | 2 |
| 10. _____ | 2 |
| 11. _____ | 2 |
| 12. _____ | 2 |
| 13. _____ | 2 |
| 14. _____ | 2 |
| 15. _____ | 2 |
| 16. _____ | 2 |

Total ☐

## 39. Eight or more reasons for "private" clubs

| Response | Score |
|---|---|
| 1. _____ | 1 |
| 2. _____ | 1 |
| 3. _____ | 1 |
| 4. _____ | 1 |
| 5. _____ | 1 |
| 6. _____ | 1 |
| 7. _____ | 1 |
| 8. _____ | 1 |

Bonus Responses

| | |
|---|---|
| 9. _____ | 2 |
| 10. _____ | 2 |
| 11. _____ | 2 |
| 12. _____ | 2 |
| 13. _____ | 2 |
| 14. _____ | 2 |
| 15. _____ | 2 |
| 16. _____ | 2 |

Total ☐

## 40. Seven or more ways to avoid getting drunk

| Response | Score |
|---|---|
| 1. _____ | 1 |
| 2. _____ | 1 |
| 3. _____ | 1 |
| 4. _____ | 1 |
| 5. _____ | 1 |
| 6. _____ | 1 |
| 7. _____ | 1 |

Bonus Responses

| | |
|---|---|
| 8. _____ | 2 |
| 9. _____ | 2 |
| 10. _____ | 2 |
| 11. _____ | 2 |
| 12. _____ | 2 |
| 13. _____ | 2 |
| 14. _____ | 2 |
| 15. _____ | 2 |
| 16. _____ | 2 |

Total ☐

## 41. Seven or more non-fuel uses of gasoline

| Response | Score |
|---|---|
| 1. _____ | 1 |
| 2. _____ | 1 |
| 3. _____ | 1 |
| 4. _____ | 1 |
| 5. _____ | 1 |
| 6. _____ | 1 |
| 7. _____ | 1 |

Bonus Responses

| | |
|---|---|
| 8. _____ | 2 |
| 9. _____ | 2 |
| 10. _____ | 2 |
| 11. _____ | 2 |
| 12. _____ | 2 |
| 13. _____ | 2 |
| 14. _____ | 2 |
| 15. _____ | 2 |
| 16. _____ | 2 |

Total ☐

## 42. Eight or more ways to avoid low mortgage payments

| Response | Score |
|---|---|
| 1. _____ | 1 |
| 2. _____ | 1 |
| 3. _____ | 1 |
| 4. _____ | 1 |
| 5. _____ | 1 |
| 6. _____ | 1 |
| 7. _____ | 1 |
| 8. _____ | 1 |

**Bonus Responses**

| | |
|---|---|
| 9. _____ | 2 |
| 10. _____ | 2 |
| 11. _____ | 2 |
| 12. _____ | 2 |
| 13. _____ | 2 |
| 14. _____ | 2 |
| 15. _____ | 2 |
| 16. _____ | 2 |

Total ☐

## 43. Six or more reasons why clouds are white and float

| Response | Score |
|---|---|
| 1. _____ | 1 |
| 2. _____ | 1 |
| 3. _____ | 1 |
| 4. _____ | 1 |
| 5. _____ | 1 |
| 6. _____ | 1 |

**Bonus Responses**

| | |
|---|---|
| 7. _____ | 2 |
| 8. _____ | 2 |
| 9. _____ | 2 |
| 10. _____ | 2 |
| 11. _____ | 2 |
| 12. _____ | 2 |
| 13. _____ | 2 |
| 14. _____ | 2 |
| 15. _____ | 2 |
| 16. _____ | 2 |

Total ☐

## 44. Six or more reasons why motorcycles are noisier than cars

| Response | Score |
|---|---|
| 1. _____ | 1 |
| 2. _____ | 1 |
| 3. _____ | 1 |
| 4. _____ | 1 |
| 5. _____ | 1 |
| 6. _____ | 1 |

**Bonus Responses**

| | |
|---|---|
| 7. _____ | 2 |
| 8. _____ | 2 |
| 9. _____ | 2 |
| 10. _____ | 2 |
| 11. _____ | 2 |
| 12. _____ | 2 |
| 13. _____ | 2 |
| 14. _____ | 2 |
| 15. _____ | 2 |
| 16. _____ | 2 |

Total ☐

## 45. Six or more things not to do with gunpowder

| Response | Score |
|---|---|
| 1. _____ | 1 |
| 2. _____ | 1 |
| 3. _____ | 1 |
| 4. _____ | 1 |
| 5. _____ | 1 |
| 6. _____ | 1 |

**Bonus Responses**

| | |
|---|---|
| 7. _____ | 2 |
| 8. _____ | 2 |
| 9. _____ | 2 |
| 10. _____ | 2 |
| 11. _____ | 2 |
| 12. _____ | 2 |
| 13. _____ | 2 |
| 14. _____ | 2 |
| 15. _____ | 2 |
| 16. _____ | 2 |

Total ☐

## 46. Six or more ways to get from New York City to Sydney, Australia, by bicycle

| Response | Score |
|---|---|
| 1. _____ | 1 |
| 2. _____ | 1 |
| 3. _____ | 1 |
| 4. _____ | 1 |
| 5. _____ | 1 |
| 6. _____ | 1 |

Bonus Responses

| | |
|---|---|
| 7. _____ | 2 |
| 8. _____ | 2 |
| 9. _____ | 2 |
| 10. _____ | 2 |
| 11. _____ | 2 |
| 12. _____ | 2 |
| 13. _____ | 2 |
| 14. _____ | 2 |
| 15. _____ | 2 |
| 16. _____ | 2 |

Total ☐

## 47. Seven or more nice things about your favorite pet

| Response | Score |
|---|---|
| 1. _____ | 1 |
| 2. _____ | 1 |
| 3. _____ | 1 |
| 4. _____ | 1 |
| 5. _____ | 1 |
| 6. _____ | 1 |
| 7. _____ | 1 |

Bonus Responses

| | |
|---|---|
| 8. _____ | 2 |
| 9. _____ | 2 |
| 10. _____ | 2 |
| 11. _____ | 2 |
| 12. _____ | 2 |
| 13. _____ | 2 |
| 14. _____ | 2 |
| 15. _____ | 2 |
| 16. _____ | 2 |

Total ☐

## 48. Six or more nice things about the person to your right

| Response | Score |
|---|---|
| 1. _____ | 1 |
| 2. _____ | 1 |
| 3. _____ | 1 |
| 4. _____ | 1 |
| 5. _____ | 1 |
| 6. _____ | 1 |

Bonus Responses

| | |
|---|---|
| 7. _____ | 2 |
| 8. _____ | 2 |
| 9. _____ | 2 |
| 10. _____ | 2 |
| 11. _____ | 2 |
| 12. _____ | 2 |
| 13. _____ | 2 |
| 14. _____ | 2 |
| 15. _____ | 2 |
| 16. _____ | 2 |

Total ☐

## 49. Six or more reasons for having justice

| Response | Score |
|---|---|
| 1. _____ | 1 |
| 2. _____ | 1 |
| 3. _____ | 1 |
| 4. _____ | 1 |
| 5. _____ | 1 |
| 6. _____ | 1 |

Bonus Responses

| | |
|---|---|
| 7. _____ | 2 |
| 8. _____ | 2 |
| 9. _____ | 2 |
| 10. _____ | 2 |
| 11. _____ | 2 |
| 12. _____ | 2 |
| 13. _____ | 2 |
| 14. _____ | 2 |
| 15. _____ | 2 |
| 16. _____ | 2 |

Total ☐

## 50. Six or more nice things about yourself

| Response | Score |
|---|---|
| 1. _____ | 1 |
| 2. _____ | 1 |
| 3. _____ | 1 |
| 4. _____ | 1 |
| 5. _____ | 1 |
| 6. _____ | 1 |

Bonus Responses

| | |
|---|---|
| 7. _____ | 2 |
| 8. _____ | 2 |
| 9. _____ | 2 |
| 10. _____ | 2 |
| 11. _____ | 2 |
| 12. _____ | 2 |
| 13. _____ | 2 |
| 14. _____ | 2 |
| 15. _____ | 2 |
| 16. _____ | 2 |

Total ☐

## 51. Seven or more reasons why men should not be free

| Response | Score |
|---|---|
| 1. _____ | 1 |
| 2. _____ | 1 |
| 3. _____ | 1 |
| 4. _____ | 1 |
| 5. _____ | 1 |
| 6. _____ | 1 |
| 7. _____ | 1 |

Bonus Responses

| | |
|---|---|
| 8. _____ | 2 |
| 9. _____ | 2 |
| 10. _____ | 2 |
| 11. _____ | 2 |
| 12. _____ | 2 |
| 13. _____ | 2 |
| 14. _____ | 2 |
| 15. _____ | 2 |
| 16. _____ | 2 |

Total ☐

## 52. Eight or more reasons for having laws

| Response | Score |
|---|---|
| 1. _____ | 1 |
| 2. _____ | 1 |
| 3. _____ | 1 |
| 4. _____ | 1 |
| 5. _____ | 1 |
| 6. _____ | 1 |
| 7. _____ | 1 |
| 8. _____ | 1 |

Bonus Responses

| | |
|---|---|
| 9. _____ | 2 |
| 10. _____ | 2 |
| 11. _____ | 2 |
| 12. _____ | 2 |
| 13. _____ | 2 |
| 14. _____ | 2 |
| 15. _____ | 2 |
| 16. _____ | 2 |

Total ☐

## 53. Seven or more ways to peel an egg

| Response | Score |
|---|---|
| 1. _____ | 1 |
| 2. _____ | 1 |
| 3. _____ | 1 |
| 4. _____ | 1 |
| 5. _____ | 1 |
| 6. _____ | 1 |
| 7. _____ | 1 |

Bonus Responses

| | |
|---|---|
| 8. _____ | 2 |
| 9. _____ | 2 |
| 10. _____ | 2 |
| 11. _____ | 2 |
| 12. _____ | 2 |
| 13. _____ | 2 |
| 14. _____ | 2 |
| 15. _____ | 2 |
| 16. _____ | 2 |

Total ☐

## 54. Six or more ways to make a reflecting surface

| Response | Score |
|---|---|
| 1. | 1 |
| 2. | 1 |
| 3. | 1 |
| 4. | 1 |
| 5. | 1 |
| 6. | 1 |

**Bonus Responses**

| | |
|---|---|
| 7. | 2 |
| 8. | 2 |
| 9. | 2 |
| 10. | 2 |
| 11. | 2 |
| 12. | 2 |
| 13. | 2 |
| 14. | 2 |
| 15. | 2 |
| 16. | 2 |

Total ☐

## 55. Eight or more ways to gain weight

| Response | Score |
|---|---|
| 1. | 1 |
| 2. | 1 |
| 3. | 1 |
| 4. | 1 |
| 5. | 1 |
| 6. | 1 |
| 7. | 1 |
| 8. | 1 |

**Bonus Responses**

| | |
|---|---|
| 9. | 2 |
| 10. | 2 |
| 11. | 2 |
| 12. | 2 |
| 13. | 2 |
| 14. | 2 |
| 15. | 2 |
| 16. | 2 |

Total ☐

## 56. Six or more ways to prevent sunburn

| Response | Score |
|---|---|
| 1. | 1 |
| 2. | 1 |
| 3. | 1 |
| 4. | 1 |
| 5. | 1 |
| 6. | 1 |

**Bonus Responses**

| | |
|---|---|
| 7. | 2 |
| 8. | 2 |
| 9. | 2 |
| 10. | 2 |
| 11. | 2 |
| 12. | 2 |
| 13. | 2 |
| 14. | 2 |
| 15. | 2 |
| 16. | 2 |

Total ☐

## 57. Seven or more people you'd like to be stranded with on a desert island

| Response | Score |
|---|---|
| 1. | 1 |
| 2. | 1 |
| 3. | 1 |
| 4. | 1 |
| 5. | 1 |
| 6. | 1 |
| 7. | 1 |

**Bonus Responses**

| | |
|---|---|
| 8. | 2 |
| 9. | 2 |
| 10. | 2 |
| 11. | 2 |
| 12. | 2 |
| 13. | 2 |
| 14. | 2 |
| 15. | 2 |
| 16. | 2 |

Total ☐

## 58. Seven or more ways to lose weight

| Response | Score |
|---|---|
| 1. _____ | 1 |
| 2. _____ | 1 |
| 3. _____ | 1 |
| 4. _____ | 1 |
| 5. _____ | 1 |
| 6. _____ | 1 |
| 7. _____ | 1 |

**Bonus Responses**

| | |
|---|---|
| 8. _____ | 2 |
| 9. _____ | 2 |
| 10. _____ | 2 |
| 11. _____ | 2 |
| 12. _____ | 2 |
| 13. _____ | 2 |
| 14. _____ | 2 |
| 15. _____ | 2 |
| 16. _____ | 2 |

Total ☐

## 59. Six or more places where you could place a second nose

| Response | Score |
|---|---|
| 1. _____ | 1 |
| 2. _____ | 1 |
| 3. _____ | 1 |
| 4. _____ | 1 |
| 5. _____ | 1 |
| 6. _____ | 1 |

**Bonus Responses**

| | |
|---|---|
| 7. _____ | 2 |
| 8. _____ | 2 |
| 9. _____ | 2 |
| 10. _____ | 2 |
| 11. _____ | 2 |
| 12. _____ | 2 |
| 13. _____ | 2 |
| 14. _____ | 2 |
| 15. _____ | 2 |
| 16. _____ | 2 |

Total ☐

# CONTRIBUTORS' SAMPLE RESPONSES

### 32. Eight or more things you could do if you weren't watching television

1. Listen to TV.
2. Listen to the radio.
3. Watch the radio.
4. Play a board game.
5. Go fishing.
6. Play pool.
7. Go swimming.
8. Explore Mars.
9. Contribute to this book.
10. Go drinking.
11. Watch a herring.
12. Go shopping.
13. Wake up.
14. Snore.
15. Play records.
16. Take a shower.
17. Go from New Orleans to Paris.
18. Take a trip to New York City.
19. Have a good time.
20. Prevent brain rot.
21. Do homework (almost).
22. Work.
23. Go to school.
24. Throw the TV away.
25. Watch grass grow.
26. Watch diamonds form.
27. Watch oil form.
28. Count the seconds between sunrise and sunset.
29. Exercise.
30. Bang my head on the street.
31. Pour cement.
32. Watch cement harden.
33. Blow glass.
34. Watch sand get washed away at the beach.
35. Pump gas.
36. Make furniture.
37. Manufacture steel in my basement.
38. Shoe horses.
39. Crash cars.
40. Jump off houses.
41. Make shoes.
42. Slaughter cattle.
43. Buy stocks.
44. Explore the city's sewer system.
45. Climb buildings.
46. Sit on flagpoles.
47. Brand cattle.
48. Brand hippos.
49. Watch ice form.
50. Get drunk.
51. Do bits from David Frye albums.
52. Play shuffleboard.
53. Lose in shuffleboard.
54. Try and drive or bomb home.
55. Go to play rehearsal.
56. Put on makeup and costumes.
57. Read.
58. Paint.
59. Ski.
60. Play football.
61. Sing in the choir.
62. Make dinner.
63. Dance.
64. Do exercises.
65. Meditate.
66. Go to a movie.
67. Talk on the telephone.
68. Wash hair.
69. Brush teeth.
70. Parachute jump.
71. Hang glide.
72. Sleep.
73. Argue with my mother.
74. Argue with my father.
75. Argue with others.
76. Practice my German accent.
77. Perpetuate underhanded schemes for taking over the student government.
78. Cheat at cards.
79. Drown.
80. Yell incoherent things in a locked bedroom.
81. Make faces at myself in the mirror.
82. Do good deeds.
83. Expose the science teacher who has been putting mind-altering drugs in the cafeteria food.
84. Alert the CIA to the Communist spy who teaches history at our school.
85. Work on being elected president of the United States.
86. Fantasize about my boyfriend/girlfriend.
87. Daydream about being an astronaut.
88. Try to understand Dulong and Petit.
89. Make voodoo dolls.
90. Look at the stars (celestial ones, that is).
91. Pick out music that a no-talent pianist can play and that a no-talent choir can sing.
92. Act like a duck.
93. Speaking as the associate editor of *Wampus*, stare people straight in the eye and yell "Wamp, Wamp."
94. Preach.
95. Place the N.H.S. (National Honor Society) in an untenable position.
96. Go to gym class and become miserable.
97. Go to a psychiatrist.
98. Decide what to say to Jesus Christ in an interview.
99. Pull your socks off and bite your toenails in earnest.
100. Go to a toga party.
101. Turn out all the lights and light all the candles in an effort to create a mysterious atmosphere.
102. Take photographs.
103. Freeze to death by doing nothing in a room owned by people trying to save on heating bills.
104. Murder that person who's been annoying you.
105. Hire a detective.
106. Steal someone's dog.
107. Talk to a plant.
108. Dye sawdust so the workroom can be color coordinated.
109. Eat.
110. Jog.
111. Talk on the phone.
112. Take various unusual tests by mail.
113. Write letters.
114. Make love.
115. Make money.
116. Bicycle.
117. Play tennis.
118. Sing.
119. Have a party.
120. Go to the bathroom.
121. Take a bath.
122. Do the dishes.
123. Walk the dog.
124. Water my plants.
125. Clean the yard.
126. Answer questions that the family keeps asking.
127. Move to a new house.
128. Go to Boston.

### 33. Six or more things to do if you're in the water without a lifejacket and you can't swim

1. Drown.
2. Swim.
3. Grab hold of a herring.
4. Yell for help.
5. Tell yourself you're such a fool for not bringing a lifejacket.
6. Count to three.
7. Blow bubbles in the water.
8. Catch your last glimpse of the world.
9. Float.
10. Stand on the bottom.
11. Walk on water.
12. Enjoy close contact with the lifeguard.
13. Scream.
14. Grab something that floats.
15. Flail your arms.
16. Swallow water.
17. Breathe.
18. Finish committing suicide.
19. Don't let go of the person who towed you out there.
20. Pray.
21. Hope it's shallow.
22. Ask yourself what you're doing in the water in the first place.
23. Evolve gills quickly.
24. See if you can float.
25. Make sure you have your wallet, so that your corpse can be identified.
26. Look for driftwood.
27. Inflate your clothing.
28. Expect sharks (as bad as things are going, they can only get worse).
29. Look for a convenient iceberg or island to climb up on.
30. Learn to swim.
31. Kick your feet.
32. Stay calm.
33. Give up.
34. Get hold of a boat.
35. Say goodbye to the world.
36. Fall asleep.
37. Play with the fish.
38. Hold your breath.
39. Get *out* of the water.
40. Hope a skier will come by and rescue you.
41. Hope a big bird will think you are a fish and pull you from the water.

### 34. Seven or more bets you should never make at a horse race

1. That your horse will lose.
2. Any bet.
3. Your horse will win.
4. Don't bet on the herring.
5. Don't bet more than $2.
6. Don't bet on a cow.
7. Don't bet on a horse with no balls.
8. Don't bet on a horse with balls.
9. Your mother will place.
10. You can make seven the hard way.
11. Secretariat will have a colt before age three.
12. The football pool.
13. The dog will get the rabbit.
14. *Kiss Me, Kate* will be a hit show.
15. Man-of-War will race again.
16. Willie Shoemaker will grow.
17. The Incredible Hulk will become a jockey.

18. A push-me-pull-you will win the race.
19. Bets on ex-plowhorses.
20. Bets against the local Mafia boss's horse.
21. Bets that none of the horses will win.
22. Bets that will leave you broke with no way home when you lose.
23. Bets that some guy with a pile of ripped-up tickets at his feet tells you are "sure things."
24. Bets at odds of 100 to 1 or worse (I'm an optimist).
25. Bets that pit a man against a horse.
26. Bets against horses owned by pharmaceutical houses.
27. Your house.
28. Your paycheck.
29. On a dead horse.
30. Daily double.
31. On the weather.
32. Honesty of the race.
33. Any horse.
34. On a sure thing.
35. On a pretty hat.
36. On good legs.
37. On the jockey.
38. On an old horse.
39. On a horse #13.
40. On the dog races.
41. On the worst horse.
42. That the horse will talk.
43. On a horse with two broken legs.
44. On a horse with a 250-lb. jockey.

---

### 35. Seven or more reasons why gold costs more than lead

1. It's worth more.
2. It has a better atomic number.
3. Would you want a lead ring?
4. It makes better beads.
5. Lead is gray.
6. What does Fort Knox have in it—lead?
7. Did you *ever* hear of a $20 lead piece?
8. How about a leaden opportunity?
9. Want a lead watch?
10. Gold is shinier.
11. It can buy more money.
12. It has a mystique.
13. Lead doesn't have the same magical properties that gold does.
14. Because people agree on the higher price.
15. Gold was traditionally valued by the ancients, and we haven't shed all of their

bad habits yet.
16. It's a better conductor of electricity.
17. It's lighter (I say this in absence of a periodic table).
18. If we decided it didn't, all of the world's currencies would come apart at the seams.
19. Gold was associated with ancient religions, gaining ritual value *before* monetary value.
20. Gold is more malleable.
21. Demand.
22. Intrinsic monetary value.
23. It's the same color as the sun.
24. It's harder to find.
25. It's more durable.
26. Ladies like jewelry.
27. No one can wear pipes.
28. Lead bracelets are too heavy.
29. Its color looks better.
30. Gold is much softer.
31. It makes into jewelry better.
32. It will not turn your skin green.
33. It looks like you have a lot of money if you have gold fillings.

---

### 36. Seven or more things to avoid while playing backgammon

1. Moving backward.
2. A six-two opening move.
3. Getting gammoned.
4. Getting backgammoned.
5. Getting prime out.
6. Getting backgammoned while the doubling cube is on 64.
7. Playing for dollars.
8. Winning.
9. Not getting doubles.
10. Leaving men open.
11. Getting hustled.
12. Picking your nose.
13. A moving front.
14. Falling over sideways.
15. A partner who puts the stones in his mouth and spits them out at you.
16. Boredom.
17. Letting your cat have kittens on the board.
18. A bad loser.
19. Poor winners.
20. Loaded dice.
21. Heavy bets.
22. Rules that your opponent tells you about, that would benefit him, that you can't verify.
23. Fistfights.
24. Handmade sets whose owners will mark you severely if you mar their

markings.
25. Opponents who shout "two no-trump" or "touchdown" at inappropriate times during the game.
26. Magnetic sets (where your opponent can move the markers from under the table with his *own* magnet).
27. Backgammon addicts who don't seem to know when to quit.
28. Trained monkeys that always win.
29. Smart opponent.
30. Your wife/husband.
31. Crooked players.
32. Advice.
33. Telephone calls.
34. Pretty girls/handsome boys.
35. Bumpy table.
36. Water.
37. Someone with a virus.
38. Someone who is color blind.
39. Someone who is deaf.
40. Someone who doesn't know how to play.
41. A fire.
42. Thinking about playing tennis.
43. Making love.
44. Don't swallow the dice.
45. Falling asleep.
46. Accidentally hitting the other player in the eye with the dice.
47. Letting the dog sleep on the field (board) while you're playing.
48. Taking a shower.
49. Watching T.V.
50. A gang of tough backgammon players.
51. Amnesia.

---

### 37. Six or more ways to win big at roulette

1. Bet big.
2. Win big.
3. Rob the casino.
4. Use magnets.
5. Don't lose.
6. Find a psychic who can tell you which number will win.
7. Use mass hypnosis so everyone thinks you won and the casino pays you.
8. Make it your object to lose and then when you do, you will have won.
9. Psychokinetically influence the wheel.
10. Throw extra balls on the wheel so they can't tell who won.
11. Get lucky.
12. Cover every space on the table.

13. Use a steel ball and magnet in #14 Red.
14. "Accidentally" bump the table a lot.
15. Sit down and note every fall the ball makes over a two-year period, then bet the most frequent winner until it wins again (perhaps you won't be broke yet).
16. Own the casino.
17. Fix the wheel.
18. Own the wheel.
19. Use a gun.
20. Bring a fortune teller.
21. Pray.
22. Pay the spinner.
23. Have a lot of money.
24. Only play once.
25. Play all the numbers.
26. Pay off the dealer.
27. Cheat.
28. Play only if you have ESP.
29. Know how to play the game well.
30. Get smashed.
31. Read a lot on the subject of roulette.
32. Don't *play*.
33. Pay an expert to play in your place.

---

### 38. Six or more reasons not to join a fraternity or sorority

1. Initiation.
2. You'll never do any work.
3. It's too much fun.
4. It sucks.
5. A bunch of loonies run them.
6. You might not like getting hazed.
7. *Animal House.*
8. Your ability to reason with any degree of sanity goes right down the tube.
9. Physical pain.
10. Walking backward for a week.
11. Crumbling fraternity/sorority house.
12. It promotes dependency.
13. Money.
14. Mensa is more fun.
15. Contagious diseases.
16. My *ex*-fiancé/fiancée was in one.
17. Members are generally snobs or turkeys.
18. Mensa women are sexier; Mensa men are more dashing (methinks I was *too* generous in the latter statement; the former, however, is dead right!).
19. They're social crutches.
20. They're expensive.

21. They isolate their members from too many enjoyable *non*-fraternal social activities.
22. They shelter members to the extent that many don't do sufficient mental or social growing-up during their four years at college.
23. They don't do enough community or social work to justify their continued survival.
24. The Greek system is archaic.
25. Discrimination.
26. Not asked.
27. Insult them.
28. None available.
29. Don't like to socialize.
30. Don't like people of the same sex.
31. Can't talk.
32. Can't communicate.
33. Don't like people.
34. You wouldn't have to swallow goldfish.
35. You don't have to run nude down Main Street.
36. No social class group stuck on you.
37. You wouldn't have to live with all those other people.
38. You wouldn't have to go through "rush."
39. No expense for rings, letters, pins, etc., with the fraternity/sorority emblem on it.

---

### 39. Eight or more reasons for "private" clubs

1. They're not public.
2. Why not?
3. Why?
4. You can charge admission.
5. They're private.
6. You can do anything you want with them.
7. You can do kinky things together.
8. To indulge people's bigotries.
9. So people can draw support from like-minded people.
10. To achieve a common goal.
11. To improve its members' professional society.
12. For recreation (to share common pursuits).
13. To enjoy illegal activities.
14. Cater to the insecure.
15. Segregate the bigoted.
16. Separate the sexist.
17. Isolate the intellectuals (ta-da!).
18. Pander to recluses.
19. Provide wells for the wealthy to sink their money into, fooling themselves into thinking that they are buying

into something "special."
20. Comfort the lonely and displaced.
21. Make people like Hugh Hefner a fortune through selective bastardization of certain moral and social tenets.
22. Provide a gathering point for people who "think right."
23. Tax shelters.
24. Keep public nuisances private.
25. Practice odd pastimes, like nudism or voodoo.
26. Prestige.
27. I can afford it.
28. Like the company.
29. Independence (show).
30. Because it's there.
31. Nobody else's business.
32. Like people of the same faith.
33. Like being friends together.
34. Like being part of a group.
35. Like people.
36. Like crowds.
37. Like people in the same category.
38. Being able to keep certain people out.
39. Being alone.
40. You can act as none of the members.
41. You can be a snob.
42. You can come out of your closet.
43. Something you can spend all your money *and* free time at.
44. Have booze at place where non-drinkers can't drink.
45. Dancing with "members" only.
46. No hassle to get in and be seated.
47. Someplace to go, all dressed up.

---

### 40. Seven or more ways to avoid getting drunk

1. Throw up after you drink.
2. Drink Kool-Aid.
3. Use your alcohol as an explosive.
4. Use your beer to wash your hair.
5. Feed it to your dog.
6. Drink on a full stomach.
7. Don't drink.
8. Know your limit.
9. Mix Coke with water and pretend it's scotch.
10. Alternate beverages with emetics and throw up each round before it can affect you.
11. Put something unpleasant in your first drink and refuse

any refills for it.
12. Announce that you're Mormon (to your host).
13. Play Carry Nation and smash every bar in your town.
14. Get imprisoned doing the Carry Nation bit (they don't serve booze in the slammer).
15. Grow up on alcohol and accustom yourself to a little alcohol every day.
16. Eat every time you're tempted to have a drink.
17. Eat better.
18. Drink milk.
19. Drink low alcoholic beverages.
20. Look at other drunks.
21. Join A.A.
22. Sip your drink.
23. Eat pizza.
24. Go to sleep.
25. Drink sodas.
26. Go swimming.
27. Let someone else drink your drinks.
28. Drink a cup of coffee after each drink.
29. Sweat a lot after drinking.
30. Pretend you haven't been drinking.
31. Keep count of how much you drink.
32. Stay at home and don't go to parties.
33. Glue your mouth shut.
34. Act as if you were bombed already—no one will really care if you drink or not.
35. Drink water with a very dry olive.

---

### 41. Seven or more non-fuel uses of gasoline

1. As an air freshener for those who like the smell of gasoline.
2. In a glass bottle as an ornament.
3. To pour out and watch evaporate.
4. As an air freshener to get rid of guests who don't like the smell of gasoline.
5. As a type of currency.
6. To clean paint brushes.
7. To degrease lawn mower parts.
8. To remove grease stains.
9. To light charcoal.
10. As cigarette lighter fluid.
11. Cleaning tools.
12. Removing tar.
13. Starting fires.
14. To commit suicide.
15. To kill plants/flowers.
16. Removing wax.
17. In chemical formulae.

18. To dispose of Buddhist priests.
19. To produce rainbow patterns in the roads.
20. To clean paint off trousers.
21. To put in tequila bottle and sell as such.
22. To carry out proper chromatography on inks.
23. To sniff.
24. To remove shoe polish so as to convert black shoes to brown.
25. To make sodium chlorate and sugar safe for ramming home in a rocket. It is packed solid: the gasoline evaporates and you have your fuel left.
26. To remove grease from hands.
27. To add sugar to make a non-fuel for a no-go automobile.
28. To make paper transparent.
29. To kill ants.
30. To remove nail varnish.
31. To clean watches.
32. To pollute rivers.
33. To elute active principles from plants.
34. To remove colour from wine gums.
35. To remove dye from hair.
36. To soften glue.
37. To make paint runnier.
38. To remove false fingernails.
39. To remove nitroglycerine from dynamite.
40. To clean oven.

---

### 42. Eight or more ways to avoid low mortgage payments

1. Live in Aruba.
2. Don't buy the house.
3. Put on dark glasses and maybe they won't recognize you.
4. Live in Switzerland.
5. Live in Denmark.
6. Live in French Guyana.
7. Buy expensive house.
8. Buy lots of houses.
9. Borrow on shorter time.
10. Don't make a down payment.
11. Wait and buy in the future.
12. Seek out high interest rates.
13. Borrow from the underworld.
14. Pay down minimum payment.
15. Obtain second mortgage.
16. Obtain third mortgage.
17. Borrow from loan sharks.
18. Borrow from public loan companies.
19. Fall behind in payments.
20. Have a short-term loan.

21. Get a high mortgage.
22. Live in England.
23. Answer no post.
24. Answer no phone.
25. Answer no door.
26. Use rented accommodation.
27. Live with in-laws.
28. Commit suicide.
29. Commit a crime and go to jail.
30. Live in a tent.
31. Go bankrupt.
32. Buy a larger house.
33. Change your name and go to South America.
34. Change your sex and say it is up to your husband/wife.
35. Have a large family and get it back in tax relief.
36. Live as a paying guest.
37. Move into an hotel.

## 43. Six or more reasons why clouds are white and float

1. To add diversity to an otherwise slightly boring sky.
2. To stir the imagination.
3. To make people wonder why clouds are white and float.
4. Because black, non-floating clouds aren't any fun.
5. So they can make funny shapes that you can laugh out loud about and people can look at you funny. You don't have to worry about hurting the clouds' feelings either.
6. To miss on perfectly clear days.
7. To make you realize how tremendous the world is.
8. To force you to wonder what is beyond them.
9. They're lighter than air.
10. There are no colors in air.
11. To be near birds.
12. They have no legs.
13. So they can move around.
14. No dust in atmosphere.
15. Lighter than atmosphere.
16. No moisture.
17. Buoyed up by heavy air below.
18. Sun cleans cloud formation.
19. Because particle size reflects light evenly with no colour bias and density is less than lower air.
20. Because we could not see them if they sank beneath the earth.
21. To give scenery for Concorde passengers.
22. For sky-starers to dissolve.
23. To presage tomorrow's weather.

24. To add variety to a skyscape.
25. For angels to sit on.
26. To hide the face of God.
27. Because sun warms earth and evaporates night moisture from soil.
28. To show the direction of the winds at different levels.
29. To surround a mountain top.
30. To hide Snoopy from the Red Baron.
31. To protect us from the sun's ultraviolet rays.
32. To give rain back to earth.
33. To show the Fata Morgana.
34. Because of the changes in the winds.
35. Because of their electric content.
36. It depends on the height of the sun above the horizon.
37. To form shapes to influence the poet.
38. To help in the greenhouse effect by insulating the earth.
39. To store rain.
40. Matthew XVI 2 & 3.
41. So that they can use cotton wool in *Magic Roundabout*.
42. To stop the stars falling through.
43. To give unease when looking at tall buildings.
44. To hide us from little green Martians.
45. To obscure satellite photography.
46. To obscure satellite television relay transmissions.

## 44. Six or more reasons why motorcycles are noisier than cars

1. The windows are open.
2. Their engines are naked.
3. Their names are loud (Suzuki).
4. The people on them are loud.
5. They are smaller than cars.
6. They have to be sure that cars can hear them.
7. They have only two wheels.
8. No room for sound proofing.
9. To sound tough.
10. To scare people.
11. To attract attention.
12. Poor mufflers.
13. Fewer cylinders.
14. Air-cooled engines.
15. No legislation to control noise.
16. Higher revs.
17. Younger men to drive them.
18. To make the traffic lights change to green.
19. Lower octane fuel.
20. Less efficient muffler.

21. Because everyone knows they are.
22. Because they only come out at night.
23. The frequency of their noise is more annoying.
24. As a signal to other road users of their presence.
25. Because they have not such good drivers.
26. Joie de vivre.
27. They serve as a mating call to young ladies.
28. They go faster.
29. To pretend they go faster.
30. As a virility symbol.
31. To show the fuzz they don't care.
32. To be heard a long way off.
33. Because they are Japanese.
34. Because engine is not enclosed.
35. Because exhaust system is shorter.
36. The gearing is different.

## 45. Six or more things not to do with gunpowder

1. Put it in cigarettes.
2. Fire bullets with it.
3. Build campfires with it.
4. Invent it.
5. Feed it to friends.
6. Or animals.
7. Don't even feed it to enemies.
8. Don't hit it.
9. Don't put it near heat.
10. Don't put match to it.
11. Play with it.
12. Throw down a sewer.
13. Give to children.
14. Make bombs.
15. Smoke it.
16. Eat it.
17. Stuff it in your ears (especially if you keep a cigarette on the ear).
18. Dampen it.
19. Put it in curry powder.
20. Use as flea powder for the cat.
21. Add to dough mixture.
22. Put in tea bags.
23. Use for moxibustion.
24. Use as vermifuge.
25. Roast it.
26. Store under House of Commons.
27. Use as fish food.
28. Send by post.
29. Carry in your pockets.
30. Use as snuff.
31. To remove false teeth.
32. To stuff children's toys.
33. To polish a dance floor.
34. Forget it.
35. Despise it.

36. To cure piles.
37. Stuff a bean bag.
38. Clean the carpet.
39. As a fuel additive.
40. Use as foot powder.
41. As wig powder.
42. As condiment.
43. Stuff it up an elephant's trunk.

## 46. Six or more ways to get from New York City to Sydney, Australia, by bicycle

1. Close your eyes.
2. Pedal fast.
3. Wait for an ice age.
4. Wear goggles.
5. Empty the ocean.
6. Use the *U.S.S. Enterprise* and let them transport you.
7. Pedal round deck of boat.
8. Cycle along on surface of water stretches using floats.
9. Use tandem and let other fellow do the pedalling.
10. Carry the bicycle and walk/canoe the trip.
11. Send yourself and bicycle by post.
12. Faith.
13. Put paddles and pontoons on.
14. Don wings and fly.
15. Sit on the bike and use commercial dialogue.
16. Swim, towing the bike.
17. Use collapsible bicycle and travel by air.
18. Pedal very fast up a long ramp and try to jump the Pacific.
19. Pedal very carefully along a very long plank.
20. Use a shorter plank and go from boat to boat.
21. Take a very deep breath for the Pacific.
22. Use scuba gear.
23. Use a submarine.
24. Try a kite.
25. Or an airship.
26. Use about ten million tons of concrete to form a bridge.
27. Use about eight million tons of concrete to form stepping stones and jump, carrying the bike.

## 47. Seven or more nice things about your favorite pet

1. She's/he's good to talk to.
2. She's/he's a good flier.
3. Cooks well.

4. Does windows.
5. She/he feels strongly about social reform.
6. Good historian.
7. Feels warm.
8. Loves me.
9. Is loyal.
10. Protects me.
11. Walks with me.
12. Has nice eyes.
13. Has nice teeth.
14. Has nice tail.
15. Makes me feel good.
16. I like him/her.
17. He/she likes me.
18. Good companion.
19. Excuse for taking a walk.
20. Breaks up weariness.
21. He/she shows appreciation.
22. Does not talk back.
23. Obeys commands.
24. Lovely long ears.
25. Only needs feeding twice a day.
26. Blond hair.
27. Does not bite.
28. Big boobs.
29. Not a lot of noise.
30. Not much mess.
31. Good teeth.
32. Cute little nose.
33. Long whiskers.
34. Neat moustache.
35. Does not eat much.
36. His/her money.
37. She/he says yes.
38. She/he never says no.
39. She/he is supercalifragilistic-expealidocious.

## 48. Six or more nice things about the person to your right

1. They are not always there.
2. They constantly change.
3. I can't depend on them.
4. He is smart.
5. She is pretty.
6. She is smart.
7. He is pretty.
8. I don't know anything about them.
9. I can get to know them.
10. Has nice hair.
11. Nice eyes.
12. Nice smile.
13. Nice legs.
14. Nice voice.
15. Nice chest.
16. Nice manners.
17. Makes me feel good.
18. Makes me feel important.
19. Nonexistent.
20. Smells good.
21. Looks good.
22. Speaks well.
23. Bright.
24. Considerate.

25. Smokes pot.
26. Soon he'll be old enough to support me.
27. His watch tells the right time.
28. Her boobs are big.
29. "A poor thing but mine own."
30. Magnetic personality.
31. Good cook.

## 49. Six or more good reasons for having justice

1. 'Cause our Declaration and Constitution say we should.
2. Because justice is a basic idea set forth and should be granted to all men.
3. I was brought up having justice and if it was taken away I would feel deprived.
4. It dictates some means of order.
5. I can't hold it, and therefore I need it.
6. To keep order.
7. To treat everyone equal.
8. To help people.
9. To provide rules.
10. Even a score.
11. Something to bitch about.
12. Carry out the laws.
13. Maintain the legal profession.
14. Appoint judges.
15. Provide political patronage.
16. To send people to jail.
17. To provide employment for cops.
18. Otherwise there would be no criminals.
19. Because lady police wear black stockings.
20. To hang people.
21. To enable me to appear at an inflated fee as an expert witness.
22. To compare with injustice.
23. So judges can wear wigs.
24. So people can complain.
25. To sublimate sadistic instincts.
26. So we can judge others.
27. So policemen can shoot innocent bystanders.
28. So presidents can overrule it.
29. So we can sue someone.
30. To fill law books.
31. Otherwise there would not be much point to a detective story.
32. To make television series.
33. Because anything else would spoil the flavour.
34. To prevent crime.
35. So men can be free.
36. So don't put gunpowder or

grass seed up an elephant's trunk.

## 50. Six or more nice things about yourself

1. I'm always here when I need myself.
2. I'm sociable.
3. I'm cute.
4. I'm wearing a Mickey Mouse T-shirt.
5. I'm great in bed.
6. I'm great out of bed.
7. Have a nice wife.
8. Have a nice car.
9. Have a nice dog.
10. Have a nice house.
11. Have a nice family.
12. Have a nice cat.
13. Have nice in-laws.
14. Have nice parents.
15. Care about people.
16. Smart.
17. Good looking.
18. Reasonable.
19. Like people.
20. Sense of humor.
21. Good companion.
22. Easy going.
23. Ad infinitum.
24. My modesty.
25. My hairy eyeballs.
26. My baby blue eyes.
27. My bank balance.
28. My dimples.
29. My Union Jack knickers.
30. My sweet smile.
31. My wife.
32. My vest.
33. My aftershave.
34. One of my feet does not smell.
35. Nor does the other.
36. Mye speling.
37. I once won a "Mr. Beautiful Legs" contest!
38. I did not win a "What Do Virgins Eat for Breakfast?" contest, though I should have, and only protested moderately (for me).
39. I do not cheat.

## 51. Seven or more reasons why men should not be free

1. They cost a lot to manufacture.
2. Because they are crazy and cannot be controlled.
3. Because leather bondage is so much fun.
4. Because freedom costs a dollar and bondage only costs 25¢.

5. Nobody would buy them.
6. Because we would never have had Roots.
7. Because if God had wanted them free he would have made them that way.
8. To maintain order.
9. To protect women.
10. To keep peace.
11. To fight wars.
12. To fill up jails.
13. To maintain police force.
14. To maintain government.
15. To prevent thefts.
16. Better controlled than women.
17. Could not commit as many crimes.
18. Could not marry.
19. Produce more.
20. Could not change jobs.
21. More easily punished.
22. Would be in at night.
23. Avoid temptation.
24. The judge said otherwise.
25. Because they are four.
26. Because everywhere they are in chains.
27. Because they owe me money.
28. Because they didn't read the small print.
29. Because women need them.
30. Someone lost the key.
31. They did it.
32. They won't pay the fine.
33. They have no friends.
34. Because women and children have to pay.
35. The witnesses were bribed.
36. Because she promised.
37. Because she's pregnant.
38. So we can have justice.

## 52. Eight or more reasons for having laws

1. Because somebody spent all that time writing them.
2. Because Congress wouldn't have much to do if we didn't.
3. Nothing would be against them and life would be boring.
4. I kinda like them.
5. Laws are fun, too.
6. Because not everybody does and we should feel honored.
7. To give lawyers something to do.
8. To protect the weak.
9. To live in peace.
10. To prevent wars.
11. To be productive.
12. Maintain law and order.
13. Inhibit society.
14. Provide for police.
15. Treat everyone the same.

16. Govern society.
17. Produce revenue.
18. Something to break.
19. So the law schools have a syllabus.
20. To send people to jail.
21. To inculcate a sense of sin.
22. To give the cops something to do.
23. To harass John Doe.
24. To catch us out.
25. So they can be broken.
26. To meet other people.
27. To impose the wishes of the majority on all.
28. To impose the wishes of a minority on the majority.
29. To hang people.
30. To punish people.
31. To avoid common sense.
32. So we can have justice.
33. Because otherwise we would put gunpowder and grass seed where we shouldn't.

## 53. Seven or more ways to peel an egg

1. With your toes.
2. Standing on your head.
3. With an electric egg peeler.
4. Carefully.
5. Hire a cheap Japanese worker to do it.
6. With a serrated knife.
7. With steel wool.
8. Raw.
9. Cooked.
10. Break it and throw away shell.
11. Burn the shell off.
12. With a knife.
13. Use your teeth.
14. Freeze it.
15. Smash it.
16. Hardboil it.
17. With a spoon.
18. Roll it.
19. Sitting down.
20. Standing up.
21. With tweezers.
22. With fingers.
23. With gloves.
24. With pinchers.
25. With pliers.
26. With monkey-wrench.
27. Roll it downhill.
28. Jump on it.
29. Bash it with another egg.
30. Stuff in a sock and use as a cosh.
31. Put it under a bus.
32. Throw off the Eiffel Tower.
33. Use as a football.
34. Dissolve shell in vinegar.
35. Soften shell with vinegar, push into bottle: throw bottle into sea: hope for collision with *Queen Elizabeth II*.
36. Attack with a sword.
37. Use as defence against a mad Samurai.
38. Substitute for karate expert's brick.
39. Use as a bookmark.
40. Put in pressure cooker: release pressure rapidly.
41. Use as a golf ball.
42. Mount under doorknocker.
43. Place under doormat.
44. Throw in air: repeat if necessary.
45. Fire from a musket.
46. Give to a squirrel.
47. Sandpaper it.
48. Grate it with a grater.
49. Put on seat before someone sits down.
50. Hide in a shoe.
51. Squeeze in the pillywinks.
52. Piece by piece with a laser beam.
53. Place at the epicentre of a thermo-nuclear reaction.
54. Place in open and wait upon wind and weather.
55. Get a little green man from Mars to zap it with his egg peeler.
56. Get an elephant to stand on it.
57. Glue it to wall and hurl *Encyclopaedia Britannica* at it.
58. Roll it between two boards.
59. Swap it for a ready-peeled egg.
60. Coat with glue and remove glue.
61. Use a diamond wheel to cut up shell: then use tiny shears to remove it.

## 54. Six or more ways to make a reflecting surface

1. Use tinfoil.
2. Rub hard.
3. Get a kit from the Edmund Scientific Company.
4. Glue millions of little crystals together and shine.
5. Use a doorknob; it looks funny.
6. Polish it.
7. Paint it.
8. Put glass on it.
9. Shine light on it.
10. Put mirror against it.
11. Put wax on it.
12. With water.
13. With oil.
14. With metal.
15. With wood.
16. Pour liquid in a dish.
17. Use fine grit, finishing with jeweller's rouge.
18. Rub with a soft cloth.
19. Take a surface and teach it to think.

20. Sand in a hot desert.
21. Breathe on it and wipe off.
22. Deposit silver, aluminum, copper, etc. in surface in a vacuum.
23. Electrodeposition of metal. Then rub down.
24. Blow a soap bubble.
25. Shine electromagnetic radiation of wavelength greater than surface irregularities.
26. Fill in irregularities with liquid.
27. Get roll of kitchen foil. Crumple it. Smooth with back of spoon.
28. Pass sheet of plain glass through benzene flame. Place in front of dark surface. Soot on rear surface will reflect.
29. Heat one of many details to melting point. Allow to cool in air.
30. Get a refraction grating and view from where light strikes it at greater than critical angle.
31. Hand a plain sheet of paper to Midas.
32. Boil a kettle. The "steam" is light reflected from the complex surface of the water vapour molecules.
33. Observe the sky, clouds, moon, etc.
34. Apply nail varnish.
35. Stop disturbing the water.
36. Pour oil on troubled waters.

## 55. Eight or more ways to gain weight

1. Eat.
2. Go to the bathroom less.
3. Put rocks in pockets.
4. Build some muscles.
5. Add body parts.
6. Feel heavy.
7. Suck in more air.
8. Eat pastries every meal.
9. Eat only sugars.
10. Drink booze.
11. Drink beer.
12. Eat a high fats diet.
13. Drink wine and soda with meals.
14. Eat all day in bed.
15. Eat more.
16. Eat between meals.
17. Eat desserts.
18. Sit all day.
19. Stay in bed.
20. Eat pasta.
21. Eat bread.
22. Overeat.
23. Swallow a cannonball.
24. Smuggle gold.
25. Carry your wife.

26. Add carbohydrates.
27. Wear a diving suit.
28. Wear wool and get it wet.
29. Let hair grow.
30. Put on extra layers of clothing.
31. Avoid the less fattening foods.
32. Use faulty scales.
33. Do not wash.
34. Do not diet.
35. Grow up.
36. Emigrate to Saturn.
37. Weigh yourself in a lift travelling upwards.
38. Go to the Dead Sea.
39. Wear another wig.
40. Shake hands with Midas.
41. Become pregnant.
42. Stop taking the pill.
43. Go on the pill.
44. Wear ear rings.
45. Throw away your contact lenses and wear glasses.
46. Drink enough to get cirrhosis and hence ascites.
47. Go into congestive heart failure.
48. Stimulate your pituitary and become acromegalic.
49. Cure your ulcer.
50. Drink polluted water and gain a "water wolf."
51. Do not cut your fingernails.
52. Have your false teeth made of osmium.
53. Have your wooden leg made of teak.
54. Carry a walking stick.
55. Fill your fountain pen.
56. Carry a parrot on your shoulder.
57. Wear a sword.
58. Grow a beard.
59. Do not trim the hairs in your nostrils.
60. Take less exercise.
61. Wear a diamond in your belly button.
62. Look at Medusa.
63. Eat Alice's biscuit.

## 56. Six or more ways to prevent sunburn

1. Spread some sort of reflective surface over your body.
2. Close the window shade.
3. Stay in shade.
4. Stay in car.
5. Wear sun screen.
6. Go out only at night.
7. Go out on cloudy days.
8. Go to North Pole.
9. Stay covered.
10. Use lotions.
11. Go out on rainy days.
12. Stay indoors.
13. Use cream.

14. Become a vampire.
15. Wear protective clothing.
16. Get tanned gradually.
17. Go to Pluto.
18. Hide under the carpet.
19. Be an elephant.
20. Be a whale.
21. Go deep-sea diving.
22. Hide in a harem.
23. Insult a witch and get changed into a frog.
24. Sunbathe behind glass opaque to U-V light.
25. Sleep in the shade of your pet elephant.
26. Send a deputy.

## 57. Seven or more people you'd like to be stranded with on a desert island

1. Ben Franklin.
2. Tom Jefferson.
3. Freud.
4. Socrates.
5. Woody Allen.
6. A helpless stereotypical stranded girl.
7. Two helpless stereotypical stranded girls.
8. Native of the island.
9. Expert in survival.
10. Beautiful girl.
11. Beautiful woman.
12. Expert sailor.
13. Well digger.
14. Priest.
15. Linda Lovelace.
16. Jane Fonda.
17. The Newlywed Gamers.
18. Dallas Cowgirls.
19. God.

20. Marilyn Chambers.
21. Jesus Christ.
22. Robinson Crusoe.
23. Leonardo da Vinci.
24. Thomas Edison.
25. Captain Bligh.
26. Patricia Blake.
27. Bugs Bunny.
28. Snow White and the Seven Dwarfs.
29. Swiss Family Robinson.
30. Brigitte Bardot.
31. Professor Challenger.
32. Hercules.
33. Hermes Trismegistus.
34. Apollonius of Tyana.
35. Mahomet.
36. Pegasus.
37. Man Friday.
38. Jack (in *Coral Island*).
39. Circe.
40. Jacques Cousteau.
41. Ragnor Hairybreeks.
42. J. W. von Goethe.
43. Isaac Newton.
44. Captain Nemo.
45. Robby the Robot (*Forbidden Planet*).
46. Twenty-seven Irishmen to dig the ditches.

## 58. Seven or more ways to lose weight

1. Cut off various body parts.
2. Adjust the scale.
3. Don't exercise.
4. Spit.
5. Remove your clothes.
6. Tighten your belt.
7. Remove intestine.
8. Wire jaw shut.
9. Play ball all day.
10. Be a dope addict.
11. Remove stomach.

12. Eat proper diet.
13. Take pills.
14. Skip lunch.
15. Eliminate sweets.
16. Eliminate pastas.
17. Eat salads.
18. Eliminate bread.
19. Fast.
20. Diet.
21. Suck a tube of cyanoacrylic resin—your lips are sealed.
22. Swallow a tapeworm.
23. Get a hair net.
24. Cut your fingernails.
25. Unscrew your wooden leg.
26. Weigh yourself in a lift traveling downward.
27. Go to the moon.
28. Go into orbit.
29. Say hello to Dracula.
30. Give blood.
31. Climb Mount Everest.
32. Cut off your head.
33. Get circumcised.
34. Go to the loo.
35. Exercise moderately.
36. Eat less.
37. Give up a meal a day.
38. Fart once weekly.
39. Take a diuretic.
40. Pick your nose.
41. Strip naked.
42. Pluck your eyebrows.
43. Remove your belly button lint.
44. Take off your glasses.
45. Clean your teeth.
46. Remove your teeth.
47. Empty your pockets.
48. Remove earrings.
49. Catch cholera.
50. Keep green monkeys.
51. Become a harem keeper.
52. Eat carcinogens.
53. Give up sugar.
54. Grow an ulcer.

55. Set fire to yourself.
56. Empty your fountain pen.
57. Take out the battery from your hearing aid.
58. Have your spleen removed.
59. Breathe out.
60. Have a shave.
61. Have an enema.
62. Take thyroxin.
63. Take amphetamines.
64. Be delivered of a baby.
65. Drink from Alice's bottle.

## 59. Six or more places where you could place a second nose

1. Directly on the back of your head.
2. Out West.
3. Norway.
4. In your pocket with your handkerchief.
5. Where that bump is on your ankle.
6. Above the existing one.
7. Beside the present one.
8. On each side of the head.
9. On your back.
10. On your belly.
11. On your forehead.
12. On your navel.
13. Under your armpits.
14. Under your chin.
15. On your big toe.
16. On your first nose.
17. On the inside.
18. Top of the mantelpiece.
19. On the clock face.
20. On a second person.
21. On his dog.
22. On a finger.

# MARCH

### Mental Calisthenic #3

Sit in a comfortable area free of distractions. As you sit there, comfortably and easily, take a deep breath and exhale very, very slowly. Now breathe normally. With each exhale think of one new English word that begins with the letter "A." Continue this exercise for five minutes. Proceed with "B," "C," "D," etc., during subsequent sessions. Go to a Mental Jogging exercise.

### 60. Six or more places never to put grass seed

| Response | Score |
|---|---|
| 1. | 1 |
| 2. | 1 |
| 3. | 1 |
| 4. | 1 |
| 5. | 1 |
| 6. | 1 |
| Bonus Responses | |
| 7. | 2 |
| 8. | 2 |
| 9. | 2 |
| 10. | 2 |
| 11. | 2 |
| 12. | 2 |
| 13. | 2 |
| 14. | 2 |
| 15. | 2 |
| 16. | 2 |

Total ☐

### 61. Seven or more reasons not to smell a rose

| Response | Score |
|---|---|
| 1. | 1 |
| 2. | 1 |
| 3. | 1 |
| 4. | 1 |
| 5. | 1 |
| 6. | 1 |
| 7. | 1 |
| Bonus Responses | |
| 8. | 2 |
| 9. | 2 |
| 10. | 2 |
| 11. | 2 |
| 12. | 2 |
| 13. | 2 |
| 14. | 2 |
| 15. | 2 |
| 16. | 2 |

Total ☐

## 62. Seven or more things to think about while descending on a parachute

| Response | Score |
|---|---|
| 1. _____ | 1 |
| 2. _____ | 1 |
| 3. _____ | 1 |
| 4. _____ | 1 |
| 5. _____ | 1 |
| 6. _____ | 1 |
| 7. _____ | 1 |

**Bonus Responses**

| | |
|---|---|
| 8. _____ | 2 |
| 9. _____ | 2 |
| 10. _____ | 2 |
| 11. _____ | 2 |
| 12. _____ | 2 |
| 13. _____ | 2 |
| 14. _____ | 2 |
| 15. _____ | 2 |
| 16. _____ | 2 |

Total ☐

## 63. Seven or more daydreams everybody has

| Response | Score |
|---|---|
| 1. _____ | 1 |
| 2. _____ | 1 |
| 3. _____ | 1 |
| 4. _____ | 1 |
| 5. _____ | 1 |
| 6. _____ | 1 |
| 7. _____ | 1 |

**Bonus Responses**

| | |
|---|---|
| 8. _____ | 2 |
| 9. _____ | 2 |
| 10. _____ | 2 |
| 11. _____ | 2 |
| 12. _____ | 2 |
| 13. _____ | 2 |
| 14. _____ | 2 |
| 15. _____ | 2 |
| 16. _____ | 2 |

Total ☐

## 64. Six or more ways to produce electricity

| Response | Score |
|---|---|
| 1. _____ | 1 |
| 2. _____ | 1 |
| 3. _____ | 1 |
| 4. _____ | 1 |
| 5. _____ | 1 |
| 6. _____ | 1 |

**Bonus Responses**

| | |
|---|---|
| 7. _____ | 2 |
| 8. _____ | 2 |
| 9. _____ | 2 |
| 10. _____ | 2 |
| 11. _____ | 2 |
| 12. _____ | 2 |
| 13. _____ | 2 |
| 14. _____ | 2 |
| 15. _____ | 2 |
| 16. _____ | 2 |

Total ☐

## 65. Seven or more important news events of your parents' lifetime

| Response | Score |
|---|---|
| 1. _____ | 1 |
| 2. _____ | 1 |
| 3. _____ | 1 |
| 4. _____ | 1 |
| 5. _____ | 1 |
| 6. _____ | 1 |
| 7. _____ | 1 |

**Bonus Responses**

| | |
|---|---|
| 8. _____ | 2 |
| 9. _____ | 2 |
| 10. _____ | 2 |
| 11. _____ | 2 |
| 12. _____ | 2 |
| 13. _____ | 2 |
| 14. _____ | 2 |
| 15. _____ | 2 |
| 16. _____ | 2 |

Total ☐

## 66. Eight or more important news events of your own lifetime

| Response | Score |
|---|---|
| 1. _____ | 1 |
| 2. _____ | 1 |
| 3. _____ | 1 |
| 4. _____ | 1 |
| 5. _____ | 1 |
| 6. _____ | 1 |
| 7. _____ | 1 |
| 8. _____ | 1 |

**Bonus Responses**

| | |
|---|---|
| 9. _____ | 2 |
| 10. _____ | 2 |
| 11. _____ | 2 |
| 12. _____ | 2 |
| 13. _____ | 2 |
| 14. _____ | 2 |
| 15. _____ | 2 |
| 16. _____ | 2 |

Total ☐

## 67. Seven or more uses for a hockey puck

| Response | Score |
|---|---|
| 1. _____ | 1 |
| 2. _____ | 1 |
| 3. _____ | 1 |
| 4. _____ | 1 |
| 5. _____ | 1 |
| 6. _____ | 1 |
| 7. _____ | 1 |

**Bonus Responses**

| | |
|---|---|
| 8. _____ | 2 |
| 9. _____ | 2 |
| 10. _____ | 2 |
| 11. _____ | 2 |
| 12. _____ | 2 |
| 13. _____ | 2 |
| 14. _____ | 2 |
| 15. _____ | 2 |
| 16. _____ | 2 |

Total ☐

## 68. Eight or more non-sport uses of a football

| Response | Score |
|---|---|
| 1. _____ | 1 |
| 2. _____ | 1 |
| 3. _____ | 1 |
| 4. _____ | 1 |
| 5. _____ | 1 |
| 6. _____ | 1 |

**Bonus Responses**

| | |
|---|---|
| 7. _____ | 2 |
| 8. _____ | 2 |
| 9. _____ | 2 |
| 10. _____ | 2 |
| 11. _____ | 2 |
| 12. _____ | 2 |
| 13. _____ | 2 |
| 14. _____ | 2 |
| 15. _____ | 2 |
| 16. _____ | 2 |

Total ☐

## 69. Six or more reasons why we have interstate highways

| Response | Score |
|---|---|
| 1. _____ | 1 |
| 2. _____ | 1 |
| 3. _____ | 1 |
| 4. _____ | 1 |
| 5. _____ | 1 |
| 6. _____ | 1 |

**Bonus Responses**

| | |
|---|---|
| 7. _____ | 2 |
| 8. _____ | 2 |
| 9. _____ | 2 |
| 10. _____ | 2 |
| 11. _____ | 2 |
| 12. _____ | 2 |
| 13. _____ | 2 |
| 14. _____ | 2 |
| 15. _____ | 2 |
| 16. _____ | 2 |

Total ☐

## 70. Six or more reasons why wells become dry

| Response | Score |
|---|---|
| 1. _____ | 1 |
| 2. _____ | 1 |
| 3. _____ | 1 |
| 4. _____ | 1 |
| 5. _____ | 1 |
| 6. _____ | 1 |

Bonus Responses

| | |
|---|---|
| 7. _____ | 2 |
| 8. _____ | 2 |
| 9. _____ | 2 |
| 10. _____ | 2 |
| 11. _____ | 2 |
| 12. _____ | 2 |
| 13. _____ | 2 |
| 14. _____ | 2 |
| 15. _____ | 2 |
| 16. _____ | 2 |

Total ☐

## 71. Seven or more reasons why water is not found in deserts

| Response | Score |
|---|---|
| 1. _____ | 1 |
| 2. _____ | 1 |
| 3. _____ | 1 |
| 4. _____ | 1 |
| 5. _____ | 1 |
| 6. _____ | 1 |
| 7. _____ | 1 |

Bonus Responses

| | |
|---|---|
| 8. _____ | 2 |
| 9. _____ | 2 |
| 10. _____ | 2 |
| 11. _____ | 2 |
| 12. _____ | 2 |
| 13. _____ | 2 |
| 14. _____ | 2 |
| 15. _____ | 2 |
| 16. _____ | 2 |

Total ☐

## 72. Six or more desserts always to avoid

| Response | Score |
|---|---|
| 1. _____ | 1 |
| 2. _____ | 1 |
| 3. _____ | 1 |
| 4. _____ | 1 |
| 5. _____ | 1 |
| 6. _____ | 1 |

Bonus Responses

| | |
|---|---|
| 7. _____ | 2 |
| 8. _____ | 2 |
| 9. _____ | 2 |
| 10. _____ | 2 |
| 11. _____ | 2 |
| 12. _____ | 2 |
| 13. _____ | 2 |
| 14. _____ | 2 |
| 15. _____ | 2 |
| 16. _____ | 2 |

Total ☐

## 73. Six or more college majors that least interest you

| Response | Score |
|---|---|
| 1. _____ | 1 |
| 2. _____ | 1 |
| 3. _____ | 1 |
| 4. _____ | 1 |
| 5. _____ | 1 |
| 6. _____ | 1 |

Bonus Responses

| | |
|---|---|
| 7. _____ | 2 |
| 8. _____ | 2 |
| 9. _____ | 2 |
| 10. _____ | 2 |
| 11. _____ | 2 |
| 12. _____ | 2 |
| 13. _____ | 2 |
| 14. _____ | 2 |
| 15. _____ | 2 |
| 16. _____ | 2 |

Total ☐

## 74. Seven or more things you'd have to change about your body to become a bird

| Response | Score |
|---|---|
| 1. _____ | 1 |
| 2. _____ | 1 |
| 3. _____ | 1 |
| 4. _____ | 1 |
| 5. _____ | 1 |
| 6. _____ | 1 |
| 7. _____ | 1 |

Bonus Responses

| | |
|---|---|
| 8. _____ | 2 |
| 9. _____ | 2 |
| 10. _____ | 2 |
| 11. _____ | 2 |
| 12. _____ | 2 |
| 13. _____ | 2 |
| 14. _____ | 2 |
| 15. _____ | 2 |
| 16. _____ | 2 |

Total ☐

## 75. The six worst movies you've ever seen

| Response | Score |
|---|---|
| 1. _____ | 1 |
| 2. _____ | 1 |
| 3. _____ | 1 |
| 4. _____ | 1 |
| 5. _____ | 1 |
| 6. _____ | 1 |

Bonus Responses

| | |
|---|---|
| 7. _____ | 2 |
| 8. _____ | 2 |
| 9. _____ | 2 |
| 10. _____ | 2 |
| 11. _____ | 2 |
| 12. _____ | 2 |
| 13. _____ | 2 |
| 14. _____ | 2 |
| 15. _____ | 2 |
| 16. _____ | 2 |

Total ☐

## 76. Six or more things that have happened to you that you wouldn't like to have happen again

| Response | Score |
|---|---|
| 1. _____ | 1 |
| 2. _____ | 1 |
| 3. _____ | 1 |
| 4. _____ | 1 |
| 5. _____ | 1 |
| 6. _____ | 1 |

Bonus Responses

| | |
|---|---|
| 7. _____ | 2 |
| 8. _____ | 2 |
| 9. _____ | 2 |
| 10. _____ | 2 |
| 11. _____ | 2 |
| 12. _____ | 2 |
| 13. _____ | 2 |
| 14. _____ | 2 |
| 15. _____ | 2 |
| 16. _____ | 2 |

Total ☐

## 77. Seven or more reasons for building a home by a lake

| Response | Score |
|---|---|
| 1. _____ | 1 |
| 2. _____ | 1 |
| 3. _____ | 1 |
| 4. _____ | 1 |
| 5. _____ | 1 |
| 6. _____ | 1 |
| 7. _____ | 1 |

Bonus Responses

| | |
|---|---|
| 8. _____ | 2 |
| 9. _____ | 2 |
| 10. _____ | 2 |
| 11. _____ | 2 |
| 12. _____ | 2 |
| 13. _____ | 2 |
| 14. _____ | 2 |
| 15. _____ | 2 |
| 16. _____ | 2 |

Total ☐

## 78. Six or more ways to move a vehicle without an engine

| Response | Score |
|---|---|
| 1. _____ | 1 |
| 2. _____ | 1 |
| 3. _____ | 1 |
| 4. _____ | 1 |
| 5. _____ | 1 |
| 6. _____ | 1 |

**Bonus Responses**

| | |
|---|---|
| 7. _____ | 2 |
| 8. _____ | 2 |
| 9. _____ | 2 |
| 10. _____ | 2 |
| 11. _____ | 2 |
| 12. _____ | 2 |
| 13. _____ | 2 |
| 14. _____ | 2 |
| 15. _____ | 2 |
| 16. _____ | 2 |

Total ☐

## 79. Seven or more reasons for headwaiters

| Response | Score |
|---|---|
| 1. _____ | 1 |
| 2. _____ | 1 |
| 3. _____ | 1 |
| 4. _____ | 1 |
| 5. _____ | 1 |
| 6. _____ | 1 |
| 7. _____ | 1 |

**Bonus Responses**

| | |
|---|---|
| 8. _____ | 2 |
| 9. _____ | 2 |
| 10. _____ | 2 |
| 11. _____ | 2 |
| 12. _____ | 2 |
| 13. _____ | 2 |
| 14. _____ | 2 |
| 15. _____ | 2 |
| 16. _____ | 2 |

Total ☐

## 80. Six or more ways to avoid stepping on ants

| Response | Score |
|---|---|
| 1. _____ | 1 |
| 2. _____ | 1 |
| 3. _____ | 1 |
| 4. _____ | 1 |
| 5. _____ | 1 |
| 6. _____ | 1 |

**Bonus Responses**

| | |
|---|---|
| 7. _____ | 2 |
| 8. _____ | 2 |
| 9. _____ | 2 |
| 10. _____ | 2 |
| 11. _____ | 2 |
| 12. _____ | 2 |
| 13. _____ | 2 |
| 14. _____ | 2 |
| 15. _____ | 2 |
| 16. _____ | 2 |

Total ☐

## 81. Eight or more routes from New Orleans, Louisiana, to Mexico City, Mexico

| Response | Score |
|---|---|
| 1. _____ | 1 |
| 2. _____ | 1 |
| 3. _____ | 1 |
| 4. _____ | 1 |
| 5. _____ | 1 |
| 6. _____ | 1 |
| 7. _____ | 1 |
| 8. _____ | 1 |

**Bonus Responses**

| | |
|---|---|
| 9. _____ | 2 |
| 10. _____ | 2 |
| 11. _____ | 2 |
| 12. _____ | 2 |
| 13. _____ | 2 |
| 14. _____ | 2 |
| 15. _____ | 2 |
| 16. _____ | 2 |

Total ☐

## 82. Six or more things you remember about the 1972 Thanksgiving dinner

| Response | Score |
|---|---|
| 1. _____ | 1 |
| 2. _____ | 1 |
| 3. _____ | 1 |
| 4. _____ | 1 |
| 5. _____ | 1 |
| 6. _____ | 1 |

**Bonus Responses**

| | |
|---|---|
| 7. _____ | 2 |
| 8. _____ | 2 |
| 9. _____ | 2 |
| 10. _____ | 2 |
| 11. _____ | 2 |
| 12. _____ | 2 |
| 13. _____ | 2 |
| 14. _____ | 2 |
| 15. _____ | 2 |
| 16. _____ | 2 |

Total ☐

## 83. Eight or more things never to say to a truck driver

| Response | Score |
|---|---|
| 1. _____ | 1 |
| 2. _____ | 1 |
| 3. _____ | 1 |
| 4. _____ | 1 |
| 5. _____ | 1 |
| 6. _____ | 1 |
| 7. _____ | 1 |
| 8. _____ | 1 |

**Bonus Responses**

| | |
|---|---|
| 9. _____ | 2 |
| 10. _____ | 2 |
| 11. _____ | 2 |
| 12. _____ | 2 |
| 13. _____ | 2 |
| 14. _____ | 2 |
| 15. _____ | 2 |
| 16. _____ | 2 |

Total ☐

## 84. Seven or more reasons why pygmies are short

| Response | Score |
|---|---|
| 1. _____ | 1 |
| 2. _____ | 1 |
| 3. _____ | 1 |
| 4. _____ | 1 |
| 5. _____ | 1 |
| 6. _____ | 1 |
| 7. _____ | 1 |

**Bonus Responses**

| | |
|---|---|
| 8. _____ | 2 |
| 9. _____ | 2 |
| 10. _____ | 2 |
| 11. _____ | 2 |
| 12. _____ | 2 |
| 13. _____ | 2 |
| 14. _____ | 2 |
| 15. _____ | 2 |
| 16. _____ | 2 |

Total ☐

## 85. Seven or more uses of bamboo

| Response | Score |
|---|---|
| 1. _____ | 1 |
| 2. _____ | 1 |
| 3. _____ | 1 |
| 4. _____ | 1 |
| 5. _____ | 1 |
| 6. _____ | 1 |
| 7. _____ | 1 |

**Bonus Responses**

| | |
|---|---|
| 8. _____ | 2 |
| 9. _____ | 2 |
| 10. _____ | 2 |
| 11. _____ | 2 |
| 12. _____ | 2 |
| 13. _____ | 2 |
| 14. _____ | 2 |
| 15. _____ | 2 |
| 16. _____ | 2 |

Total ☐

## 86. Eight or more famous people you've always wanted to meet

| Response | Score |
|---|---|
| 1. | 1 |
| 2. | 1 |
| 3. | 1 |
| 4. | 1 |
| 5. | 1 |
| 6. | 1 |
| 7. | 1 |
| 8. | 1 |

Bonus Responses

| | |
|---|---|
| 9. | 2 |
| 10. | 2 |
| 11. | 2 |
| 12. | 2 |
| 13. | 2 |
| 14. | 2 |
| 15. | 2 |
| 16. | 2 |

Total ☐

## 87. Nine or more uses of dust

| Response | Score |
|---|---|
| 1. | 1 |
| 2. | 1 |
| 3. | 1 |
| 4. | 1 |
| 5. | 1 |
| 6. | 1 |
| 7. | 1 |
| 8. | 1 |
| 9. | 1 |

Bonus Responses

| | |
|---|---|
| 10. | 2 |
| 11. | 2 |
| 12. | 2 |
| 13. | 2 |
| 14. | 2 |
| 15. | 2 |
| 16. | 2 |

Total ☐

## 88. Eight or more places in the world you would never want to visit

| Response | Score |
|---|---|
| 1. | 1 |
| 2. | 1 |
| 3. | 1 |
| 4. | 1 |
| 5. | 1 |
| 6. | 1 |
| 7. | 1 |
| 8. | 1 |

Bonus Responses

| | |
|---|---|
| 9. | 2 |
| 10. | 2 |
| 11. | 2 |
| 12. | 2 |
| 13. | 2 |
| 14. | 2 |
| 15. | 2 |
| 16. | 2 |

Total ☐

## 89. Nine or more things never to throw out

| Response | Score |
|---|---|
| 1. | 1 |
| 2. | 1 |
| 3. | 1 |
| 4. | 1 |
| 5. | 1 |
| 6. | 1 |
| 7. | 1 |
| 8. | 1 |
| 9. | 1 |

Bonus Responses

| | |
|---|---|
| 10. | 2 |
| 11. | 2 |
| 12. | 2 |
| 13. | 2 |
| 14. | 2 |
| 15. | 2 |
| 16. | 2 |

Total ☐

## 90. Eight or more reasons why males are physically stronger than females

| Response | Score |
|---|---|
| 1. _____ | 1 |
| 2. _____ | 1 |
| 3. _____ | 1 |
| 4. _____ | 1 |
| 5. _____ | 1 |
| 6. _____ | 1 |
| 7. _____ | 1 |
| 8. _____ | 1 |

**Bonus Responses**

| | Score |
|---|---|
| 9. _____ | 2 |
| 10. _____ | 2 |
| 11. _____ | 2 |
| 12. _____ | 2 |
| 13. _____ | 2 |
| 14. _____ | 2 |
| 15. _____ | 2 |
| 16. _____ | 2 |

Total ☐

# CONTRIBUTORS' SAMPLE RESPONSES

## 60. Six or more places never to put grass seed

1. Behind your ear.
2. In your shoes.
3. On unpeeled eggs.
4. Where it might not grow.
5. In the ocean.
6. On top of another piece of grass (jealousy).
7. Where the sun doesn't shine.
8. In the soup.
9. In the gas tank.
10. In the well.
11. In the mashed potatoes.
12. In the stew.
13. In all food.
14. In the coffee.
15. In the computer.
16. On the sidewalk.
17. In the basement.
18. On the rugs.
19. In the garage.
20. In your ears.
21. Up nose.
22. Between your toes.
23. In a seed cake.
24. In a salt cellar.
25. On toast.
26. In your bed.
27. In a watch.
28. In a breast prosthesis.
29. In cold water tank of a house.
30. In a tube of toothpaste.
31. In eye lotion.
32. In an electrical socket.
33. On your concrete path.
34. On the floor of your car.
35. In your fountain pen.
36. In your teabags.
37. In the coffee percolator.
38. On the moon.
39. Under the plaster cast on your broken leg.
40. In your belly button.
41. Under your undervest.
42. In your radiator.
43. In library books.
44. In a baby's diaper.
45. Up an elephant's trunk.
46. On a snooker table.
47. In an asthmatic's inhaler.
48. In your grandma's corsets.

## 61. Seven or more reasons not to smell a rose

1. You are not a flower hater.
2. You are in a hurry.
3. You have a cold.
4. You have no sense of smell.
5. You have just smelled something better.
6. It might not smell at all.
7. It might be a plastic one.
8. It might make you sneeze.
9. It might be sprayed with a deadly vapor.
10. There might be an insect inside.
11. It might not like your nose near it.
12. A dog might have wet it.
13. It has not been sterilised.
14. It might make you cough.
15. It could give you nightmares.
16. You might not enjoy it.
17. You might want to keep it.
18. You might be allergic to it.
19. You could start a habit.
20. Someone else might be envious.
21. Others might think you too sensuous.
22. You could prick yourself.
23. You could tear your clothes on a bush.
24. You could knock over a vase.
25. You might trample on other plants to reach it.
26. You might need to stand on a chair to reach it.
27. It could be downwind of a sewer.
28. You could frighten it.
29. It might conceal a microbomb.
30. Could be a sign for a secret agent nearby.
31. It might change into a monster.
32. There are more fragrant flowers to smell.
33. You can easily irritate your nostrils.
34. It takes too long.
35. There might be a stench in the air.
36. If it's weak, you might break it or kill it.
37. It could be addictive.
38. It might distract you from what you have to do at the time.
39. The other flowers would become jealous.
40. A squirrel might become interested. Then he might decide to eat it.
41. To keep from missing the smell of other flowers.
42. Because you don't like the smell.
43. To keep at a short distance in order to be able to enjoy the beauty of nature as well.
44. To avoid bees.
45. So a conversation will not be interrupted.
46. People might not want you on their property.
47. It's dead.
48. There's a vicious dog next to it.
49. You can't find one.
50. You're stepping on it.
51. You've got a stuffed nose.
52. You haven't got a nose.
53. The rose has gas all over it.

## 62. Seven or more things to think about while descending on a parachute

1. If there's a hole in the parachute.
2. The plane flying towards you.
3. Your great-aunt in Alabama.
4. The color of your parachute.
5. Whether or not you locked your car.
6. Why you're descending on a parachute.
7. How to get home when you land.
8. How your parachute got stuck on the wing of the plane.
9. The bird chewing on your parachute.
10. Whose house you're about to land on.
11. The speed at which you're descending.
12. How the wind feels.
13. The temperature of the air.
14. The view.
15. How far you have descended.
16. How much farther you will descend.
17. The weather.
18. How warmly you're dressed.
19. What you're wearing.
20. If you brought a spare parachute.
21. Who will help you get the parachute off.
22. Do you want to go up again?
23. How you feel?
24. Was the trip (i.e., descent) worth it.
25. Are you risking your life?
26. Is it harder to breathe at a higher altitude?
27. How the air smells.
28. Are there clouds above you.
29. Is the sun warm?
30. Will you bring a friend next time?
31. What would you normally be doing now?
32. How does this jump compare to others?
33. Should you have worn sunglasses?
34. What would happen if the parachute broke?
35. Hitting a bird.
36. Landing in a tree or a lake.
37. Hitting the person parachuting below you.
38. The cost.
39. What it would be like to fly.
40. Where you will land.
41. How to avoid seriously maiming your body.
42. How to avoid being hit by a foreign object.
43. What you will do when you land.
44. How to convince your friends that you were on a parachute.
45. The weather around you.
46. Who is going to pay for your funeral.
47. When to pull the cord.
48. How to make the landing.
49. The force of the wind.
50. Is this thing safe?
51. Why are you doing this?
52. What will your friends think?
53. What's for dinner?
54. How quiet it is.
55. How afraid you are.
56. How you are enjoying it.
57. How much longer before you land.
58. What to do if you land on a ferocious bull.
59. How the family are feeling.
60. Has the plane landed yet?
61. Is your will in order?
62. Are there any reporters below?
63. Will your picture be in the paper?
64. Will you be on television local news?
65. Will you make a fool of yourself on landing?
66. Will everyone cheer?
67. What are those dots down there?
68. Isn't the landscape lovely?
69. Will you collide with a bird?
70. How lovely the clouds are.
71. Is a broken leg very painful?
72. There is no one to talk to.
73. No one would hear you if you screamed.
74. No one could criticise your singing.
75. Everything's getting bigger.
76. Christmas will soon be here.
77. You might sleep better tonight.
78. What's it like in Heaven?
79. Or the other place?
80. Perhaps it's really a dream anyway.
81. Remember to thank the pilot when you next see him.

1. Getting into first choice of colleges.
2. Getting out of high school.
3. Living a leisurely life in Hawaii.
4. Owning a large farm.
5. Accumulating a lot of wealth.
6. Gaining power.
7. Being respected.
8. Being successful.
9. Feeling fulfilled.
10. Being happy in your work.
11. Being valuable.
12. Being wanted.
13. Being needed.
14. Having sex with some sex-symbol.
15. Lying on the beach (this usually occurs in the winter).
16. Skiing down three feet of powder on expert trails in Vermont while simultaneously missing school (usually occurs during spring and fall).
17. If you're younger than seventeen in New Jersey, driving.
18. Eating a big, tasty, juicy steak.
19. Enjoying hedonism on some remote, almost-deserted island.
20. Being president of the U.S.
21. Becoming involved in a grandiose scandal.
22. Being the most popular person in the country.
23. Attending a school where there is no grading.
24. Being a star baseball player.
25. Becoming the lead in a new feature movie.
26. Being offered the automobile of your own choosing.
27. Willing servants.
28. An extra-sensitive spouse.
29. Special popularity among friends.
30. A position of influence.
31. Having a famous face.
32. Inventing something brilliantly simple.
33. Admiration from others.
34. Finding treasure.
35. Inheriting a fortune.
36. Winning a competition.
37. Finding you have a deep unknown talent.
38. A dream house.
39. A garden with a swimming pool.
40. The most expensive car.
41. Lavish clothes in abundance.
42. Going on a luxury holiday.
43. Visiting isolated corners of the world.
44. Flying in Concorde.
45. Going on a Mediterranean cruise.
46. Owning a yacht.
47. Meeting a favourite film star.
48. Winning at a casino.
49. Having a private desert island.
50. Winning a lottery.
51. Real jewels for every occasion.
52. Driving a racing car.
53. Driving a train.
54. Having a secret lover.
55. Rivalry among several lovers.
56. Meeting a long lost friend.
57. Meeting a friendly ghost.
58. Appearing on television.
59. Solving a national problem.
60. Visiting the moon.
61. Printing your own money.
62. Robbing a bank and not getting caught.
63. Winning a beauty contest.
64. Speaking many languages.
65. Growing prize vegetables.
66. Swimming the English Channel.
67. Having tea with the Queen.
68. Running a small business.
69. Running away for a while.
70. Working only when you feel like it.
71. Being able to fly.
72. Seeing into the future.
73. Making a complaint without being nervous.
74. Eating chocolates and staying slim.
75. Having children who realise our own ambitions.

1. Go fly a kite.
2. Hold a long metal bar in the air during a thunderstorm.
3. Combing your hair in the winter.
4. Walking on wool carpets and touching metal.
5. Waterwheel.
6. Windmill.
7. Capture and utilize lightning.
8. Harness a river.
9. Rub your feet on a rug.
10. Rub objects on a sweater (e.g., balloon).
11. Harness the energy of the sun and give it a charge.
12. Using a hydro-powered generator.
13. Harnessing an electric eel.
14. Making your enemy run on a treadmill.
15. Get some lightning and store it.
16. Build a nuclear reactor in your backyard.
17. Pray for it.
18. Steal it.
19. Grow it in place of your front lawn.
20. Put Sonny and Cher in the same bedroom.
21. Watch television in the bathtub.
22. Using a simple battery.
23. Moving a magnet past a coil of wire.
24. The action of acids on various metals.
25. Through the use of a thermocouple.
26. Photo electric cells—conversion of light energy to electrical energy.
27. Oil-fired power station.
28. Coal-fired power station.
29. Gas-fired power station.
30. Nuclear power station.
31. Subterranean hot springs.
32. Solar energy.
33. From a waterfall.
34. From the waves of the sea.
35. From the wind.
36. A line of men pedalling bicycles.
37. Harnessing lightning.
38. Harnessing a volcano.
39. From an earthquake.
40. Through the movement of a car.
41. Putting a generator under an aeroplane wing.
42. Putting a generator on top of a train.
43. From a sewing machine treadle.
44. From a donkey wheel.
45. Firing a machine gun at the blades of a paddle wheel.
46. Releasing a fire extinguisher at the blades of a paddle wheel.
47. From a tornado.
48. From an avalanche.
49. From a whirlpool.
50. Wearing nylon next to your body.

1. Depression.
2. Beginning of Vietnam War.
3. Launching of Sputnik.
4. First man into space.
5. Polio vaccine.
6. Stock market crash.
7. First transatlantic flight.
8. Coronation of George VI.
9. Assassination of John F. Kennedy.
10. Man on moon.
11. Watergate.
12. Vietnam.
13. McCarthyism.
14. The Cold War.
15. Advent of the jet.
16. Invention of transistor.
17. Election of Franklin Delano Roosevelt in 1933.
18. Japanese attack on Pearl Harbor.
19. Apprehension of John Dillinger.
20. End of World War II in Europe (VE Day).
21. Dropping of first atomic bomb at Hiroshima.
22. Death of Franklin Delano Roosevelt in 1945.
23. Election of Harry Truman in 1948.
24. Execution of Julius and Ethel Rosenberg.
25. McCarthy's announcement of Communists in the government.
26. The development of the hydrogen bomb.
27. The discovery of a cure for polio.
28. The beginning of the Korean War.
29. Outbreak of World War I.
30. Peace after World War I.
31. Outbreak of World War II.
32. Sinking of the *Titanic*.
33. Russian Revolution.
34. Invention of television.
35. First sound movie.
36. Death of Rasputin.
37. Launching of the S.S. *Queen Mary*.
38. Discovery of penicillin.
39. Abdication of Edward VIII.

1. Peace after World War II.
2. Death of George VI.
3. Coronation of Queen Elizabeth II.
4. Assassination of President Kennedy.
5. Watergate scandal.
6. Launching of first space flight.
7. Yuri Gagarin in space.
8. Death of Winston Churchill.
9. Conquering of Mount Everest.
10. England won World Cup, 1966.
11. Running the four-minute mile.
12. Bombings in Ireland.
13. Earthquake in Iran.
14. Floods in India.
15. Woodstock.

16. Closing of the Suez Canal.
17. Death of Pope Paul.
18. Ban-the-bomb marches.
19. Opening the first motorway.
20. First hovercraft trials.
21. Heart transplants.
22. Fertility drugs and multiple births.
23. Test tube babies.
24. Death of Elvis Presley.
25. Beatlemania.
26. Elizabeth Taylor marries Richard Burton.
27. Cuban missile crisis.
28. Assassination of Bobby Kennedy.
29. Attempt to kill George Wallace.
30. Assassination of Martin Luther King.
31. Death of Howard Hughes.
32. Resignation of Richard Nixon.
33. Neil Armstrong is first man to walk on the moon.
34. Ending of the Vietnam War.
35. Election of Jimmy Carter to the presidency.
36. The apprehension of David Berkowitz, the .44 caliber killer.
37. 1969 World Championship for N. Y. Mets.
38. Super Bowl Championship for N. Y. Jets.
39. Nixon's trip to China.
40. Murdering of Israeli Olympic team at the 1972 games in Munich.
41. President Ford's pardon of Richard Nixon.
42. Watergate.
43. Vietnam War.
44. Israeli-Palestinian conflict.
45. President Carter's Polish (mis)interpreter.
46. The death of Francisco Franco.
47. Successful separation of Siamese twins.
48. Worst winter since 1800's.
49. Release of killer bees.
50. Imprisonment of Nixon's aides.
51. Neutron bomb.
52. End of draft.
53. Astronauts sent to the moon.
54. Concorde.

## 67. Seven or more uses for a hockey puck

1. To play hockey.
2. As substitute for a ball.
3. To hit someone.
4. To lengthen drying socks.
5. As a candle holder.
6. To draw a circle round.
7. Learn about geometry.
8. Learn about science.
9. Bang in a nail.
10. Put in someone's mouth to stop them from screaming.
11. Stand on to be a bit taller.
12. Block a hole of the same size.
13. As a table for a pet mouse.
14. As a door handle.
15. As a table mat.
16. Knock over skittles.
17. Make a banging noise.
18. A base for a door knocker.
19. As a jockey wheel.
20. To catch a fly in a jam jar.
21. Spin on the water.
22. Balance on your head.
23. Darn a sock.
24. As a target.
25. Hollow out to make an ashtray.
26. Fit to the front of bumpers.
27. Weigh down a fishing line.
28. Break a window.
29. Put pressure on a leg wound.
30. Play "Hunt the Hockey Puck."
31. As a paper weight.
32. As a defense weapon.
33. As a mini-discus.
34. As a good luck charm.
35. As a device for inflicting *unbearable* pain.
36. Give it as a present to President Carter.
37. Mail it to lose money on postage.
38. Use it as a Kleenex.
39. To be a period on a billboard.
40. To provide work relief for unemployed young hockey players.
41. To test the laws of gravity with.
42. To weigh.
43. To grill in place of hamburgers.
44. To drop on people's fingers or toes.
45. To plant it and harvest a whole crop of hockey pucks and then change your name to Spalding.
46. As something to kick around in order to vent aggression.
47. Plant stand (base for a small pot).
48. Door stop.
49. Coaster.
50. Toy for a dog.
51. To place under the leg of a table in order to make the table level.
52. To throw at your brother.
53. To roll it down the street.
54. To hide in the closet.
55. To paint it red.
56. Conducting a study on whether or not it's alive.
57. Knocking out teeth.

## 68. Eight non-sport uses of a football

1. Play with in the bath.
2. Punch when in a temper.
3. As a buoy.
4. Feel in the dark.
5. Blow up.
6. As a base for a papier mâché face.
7. Throw at someone.
8. Compare with a golf ball.
9. Learn about geometry.
10. Learn about science.
11. Give as a present.
12. As a lottery prize.
13. Collect autographs.
14. Test-paint colour.
15. Cut up and wear as a hat.
16. Draw a face on.
17. Transmit vibrations.
18. In a circus.
19. For a dolphin.
20. Exercise a dog.
21. Stretch a tapestry.
22. Sit on when you don't want to fall asleep.
23. Make a lampshade.
24. Cause a car accident.
25. Draw a map of the world on.
26. Deflate under water to make bubbles.
27. Smuggle drugs in.
28. Trip up guests.
29. Imitate a pregnant woman.
30. As a bookend.
31. As a paperweight.
32. As a teething toy for a pet dog.
33. As an attack weapon.
34. As shirt stuffer.
35. As a fake watermelon.
36. Chair.
37. Put a hole in it and make a birdhouse.
38. Make a wallet out of its leather.
39. Window breaker.
40. Drop it on insects.
41. Flatten it out and use it as a frisbee.
42. Alienate pacifists.
43. To be signed by Fran Tarkenton.
44. As a trophy.
45. Cut in half and use as a flower pot.
46. Make it into a lamp for a youngster.
47. Bronze it and use it as a doorstop.
48. Hang it up and make a punching bag out of it.
49. Cut it in half and make a bird feeder.
50. To use as a pillow.
51. To decorate a cake.
52. To read in the bathroom.
53. To hold an extra shoelace.
54. As a float for a fishing line.
55. As a centerpiece.

## 69. Six or more reasons why we have interstate highways

1. To drive to other states.
2. Move goods to other states.
3. For businessmen.
4. For tourists.
5. For those who dislike small routes.
6. For those who dislike railways.
7. For those who dislike air travel.
8. To provide locations for motels.
9. Provide locations for restaurants.
10. Demonstrate modern technology.
11. Occupy the police.
12. Occupy the maintenance workers.
13. Prevent the traffic driving over fields.
14. Stimulate the accident rate.
15. Play chicken.
16. See how fast the car goes.
17. Provide quick escape for the law breakers.
18. Dodge the interstate laws.
19. Use white paint.
20. Give Alfred Hitchcock a location for films.
21. For emergency landing of aircraft.
22. Obliterate farmland.
23. Spoil the view.
24. Provide a hazardous pastime in the fog.
25. Create a challenge in icy conditions.
26. Shoot pellets from bridges.
27. Occupy the traffic sensors.
28. Increase the number of radio listeners.
29. Greater traveling speeds.
30. Closer cooperation between states.
31. They have been expressly authorized.
32. To waste gas.
33. To kill time.
34. Kill all surrounding life by fumigation.
35. Support the car companies.
36. As a place to get killed or commit suicide.
37. For drag racing.
38. As a proving ground for tinsel heroes.
39. To travel more quickly between states.
40. To avoid local traffic.
41. To reduce traffic tieups.
42. To collect tax money.
43. To hire more employees.
44. To stimulate the economy.
45. So you have somewhere to stand when you're hitching.
46. So they can put up toll

booths.

47. So you don't have to worry about driving behind a horse.
48. So you can get to a good restaurant in another state.
49. So they can get rid of extra speed-limit signs.

## 70. Six or more reasons why wells become dry

1. Lack of rainfall.
2. Source of supply dries up.
3. Supply diverted.
4. Change of climate.
5. Lack of maintenance.
6. Used for the disposal of corpses.
7. Over-consumption before water can reach well.
8. Oil supplies used up.
9. Oil is burnt out.
10. The original source runs out.
11. The pumping system breaks down.
12. The water supply freezes.
13. The well is devastated.
14. Poor farmers have no luck.
15. They get tired.
16. Sometimes they grow old and die.
17. They are recalled by the well company, which is eventually forced to scrap them, i.e., dry them out.
18. Their water evaporates.
19. They realize finally that alcohol has been controlling their lives.
20. They figure that the chic female wells like that type of humor better.
21. The source is depleted.
22. High temperatures.
23. Low humidity.
24. Resources used without being replaced.
25. Many thirsty animals.
26. People drink it.
27. Because the sides collapse and splash the water out.
28. The stream that leads to the well becomes blocked.

## 71. Seven or more reasons why water is not found in deserts

1. Deserts are too dry.
2. It does not rain.
3. Sun evaporates water.
4. Deserts have no streams.
5. They have no rivers.
6. No reservoirs.
7. No floods.
8. No lakes.
9. No snow.
10. No wells.
11. Desert animals survive well on little water.
12. Desert plants survive well on little water.
13. The surface lets all the water through.
14. No trees or grass to retain water.
15. The natives drink it all.
16. A place with a plentiful water supply is not a desert.
17. Deserts and water make poor companions.
18. Nobody has looked hard enough.
19. Somebody has drunk all of it.
20. No water makes fewer floods.
21. All the water has evaporated, never to return.
22. All earthly rainfall somehow avoids the desert lands.
23. The cacti have the market cornered on water so nothing else in the desert can get it, including the desert itself.
24. There's too much sand, and the water hates sand.
25. Rain clouds don't like the neighborhood.
26. The rain evaporates before it hits the sand.
27. Since there's no television or social life in the desert, whereas the beach is teeming with such activity, the rain and water avoid it as a rule and tend to spend their time at the beach.
28. If you were rain, would you want to fall 25,000 feet onto 120° sand only to burn into steamy oblivion?
29. Rain won't go anywhere where it can't be snow, unless it gets to feed plants, as it does in the tropics.
30. Dry air.
31. High temperatures.
32. Lot of sand to absorb water.
33. The limited supply is used by the animal life.
34. The supply is used by plants.
35. Low humidity.
36. No cloud cover so the sun quickly causes the water to evaporate.
37. It's hot and the water dries up.
38. The camels drink it.
39. It's too hot to go looking for it, so no one can find it.
40. It's not found in deserts because it's not there.

## 72. Six or more desserts always to avoid

1. Jelly.
2. Sour grapes.
3. Melted ice cream.
4. Prunes and custard.
5. Apples with cinnamon.
6. Figs (if you wear dentures).
7. Squashy bananas.
8. Tapioca pudding.
9. Cold rice.
10. Spotted duck with no currants.
11. Suet pudding if on a diet.
12. "Just desserts" when you have done something wrong.
13. Butterscotch ice cream.
14. Peach melba.
15. Apricot strudel.
16. Sweet rum cake.
17. Shoo-fly pie.
18. Pecan pie.
19. Coffee ice cream.
20. Bananas flambé.
21. Frog.
22. Ram's bladder cup.
23. Glass fragments and razor blades.
24. Death.
25. Rotten fruit.
26. Basketball.
27. Electricity.
28. Rock.
29. Sixty crazed aborigines.
30. Tyrannosaurus Rex.
31. Any work of art.
32. Metal.
33. Perchloric acid.
34. Lye.
35. Bicycles.
36. Cheese cake.
37. Banana splits.
38. Sundaes.
39. Milk shakes.
40. Chocolate éclair.
41. Cotton candy.
42. Red licorice.
43. Chocolate candy.
44. Green Jell-O.
45. Prune whip.
46. Bubblegum ice cream.
47. A mealy apple.
48. Apple pie with cheese.

## 73. Six or more college majors that least interest you

1. History.
2. Needlecraft.
3. Agriculture.
4. Botany.
5. Anthropology.
6. Classical literature.
7. Hebrew.
8. Music theory.
9. African studies.
10. Religion.
11. Drama.
12. Fine arts.
13. Chair-building.
14. Spanish.
15. Economics.
16. Business.
17. Physics.
18. Statistics.
19. Nursing.
20. Political science.
21. Law.
22. Sociology.
23. Poetry.
24. Philosophy.

## 74. Seven or more things you'd have to change about your body to become a bird

1. Learn to tweet.
2. Have to shrink.
3. Lose a lot of weight.
4. Grow claws.
5. Shorten your legs.
6. Grow a tail.
7. Your nose.
8. Your mouth.
9. Your skin.
10. Your arms.
11. Your eyes.
12. Your legs.
13. Your digestive system.
14. Your hair.
15. Your ears.
16. Hands.
17. Vocal cords.
18. Feet.
19. Toes.
20. Fingers.
21. Nails.
22. I'd have to become more streamlined.
23. Learn how to build a nest with my beak.
24. Grow talons.
25. Longer nose.
26. Wings instead of arms.
27. Stronger legs.
28. More agility.
29. Stronger teeth.
30. Grow a beak.
31. Nostrils to disappear almost.
32. Grow feathers.
33. Arms to become wings.
34. Eyes to be placed on either side of the head.
35. Bones to become lighter.
36. Legs to thin out.
37. One toe to disappear.
38. Other four to be re-arranged.
39. Taste buds to find worms acceptable.
40. More shoulder muscles.
41. Better eyesight.
42. More sensitive hearing.
43. Women's lactation apparatus to disappear.

44. Sexual attraction for other birds.
45. Adapt "rear end" to pass an egg (without breaking it).
46. Adapt bottom to sit on eggs.

## 75. The six worst movies you've ever seen

1. *Airport.*
2. *Airport '75.*
3. *Murder by Death.*
4. *Harry and Walter Go to New York.*
5. *Silent Movie.*
6. *The Last Picture Show.*
7. *They Shoot Horses, Don't They?*
8. Home movies.
9. *Mask of the Red Death.*
10. *Easy Rider.*
11. *Sinbad.*
12. *Giant.*
13. Any old Western.
14. *An Unmarried Woman.*
15. All Japanese monster movies with English dubbed in.
16. *Earthquake.*
17. *The Day of the Dolphin.*
18. *Scenes from a Marriage.*
19. *Audrey Rose.*
20. *Aloha, Bobby and Rose.*
21. *Let the Good Times Roll.*
22. *Celebration at Big Sur.*
23. *Star Wars.*
24. *Week-End.*
25. *Pierrot le Fou.*
26. *Zazi dans le Métro.*
27. *Count Dracula.*
28. *Frankenstein.*

## 76. Six or more things that have happened to you that you wouldn't like to have happen again

1. My dog was given away.
2. Eating cheese blintzes.
3. Having my parakeet die.
4. Getting braces.
5. Hair cut too short.
6. Playing softball for my school.
7. Diving into the pool with glasses on.
8. Having the air let out of my tires.
9. Getting drunk and ill.
10. Having an argument with a professor.
11. Getting married.
12. Get caught in an undertow.
13. Going on rides on the boardwalk that go in circles.
14. Spilling a drink on someone.
15. Chicken pox.
16. Car crash.

17. Little League baseball.
18. Seventh grade.
19. Walking backwards into a car.
20. Getting seasick.
21. My bar mitzvah.
22. A broken arm.
23. I forgot my canteen on a twenty-mile hike.
24. I fell off my bicycle coming down a hill.
25. The junior high school prom.
26. Getting an "F" on a history test.
27. Adding to the family.
28. Taking a driving test.
29. Breaking a collar bone.
30. Walking on crutches.
31. Having an operation.
32. Catching German measles.
33. Evacuating a burning building.
34. Coming home to find burglars have been.
35. Discovering an intruder in the garden.
36. Hearing screams of a mugging victim.
37. Toothache.
38. Losing a suitcase in a foreign port.
39. Having a car catch fire.
40. Riding in a coach when the front tyre blows out.
41. Staying awake all night.
42. Sleeping in a cave in sub-zero temperatures.
43. Ripping off someone's bumper when parking.
44. Teaching eight-year-olds.
45. Working in a lampshade factory.
46. Fridge blowing up.
47. Finding no money to pay in a restaurant.
48. Waking up to find condensed milk over my hair.
49. Pulling a screaming child home from school.

## 77. Seven or more reasons for building a home by a lake

1. So you can tell someone to go jump in a lake.
2. So you can drown your enemies without going out of your way.
3. So you have somewhere to keep your canoe.
4. So your pet whale can still feel like a part of the family.
5. So you can ice skate in the winter.
6. Won't ever get thirsty.
7. Can buy a boat.
8. To be able to go boating.
9. Can walk around it.

10. If life is really bad, you can drown yourself in it.
11. Lots of girls.
12. To enjoy the scenery.
13. To be able to swim.
14. To be able to waterski.
15. To be able to fish.
16. To increase the value of the home.
17. To relax by the water.
18. To have a supply of fresh water.
19. To meet people.
20. To avoid vacationers.
21. To keep cool in the summer.
22. Social status.
23. Opportune location for parties.
24. Provides one with a sense of "insular" security.
25. A nice view.
26. Mooring for a boat.
27. Peace and quiet.
28. To see reflections.
29. To study fish.
30. Study birds.
31. Study insects.
32. Study water vegetation.
33. Have a more fertile garden.
34. To attract friends.
35. Go for amorous walks.
36. Watch children fishing.
37. Learn sub aqua.
38. Dump rubbish.
39. Watch people drown.
40. Learn rescue skills.
41. Watch the sunset.
42. Hold a party on a boat.
43. Watch the sun shimmering.
44. Take photographs.
45. Compose music.
46. Write stories.
47. Write poems.
48. Throw stones in the water.
49. Dispose of a corpse easily.
50. Feed the ducks.
51. Notice the changing seasons.
52. Feed the geese.
53. Get attacked by the swans.
54. Feel healthy.
55. Cure hydrophobia.

## 78. Six or more ways to move a vehicle without an engine

1. Pull it with a team of horses.
2. Lift it with a crane.
3. Push it down a hill.
4. Tie helium balloons to it.
5. Feed it milk of magnesia.
6. Put a jet plane in its trunk.
7. Tell it there are several nice-looking cars over yonder.
8. Kick it.
9. Use a sail—i.e., wind.
10. Use oars.
11. Use manpower.
12. Use horses.
13. Construct only downhill roadways—thus the vehicle

could move simply by virtue of its own potential and kinetic energy.
14. Use cables.
15. Use pulleys.
16. Use wild Alaskan huskies.
17. Push it.
18. Pull it.
19. Tow it with a rope.
20. Lever it with a bar.
21. Ram it with another vehicle.
22. Charge it.
23. Blow it up.
24. Fire a missile at it.
25. Fix it on a trailer.
26. Hitch it to another vehicle.
27. Pedal it.
28. Roll it over.
29. Hitch it to a helicopter.
30. Tie it to an elephant.
31. Dismantle it.

## 79. Seven or more reasons for headwaiters

1. To show people to their tables.
2. To hand out menus.
3. To pull out chairs for people.
4. To make a restaurant seem classy.
5. To ask if everything was O.K.
6. To collect tips.
7. To act friendly so people will return.
8. To stand in front of lines.
9. To look important.
10. To make sure the waiters don't go crazy.
11. To pour wine.
12. To make the other waiters wait.
13. To support the American economy.
14. Otherwise, his kids would go hungry.
15. To organize other waiters.
16. To find you a table.
17. To correct mistakes made by waiters.
18. Pacify angry customers.
19. To keep customers happy.
20. To make reservations.
21. Creates greater employment opportunities.
22. More efficient and more courteous dining service.
23. Increased gratuity charges.
24. More professional atmosphere.
25. A feeling of *subordination.*
26. It makes things easier for the rest of the waiters.
27. It keeps the management more satisfied.
28. Welcome the diners.
29. Smile.
30. Be solicitous.
31. Answer queries.

32. Look decorative.
33. Look disdainful.
34. Set an example.
35. Inspect the tables.
36. Consult with the chef.
37. Represent the management.
38. Recommend the wine.
39. Translate the menu.
40. Keep an eye on the proceedings.
41. Instruct new staff.
42. Resolve arguments.
43. Vet guests' appearance.
44. Dress as penguins.

## 80. Six or more ways to avoid stepping on ants

1. Ask them to move out of your way.
2. Travel *everywhere* by plane.
3. Walk only in water.
4. Roll wherever you want to go.
5. Walk on your hands.
6. Use a pogo stick.
7. Don't walk.
8. Make all ants glow for higher visibility.
9. Kill *all* of them.
10. Confine them to certain areas, with streets, porches, etc., off limits.
11. Let ants fly instead of crawl.
12. Watch where you're walking.
13. Don't walk where they are.
14. Move about in a car.
15. Stay indoors.
16. Ride a bicycle.
17. Put a red marker on all ant colonies.
18. Do not walk where the ground is porous.
19. Construct raised walking surfaces for human beings.
20. Do away with the ant population.
21. Contain all ants below earth's surface.
22. Transport all ants to a giant ant farm.
23. Walk on cushioned stilts.
24. Carry an ant detector on any walk you take.
25. Jump over them.
26. Walk round them.
27. Learn to fly.
28. Keep still.
29. Pick them up.
30. Sweep them away.
31. Blow them away.
32. Suck them up a vacuum cleaner.
33. Make a noise to scare them.
34. Wash them away with a hose.
35. Look very carefully.
36. Examine the ground with a magnifying glass.

37. Ask someone to carry you.
38. Use a pedal car.
39. Ride a horse.
40. Ride on a dog.
41. Take giant leaps.
42. Walk on a line of chairs.

## 81. Eight or more routes from New Orleans, Louisiana, to Mexico City, Mexico

1. Let your fingers do the walking.
2. Look on a map for the nearest route.
3. Divide the journey into six parts—the first by land, the next two by sea, and the last three by air.
4. Ask a Mexican.
5. Sail across the Gulf of Mexico, then go from Vera Cruz to Puebla to Mexico City.
6. Travel in your mind by reading travel books.
7. Invite a group of Mexico City people to visit you in New Orleans and imagine you are in Mexico City.
8. Hitchhike to get as close as possible—walk the rest of the way.
9. Through the Arctic.
10. Back roads.
11. Interstate highways.
12. Telephone pole wires.
13. As the crow flies.
14. Ferry to Tampico and burro to Mexico City.
15. New Orleans to San Diego to Encinada ferry to mainland, donkey cart to Mexico City.
16. I-10 to Dallas, take left straight to Mexico City.
17. Steamer to Panama Canal, head north.
18. New Orleans to North Pole, head due south to Mexico City.
19. Go to nearest Taco Bell for directions.
20. Go to travel show.
21. Through Gulf of Mexico, past Cuba into the Caribbean, through Panama Canal, up the Pacific, land at Colima, and travel east.
22. Through Gulf of Mexico, south through Atlantic, round Tierra del Fuego, up the Pacific, land at Colima, and travel east.
23. Through Gulf of Mexico, north up Atlantic to Greenland, through Baffin Bay to Arctic Ocean, through Bering Strait, south through

Pacific to Colima, and travel east.
24. Through Gulf of Mexico, north up Atlantic to St. John's, follow Canadian border to Vancouver Island, south through Pacific to Colima, and travel east.
25. Direct by air.
26. Direct by underground tunnel.
27. By car.
28. By rail.
29. On foot.
30. Don't go at all.
31. By writing to my sister-in-law in Chile and asking her.
32. Via London.
33. Via Tokyo.
34. Via Bombay.
35. Go east around world over Africa and Asia (scenic route)—*or* spiral west.
36. Go north over North and South poles (another scenic route)—or start off south.
37. You could always hijack a plane (specific route depending on where it was at the time you hijacked it).
38. Via anywhere else you would like to go. For example: "I'd like to go to Mexico City via Afghanistan and Kenya, please." This would get you some odd looks at the travel agency, but. . .
39. By rocket (bounce yourself off a satellite).
40. Go to the highest place in New Orleans, then jump off in a hang glider and hope for a good wind.

## 82. Six or more things you remember about the 1972 Thanksgiving dinner

1. My father was alive at the time.
2. My inlaws stayed home and were not in town.
3. The turkey we crossed with a centipede so that we could have enough drumsticks for everyone bore offspring, but we couldn't catch any of them.
4. The Pilgrims did not attend.
5. The dishes are done.
6. Stuffing.
7. Gravy.
8. Forks.
9. Knives.
10. Napkins.
11. Alka-Seltzer.
12. Potatoes.

13. Pumpkin pie.
14. Milk.
15. Apple pie.
16. Ice cream.
17. Cold weather.
18. Drunk Uncle Joe.
19. Aunt Mary's grace (meal prayer).
20. Grandma's meal prayer (Polish).
21. Being expectant parents.
22. Aunt Mary's cookies (yuk).
23. Pecan pie spiked with rum.
24. Playing cards for money.
25. High school football on T.V.
26. Butchering turkey with carving knife.
27. Nice weather.
28. Shrimp cocktails.
29. The leftovers that everyone nibbled on all evening.
30. Drive from Rhode Island.
31. 1969 Oldsmobile.
32. Met new cousin-in-law.
33. Being in navy.
34. Moody neighbor "dropped in."
35. Crowded refrigerator.
36. Wine.
37. Coats piled on bed.
38. Nonny and Maureen's big fight.
39. Relatives badger old maid sister (age 18), i.e. "Any new boyfriends?" "How's school?", etc.
40. Unborn baby kicking.
41. Susan's boyfriend.
42. Father getting mad during cardgame.
43. Boredom after dessert.
44. Talk of Grandma's funeral.
45. Garbage disposal didn't work.
46. *Women* stuck with doing dishes!!!
47. Lots of booze.
48. Nonny and Maureen leave early.
49. Meal hurried along so dishes could get washed.
50. Conversation loud and boring.
51. All had to talk to Uncle Casey on telephone (Connecticut to Florida).
52. Aunt Mary talks of tranquilizers to keep down weight.
53. Trying to explain to relatives that navy still has propeller planes.
54. Relatives making me feel inferior because I flew props.
55. Nothing, we don't have one in this country.
56. It was in 1972.
57. It rained all day.
58. It was a Tuesday.
59. That I don't really know what Thanksgiving is.
60. Runny mashed potatoes

(with almonds, yet).
61. The leftovers that everyone nibbled at all evening.
62. All that $¢#@&*¢% football.

---

## 83. Eight or more things never to say to a truck driver

1. "You ugly truck driver."
2. "Run me over."
3. "Stop."
4. "Move it, buster!"
5. "Why don't you drive the speed limit?"
6. "You're too lazy to get a *real* job."
7. "Pull off the road and let me get ahead of you."
8. "Do you have a girlfriend at every stop?"
9. "What really goes on at a truck stop?"
10. "Do you earn minimum wage?"
11. "Keep on truckin'."
12. "What's the weather like up there?"
13. "Get off the road, Bub!"
14. "I hate the teamsters union."
15. "Trucks should only be allowed on the road at night!"
16. "We don't serve truckers here."
17. "CB radios are outlawed."
18. "We're out of diesel fuel."
19. "You missed your exit by fifty miles."
20. "I believe you're taking up more than one parking space."
21. "Wanna drag?!"
22. "Your mother wears combat boots!"
23. "You have to drive back tonight!"
24. "Stuff your truck, mate!"
25. "Run out of petrol have you?"
26. "Sorry, mate, we're just closing."
27. "You don't look very strong to me."
28. "Call that driving?"
29. "You want to get yourself a decent truck."
30. "Hey, can you read?"
31. "How should I know? Buy yourself a map."
32. "I don't care how long you've been on the road, we're still closed."
33. "I want no truck with you."
34. "Fuck off, truck."
35. "Truck off, fuck."
36. "Get off my toe."
37. "Balls."
38. "Your slip is showing."
39. "And why not?"
40. "Back into that drive."
41. "Go by rail."
42. "Boy, what a hunk of junk! Ya call *that* a truck?!"
43. "Truckers sure are lousy drivers!"
44. "Truck drivers are all alike—a loudmouthed lot of pushy, scroungy. . ."
45. "I'd rather drive a seventy-two Pinto than be caught in *that* rig!"
46. (as a practical joke): "Hey, the back end of your truck just fell off and you're spilling stuff all over the road!"
47. "Your truck is so dirty that I can't tell where it stops and the ground begins."

---

## 84. Seven or more reasons why pygmies are short

1. Because of their genes.
2. Because of their chromosomes.
3. From hanging around with Randy Newman, singer of "Short People."
4. They don't have a proper diet.
5. The sun stunts their growth.
6. The elephants stomped on them.
7. They smoked dried jungle leaves when they were young.
8. They don't think tall.
9. To conserve the amount of material needed to make a garment.
10. So that the phrase "short and sassy" would apply to them.
11. Somebody else is too tall and the pygmies are short to make the average person just normal in height.
12. Geographical reasons.
13. Built close to ground.
14. Inbreeding.
15. To fit in their clothes.
16. Easy to hide.
17. Crawl under door of pay toilet.
18. To fit in their houses.
19. Didn't grow tall.
20. Don't stand straight.
21. Drank coffee as children.
22. Smoked as children.
23. So they can stuff more pygmies into a phone booth.
24. So they can make bite-sized morsels for tigers.
25. So they can use hankies for loincloths.
26. So one "side of rabbit" will fill their freezer.
27. So they can enter building through mail slot.
28. A meteorite fell on entire colony.
29. From breaking coconuts with their heads.
30. From carrying large loads on their heads.
31. So they can walk under trains.
32. So they don't outgrow clothes.
33. Everyone else is taller.
34. They build small houses.
35. In the dark forests the sun doesn't get at them.
36. They were made that way.
37. They don't eat enough to grow.
38. Squashed genes.
39. Pygmies value shortness and select marriage partners that way.
40. Tall pygmies are put to death at birth.
41. Pregnant pygmy women carry weights on their hump.
42. They spent it all already.
43. In an initiation ceremony, their legs are cut off and shortened. They are so healthy that the bones knit well.
44. So high openings raise troubles.
45. To walk around in the jungle without bumping their heads on low branches.
46. Conserves food—small people eat less.
47. Need less clothing—save money by buying smaller sizes.
48. So they can hide in bushes more easily.
49. None of them want to be basketball players.
50. Saves on burial plots.

---

## 85. Seven or more uses of bamboo

1. To build houses.
2. To torture people by sticking it up their fingernails.
3. As food in chow-mein.
4. To pole-vault.
5. Furniture.
6. Fishing pole.
7. Make a whistle.
8. Cut the bamboo stalk and make napkin rings.
9. Use some for scenery in a play about Vietnam.
10. To boo whatever a bam is.
11. Back scratcher for an elephant.
12. Use bamboo shoots to make baskets.
13. As a pole for climbing beans to grow on.
14. Make a bird cage.
15. As a hedge to give privacy.
16. As a paint-stirring stick.
17. Goal posts.
18. Flagpole.
19. Blinds.
20. Divider screen.
21. Fence.
22. Straw.
23. Blowgun.
24. Mats.
25. Tourist shop junk.
26. Trays.
27. Place mats.
28. Dolls.
29. Landscaping.
30. Bridge.
31. Wall hanging.
32. Cigarette holder.
33. Cup.
34. Eating utensils (chopsticks).
35. Curtain.
36. Tree house.
37. Need (for underwater survival).
38. Kite.
39. Weapons.
40. Hats.
41. Rickshaw.
42. Fan.
43. Trough.
44. Irrigation system.
45. Waterwheel.
46. Jails.
47. Backpack.
48. Tent poles.
49. Crutches, cane.
50. Funnel.
51. Coat rack.
52. Corral.
53. Batons.
54. Bat.
55. Flyswatter.
56. Pen.
57. Javelin.
58. Stair rail.
59. Prop open window.
60. Jewelry.
61. Back scratcher.
62. Holding up plants.
63. Building bridges.
64. Shaft of spear.
65. Arrow.
66. Blowing darts through.
67. Crossword puzzle clue.
68. Backing words for pop singers.
69. Giving "b" plenty of practice on typewriter.
70. Cane in the garden.
71. Blow pipe.
72. Fuel pipe.
73. Splints for broken bones.
74. New Batman words, viz, "Zip Bam Pow Boo."
75. Peashooter.
76. Carve it.
77. Wind chimes.
78. Make it into a flute and play it.
79. Use it as drumsticks.
80. Use it as a drinking straw.
81. Make a raft.
82. Make a picture frame.

83. Build a hut.
84. Use it as a cane.
85. Carve it into toothpicks.
86. Prop something up with it, in case you have anything that needs propping up.

## 86. Eight or more famous people you've always wanted to meet

1. Richard Nixon.
2. George Washington.
3. Raquel Welch.
4. Dr. Reid Daitzman.
5. Robert Redford.
6. Margaret Mead.
7. John Denver.
8. Ralph Nader.
9. Pythagoras.
10. Isaac Newton.
11. Carl Gauss.
12. Archimedes.
13. Charles Schulz ("Peanuts" creator).
14. John Doe.
15. Billy Graham.
16. Robert Frost.
17. Nancy Walker.
18. Dolly Parton.
19. James Michener.
20. Pericles.
21. Captain Kangaroo.
22. Neil Sedaka.
23. Pope John Paul II.
24. Barbara Walters.
25. George Burns.
26. Peter Sellers.
27. Hal Halbrook.
28. Farah Fawcett-Majors.
29. Leonardo da Vinci.
30. Thomas Edison.
31. Teddy Roosevelt.
32. The vice-president's secretary.
33. Ted Williams.
34. Stan Musial.
35. Burt Reynolds.
36. Sophia Loren.
37. Napoleon.
38. Julius Caesar.
39. Jesus Christ.
40. Simon Peter.
41. Judas Iscariot.
42. Pope John XXIII.
43. St. Augustine.
44. St. Martin de Porres.
45. Bertrand Russell.
46. My soul.
47. Montgomery of Alamein.
48. Paulette Goddard.
49. Lucille Ball.
50. Betty Grable.
51. Louis Armstrong.
52. Woody Herman.
53. Beatrix Potter.
54. Noam Chomsky.
55. Prince Charles.
56. T. S. Eliot.
57. Abraham Lincoln.
58. Adolf Hitler.
59. Captain Kirk (of *Star Trek*) and Mr. Spock (ditto).
60. Woody Allen.
61. Everyone on *Monty Python*.
62. W. G. Grace.
63. The man who invented the wheel.
64. Carol Burnett.
65. Sherlock Holmes.
66. Helen Keller.
67. Salvador Dali.
68. Karl Marx.
69. Isaac Asimov.
70. Alexander Solzhenitsyn.
71. Jacques-Yves Cousteau.
72. J. R. R. Tolkien.

## 87. Nine or more uses of dust

1. To make a vacuum cleaner necessary.
2. Make raindrops possible.
3. Create allergies.
4. To fill up a dustpan.
5. To make it possible to write your name on furniture.
6. So that duster, as in Dodge Duster, makes sense.
7. To be a synonym for powder.
8. To rhyme with bust, lust, must, rust.
9. The short version of does't. ("Dust thou take this man?" as opposed to "Does't thou take this man?")
10. To keep people out of your house.
11. To clean.
12. To sneeze at.
13. To make fingerprints.
14. Embarrass hostess.
15. Show missed spots during cleaning.
16. Show shoes that haven't been worn in awhile.
17. Keep housewife busy.
18. For dust storm.
19. Make cobwebs.
20. To aggravate homeowner.
21. To show how long groceries have been on shelf in store.
22. To make mud.
23. To enhance the appearance of wrought-iron ornaments.
24. To give an object that "not used" look.
25. Furniture covering.
26. Fingerprint powder.
27. Face black.
28. Base for various pastes.
29. To clog up machinery.
30. To mark out an area.
31. Fill boxes with it for ballast.
32. To create a smoke screen.
33. Make work for housewives.
34. To turn into an anagram, i.e., stud, to make this game easier, hence.
35. Fix collar to shirt.
36. Give horses.
37. Make me feel guilty for cheating.
38. To explain what it was like in the Dust Bowl.
39. To frighten people with the cloud.
40. For interstellar space, as fuel for stars.
41. To wear out duster.
42. To describe gold.
43. To fill bins.
44. As raw material for school demonstrations of Brownian motion.
45. For testing vacuum cleaners.
46. For compost.
47. As a regular verb in an English grammar.
48. Writing messages in.
49. Snuff substitute.
50. As weapon to throw in eyes of enemies.
51. To use in a fire demonstration.
52. For allergy testing.
53. For hiding under carpets.
54. For lining the floor of caves.
55. Subject for meditation or prayer.
56. Stuff pillows with it.
57. Insulation.
58. Tells you where things were when you pick them up (so you can put them back right).
59. Glue it to things that you'd like to be gray and fuzzy.
60. Cheap confetti (dye it different colors).
61. Use it as packing material for fragile things you are packing or mailing.
62. Dust things off when there's nothing else to do.

## 88. Eight or more places in the world you would never want to visit

1. Central Park, New York, at night.
2. Texas (yes, yes, I *know* I live there—that doesn't mean I like it).
3. Any swamp, especially a leech-, mosquito-, and/or malaria-infested one.
4. The sun (too hot).
5. Alaska (too cold).
6. The very top outside roof of any tall building.
7. India.
8. Any desert.
9. Antarctica.
10. America.
11. The sky.
12. Arctic.
13. Snake pits.
14. Jungles.
15. Inside volcanoes.
16. Ocean beds.
17. Wigan Pier.
18. The ladies lavatory at Fenchurch St. Station.
19. Baton Rouge.
20. Birmingham, Alabama.
21. Birmingham, England.
22. Manchester, England.
23. Uganda.
24. Leeds, England.
25. Liverpool, England.
26. Belfast.
27. Derry.
28. Newington, Connecticut.
29. County jail.
30. Poland.
31. Jacksonville, Florida.
32. Elberta, Alabama.
33. Meridian, Mississippi.
34. Topeka, Kansas.
35. Enfield, Connecticut.
36. Confessional.
37. Harlem.
38. Philippines.
39. City Sewage Plant.
40. Africa—South of Sahara.
41. Iraq.
42. Iran.
43. Sweden.
44. Hawaii.
45. Mexico.
46. South America.
47. Vietnam.
48. Korea.
49. Siberia.
50. South Pole.
51. Eniwetok (H-bomb test site).
52. New York City.
53. Newark, New Jersey.
54. Palermo, Italy.
55. Algeria.
56. Hong Kong.
57. Neiria Hotel, Madrid, Spain.
58. Rota, Spain.
59. Figaro Restaurant, Enfield, Connecticut.
60. Friendly Acre Motel, Newington, Connecticut.
61. Detroit, Michigan.
62. Abortion clinic.
63. Sing Sing.
64. Baldwin, Florida.
65. Jungle ride at Riverside Park, Agawam, Massachusetts.
66. Naval Air Station, Brooklyn, New York.
67. Suburbia, Washington, D.C.
68. House of ill-repute, Cania, Crete.
69. Mud flat housing, Millington, Tennessee.
70. "South of the Border," South Carolina.
71. Nebraska.
72. "Polka," WHYN-TV, Channel 40, Springfield, Massachusetts.
73. Marineland, St. Augustine, Florida.
74. Phyllis Newman's house.

75. Don Rickles' house.
76. Life insurance agent's office.
77. Mortician's place.
78. Hell.
79. Montana.
80. Latin America.
81. Iceland.
82. China.
83. The corner I had to sit in for punishment.
84. Under the bed.
85. In a rabbit cage or chicken coop.
86. An occupied lion's cage.

## 89. Nine or more things never to throw out

1. Babies with bathwater.
2. Challenges.
3. Dirty banknote.
4. Your arms in a crowd.
5. Seeds on stony ground.
6. Things in the "in tray."
7. Postage stamps.
8. Things that might come in useful.
9. Invited guests.
10. Rubbish in the street.
11. Good food.
12. Personal letters.
13. Uncashed checks.
14. Friends.
15. Receipts.
16. Clothes in good repair.
17. Daughter's boyfriends.
18. Reference books.
19. Written guarantees.
20. Bows from gift packages.
21. Plastic margarine containers.
22. Nails, nuts, bolts.
23. Grocery bags.
24. Common pins.
25. Rubber bands.
26. Negatives.
27. Service memorabilia (military).
28. Term papers.
29. Scrap material.
30. *National Geographic*s.
31. Children's art work.
32. String.
33. Honeymoon memorabilia.
34. Paperclips.
35. Sneakers.
36. NATOPS manual.
37. Baby's first clip of hair.
38. Cigar boxes.
39. Baby food jars.
40. Golf balls.
41. Your eye-glasses.
42. Your contact lenses.
43. Your telephone.
44. Your toothpaste.
45. Your key.
46. My original Snoopy drawing by Charles Schulz.
47. Money.
48. Myself.
49. The garbage can.
50. My wedding pictures.
51. What should be thrown in.
52. The car and house keys.
53. The garbage man.
54. Trash, while driving down the highway.
55. My husband.
56. The mattress with my millions in it.
57. The urn with Grandpa's ashes in it.
58. Driver's license.
59. Good blank paper.
60. Pens, pencils, or any other writing implements.
61. Important documents.
62. Games, if they're good ones.

23. Hereditary traits.
24. Superiority.
25. God made them that way.
26. To beat up on the females.
27. To carry packages for the females.
28. To work on the car.
29. They are descendants of Adam.
30. They have nothing better to do.
31. So they can hold them down when committing rape.
32. So they can assert themselves.
33. So they can carry their cases.
34. Because they eat more.
35. Because females don't envy Tarzan his strength.
36. They've got to have some compensations.
37. So that economists could invent the division of labour when applied to prehistoric settlements.

## 90. Eight or more reasons why males are physically stronger than females

1. Prehistoric males probably hunted more than females.
2. Greater emphasis placed on male strength by society.
3. Males have larger muscles.
4. Males generally have more strength-oriented jobs.
5. Until previously the only sports figures were male.
6. Males place a lot on being "macho" so they exercise and work out more.
7. Little emphasis on female sports in school (most schools).
8. Until recently, females were taught to be inferior to males.
9. Males are larger.
10. Males do more manual work.
11. Males have a more aggressive instinct leaning to more use of muscle power.
12. Females tend to sit around a lot more.
13. Females are more inclined to take a bus whereas a male would walk.
14. Females deliberately do not build up their musclepower in order to play on their femininity.
15. Hormones.
16. To make up for brains.
17. Have to play more strenuous sports.
18. They flex their muscles more.
19. They're expected to be.
20. Because ice cream doesn't have bones (neither do hot dogs).
21. Daddies play rougher with little boys.
22. So they can lug the bride over the threshold.

# APRIL

### Mental Calisthenic #4

Take a drink of plain water. Close your eyes and try to imagine the taste of SUGAR. Now place some sugar* on your tongue. Rinse your mouth. Repeat this sequence with a LEMON, SALT, and BREAD. Go to a Mental Jogging exercise.

*Not for diabetics

## 91. Seven or more reasons why we keep sports records

| Response | Score |
|---|---|
| 1. _____ | 1 |
| 2. _____ | 1 |
| 3. _____ | 1 |
| 4. _____ | 1 |
| 5. _____ | 1 |
| 6. _____ | 1 |
| 7. _____ | 1 |
| **Bonus Responses** | |
| 8. _____ | 2 |
| 9. _____ | 2 |
| 10. _____ | 2 |
| 11. _____ | 2 |
| 12. _____ | 2 |
| 13. _____ | 2 |
| 14. _____ | 2 |
| 15. _____ | 2 |
| 16. _____ | 2 |

Total ☐

## 92. Six or more reasons why handkerchiefs are square

| Response | Score |
|---|---|
| 1. _____ | 1 |
| 2. _____ | 1 |
| 3. _____ | 1 |
| 4. _____ | 1 |
| 5. _____ | 1 |
| 6. _____ | 1 |
| **Bonus Responses** | |
| 7. _____ | 2 |
| 8. _____ | 2 |
| 9. _____ | 2 |
| 10. _____ | 2 |
| 11. _____ | 2 |
| 12. _____ | 2 |
| 13. _____ | 2 |
| 14. _____ | 2 |
| 15. _____ | 2 |
| 16. _____ | 2 |

Total ☐

## 93. Seven or more reasons why most males shave their beard and most women shave their legs

| Response | Score |
|---|---|
| 1. _____ | 1 |
| 2. _____ | 1 |
| 3. _____ | 1 |
| 4. _____ | 1 |
| 5. _____ | 1 |
| 6. _____ | 1 |
| 7. _____ | 1 |

**Bonus Responses**

| | |
|---|---|
| 8. _____ | 2 |
| 9. _____ | 2 |
| 10. _____ | 2 |
| 11. _____ | 2 |
| 12. _____ | 2 |
| 13. _____ | 2 |
| 14. _____ | 2 |
| 15. _____ | 2 |
| 16. _____ | 2 |

Total ☐

## 94. Seven or more reasons why books are usually printed on white paper

| Response | Score |
|---|---|
| 1. _____ | 1 |
| 2. _____ | 1 |
| 3. _____ | 1 |
| 4. _____ | 1 |
| 5. _____ | 1 |
| 6. _____ | 1 |
| 7. _____ | 1 |

**Bonus Responses**

| | |
|---|---|
| 8. _____ | 2 |
| 9. _____ | 2 |
| 10. _____ | 2 |
| 11. _____ | 2 |
| 12. _____ | 2 |
| 13. _____ | 2 |
| 14. _____ | 2 |
| 15. _____ | 2 |
| 16. _____ | 2 |

Total ☐

## 95. Six or more reasons why silk is usually more expensive than cotton

| Response | Score |
|---|---|
| 1. _____ | 1 |
| 2. _____ | 1 |
| 3. _____ | 1 |
| 4. _____ | 1 |
| 5. _____ | 1 |
| 6. _____ | 1 |

**Bonus Responses**

| | |
|---|---|
| 7. _____ | 2 |
| 8. _____ | 2 |
| 9. _____ | 2 |
| 10. _____ | 2 |
| 11. _____ | 2 |
| 12. _____ | 2 |
| 13. _____ | 2 |
| 14. _____ | 2 |
| 15. _____ | 2 |
| 16. _____ | 2 |

Total ☐

## 96. Six or more reasons why fish die after exposure to the air

| Response | Score |
|---|---|
| 1. _____ | 1 |
| 2. _____ | 1 |
| 3. _____ | 1 |
| 4. _____ | 1 |
| 5. _____ | 1 |
| 6. _____ | 1 |

**Bonus Responses**

| | |
|---|---|
| 7. _____ | 2 |
| 8. _____ | 2 |
| 9. _____ | 2 |
| 10. _____ | 2 |
| 11. _____ | 2 |
| 12. _____ | 2 |
| 13. _____ | 2 |
| 14. _____ | 2 |
| 15. _____ | 2 |
| 16. _____ | 2 |

Total ☐

## 97. Seven or more sensations you would have if you were scuba diving at one hundred feet below sea level

| Response | Score |
|---|---|
| 1. _____ | 1 |
| 2. _____ | 1 |
| 3. _____ | 1 |
| 4. _____ | 1 |
| 5. _____ | 1 |
| 6. _____ | 1 |
| 7. _____ | 1 |

Bonus Responses

| | |
|---|---|
| 8. _____ | 2 |
| 9. _____ | 2 |
| 10. _____ | 2 |
| 11. _____ | 2 |
| 12. _____ | 2 |
| 13. _____ | 2 |
| 14. _____ | 2 |
| 15. _____ | 2 |
| 16. _____ | 2 |

Total ☐

## 98. Six or more non-dietary uses of cheese

| Response | Score |
|---|---|
| 1. _____ | 1 |
| 2. _____ | 1 |
| 3. _____ | 1 |
| 4. _____ | 1 |
| 5. _____ | 1 |
| 6. _____ | 1 |

Bonus Responses

| | |
|---|---|
| 7. _____ | 2 |
| 8. _____ | 2 |
| 9. _____ | 2 |
| 10. _____ | 2 |
| 11. _____ | 2 |
| 12. _____ | 2 |
| 13. _____ | 2 |
| 14. _____ | 2 |
| 15. _____ | 2 |
| 16. _____ | 2 |

Total ☐

## 99. Six or more ways to tell a basketball player from a football player

| Response | Score |
|---|---|
| 1. _____ | 1 |
| 2. _____ | 1 |
| 3. _____ | 1 |
| 4. _____ | 1 |
| 5. _____ | 1 |
| 6. _____ | 1 |

Bonus Responses

| | |
|---|---|
| 7. _____ | 2 |
| 8. _____ | 2 |
| 9. _____ | 2 |
| 10. _____ | 2 |
| 11. _____ | 2 |
| 12. _____ | 2 |
| 13. _____ | 2 |
| 14. _____ | 2 |
| 15. _____ | 2 |
| 16. _____ | 2 |

Total ☐

## 100. Six or more reasons why you should never steal home plate

| Response | Score |
|---|---|
| 1. _____ | 1 |
| 2. _____ | 1 |
| 3. _____ | 1 |
| 4. _____ | 1 |
| 5. _____ | 1 |
| 6. _____ | 1 |

Bonus Responses

| | |
|---|---|
| 7. _____ | 2 |
| 8. _____ | 2 |
| 9. _____ | 2 |
| 10. _____ | 2 |
| 11. _____ | 2 |
| 12. _____ | 2 |
| 13. _____ | 2 |
| 14. _____ | 2 |
| 15. _____ | 2 |
| 16. _____ | 2 |

Total ☐

## 101. Seven or more ways you can tell a dog from a cat without seeing one

| Response | Score |
|---|---|
| 1. _____ | 1 |
| 2. _____ | 1 |
| 3. _____ | 1 |
| 4. _____ | 1 |
| 5. _____ | 1 |
| 6. _____ | 1 |
| 7. _____ | 1 |

Bonus Responses

| | |
|---|---|
| 8. _____ | 2 |
| 9. _____ | 2 |
| 10. _____ | 2 |
| 11. _____ | 2 |
| 12. _____ | 2 |
| 13. _____ | 2 |
| 14. _____ | 2 |
| 15. _____ | 2 |
| 16. _____ | 2 |

Total ☐

## 102. Eight or more reasons not to drink alcohol when driving

| Response | Score |
|---|---|
| 1. _____ | 1 |
| 2. _____ | 1 |
| 3. _____ | 1 |
| 4. _____ | 1 |
| 5. _____ | 1 |
| 6. _____ | 1 |
| 7. _____ | 1 |
| 8. _____ | 1 |

Bonus Responses

| | |
|---|---|
| 9. _____ | 2 |
| 10. _____ | 2 |
| 11. _____ | 2 |
| 12. _____ | 2 |
| 13. _____ | 2 |
| 14. _____ | 2 |
| 15. _____ | 2 |
| 16. _____ | 2 |

Total ☐

## 103. Seven or more reasons why alcohol was made illegal during the twenties

| Response | Score |
|---|---|
| 1. _____ | 1 |
| 2. _____ | 1 |
| 3. _____ | 1 |
| 4. _____ | 1 |
| 5. _____ | 1 |
| 6. _____ | 1 |
| 7. _____ | 1 |

Bonus Responses

| | |
|---|---|
| 8. _____ | 2 |
| 9. _____ | 2 |
| 10. _____ | 2 |
| 11. _____ | 2 |
| 12. _____ | 2 |
| 13. _____ | 2 |
| 14. _____ | 2 |
| 15. _____ | 2 |
| 16. _____ | 2 |

Total ☐

## 104. Eight or more foods never to order for lunch

| Response | Score |
|---|---|
| 1. _____ | 1 |
| 2. _____ | 1 |
| 3. _____ | 1 |
| 4. _____ | 1 |
| 5. _____ | 1 |
| 6. _____ | 1 |
| 7. _____ | 1 |
| 8. _____ | 1 |

Bonus Responses

| | |
|---|---|
| 9. _____ | 2 |
| 10. _____ | 2 |
| 11. _____ | 2 |
| 12. _____ | 2 |
| 13. _____ | 2 |
| 14. _____ | 2 |
| 15. _____ | 2 |
| 16. _____ | 2 |

Total ☐

## 105. Six or more things never to say to a policeman

| Response | Score |
|---|---|
| 1. _____ | 1 |
| 2. _____ | 1 |
| 3. _____ | 1 |
| 4. _____ | 1 |
| 5. _____ | 1 |
| 6. _____ | 1 |

**Bonus Responses**

| | |
|---|---|
| 7. _____ | 2 |
| 8. _____ | 2 |
| 9. _____ | 2 |
| 10. _____ | 2 |
| 11. _____ | 2 |
| 12. _____ | 2 |
| 13. _____ | 2 |
| 14. _____ | 2 |
| 15. _____ | 2 |
| 16. _____ | 2 |

Total ☐

## 106. Six or more reasons not to have a pet

| Response | Score |
|---|---|
| 1. _____ | 1 |
| 2. _____ | 1 |
| 3. _____ | 1 |
| 4. _____ | 1 |
| 5. _____ | 1 |
| 6. _____ | 1 |

**Bonus Responses**

| | |
|---|---|
| 7. _____ | 2 |
| 8. _____ | 2 |
| 9. _____ | 2 |
| 10. _____ | 2 |
| 11. _____ | 2 |
| 12. _____ | 2 |
| 13. _____ | 2 |
| 14. _____ | 2 |
| 15. _____ | 2 |
| 16. _____ | 2 |

Total ☐

## 107. Eight or more things you could be doing now if you were not using this book

| Response | Score |
|---|---|
| 1. _____ | 1 |
| 2. _____ | 1 |
| 3. _____ | 1 |
| 4. _____ | 1 |
| 5. _____ | 1 |
| 6. _____ | 1 |
| 7. _____ | 1 |
| 8. _____ | 1 |

**Bonus Responses**

| | |
|---|---|
| 9. _____ | 2 |
| 10. _____ | 2 |
| 11. _____ | 2 |
| 12. _____ | 2 |
| 13. _____ | 2 |
| 14. _____ | 2 |
| 15. _____ | 2 |
| 16. _____ | 2 |

Total ☐

## 108. Seven or more reasons not to have the Olympic Games

| Response | Score |
|---|---|
| 1. _____ | 1 |
| 2. _____ | 1 |
| 3. _____ | 1 |
| 4. _____ | 1 |
| 5. _____ | 1 |
| 6. _____ | 1 |
| 7. _____ | 1 |

**Bonus Responses**

| | |
|---|---|
| 8. _____ | 2 |
| 9. _____ | 2 |
| 10. _____ | 2 |
| 11. _____ | 2 |
| 12. _____ | 2 |
| 13. _____ | 2 |
| 14. _____ | 2 |
| 15. _____ | 2 |
| 16. _____ | 2 |

Total ☐

## 109. Seven or more reasons for having a pet dog

| Response | Score |
|---|---|
| 1. _____ | 1 |
| 2. _____ | 1 |
| 3. _____ | 1 |
| 4. _____ | 1 |
| 5. _____ | 1 |
| 6. _____ | 1 |
| 7. _____ | 1 |

Bonus Responses

| | |
|---|---|
| 8. _____ | 2 |
| 9. _____ | 2 |
| 10. _____ | 2 |
| 11. _____ | 2 |
| 12. _____ | 2 |
| 13. _____ | 2 |
| 14. _____ | 2 |
| 15. _____ | 2 |
| 16. _____ | 2 |

Total ☐

## 110. Seven or more reasons why dogs should run loose

| Response | Score |
|---|---|
| 1. _____ | 1 |
| 2. _____ | 1 |
| 3. _____ | 1 |
| 4. _____ | 1 |
| 5. _____ | 1 |
| 6. _____ | 1 |
| 7. _____ | 1 |

Bonus Responses

| | |
|---|---|
| 8. _____ | 2 |
| 9. _____ | 2 |
| 10. _____ | 2 |
| 11. _____ | 2 |
| 12. _____ | 2 |
| 13. _____ | 2 |
| 14. _____ | 2 |
| 15. _____ | 2 |
| 16. _____ | 2 |

Total ☐

## 111. Six or more recipes for mixed drinks

| Response | Score |
|---|---|
| 1. _____ | 1 |
| 2. _____ | 1 |
| 3. _____ | 1 |
| 4. _____ | 1 |
| 5. _____ | 1 |
| 6. _____ | 1 |

Bonus Responses

| | |
|---|---|
| 7. _____ | 2 |
| 8. _____ | 2 |
| 9. _____ | 2 |
| 10. _____ | 2 |
| 11. _____ | 2 |
| 12. _____ | 2 |
| 13. _____ | 2 |
| 14. _____ | 2 |
| 15. _____ | 2 |
| 16. _____ | 2 |

Total ☐

## 112. Seven or more things never to say to a dentist

| Response | Score |
|---|---|
| 1. _____ | 1 |
| 2. _____ | 1 |
| 3. _____ | 1 |
| 4. _____ | 1 |
| 5. _____ | 1 |
| 6. _____ | 1 |
| 7. _____ | 1 |

Bonus Responses

| | |
|---|---|
| 8. _____ | 2 |
| 9. _____ | 2 |
| 10. _____ | 2 |
| 11. _____ | 2 |
| 12. _____ | 2 |
| 13. _____ | 2 |
| 14. _____ | 2 |
| 15. _____ | 2 |
| 16. _____ | 2 |

Total ☐

## 113. Six or more reasons why diamonds cost more than coal

| Response | Score |
|---|---|
| 1. _____ | 1 |
| 2. _____ | 1 |
| 3. _____ | 1 |
| 4. _____ | 1 |
| 5. _____ | 1 |
| 6. _____ | 1 |

Bonus Responses

| | |
|---|---|
| 7. _____ | 2 |
| 8. _____ | 2 |
| 9. _____ | 2 |
| 10. _____ | 2 |
| 11. _____ | 2 |
| 12. _____ | 2 |
| 13. _____ | 2 |
| 14. _____ | 2 |
| 15. _____ | 2 |
| 16. _____ | 2 |

Total ☐

## 114. Seven or more reasons why we shake hands

| Response | Score |
|---|---|
| 1. _____ | 1 |
| 2. _____ | 1 |
| 3. _____ | 1 |
| 4. _____ | 1 |
| 5. _____ | 1 |
| 6. _____ | 1 |
| 7. _____ | 1 |

Bonus Responses

| | |
|---|---|
| 8. _____ | 2 |
| 9. _____ | 2 |
| 10. _____ | 2 |
| 11. _____ | 2 |
| 12. _____ | 2 |
| 13. _____ | 2 |
| 14. _____ | 2 |
| 15. _____ | 2 |
| 16. _____ | 2 |

Total ☐

## 115. Six or more reasons we have gates

| Response | Score |
|---|---|
| 1. _____ | 1 |
| 2. _____ | 1 |
| 3. _____ | 1 |
| 4. _____ | 1 |
| 5. _____ | 1 |
| 6. _____ | 1 |

Bonus Responses

| | |
|---|---|
| 7. _____ | 2 |
| 8. _____ | 2 |
| 9. _____ | 2 |
| 10. _____ | 2 |
| 11. _____ | 2 |
| 12. _____ | 2 |
| 13. _____ | 2 |
| 14. _____ | 2 |
| 15. _____ | 2 |
| 16. _____ | 2 |

Total ☐

## 116. Seven or more reasons why cars have brakes

| Response | Score |
|---|---|
| 1. _____ | 1 |
| 2. _____ | 1 |
| 3. _____ | 1 |
| 4. _____ | 1 |
| 5. _____ | 1 |
| 6. _____ | 1 |
| 7. _____ | 1 |

Bonus Responses

| | |
|---|---|
| 8. _____ | 2 |
| 9. _____ | 2 |
| 10. _____ | 2 |
| 11. _____ | 2 |
| 12. _____ | 2 |
| 13. _____ | 2 |
| 14. _____ | 2 |
| 15. _____ | 2 |
| 16. _____ | 2 |

Total ☐

## 117. Seven or more reasons not to wear a helmet while driving a motorcycle

| Response | Score |
|---|---|
| 1. _____ | 1 |
| 2. _____ | 1 |
| 3. _____ | 1 |
| 4. _____ | 1 |
| 5. _____ | 1 |
| 6. _____ | 1 |
| 7. _____ | 1 |

Bonus Responses

| | |
|---|---|
| 8. _____ | 2 |
| 9. _____ | 2 |
| 10. _____ | 2 |
| 11. _____ | 2 |
| 12. _____ | 2 |
| 13. _____ | 2 |
| 14. _____ | 2 |
| 15. _____ | 2 |
| 16. _____ | 2 |

Total ☐

## 118. Eight or more persons who may be President of the United States in the year 2000

| Response | Score |
|---|---|
| 1. _____ | 1 |
| 2. _____ | 1 |
| 3. _____ | 1 |
| 4. _____ | 1 |
| 5. _____ | 1 |
| 6. _____ | 1 |
| 7. _____ | 1 |
| 8. _____ | 1 |

Bonus Responses

| | |
|---|---|
| 9. _____ | 2 |
| 10. _____ | 2 |
| 11. _____ | 2 |
| 12. _____ | 2 |
| 13. _____ | 2 |
| 14. _____ | 2 |
| 15. _____ | 2 |
| 16. _____ | 2 |

Total ☐

## 119. Eight or more problems that had to be overcome to fly to the moon

| Response | Score |
|---|---|
| 1. _____ | 1 |
| 2. _____ | 1 |
| 3. _____ | 1 |
| 4. _____ | 1 |
| 5. _____ | 1 |
| 6. _____ | 1 |
| 7. _____ | 1 |
| 8. _____ | 1 |

Bonus Responses

| | |
|---|---|
| 9. _____ | 2 |
| 10. _____ | 2 |
| 11. _____ | 2 |
| 12. _____ | 2 |
| 13. _____ | 2 |
| 14. _____ | 2 |
| 15. _____ | 2 |
| 16. _____ | 2 |

Total ☐

## 120. Seven or more ways to carry ten wooden coat hangers

| Response | Score |
|---|---|
| 1. _____ | 1 |
| 2. _____ | 1 |
| 3. _____ | 1 |
| 4. _____ | 1 |
| 5. _____ | 1 |
| 6. _____ | 1 |
| 7. _____ | 1 |

Bonus Responses

| | |
|---|---|
| 8. _____ | 2 |
| 9. _____ | 2 |
| 10. _____ | 2 |
| 11. _____ | 2 |
| 12. _____ | 2 |
| 13. _____ | 2 |
| 14. _____ | 2 |
| 15. _____ | 2 |
| 16. _____ | 2 |

Total ☐

# CONTRIBUTORS' SAMPLE RESPONSES

## 91. Seven or more reasons why we keep sports records

1. So we can know if someone does anything better than before.
2. For hero-worshippers of sports fans (so they can rattle off statistics).
3. For people who study the history of human height, weight, strength, stamina, etc.
4. If we didn't, the sections of encyclopedias and world almanacs devoted to records would consist of blank errors.
5. It makes the sports heroes feel good.
6. So players can set goals.
7. Heightens competition.
8. To see who won.
9. To see who lost.
10. For use in training programmes.
11. To settle arguments in pubs.
12. As a matter of prestige.
13. People like to see their name in print.
14. Keep statistics in business.
15. To fill the record book.
16. To give Howard Cosell a job.
17. So athletes will have statistics to bargain with at contract negotiation time.
18. To sell books.
19. To have something to print on the back of baseball bubblegum trading cards.
20. To see who is best.
21. To see who is worst.
22. To make it official.
23. For history.
24. For the hell of it.
25. To increase the supply and demand to drive up the price of writing instruments, calculators, papers, etc.
26. So that we can break them.
27. To have something to help fill up the sports pages.
28. To have an idea of what it means to be a good sport.
29. So we'll know who is Number 1.
30. To provide a challenge for those who need it.
31. Because of natural competitiveness.
32. To play when we're fed up with musical records.
33. Because the Greeks began it.
34. So we don't lose them.
35. To have a purpose for the Olympic games.
36. As a substitute for war.
37. To put in the *Guinness Book of Records*.

## 92. Six or more reasons why handkerchiefs are square

1. Because tissues are with it.
2. So they can be used to keep the sun off by tying knots in the corners.
3. To fit into square boxes.
4. Because trendy people don't blow their noses.
5. Because what's good enough for my grandfather is good enough for me.
6. Because it's more modern to use a paper tissue.
7. To facilitate their manufacture.
8. To make them easy to iron.
9. Noses fit in them nicely.
10. Easy folding.
11. To remember four things.
12. To wrap sandwich in.
13. Stork to deliver baby in.
14. Tie on a stick, filled with wordly possessions to run away.
15. Make a kite with.
16. Use as diaper.
17. Use as mask in holdup.
18. Use as sling.
19. Use as surrender flag.
20. Tie on car door in emergency.
21. Use as bed linen (but not on a kingsized bed).
22. Wrap bread and cheese in for lunch.
23. To differentiate them from round place mats.
24. They are easier to sew an edge onto.
25. So that they will have corners for cleaning ears.
26. No one has ever thought of making them any other way.
27. Look better folded up in a pocket.
28. You can hold it by a corner to wave or do magic tricks.
29. You can't make a bunny pop out of a round handkerchief.
30. Eliminate waste when making them.
31. Can get it wet and "pop" people with it more easily.
32. Can hang it on a clothesline better.
33. Can roll it up like a tourniquet.

## 93. Seven or more reasons why most males shave their beard and most women shave their legs

1. So they can use the same razor blade.
2. So as not to outdo each other.
3. To save embarrassment to hairy-legged men and bearded women.
4. For smoother male kissing of female legs.
5. Because hair grows there.
6. To increase their sexual attractiveness.
7. To emphasize that we have evolved long past the hairy stage, i.e., are naked apes.
8. Society insists that we do.
9. To prevent ingrown hairs.
10. To get hair clippings to stuff a pillow with.
11. To make razor blades and electric shavers necessary.
12. So that there can be something called "shaving cream."
13. So that a shave and a haircut can cost two bits (quarters).
14. They don't like chemical hair removers.
15. To avoid having to comb the hair.
16. Men's facial hair is more noticeable.
17. Women's legs are supposed to be nice and smooth.
18. Smooth skin.
19. To prevent itching.
20. Looks better.
21. To keep cool.
22. For adventure.
23. To conform.
24. To please opposite sex.
25. Hair does not grow on women's faces.
26. People see men's legs more than their faces.
27. Hair on woman's legs is held to be unattractive.
28. To keep razor manufacturers in business.
29. The effect of social conventions.
30. Some men feel that a beard hides a weak chin.
31. Women feel that hairy legs are unfeminine.
32. It helps to pass the time.
33. Because people have always done that.
34. Beards get crumbs in them when the owner eats.
35. It costs too much to permanent-wave your chin or legs.
36. It gives them something to do if they're bored ("What do you want to do?" "Oh, I don't know—let's go shave.").
37. They think it makes them look better.
38. Pantyhose over hairy legs look *yecch!*
39. A criminal can shave off his beard to change his looks.

## 94. Seven or more reasons why books are usually printed on white paper

1. So the paper doesn't have to be dyed.
2. Because ink is black.
3. Soothing to the eyes.
4. In case printing factors are too dark.
5. You wouldn't print houses on white paper.
6. You couldn't print books on white grass.
7. Ask Caxton.
8. Easier to read.
9. Symbolism of purity.
10. The bleach industry has a strong lobby.
11. It won't show spilt milk.
12. You can see insects on it.
13. So the black type will show up better.
14. So the people with dirty hands can have a dirty book to read.
15. White paper is cheaper.
16. Greater abundance of white paper.
17. Tradition.
18. Print won't show up on black paper.
19. Reflective factor.
20. So you can write notes in margins.
21. So you can use a yellow "hilighter."
22. So you don't confuse a book with the Sunday comic strips.
23. Looks neater.
24. Reproduces easier, more clearly.
25. Black ink is less expensive to make and it shows up best on white paper.
26. So coffee stains will show up with greater definition.
27. It is easier to read from than colored paper.
28. White is easier to produce.
29. It is easier than having to change the colour of ink if it is to be as clearly seen.
30. White goes with any home colour scheme.
31. People associate colours with factions.

conservative would not buy a red book regardless of content.

32. White is cheaper.
33. White paper looks classier.
34. Paper is nice and light so even a long book is not too heavy.
35. During book burnings, who wants to smell dyes used to dye the paper?
36. So they'll be cheaper (as compared to gold pages).

## 95. Six or more reasons why silk is usually more expensive than cotton

1. The silkworms' trade union has done a good job.
2. Silk is rarer.
3. Silk is finer, smoother.
4. Cotton prices are held down by competition from man-made fibres.
5. It's purely the snob appeal of silk.
6. More capital has been invested in cotton.
7. The worms have been unionized longer, and demand more money.
8. Because people are willing to pay more to feel "silkier."
9. The sheen from the silk blinds your eyes to the price tag.
10. The worms see you coming.
11. There are more cotton plants than silkworms.
12. Because Eli Whitney did not invent a silk gin.
13. Cotton is more "seedy."
14. It's softer.
15. Silkworms are so tiny.
16. Cotton is produced in more areas of world.
17. Cotton harvesting is cheaper.
18. Silk is rare, cotton isn't.
19. Silk feels better.
20. Silk is shinier.
21. It takes more silk thread per square inch to make a fabric than cotton yarn per square inch.
22. Fertilizer is cheaper than mulberry leaves.
23. Silkworms require more man hours to care for them than does a cotton field.
24. Silk yarn/finished goods have to be shipped farther to mills/merchant than does cotton.
25. Cotton is more plentiful.
26. Silk is more expensive to make.
27. There is a greater demand for silk.
28. Silk looks better.
29. Silk lasts longer.
30. Silk is regarded as being more classy.
31. One can increase the number of cotton plants whereas silkworms can't work overtime.
32. Silkworms eat more than cotton plants.
33. Silk fabric feels nicer than cotton.
34. Silk is harder to make.
35. Silk is a status symbol.
36. Silk generally looks better.
37. Watered silk looks great—watered cotton just gets wet.

## 96. Six or more reasons why fish die after exposure to the air

1. Their scales harden and they can't move.
2. They know when they're beaten.
3. They don't wear enough clothing.
4. Oversea breathing apparatus has not been invented yet.
5. So they can be cooked and eaten.
6. They don't have lungs.
7. They are more susceptible to lung cancer.
8. Because they are fishes out of water.
9. The air isn't fishy enough.
10. There's nothing to support his backstroke.
11. His mother won't think to look for him there.
12. Out of natural environment.
13. Too much oxygen.
14. Suffocation.
15. Oxygen obtained only through water flowing through gills.
16. They dry out.
17. Somebody cuts off their heads.
18. Hook stuck in jugular vein.
19. Food source cut off.
20. They get homesick.
21. They die of shock.
22. Exhaustion from flipping around.
23. Wind up in a cannery or fish market.
24. Old age.
25. Pollution.
26. Fish cannot move on land.
27. The difference in air pressure weakens them.
28. They cannot feed out of water.
29. Their bodies dry up without water.
30. Get too hot (or cold).
31. Get scared.
32. Miss their fish friends.
33. Get bored.

## 97. Seven or more sensations you would have if you were scuba diving at one hundred feet below sea level

1. Isn't this fun?
2. How much air do I have?
3. Look at the fish!
4. Boy, it's cold!
5. Hope there's no sharks around!
6. Where's the ship (or shore)?
7. I'm free to do whatever I want!
8. This is like flying—up or down and wherever I want to go!
9. Wonder.
10. Awe.
11. Loneliness.
12. Lack of weight.
13. Difference in air pressure.
14. Freedom.
15. Speed.
16. Power.
17. Intruder into another world.
18. Breathing more difficult.
19. Serenity.
20. Curiosity.
21. Hunger.
22. Fear.
23. Sense of self.
24. Loss of sense of direction.
25. Ears popping.
26. Nausea.
27. "Bends."
28. Fear of squid.
29. Fear of whales.
30. Fear of sting-rays.
31. Fear of barracudas.
32. Fear of Russian submarines.
33. Fear of jelly fish.
34. Possible lack of air.
35. Uneasiness.
36. Happiness.
37. The feeling of being in an aquarium.
38. Darkness.
39. Isolated.
40. Helpless.
41. Exposure to new colors.
42. Sounds of silent deep.
43. Boredom.
44. Wetness.
45. Guts ache.
46. Excitement.
47. Changed weight.
48. Realization that I don't know what a scuba looks like.
49. Wondering what's for dinner.

## 98. Six or more non-dietary uses of cheese

1. To display in grocer's window.
2. For training cheese cutters.
3. Dutch cheese for cannon balls.
4. For weightlifting.
5. For use in Tom and Jerry film.
6. Catch mice.
7. Soothe a black eye.
8. Stick up poster.
9. Deodorizer—air freshener.
10. Grow fungi.
11. Put it between your sheets to serve as a conversation piece.
12. Put a piece on your camera so you can tell people to say "cheese."
13. Decoration (i.e. cheese ball).
14. Fishing bait.
15. Smell up refrigerator.
16. Wheels on go-cart.
17. Wood filler.
18. Ward off vampires (mix with garlic).
19. Use Swiss cheese for sewing card.
20. Build a cheese house.
21. Resole your shoes with it.
22. Plug up a leak in your boat.
23. Swiss cheese should make an excellent substitute for computer data processing cards.
24. Can cut designs in a slice of cheese and use as a template.
25. Take a sharp object and write messages on cheese.
26. As a dull topic of conversation.
27. Make a depression in a large piece of cheese and use as a bowl.
28. As a weapon.
29. Rub on gun barrel to dull the finish.
30. As a book marker.
31. Draw numerals and symbols on fifty-two slices and use as a deck of cards.
32. As a pincushion.
33. Use as ball to play catch.
34. Drop pieces along trail as you walk through the woods so you won't lose your way.
35. Plug gaps in walls.
36. Door stops.
37. Seal window frames.
38. Sculpture medium.
39. Use as targets on military ranges.
40. Thin sheets of processed cheese can be used as temporary notepads.
41. Thin sheets can be used as wallpaper.
42. A medium for bacteria culture.
43. Paperweights.
44. Table ornaments.
45. Carve a statue.

46. Make a dartboard from a wheel of it.
47. Smear limburger all over yourself to keep bugs (and muggers) away.
48. Wear it around your neck as a combination good-luck charm and emergency snack.
49. Roll the cheese into tiny balls and shoot them out of a pea-shooter.
50. Make cheese catfish-bait.

## 99. Six or more ways to tell a basketball player from a football player

1. A basketball player's shooting arm is longer.
2. A football player's back is bent from wearing pads.
3. A football player won't do anything until you say "Hike."
4. Say "Jump" and only the basketball player will do so.
5. The basketball player will be more forward—have you ever tried to talk to a fullback?
6. The basketball player is a roundhead—the football player, an egghead.
7. Uniform.
8. Equipment used.
9. Shoes.
10. Place where they are playing.
11. Height.
12. Footwear.
13. Uniform.
14. Headgear.
15. Playing field.
16. Amount of skin showing.
17. Build.
18. Basketball players always walk around practicing jump shots.
19. Basketball players dribble, football players fumble.
20. Footballers do not handle the ball (in U.K.).
21. Footballers wear a different type of boots (in U.K.).
22. If involved in a scandal he is not a basketball player.
23. Basketball players do not feign injury.
24. Basketball players do not cripple their opponents.
25. If he owns two pubs and a hotel he is a football player.
26. Basketball player is taller.
27. Football player is probably more muscular.
28. Different fields, if they're on them.
29. Football player is probably more beaten up.

30. They have baskets growing at the end of their legs.
31. Ask them which they are.
32. Give them a football and see what they do with it.
33. Give them a basketball and see what they do with it.
34. Shout "goal" and see if their eyes light up.
35. Write "from a football player" on paper and show it to the basketball player.

## 100. Six or more reasons why you should never steal home plate

1. Because I sometimes steal home drunk.
2. Because my mother told me not to.
3. Because you might get caught.
4. Because the owners will miss it.
5. Because you've got enough already and don't need any more.
6. Your mother won't let you eat off it.
7. You might break it.
8. The umpire won't have anything to sweep.
9. The catcher will squat at the wrong place.
10. Then it would be a visiting plate.
11. There's no basis for it.
12. Too long a distance.
13. Might get hurt.
14. Will probably be out.
15. Could cause a fight.
16. You could get arrested if caught.
17. Other team wouldn't like it (if you were safe).
18. Could get benched.
19. Could get thrown off team.
20. Could get killed.
21. Against the law.
22. Could get—OUT.
23. It you stole it, where would you sell it?
24. Could disrupt game.
25. No place for batter to stand.
26. Could trip and embarrass self.
27. Could get uniform soiled.
28. Could swallow ball if hit by batter.
29. Could get in 3rd Baseman's way.
30. Could distract pitcher.
31. Could rub out 3rd base foul line.
32. Could kick up dust storm.
33. Other team might win if you fail.
34. Other team might lose if you succeed.

35. Might step on an ant.
36. Might cause the manager to lose his job if you fail.
37. You might work up a sweat.
38. You might get a run in your nylon uniform stocking.
39. Might distract batter so he takes his eye off ball and swings and misses.
40. Might get mobbed by jubilant fans.
41. Might get hit in the nuts by a line drive.
42. Might sprain an ankle.
43. Difficult to paste in scrapbook.
44. Difficult to sneak out of ballpark with.
45. Could run the wrong way and steal 2nd.
46. Could miss touching homeplate.
47. Would slide and spike the batter by mistake.
48. Could fail and get fired.
49. Could fail and get sent to minors.
50. Could ruin nice shine on your shoes.
51. Could cause a fan to get excited and spill a beer on man in front of him.
52. It does not belong to you.
53. Its owner may be annoyed.
54. It's not the done thing.
55. Away plate is more valuable.
56. Theft is an indictable offense.
57. It spoils the game.
58. You could run into the catcher—or even worse, the umpire.
59. Too risky.
60. If you steal the base, no one else could score.
61. Batter might miss swing and hit you.

## 101. Seven or more ways you can tell a dog from a cat without seeing one

1. Smell then breathe.
2. Feel their tails.
3. Feel their ears.
4. By the sounds they make when angry.
5. By their cleanliness.
6. By whether or not they can climb a tree.
7. Whether or not they jump a large fence.
8. Listen to it.
9. Take a dog's eye out and a cat's eye out and compare them.
10. Ask them.
11. Feed each one a steak and the one who finishes first is the dog.

12. Length of its tail.
13. Fur texture.
14. Bone structure.
15. Diet.
16. Shape of eyes.
17. Body proportions.
18. Body weight compared to volume of body.
19. Nocturnal habits.
20. How high can it jump?
21. Does it fall on its feet?
22. Get it angry—does it keep its tail still?
23. Does it bite you or claw you (first)?
24. When it bites you does it hang on (as I *think* dogs do)?
25. Will it protest if made to sleep outside?
26. Can it swim?
27. Does it swim for pleasure?
28. Does it ever bury its food?
29. Can it move fast enough to kill a mouse?
30. A dog barks.
31. A cat purrs.
32. A cat leaves generally smaller feces than a dog.
33. A normal dog will not take cover in a six-foot tree.
34. A normal dog also will not enjoy caressing your legs with its body.
35. A cat will make one sneeze while a dog will only give one sniffles.
36. A cat will use one's leg as a scratching post while a dog will use one's leg as a fire hydrant.
37. If one is missing some food nine out of ten times it will be a dog rather than a cat.

## 102. Eight or more reasons not to drink alcohol when driving

1. Impaired vision.
2. Impaired reaction time.
3. Lack of responsible decision making.
4. Sleepiness.
5. Bad breath.
6. Lack of attention to driving.
7. Need to stop and go to the bathroom.
8. Need to stop and throw up.
9. Might pass out.
10. The drink could spill all over.
11. Because there is no bar in the car.
12. Because it is hard to do two things at once.
13. Because it is better to drink at home in front of a football game.
14. The alcohol would splash all over the driver's face.

15. The bottle or can gets in the way.
16. If there are too many alcoholic fumes the car would explode.
17. Because there isn't a bartender to talk to.
18. If caught, penalty's severe.
19. If have an accident, penalty's extremely severe.
20. Drinking costs money, anyway.
21. If you did have an accident you might not be able to get clear of a fire.
22. You may forget to lock your car when you leave it, or it would be stolen (properly).
23. Lose sense of balance.
24. Lose judgment.
25. It's illegal.
26. One can strip the gears on a standard transmission.
27. Distraction.
28. Both hands needed for driving.
29. Damage of property.
30. Injury to others.
31. Injury to yourself.

## 103. Seven or more reasons why alcohol was made illegal during the twenties

1. Give law-enforcement people work.
2. Make money from fines.
3. Discourage public drunkenness.
4. Give moonshiners something to do.
5. To sell equipment for making your own.
6. Discourage children from drinking.
7. Improve automobile safety.
8. To give government agents something to do.
9. To find out whether or not alcohol could become a backyard industry.
10. So Coca-Cola could become popular.
11. Because bartenders were threatening to go on strike.
12. Everyone was so happy during the twenties, and since you can't have too much of a good thing they took their booze away.
13. Because 1924 was a bad year for wine.
14. Because it was time for another amendment to the Constitution.
15. So the syndicate could make $.
16. So bootleggers could make $.

17. Because it was decided that drinking was not healthy.
18. Because drinking causes boisterous behavior.
19. Because drinking causes loss in judgment.
20. Because it is addictive (thought to be).
21. Because it was a sign of the devil.
22. Because it was a sin.
23. Saloons' encouragement of drunkenness.
24. Loss of family income to saloons.
25. Carry Nation.
26. WCTU (Women's Christian Temperance Union).
27. Play "The Drunkard."
28. Some congressmen wanting to be elected back to office.
29. By passing such a law.

## 104. Eight or more foods never to order for lunch

1. Sub with onions.
2. Greasy fried chicken.
3. Alcoholic beverages.
4. Liver and onions.
5. Pizza.
6. Spaghetti.
7. Brussels sprouts.
8. Crabs (in shell).
9. Lobster (in shell).
10. Cold cereal.
11. Frogs legs.
12. Pigs feet.
13. Brains in wine sauce.
14. Sweetbreads.
15. Oatmeal.
16. Kelp.
17. Syrup of Ipecac surprise.
18. Caviar sandwich.
19. Vanilla ice cream with hot melted tar.
20. Eels with vinegar oil.
21. Chipped beef.
22. Yak testicle stew.
23. Rocky Mountain oysters.
24. Sandwich with penicillin-type bread.
25. Peanut butter.
26. Milk.
27. Tea.
28. Sticky rice (Philippines).
29. Fried worms (Mexico).
30. Chocolate-covered ants (Mexico).
31. Amanita mushrooms (Siberia).
32. Candied catfish eyeballs ("Li'l Abner").
33. Processed whale blubber (Japan).

## 105. Six or more things never to say to a policeman

1. Call him "boy."
2. "Flatfoot."
3. Offer to bribe him.
4. Admit you're guilty.
5. Threaten him.
6. Insult his intelligence.
7. Make reference to his mother.
8. "Hey, Clancy!"
9. "You idiot."
10. "Hey stupid!"
11. "Your mother wears army boots."
12. "Will this fifty dollars cover my fine?"
13. "All policemen are jerks."
14. "Take any good bribes lately?"
15. "Uniforms turn me on."
16. "Maybe you're more clever than Bannon, but he's better looking."
17. "Fuzz."
18. "Where'd you rent the uniform?"
19. "Want to know what to do with your rifle?"
20. "Your wife's the hooker, isn't she?"
21. "You're under arrest."
22. "Whatever I did, I admit it."
23. "I'd like to be a cop, going round being a nuisance."
24. "I know you're getting WCCK on that radio."
25. "Interrogate me—I *love* being beaten."
26. "Didn't you used to be on *Car 54, Where Are You?*"
27. "Piggy, piggy, piggy."
28. "Hey, I bet you can't shoot me."
29. "I dare you to put me in jail."
30. "Bet you can't catch me."
31. "Oink, oink, oink."
32. "I just killed your partner."
33. "You can't stop me."
34. "You can't see my drivers license."
35. "You can't see my registration."
36. "I'll report you."
37. "I'll hit you in your face."
38. "I'll kill you for this."

## 106. Six or more reasons not to have a pet

1. Expense of buying.
2. Expense of feeding.
3. Veterinarian bills.
4. Cost of license.
5. Mess up yard.
6. Ruin furniture.
7. Noise.

8. Cannot be away from home for any length of time.
9. They might urinate all over the house.
10. They may steal off your plate.
11. They may want to go outside in the middle of the night.
12. They eat too much.
13. They are boring.
14. Get hairs or feathers on furniture.
15. Eats.
16. Attracts fleas.
17. Can bite you.
18. Takes up space.
19. Can get lost.
20. Can claw furniture.
21. Can dig up or crap in the garden.
22. What do you do if it gets pregnant?
23. Can intimidate friends.
24. You can get too attached to it.
25. You can't marry someone who doesn't like it.
26. Keep you awake at night.
27. Rabies?
28. What if it bites someone?
29. Chew up clothes (sometimes).
30. Gets in your way.
31. Needs playing with.
32. No bother.
33. Doesn't give bad odor.
34. I like to walk barefoot.
35. Care problem during vacation.
36. Attention requirements at normal times.
37. Attention requirements at abnormal times.
38. Sorrow at their death.
39. Allergies.
40. Landlord won't allow pets.

## 107. Eight or more things you could be doing now if you were not using this book

1. Shopping.
2. Swimming.
3. Eating.
4. Watching TV.
5. Visiting theater.
6. Laundry.
7. Feeding the cats.
8. Calling home.
9. Mowing the lawn.
10. Sleeping.
11. Robbing a bank.
12. Counting my money.
13. Pacing back and forth.
14. Banging my head against the wall.
15. Breaking all of our plates.
16. Changing a light bulb.
17. Studying.

18. Listening to a record.
19. Reading (for pleasure).
20. Go out drinking.
21. Visiting friend next door.
22. Working overtime.
23. Writing a letter.
24. Jogging.
25. Rowing.
26. Making my sandwiches for lunch tomorrow.
27. Having supper.
28. Planning budget (got paid today!).
29. Rearranging posters.
30. Playing Monopoly with landlord's kids.
31. Doing laundry.
32. Washing-up.
33. Putting clothes away.
34. Cleaning shoes.
35. Trying to find broken alarm clock.
36. Making out Christmas present list.
37. Trying to reread old lecture notes.
38. Making obscene phone calls to someone called, say, Hoare or Bhumm.
39. Sorting out newspaper cutting collection.
40. Starting a diary.
41. Using all my spent matches to make a model.
42. Attending Mensa meeting.
43. Filling out a job application.
44. Making paper aeroplanes.
45. Going to a soccer game.
46. Cleaning my windows.
47. Washing my hair.
48. Having a bath.
49. Driving.
50. Having sex.
51. Doing homework.
52. Talking.
53. Working on my car.
54. Yelling at my sister.
55. Playing golf.
56. Talking to my wife.
57. Raking leaves.

## 108. Seven or more reasons not to have the Olympic Games

1. Disagreement between countries about where to hold them.
2. Need for security precautions.
3. Expense.
4. Problem of what to do with the facilities when the games are over.
5. Impossibility of impartial judging.
6. Encourages competition rather than cooperation.
7. Too much emphasis on physical superiority.
8. Need to control for cheating

and use of illegal drugs.
9. Because the same countries win all the time.
10. Because you have to listen to Jim McKay all the time.
11. Because there are so many other international competitions.
12. Because the Russians have more medals than the U.S.
13. Because you can only watch finals and never heats.
14. Because there are always fights.
15. Too many athletes are professionals.
16. Too much disturbance in the host city.
17. Too useful as an opportunity for political protest.
18. Too many officials involved.
19. Too-officious officials.
20. Tourists get ripped off.
21. Thieves' paradise.
22. Transport facilities overloaded.
23. Vice grows.
24. Great Britain never wins.
25. Take up too much time on TV.
26. Unfair distribution of tickets by organizers.
27. Sign of "approval" of country—e.g., Germany 1936, USSR 1980.
28. Too many deaths ('72).
29. Too much competitiveness.
30. Wastes too much energy.
31. Makes weakling feel bad.
32. Gives runners shin splints and blisters.
33. Makes losers feel bad.
34. Fear of terrorist groups.
35. Lack of interest.

## 109. Seven or more reasons for having a pet dog

1. Companionship.
2. Protection.
3. To have something to do with leftover bones.
4. Something to play with.
5. Something to wash food off your face.
6. To dig yard up so you can plant.
7. Provide fertilizer for garden.
8. So you don't get lonely.
9. To act as a vacuum cleaner.
10. To keep out any unwanted visitors.
11. Because they spot insects in your house.
12. Because they can bark when someone comes.
13. Friendship.
14. Something to talk to when the wife/husband is out.
15. Use it as a hot water bottle.

16. Could go shopping if properly trained.
17. Wrestle with it if you feel reckless (or suicidal?).
18. You can marry someone who likes dogs but not you.
19. I like the pain when it bites me.
20. Make money breeding dogs.
21. Satisfies a paternal/maternal instinct in some people.
22. Makes *you* take exercise, too.
23. To keep you awake.
24. To use up your $.
25. To use up your tablescraps.
26. To chase your cat.
27. To fight with other dogs.
28. You're blind.
29. You're deaf.
30. For children.

## 110. Seven or more reasons why dogs should run loose

1. They prefer it.
2. Leashes can choke them.
3. To chase away intruders.
4. They'll bark less.
5. They'll find their own food.
6. So they'll mess up the neighbor's yard instead of yours.
7. To play with the children in the neighborhood.
8. So they get more exercise.
9. So the city can employ more dog catchers.
10. To see where they go.
11. So they can see the sights.
12. So they can go to a movie.
13. So you don't have to walk them.
14. So they can meet other dogs.
15. Their natural instinct.
16. May bite if you don't let them run free.
17. May crap around the place if you keep them inside.
18. Can find food so you needn't feed them.
19. Saves *you* running with them on a leash.
20. May catch food for you.
21. It can mate with other dogs and not get frustrated and irritable.
22. Tire itself out so it sleeps all day and keeps quiet.
23. Probably cheaper to watch than a TV.
24. Give your lungs exercise shouting at it.
25. Give your legs exercise running to catch it.
26. No feces in your yard.
27. Spread rabies.
28. Bite mailman.
29. Cause auto accidents.
30. Save expense of leash.

31. Scare people.
32. Get killed.
33. Too big for the house.
34. You live on a farm.
35. More protection from passersby.
36. You do not care if something happens to dog.
37. You do not abide by law.
38. Do not want any flies in house.

## 111. Six or more recipes for mixed drinks

1. Bourbon and arsenic.
2. Gasoline and a drop of oil.
3. Hydrochloric acid and brandy.
4. Sake and prune juice.
5. Carrot juice and vodka.
6. Chocolate milk and whiskey.
7. Strawberry soda and gin.
8. Gin and tomato juice.
9. Vodka and lemon juice.
10. Rum and grapefruit.
11. Whiskey and black currant.
12. Whiskey and tomato juice.
13. Rum and tomato juice.
14. Whiskey and Coke.
15. Gin and ginger ale.
16. Vodka and black currant.
17. Martini and black currant.
18. Gin and ice.
19. Gin with one jigger Drano.
20. ½ bourbon and ½ scotch.
21. ½ bourbon, ¼ scotch, ⅛ $H_2O$, ⅛ melted Jell-O.
22. ½ vinegar, ¼ oil, ¼ bourbon.
23. ¼ vodka, ¼ gin, ½ Mogen David.
24. Beer and tomato juice.
25. Rum and rough alcohol.
26. Creme de menthe and vodka.
27. Apple juice and brandy.

## 112. Seven or more things never to say to a dentist

1. "Will this hurt?"
2. "Tell me all you know about teeth."
3. "How much does the bill come out to be?"
4. "Do you have any cavities?"
5. "Your drill is on fire."
6. "Get your hands out of my mouth."
7. "Your hands are dirty."
8. "Is that all it costs?"
9. "Are you sure I need anesthesia?"
10. "I'd like to have a root canal."
11. "Don't touch me."
12. "I had onions for lunch."
13. "I haven't had a chance to brush my teeth lately."

14. "I don't mind pain."
15. "I laid your wife last night."
16. "Ever applied to be a Soviet interrogator?"
17. "I inherited a quarter million dollars yesterday."
18. "No, that doesn't hurt" (when it does).
19. "I didn't *mean* to bite you."
20. "Uniforms turn me on. . . ."
21. "Your nurse . . . $80 a night?"
22. "I can think of better places for you to inject."
23. "Most dentists are failed doctors, aren't they?"
24. "Anyone ever tell you you've got buck teeth?"
25. "My tooth hurts."
26. "I bet you can't hurt me."
27. "My, that drill spins fast!"
28. "Money is no object."
29. "Why do you wear dentures?"
30. "I don't have any money."
31. "I have halitosis."
32. "Pull my tooth."
33. "I like to come here every day."
34. "Please use your drill on my teeth."
35. "Pull all my teeth."
36. "Remove all my fillings."
37. "Take an X-ray."
38. "Don't put my nerves to sleep when extracting my teeth."

## 113. Six or more reasons why diamonds cost more than coal

1. Diamonds are shinier.
2. Coal doesn't look good in rings.
3. Coal is messier.
4. Supply.
5. Demand.
6. More attractive.
7. Harder.
8. Need to be cut.
9. Diamonds can do useful things like cut glass or rock.
10. Diamonds don't burn.
11. Coal is opaque.
12. Elizabeth Taylor doesn't wear coal.
13. Wearing coal on your finger would dirty your clothes.
14. You can't make plastics from diamonds.
15. You can't keep diamonds in a shed in the yard.
16. Diamonds are pure carbon.
17. Coal is cheap.
18. Coal burns.
19. Ladies like wearing diamonds.
20. Coal is black.
21. Cost of mining.
22. Diamonds are a girl's best friend.
23. Market is soaring.
24. You have them all your life.

## 114. Seven or more reasons we shake hands

1. So we can feel what the other person's hand is like.
2. So we can tell if the other person is sweating.
3. Because it's too hard to shake feet.
4. So we know the other person isn't up to something.
5. To tell if the person is honest.
6. To show we don't have a gun.
7. To exchange scents.
8. To show warmth.
9. To keep the person at arm's length.
10. To show our strength.
11. To gauge how the other person feels about us.
12. To appear formal.
13. To appear professional.
14. The other guy can't hit you quite so soon.
15. I like holding hands.
16. See if they use a secret identifying signal.
17. See if he has calluses and works a lot with his hands.
18. You can get near and smell his breath.
19. You can get close and see his pupils (does he take drugs?).
20. To say "Hi."
21. To say "Bye."
22. To make contact.
23. To act cool.
24. To impress your peers.
25. Because you are a pickpocket and want his watch.
26. Because your palm itches.

## 115. Six or more reasons we have gates

1. Because the gate manufacturers say so.
2. To mark driveways.
3. For appearance.
4. It is a place to put our gold.
5. To let people in.
6. To keep people out.
7. To swing on.
8. So we don't have to climb the fence.
9. To see through.
10. Keep animals out.
11. Keep children in.
12. Mark out our own property.
13. Put home name or number on.
14. Give work to carpenters and metalworkers.
15. The squeaks sound nice.
16. Stick messages for the milkman on them.
17. Fix mailbox on it.
18. To keep people in.
19. To keep animals in.
20. To obstruct an ugly view.
21. To have privacy.
22. They look great.
23. Protect children.
24. Protect pets.
25. Protect your property.
26. Protect your livestock.
27. Added value to property.

## 116. Seven or more reasons why cars have brakes

1. Because there was empty floor space.
2. So you have a place to put your foot when you take it off the gas pedal.
3. To provide use for brake fluid.
4. Because car manufacturers put them in.
5. So we can have brake repairmen.
6. Because Ralph Nader says we need them.
7. To slow down the car.
8. To stop the car.
9. To make the brake lights go on.
10. To keep the accelerator foot from going to sleep.
11. To help us skid on ice.
12. To propel us through the windshields.
13. To give seatbelts something to do.
14. To fill up space under the hood.
15. Add extra weight.
16. Add to the price.
17. Give work to mechanics.
18. To make nice squealing noises.
19. Use up asbestos.
20. To have an extra pedal.
21. To keep from going up.
22. To keep from going down.
23. So you don't hit things.
24. Cars wouldn't sell well without them.
25. Not to hit people.
26. Not to hit houses.
27. Not to hit animals.
28. Required by law.
29. To stop for red light.
30. To stop for stop sign.

## 117. Seven or more reasons not to wear a helmet while driving a motorcycle

1. It doesn't look nice.
2. Helmets hurt your head.
3. You can't scratch your scalp.
4. You can't show off your hairdo.
5. They are too fancy.
6. They slip and slide on your head sometimes.
7. They might hurt your ears.
8. Impaired vision.
9. Impaired hearing.
10. Impaired taste.
11. Impaired smell.
12. Keeps your hair from blowing.
13. More comfortable.
14. Decreased weight.
15. Feel freer.
16. Let's your hair dry if you've just washed it.
17. Shows bravery (or stupidity).
18. Have money, don't need to buy one.
19. Don't have marks on your head from it rubbing.
20. Easier to talk to people.
21. To cut down drag.
22. So if you hit something you'll die easier.
23. Because it looks neat.
24. Because your friends do it.
25. Hot.
26. Heavy.
27. Bulky.
28. Decreases amount of fresh air.
29. Something else to have stolen.

## 118. Eight or more persons who may be President of the United States in the year 2000

1. Amy Carter.
2. Howard Cosell.
3. Muhammad Ali.
4. Bert Lance.
5. Bella Abzug.
6. Ed Koch.
7. Bill Bradley.
8. Truman Capote.
9. Julian Bond.
10. Donnie Osmond.
11. Marie Osmond.
12. John Travolta.
13. Michael Jackson.
14. Karen Carpenter.
15. John-John Kennedy.
16. Caroline Kennedy.
17. My fiancée.

18. My fiancée's brother.
19. The girl who lives next door to my fiancée.
20. The brother of a Canadian guy I know, who was born in Detroit.
21. My kid, if he's born in the USA.
22. Charlie Brown.
23. Bob Dylan.
24. Shirley Temple Black.
25. Farrah Fawcett-Majors.
26. Cheryl Ladd.
27. Joni Mitchell.
28. Starsky.
29. Hutch.
30. John Updike.
31. Jerry Brown.
32. Lee Majors.
33. Batman.
34. Hugh Hefner.
35. This month's Playmate.
36. Nelson Rockefeller IV.
37. Kennedy grandchild.
38. Socialist.
39. Midwestern woman.

---

119. Eight or more problems that had to be overcome to fly to the moon

1. Gravity.
2. Astronauts' relationships.
3. Determining where the moon would be.
4. How to get the money from Congress.
5. Making sure the Russians didn't get there first.
6. Finding a flag to put up.
7. Finding time when the television networks are willing to be there.
8. Getting enough fuel to fly the rocket.
9. Eating in weightless conditions.
10. Drinking.
11. Bathing.
12. Mercury subortibal—then orbital flight.
13. Where to invest money received for testimonials.
14. Shield to re-enter the atmosphere.
15. Boredom.
16. Loneliness.
17. Long-distance radio communications.
18. Determining if it is safe to land on the moon.
19. Working out the correct time of launch.
20. Training the right people to control rocket systems.
21. Making sure everything worked.
22. Building the rocket.
23. Building the launch facilities.
24. Air mixture that's best to breathe.
25. Excretion in weightless conditions.
26. Recovering the capsule on return.
27. Training people in geology..
28. Training people to walk on the moon.
29. Determining what the moon was made of.
30. Determining how much astronauts should be paid.
31. Getting enough computer power available to do all the necessary news.
32. Simple fear of the unknown.
33. Finding enough people to work all the systems on the ground.
34. Cutting down drag.
35. Increasing momentum.
36. Finding brave men.
37. Having Scientific data.
38. Finding correct-type transport.
39. Having way to get back.

---

120. Seven or more ways to carry ten wooden coat hangers

1. Hang them on a metal bar and carry the bar.
2. Put them in your mouth.
3. Pay someone to carry them for you.
4. Hang them on your belt.
5. Tie them to a string and tie a string around your neck.
6. Put them in a backpack.
7. Strung onto each other.
8. In a large truck.
9. With clothes on them.
10. Burned up with the ashes in a bottle.
11. Hanging from ears and arms.
12. One on each finger.
13. In a box; jumbled anyhow.
14. Hook each over the other and carry them by the topmost one.
15. Stacked on top of each other.
16. Side by side in your fist, like a bunch of flowers.
17. Under your arms.
18. In your hands.
19. In a little red wagon.
20. Balanced on your head.
21. In a paper bag.
22. In plastic bag.

# MAY

### Mental Calisthenic #5

Sit in a comfortable area free of distractions and NOISE. Use earplugs if necessary, or wait until late at night when all is quiet. Now, close your eyes and imagine the sound of THUNDER, a TRUCK, POLICE SIREN, WHISTLE, CROWD, DISHWASHER, a LARGE RIVER, a PING-PONG MATCH, a TENNIS MATCH, a BABY CRYING. Which ones were easy? Which ones were difficult? Go to a Mental Jogging exercise.

## 121. Seven or more reasons not to follow road signs

| Response | Score |
|---|---|
| 1. | 1 |
| 2. | 1 |
| 3. | 1 |
| 4. | 1 |
| 5. | 1 |
| 6. | 1 |
| 7. | 1 |
| Bonus Responses | |
| 8. | 2 |
| 9. | 2 |
| 10. | 2 |
| 11. | 2 |
| 12. | 2 |
| 13. | 2 |
| 14. | 2 |
| 15. | 2 |
| 16. | 2 |

Total ☐

## 122. Six or more ways to light a pipe without a match

| Response | Score |
|---|---|
| 1. | 1 |
| 2. | 1 |
| 3. | 1 |
| 4. | 1 |
| 5. | 1 |
| 6. | 1 |
| Bonus Responses | |
| 7. | 2 |
| 8. | 2 |
| 9. | 2 |
| 10. | 2 |
| 11. | 2 |
| 12. | 2 |
| 13. | 2 |
| 14. | 2 |
| 15. | 2 |
| 16. | 2 |

Total ☐

## 123. Six or more reasons we use gasoline instead of water for car fuel

| Response | Score |
|---|---|
| 1. _____ | 1 |
| 2. _____ | 1 |
| 3. _____ | 1 |
| 4. _____ | 1 |
| 5. _____ | 1 |
| 6. _____ | 1 |

Bonus Responses

| | |
|---|---|
| 7. _____ | 2 |
| 8. _____ | 2 |
| 9. _____ | 2 |
| 10. _____ | 2 |
| 11. _____ | 2 |
| 12. _____ | 2 |
| 13. _____ | 2 |
| 14. _____ | 2 |
| 15. _____ | 2 |
| 16. _____ | 2 |

Total ☐

## 124. Eight or more reasons why rainbows cannot be seen at night

| Response | Score |
|---|---|
| 1. _____ | 1 |
| 2. _____ | 1 |
| 3. _____ | 1 |
| 4. _____ | 1 |
| 5. _____ | 1 |
| 6. _____ | 1 |
| 7. _____ | 1 |
| 8. _____ | 1 |

Bonus Responses

| | |
|---|---|
| 9. _____ | 2 |
| 10. _____ | 2 |
| 11. _____ | 2 |
| 12. _____ | 2 |
| 13. _____ | 2 |
| 14. _____ | 2 |
| 15. _____ | 2 |
| 16. _____ | 2 |

Total ☐

## 125. Seven or more colors you've never seen

| Response | Score |
|---|---|
| 1. _____ | 1 |
| 2. _____ | 1 |
| 3. _____ | 1 |
| 4. _____ | 1 |
| 5. _____ | 1 |
| 6. _____ | 1 |
| 7. _____ | 1 |

Bonus Responses

| | |
|---|---|
| 8. _____ | 2 |
| 9. _____ | 2 |
| 10. _____ | 2 |
| 11. _____ | 2 |
| 12. _____ | 2 |
| 13. _____ | 2 |
| 14. _____ | 2 |
| 15. _____ | 2 |
| 16. _____ | 2 |

Total ☐

## 126. Seven or more reasons for wearing lipstick

| Response | Score |
|---|---|
| 1. _____ | 1 |
| 2. _____ | 1 |
| 3. _____ | 1 |
| 4. _____ | 1 |
| 5. _____ | 1 |
| 6. _____ | 1 |
| 7. _____ | 1 |

Bonus Responses

| | |
|---|---|
| 8. _____ | 2 |
| 9. _____ | 2 |
| 10. _____ | 2 |
| 11. _____ | 2 |
| 12. _____ | 2 |
| 13. _____ | 2 |
| 14. _____ | 2 |
| 15. _____ | 2 |
| 16. _____ | 2 |

Total ☐

## 127. Six or more reasons why some people make more money than others

| Response | Score |
|---|---|
| 1. _____ | 1 |
| 2. _____ | 1 |
| 3. _____ | 1 |
| 4. _____ | 1 |
| 5. _____ | 1 |
| 6. _____ | 1 |

Bonus Responses

| | |
|---|---|
| 7. _____ | 2 |
| 8. _____ | 2 |
| 9. _____ | 2 |
| 10. _____ | 2 |
| 11. _____ | 2 |
| 12. _____ | 2 |
| 13. _____ | 2 |
| 14. _____ | 2 |
| 15. _____ | 2 |
| 16. _____ | 2 |

Total ☐

## 128. Six or more reasons for eating three meals a day

| Response | Score |
|---|---|
| 1. _____ | 1 |
| 2. _____ | 1 |
| 3. _____ | 1 |
| 4. _____ | 1 |
| 5. _____ | 1 |
| 6. _____ | 1 |

Bonus Responses

| | |
|---|---|
| 7. _____ | 2 |
| 8. _____ | 2 |
| 9. _____ | 2 |
| 10. _____ | 2 |
| 11. _____ | 2 |
| 12. _____ | 2 |
| 13. _____ | 2 |
| 14. _____ | 2 |
| 15. _____ | 2 |
| 16. _____ | 2 |

Total ☐

## 129. Eight or more reasons for coughing

| Response | Score |
|---|---|
| 1. _____ | 1 |
| 2. _____ | 1 |
| 3. _____ | 1 |
| 4. _____ | 1 |
| 5. _____ | 1 |
| 6. _____ | 1 |
| 7. _____ | 1 |
| 8. _____ | 1 |

Bonus Responses

| | |
|---|---|
| 9. _____ | 2 |
| 10. _____ | 2 |
| 11. _____ | 2 |
| 12. _____ | 2 |
| 13. _____ | 2 |
| 14. _____ | 2 |
| 15. _____ | 2 |
| 16. _____ | 2 |

Total ☐

## 130. Seven or more ways to prevent a candle from burning down

| Response | Score |
|---|---|
| 1. _____ | 1 |
| 2. _____ | 1 |
| 3. _____ | 1 |
| 4. _____ | 1 |
| 5. _____ | 1 |
| 6. _____ | 1 |
| 7. _____ | 1 |

Bonus Responses

| | |
|---|---|
| 8. _____ | 2 |
| 9. _____ | 2 |
| 10. _____ | 2 |
| 11. _____ | 2 |
| 12. _____ | 2 |
| 13. _____ | 2 |
| 14. _____ | 2 |
| 15. _____ | 2 |
| 16. _____ | 2 |

Total ☐

## 131. Eight or more things we couldn't do if we didn't have fingernails

| Response | Score |
|---|---|
| 1. _____ | 1 |
| 2. _____ | 1 |
| 3. _____ | 1 |
| 4. _____ | 1 |
| 5. _____ | 1 |
| 6. _____ | 1 |
| 7. _____ | 1 |
| 8. _____ | 1 |

**Bonus Responses**

| | |
|---|---|
| 9. _____ | 2 |
| 10. _____ | 2 |
| 11. _____ | 2 |
| 12. _____ | 2 |
| 13. _____ | 2 |
| 14. _____ | 2 |
| 15. _____ | 2 |
| 16. _____ | 2 |

Total ☐

## 132. Seven or more ways to prevent the red dye in pistachio nuts from getting all over your fingers

| Response | Score |
|---|---|
| 1. _____ | 1 |
| 2. _____ | 1 |
| 3. _____ | 1 |
| 4. _____ | 1 |
| 5. _____ | 1 |
| 6. _____ | 1 |
| 7. _____ | 1 |

**Bonus Responses**

| | |
|---|---|
| 8. _____ | 2 |
| 9. _____ | 2 |
| 10. _____ | 2 |
| 11. _____ | 2 |
| 12. _____ | 2 |
| 13. _____ | 2 |
| 14. _____ | 2 |
| 15. _____ | 2 |
| 16. _____ | 2 |

Total ☐

## 133. Six or more ways to prevent yourself from swallowing sea water while swimming

| Response | Score |
|---|---|
| 1. _____ | 1 |
| 2. _____ | 1 |
| 3. _____ | 1 |
| 4. _____ | 1 |
| 5. _____ | 1 |
| 6. _____ | 1 |

**Bonus Responses**

| | |
|---|---|
| 7. _____ | 2 |
| 8. _____ | 2 |
| 9. _____ | 2 |
| 10. _____ | 2 |
| 11. _____ | 2 |
| 12. _____ | 2 |
| 13. _____ | 2 |
| 14. _____ | 2 |
| 15. _____ | 2 |
| 16. _____ | 2 |

Total ☐

## 134. Seven or more reasons why police cars have sirens

| Response | Score |
|---|---|
| 1. _____ | 1 |
| 2. _____ | 1 |
| 3. _____ | 1 |
| 4. _____ | 1 |
| 5. _____ | 1 |
| 6. _____ | 1 |
| 7. _____ | 1 |

**Bonus Responses**

| | |
|---|---|
| 8. _____ | 2 |
| 9. _____ | 2 |
| 10. _____ | 2 |
| 11. _____ | 2 |
| 12. _____ | 2 |
| 13. _____ | 2 |
| 14. _____ | 2 |
| 15. _____ | 2 |
| 16. _____ | 2 |

Total ☐

## 135. Six or more ways to prevent ice cubes from melting

| Response | Score |
|---|---|
| 1. _____ | 1 |
| 2. _____ | 1 |
| 3. _____ | 1 |
| 4. _____ | 1 |
| 5. _____ | 1 |
| 6. _____ | 1 |

Bonus Responses

| | |
|---|---|
| 7. _____ | 2 |
| 8. _____ | 2 |
| 9. _____ | 2 |
| 10. _____ | 2 |
| 11. _____ | 2 |
| 12. _____ | 2 |
| 13. _____ | 2 |
| 14. _____ | 2 |
| 15. _____ | 2 |
| 16. _____ | 2 |

Total ☐

## 136. Seven or more reasons why there are more forty-year-old single females than single males

| Response | Score |
|---|---|
| 1. _____ | 1 |
| 2. _____ | 1 |
| 3. _____ | 1 |
| 4. _____ | 1 |
| 5. _____ | 1 |
| 6. _____ | 1 |
| 7. _____ | 1 |

Bonus Responses

| | |
|---|---|
| 8. _____ | 2 |
| 9. _____ | 2 |
| 10. _____ | 2 |
| 11. _____ | 2 |
| 12. _____ | 2 |
| 13. _____ | 2 |
| 14. _____ | 2 |
| 15. _____ | 2 |
| 16. _____ | 2 |

Total ☐

## 137. Seven or more reasons not to make a lot of money

| Response | Score |
|---|---|
| 1. _____ | 1 |
| 2. _____ | 1 |
| 3. _____ | 1 |
| 4. _____ | 1 |
| 5. _____ | 1 |
| 6. _____ | 1 |
| 7. _____ | 1 |

Bonus Responses

| | |
|---|---|
| 8. _____ | 2 |
| 9. _____ | 2 |
| 10. _____ | 2 |
| 11. _____ | 2 |
| 12. _____ | 2 |
| 13. _____ | 2 |
| 14. _____ | 2 |
| 15. _____ | 2 |
| 16. _____ | 2 |

Total ☐

## 138. Eight or more new uses for cellophane tape

| Response | Score |
|---|---|
| 1. _____ | 1 |
| 2. _____ | 1 |
| 3. _____ | 1 |
| 4. _____ | 1 |
| 5. _____ | 1 |
| 6. _____ | 1 |
| 7. _____ | 1 |
| 8. _____ | 1 |

Bonus Responses

| | |
|---|---|
| 9. _____ | 2 |
| 10. _____ | 2 |
| 11. _____ | 2 |
| 12. _____ | 2 |
| 13. _____ | 2 |
| 14. _____ | 2 |
| 15. _____ | 2 |
| 16. _____ | 2 |

Total ☐

## 139. Seven or more things you see when you close your eyes

| Response | Score |
|---|---|
| 1. _____ | 1 |
| 2. _____ | 1 |
| 3. _____ | 1 |
| 4. _____ | 1 |
| 5. _____ | 1 |
| 6. _____ | 1 |
| 7. _____ | 1 |

**Bonus Responses**

| | |
|---|---|
| 8. _____ | 2 |
| 9. _____ | 2 |
| 10. _____ | 2 |
| 11. _____ | 2 |
| 12. _____ | 2 |
| 13. _____ | 2 |
| 14. _____ | 2 |
| 15. _____ | 2 |
| 16. _____ | 2 |

Total ☐

## 140. Eight or more words you have never seen or heard

| Response | Score |
|---|---|
| 1. _____ | 1 |
| 2. _____ | 1 |
| 3. _____ | 1 |
| 4. _____ | 1 |
| 5. _____ | 1 |
| 6. _____ | 1 |
| 7. _____ | 1 |
| 8. _____ | 1 |

**Bonus Responses**

| | |
|---|---|
| 9. _____ | 2 |
| 10. _____ | 2 |
| 11. _____ | 2 |
| 12. _____ | 2 |
| 13. _____ | 2 |
| 14. _____ | 2 |
| 15. _____ | 2 |
| 16. _____ | 2 |

Total ☐

## 141. Seven or more reasons for not having computers

| Response | Score |
|---|---|
| 1. _____ | 1 |
| 2. _____ | 1 |
| 3. _____ | 1 |
| 4. _____ | 1 |
| 5. _____ | 1 |
| 6. _____ | 1 |
| 7. _____ | 1 |

**Bonus Responses**

| | |
|---|---|
| 8. _____ | 2 |
| 9. _____ | 2 |
| 10. _____ | 2 |
| 11. _____ | 2 |
| 12. _____ | 2 |
| 13. _____ | 2 |
| 14. _____ | 2 |
| 15. _____ | 2 |
| 16. _____ | 2 |

Total ☐

## 142. Seven or more reasons not to have a Bloody Mary for breakfast

| Response | Score |
|---|---|
| 1. _____ | 1 |
| 2. _____ | 1 |
| 3. _____ | 1 |
| 4. _____ | 1 |
| 5. _____ | 1 |
| 6. _____ | 1 |
| 7. _____ | 1 |

**Bonus Responses**

| | |
|---|---|
| 8. _____ | 2 |
| 9. _____ | 2 |
| 10. _____ | 2 |
| 11. _____ | 2 |
| 12. _____ | 2 |
| 13. _____ | 2 |
| 14. _____ | 2 |
| 15. _____ | 2 |
| 16. _____ | 2 |

Total ☐

## 143. Six or more reasons why some people have never played chess

| Response | Score |
|---|---|
| 1. | 1 |
| 2. | 1 |
| 3. | 1 |
| 4. | 1 |
| 5. | 1 |
| 6. | 1 |

**Bonus Responses**

| | |
|---|---|
| 7. | 2 |
| 8. | 2 |
| 9. | 2 |
| 10. | 2 |
| 11. | 2 |
| 12. | 2 |
| 13. | 2 |
| 14. | 2 |
| 15. | 2 |
| 16. | 2 |

Total ☐

## 144. Seven or more feelings you have when you see a policeman in your rearview mirror

| Response | Score |
|---|---|
| 1. | 1 |
| 2. | 1 |
| 3. | 1 |
| 4. | 1 |
| 5. | 1 |
| 6. | 1 |
| 7. | 1 |

**Bonus Responses**

| | |
|---|---|
| 8. | 2 |
| 9. | 2 |
| 10. | 2 |
| 11. | 2 |
| 12. | 2 |
| 13. | 2 |
| 14. | 2 |
| 15. | 2 |
| 16. | 2 |

Total ☐

## 145. Six or more places the sun never shines

| Response | Score |
|---|---|
| 1. | 1 |
| 2. | 1 |
| 3. | 1 |
| 4. | 1 |
| 5. | 1 |
| 6. | 1 |

**Bonus Responses**

| | |
|---|---|
| 7. | 2 |
| 8. | 2 |
| 9. | 2 |
| 10. | 2 |
| 11. | 2 |
| 12. | 2 |
| 13. | 2 |
| 14. | 2 |
| 15. | 2 |
| 16. | 2 |

Total ☐

## 146. Seven or more reasons why most paintings are more expensive than photographs

| Response | Score |
|---|---|
| 1. | 1 |
| 2. | 1 |
| 3. | 1 |
| 4. | 1 |
| 5. | 1 |
| 6. | 1 |
| 7. | 1 |

**Bonus Responses**

| | |
|---|---|
| 8. | 2 |
| 9. | 2 |
| 10. | 2 |
| 11. | 2 |
| 12. | 2 |
| 13. | 2 |
| 14. | 2 |
| 15. | 2 |
| 16. | 2 |

Total ☐

## 147. Six or more reasons we use checks

| Response | | Score |
|---|---|---|
| 1. _____ | | 1 |
| 2. _____ | | 1 |
| 3. _____ | | 1 |
| 4. _____ | | 1 |
| 5. _____ | | 1 |
| 6. _____ | | 1 |

Bonus Responses

| | | |
|---|---|---|
| 7. _____ | | 2 |
| 8. _____ | | 2 |
| 9. _____ | | 2 |
| 10. _____ | | 2 |
| 11. _____ | | 2 |
| 12. _____ | | 2 |
| 13. _____ | | 2 |
| 14. _____ | | 2 |
| 15. _____ | | 2 |
| 16. _____ | | 2 |

Total ☐

## 148. Seven or more reasons for not using postage stamps

| Response | | Score |
|---|---|---|
| 1. _____ | | 1 |
| 2. _____ | | 1 |
| 3. _____ | | 1 |
| 4. _____ | | 1 |
| 5. _____ | | 1 |
| 6. _____ | | 1 |
| 7. _____ | | 1 |

Bonus Responses

| | | |
|---|---|---|
| 8. _____ | | 2 |
| 9. _____ | | 2 |
| 10. _____ | | 2 |
| 11. _____ | | 2 |
| 12. _____ | | 2 |
| 13. _____ | | 2 |
| 14. _____ | | 2 |
| 15. _____ | | 2 |
| 16. _____ | | 2 |

Total ☐

## 149. Six or more reasons for picture frames

| Response | | Score |
|---|---|---|
| 1. _____ | | 1 |
| 2. _____ | | 1 |
| 3. _____ | | 1 |
| 4. _____ | | 1 |
| 5. _____ | | 1 |
| 6. _____ | | 1 |

Bonus Responses

| | | |
|---|---|---|
| 7. _____ | | 2 |
| 8. _____ | | 2 |
| 9. _____ | | 2 |
| 10. _____ | | 2 |
| 11. _____ | | 2 |
| 12. _____ | | 2 |
| 13. _____ | | 2 |
| 14. _____ | | 2 |
| 15. _____ | | 2 |
| 16. _____ | | 2 |

Total ☐

## 150. Seven or more common things kept in most wallets

| Response | | Score |
|---|---|---|
| 1. _____ | | 1 |
| 2. _____ | | 1 |
| 3. _____ | | 1 |
| 4. _____ | | 1 |
| 5. _____ | | 1 |
| 6. _____ | | 1 |
| 7. _____ | | 1 |

Bonus Responses

| | | |
|---|---|---|
| 8. _____ | | 2 |
| 9. _____ | | 2 |
| 10. _____ | | 2 |
| 11. _____ | | 2 |
| 12. _____ | | 2 |
| 13. _____ | | 2 |
| 14. _____ | | 2 |
| 15. _____ | | 2 |
| 16. _____ | | 2 |

Total ☐

## 151. Seven or more things impossible to store in most airport lockers

| Response | Score |
|---|---|
| 1. _____ | 1 |
| 2. _____ | 1 |
| 3. _____ | 1 |
| 4. _____ | 1 |
| 5. _____ | 1 |
| 6. _____ | 1 |
| 7. _____ | 1 |

### Bonus Responses

| | |
|---|---|
| 8. _____ | 2 |
| 9. _____ | 2 |
| 10. _____ | 2 |
| 11. _____ | 2 |
| 12. _____ | 2 |
| 13. _____ | 2 |
| 14. _____ | 2 |
| 15. _____ | 2 |
| 16. _____ | 2 |

Total ☐

# CONTRIBUTORS' SAMPLE RESPONSES

## 121. Seven or more reasons not to follow road signs

1. They might be wrong.
2. You might have a better route.
3. There may be interesting things you might miss if you follow the signs.
4. They may be outdated.
5. They may not apply.
6. They may try to fool you.
7. A map may be better.
8. To get where you're going faster.
9. To live dangerously.
10. To test a law.
11. Can't read.
12. An alien attack.
13. So you can get a ticket.
14. Somebody stole the signs.
15. Because they're yellow.
16. Because you don't want to.
17. Because there are too many of them.
18. You like driving the wrong way.
19. To fly thirty feet from your car.
20. To be in a real-life bumper car.
21. Because Evel Knievel is your hero.

## 122. Six or more ways to light a pipe without a match

1. Light it with a burning cigarette.
2. Light it with a burning stick.
3. From gas burner on stove.
4. With a blowtorch.
5. Rub two sticks together.
6. With a Bunsen burner.
7. Use electrical wires.
8. Use Solar collectors.
9. With a magnesium ribbon.
10. A fireplace.
11. Soak tobacco in gasoline, and strike a flint.
12. Put pipe under extreme pressure.
13. A lighter.
14. A piece of molten iron.
15. A bonfire.
16. A burning marshmallow.
17. Use a firecracker.
18. Call a Boy Scout.
19. Stand near a barbecue.
20. Become a fireman.

21. Use a flamethrower.
22. Stand in an electrical storm.
23. Visit Mt. Vesuvius.

## 123. Six or more reasons we use gasoline instead of water for car fuel

1. Car wouldn't run on water.
2. Water engines haven't been developed.
3. Might ruin the engine.
4. Inefficient.
5. Too slow.
6. Not enough power.
7. Water does not burn.
8. Oil companies make more profits on gas.
9. Water would cause gas tanks to rust.
10. Gasoline has more smell.
11. Gas has more taste.
12. Water is better for other things.
13. Gas stations don't have pumps with water.
14. It's too hard to fit the car into the sink.
15. Because it begins with a "G."
16. There is a smaller supply of gasoline.
17. Water has too many calories.
18. Gasoline is more combustible.
19. Why not?

## 124. Eight or more reasons why rainbows cannot be seen at night

1. It's dark.
2. Rainbows don't form at night.
3. They require a source of light.
4. People are asleep.
5. They are invisible.
6. It's cloudy.
7. It's foggy.
8. Nobody looks for rainbows at night.
9. Rainbows are afraid of the dark.
10. Rainbows do not have lights.
11. Rainbows close down at 5:30.
12. Rainbows moonlight as cab drivers at night.
13. There is a curfew on rainbows.
14. Rainbows eat stars, and they can only find stars at night— so they are out to dinner when it is dark.
15. Union rules prohibit rainbows to work past dusk.

16. The painter doesn't work overtime.
17. Because the leprechauns are asleep at night.
18. Because no one wears their sunglasses.
19. Because people don't look for them at night.
20. The stars are covering them.

## 125. Seven or more colors you've never seen

1. Gerpil.
2. Zappil.
3. Laronge.
4. Rosell.
5. Mauvret.
6. Velour.
7. Ultraviolet.
8. Infrared.
9. Sky green.
10. Lemon blue.
11. Battleship pink.
12. Charcoal white.
13. Blood yellow.
14. Clear.
15. The color of air.
16. Total darkness.
17. Gringo.
18. Belgian blue.
19. Army avocado.
20. Head game green.
21. Aggravation orange.

## 126. Seven or more reasons for wearing lipstick

1. Soothes chapped lips.
2. Looks pretty.
3. Prevents chapped lips.
4. Makes lips look larger.
5. Makes lips look smaller.
6. Enhances outfit you're wearing.
7. Looks sexy.
8. It's in fashion.
9. Vanity.
10. To leave marks on people's faces for later identification.
11. To be able to kiss someone without really ever touching them.
12. Give cosmetic companies business.
13. To see lip imprint on a napkin.
14. It's better than wearing oil base paint.
15. So you can whistle louder.
16. It's easier to remove than nail polish.
17. To feel grownup.
18. So you have more glasses to wash.
19. As an incentive to brush your teeth.

## 127. Six or more reasons why some people make more money than others

1. Some people are smarter.
2. Some people are shrewder.
3. Some people inherit it.
4. Some people have money.
5. Some people know the right people.
6. Extortion.
7. Some people are worth more than others.
8. Some people are harder to replace than others.
9. Some people try harder than others.
10. Some people deserve more than others.
11. Some people are luckier than others.
12. So that people who make less can look up to something.
13. To put the graduated income tax to use.
14. So that people who make more can feel superior.
15. One has a luckier rabbit's foot than the other.
16. Because they can't make anything else.
17. Because they have good printing presses and plates.
18. Because their fathers are the chiefs of police.
19. They have bigger cash registers.

## 128. Six or more reasons for eating three meals a day

1. Nutrition.
2. Gain weight.
3. Lose weight.
4. Keep your strength.
5. Stay healthy.
6. Prevent food from spoiling.
7. Enjoyment.
8. Socializing.
9. Recreation.
10. Three divides evenly into twenty-four hours.
11. Three meals leaves enough time for between-meal snacks.
12. More than three meals costs too much.
13. Tradition.
14. Nobody can think of another reason for an entire meal.
15. To prove we are three times as important as our dogs— who eat once a day.
16. Because there is nothing else we have three of.
17. Three is your lucky number.

18. Because you don't take Geritol.
19. To exercise your false teeth.
20. To stretch the elastics on the braces.
21. We only have three chickens.
22. Because our mothers told us to.

## 129. Eight or more reasons for coughing

1. Reflex action.
2. Clearing your throat.
3. Clearing your lungs.
4. Clearing your sinuses.
5. Allergic reaction.
6. Nervousness.
7. To get someone's attention.
8. To test if you can still make a noise.
9. To put a Lifesafer in your mouth without having anyone notice.
10. To find time to think of something else to say.
11. To prove you are sick.
12. To break a silence.
13. To see if your throat hurts.
14. Because you forgot your lines.
15. To get a noise you made on a tape.
16. To see your "insides."
17. To give someone else what you have.
18. It's a mating signal.
19. To catch flies.
20. To try a new cough medicine.
21. To be chosen for a commercial.
22. To go to that "cute" doctor.

## 130. Seven or more ways to prevent a candle from burning down

1. Put more wax on it.
2. Put it in a tub of wax.
3. Put a protective covering around it.
4. Do not light it.
5. Make a candle out of iron.
6. Keep a fan directed at the candle.
7. Put a fire wall between the flame and the candle.
8. Keep the candle in a vacuum.
9. Drop it in the ocean.
10. Eat it.
11. Blow it up.
12. Turn it upside down, then it will burn up.
13. Flatten it out.

## 131. Eight or more things we couldn't do if we didn't have fingernails

1. Couldn't polish them.
2. Couldn't have manicures.
3. Couldn't jab as well.
4. Couldn't flick as well.
5. Couldn't use them as tweezers.
6. Couldn't open very tiny knots.
7. Pick your teeth.
8. Peel a sticker.
9. Change the time on your watch.
10. Open a new record.
11. Get an ingrown nail.
12. Pinch somebody.
13. Pick up a card from a flat table.
14. Rip tape.
15. Peel an orange.
16. Get that dime from the telephone machine.
17. Tear open mail.
18. Bite them.
19. Scratch people.
20. Scratch your head.
21. File them.

## 132. Seven or more ways to prevent the red dye in pistachio nuts from getting all over your fingers

1. Get undyed pistachios.
2. Buy them shelled.
3. Don't touch them with your hands.
4. Paint them first.
5. Crack them with a hammer.
6. Don't eat pistachio nuts.
7. Keep your hands completely dry.
8. Use a fork and knife.
9. Wash the nuts.
10. Hire somebody to open the nuts.
11. Crack them by stepping on them.
12. Wear surgical gloves.
13. Ask your friend to open them.
14. Dye them blue.

## 133. Six or more ways to prevent yourself from swallowing sea water while swimming

1. Spit the water out.
2. Swim on your back.
3. Look where you are going.

4. Tape your mouth shut.
5. Wear a diving mask.
6. Stuff a plastic shield into the back of your mouth.
7. Swim in fresh-water oceans only.
8. Keep your head out of the water.
9. Fill the ocean with more water to dilute the salt.
10. Boil off the water in the ocean and collect it in a non-salty area.
11. Have your esophagus removed.
12. Kiss your mate.
13. Drain the water.
14. Swallow the sand.
15. Suck on a lollipop.
16. Bite a nearby fish.
17. Stare at the sky.
18. Stand on someone's shoulders.

## 134. Seven or more reasons why police cars have sirens

1. To get people to stop.
2. To identify themselves.
3. To enable other people to identify them.
4. To make policemen feel important.
5. So people will hear them coming.
6. To scare dogs out of the way of police cars.
7. To attract young children.
8. To wake up lazy people who are asleep.
9. To scare away any criminals so that the police can't arrest anyone and crime statistics will improve.
10. To give police something to play with.
11. To give police something to sing along with.
12. To accompany the light show given by the flashing lights.
13. So they can make it home for dinner on time.
14. Because their horns don't work.
15. Because they get tired of yelling.
16. So they can go through red lights.
17. To give policemen a longer coffee break.

## 135. Six or more ways to prevent ice cubes from melting

1. Put them in the cooler.

2. Insulate them.
3. Turn down the heat.
4. Put them in a vacuum.
5. Put them in the North Pole.
6. Put them in snow.
7. Constantly spray freon on them.
8. Put them in a glacier.
9. Take them to Pluto.
10. Wrap them in a ton of tinfoil with layers of vacuum.
11. Keep them in liquid nitrogen.
12. Chew them.
13. Make them out of plastic.
14. Drink in a freezer.
15. Avoid fires.
16. Freeze the drink.
17. Remove if melting begins.

## 136. Seven or more reasons why there are more forty-year-old single females than single males

1. There are more women than men.
2. Harder for women to remarry.
3. They are more screwed-up.
4. They are less attractive.
5. They don't produce children.
6. Men want younger women.
7. Because females were more popular in 1939.
8. More men fought and died in wars.
9. More men get heart attacks.
10. Women practice polygamy.
11. A higher percentage of men are suited for marriage.
12. Women born in 1939 do not get along with anybody.
13. Women born in 1940 are prettier than those born in 1939.
14. Females live longer.
15. Females are chicken.
16. Men are better chefs than women.
17. Men like wedding bands.
18. All of the men marry at age forty.

## 137. Seven or more reasons not to make a lot of money

1. Takes time.
2. Takes effort.
3. Cuts into recreation.
4. Shortens time with spouse.
5. Shortens time with children.
6. Shortens time with dating.
7. Shortens time with hobbies.
8. Hurts people.
9. Immoral.
10. Greedy.

11. Deprives people of jobs.
12. To be in a lower tax bracket.
13. To avoid fortune-hunters.
14. To avoid being kidnapped.
15. So you have no investments to lose in a depression.
16. So nobody will want money from you.
17. To get sympathy.
18. Your mattress is too small.
19. So you don't get robbed.
20. You don't like the color green.
21. You don't like to spend.
22. Change is too heavy.

## 138. Eight or more new uses for cellophane tape

1. Starting a fire.
2. Picking up lint.
3. Acting as a bandage.
4. Picking up bugs.
5. Making a necklace.
6. Facial mask.
7. Insulation around edge of screen doors.
8. Patching holes in screen doors.
9. A cleaner.
10. Fixing broken trees.
11. As a hook on a tow truck.
12. To collect and trade.
13. Making glass windows.
14. Using as shoelaces.
15. To hold your socks up.
16. To keep your trees from falling.
17. To make a pool.
18. As clothing.
19. To make an invisible man.

## 139. Seven or more things you see when you close your eyes

1. Spots.
2. Colors.
3. Darkness.
4. Depth.
5. Lines.
6. Light flashes.
7. Dreams.
8. Fantasies.
9. Calmness.
10. The backs of your eyelids.
11. The desert when it's dark.
12. Kansas when it's dark.
13. The top of a mountain when it's dark.
14. The boogie man.
15. Robert Redford.
16. Myself.
17. What's in front of me.
18. My teddy bear.

## 140. Eight or more words you have never seen or heard

1. Arbortrim.
2. Salofel.
3. Lotul.
4. Grumler.
5. Perkop.
6. Miffid.
7. Tavil.
8. Boffcil.
9. Gwagwa.
10. Latrony.
11. Arnth.
12. Slarble.
13. Glurd.
14. Badada.
15. Hekiis.
16. Berauip.
17. Arpt.
18. Oo-bok-ē-koo.
19. Blort.
20. Deah Samag.
21. Yart.
22. Ilgoo.
23. Sority.
24. Yawbus.

## 141. Seven or more reasons for not having computers

1. Creates dependence.
2. Impersonal.
3. Fear.
4. Not easily understood by laymen.
5. Software not easily debugged—perpetuates mistakes.
6. They use electricity.
7. They need special environments (air conditioning).
8. They make white-collar crime easier.
9. Output is taken as "truth."
10. Non-creative.
11. Create more jobs.
12. Leave unsolved problems.
13. Rely more on math's insight and style.
14. See a problem through from start to finish.
15. Do things by trial and error.
16. Credit good guesses.
17. Give feasibility checks.
18. Get the decimal point by inspection.
19. Save delays.
20. Prevent centralization.
21. Restrain individuality.
22. Promote general understanding.
23. Get people together.
24. Reduce loneliness.
25. Promote responsibility for decisions.
26. To reduce the amount of filed private information.
27. To make people use their own minds.
28. To prevent the possibility of the computer blowing up.
29. If the computer made one mistake, that would ruin the whole system.
30. To prevent the waste of metals.
31. To prevent the waste of paper.
32. Because they can't play Frisbee.
33. If one drops, it breaks.
34. They become obsolete.
35. No tener dinero para comprarlas.
36. Gimnasia mental.
37. Desconfianza de los resultados.
38. Ser muy tradicionalista.
39. No tomar posición entre abacistas y calculistas.
40. No querer parecer abacista.
41. Ser calculista.
42. Haber vivido antes de su invención.
43. Cumplir promesa de no usarlas.
44. Por apuesta.
45. Ser ciego y no haber computadoras en braille.
46. No saber usarlas.
47. Tener una y querer mantenerla sin uso.
48. Vivir cuando ya no se usen.
49. Tenerlas fobia.
50. No haberse enterado de que existen.
51. No saber leer los resultados.
52. Preferir el ábaco soroban.
53. No tener nada para computar.
54. Vivir en una zona donde el campo magnético interfiere.

## 142. Seven or more reasons not to have a Bloody Mary for breakfast

1. Could lead to alcohol problems.
2. Bad example for children.
3. Out of tomato juice.
4. Alters perception.
5. Acts as depressant.
6. Can harm your reputation.
7. Can harm self-image.
8. Not effective hangover cure.
9. Can become habitual.
10. Costs more than juice alone.
11. Spoils the flavour of grapefruit.
12. Stay sober for the boss.
13. Spouse wants one, too.
14. Quite expensive.
15. High in calories.
16. Milkman won't deliver vodka.
17. Don't like alcohol.
18. Smelly breath.
19. Got a hangover already.
20. Get fresh with secretary.
21. Break with routine.
22. Drinking needs thought.
23. Wake up too fast.
24. Nothing left for lunch.
25. Mustn't drink alone.
26. Mustn't drink and drive.
27. Tomato juice phobia.
28. Forget things.
29. Catch the wrong bus.
30. Give them housework.
31. Put down by neighbours.
32. No glasses.
33. Double vision—can't pour.
34. Prefer Harvey Wallbangers.
35. Not normal.
36. Can't take liquid in morning.
37. To prevent regurgitation.
38. To prevent falling down the stairs.
39. To get a more nutritious drink.
40. To be aware at school or work.
41. A daiquiri would taste better.
42. To prevent spilling it all over the place.
43. Dispepsia.
44. Gastritis.
45. Ulcera.
46. Confusion con "bloomary."
47. Por ser temprano.
48. Preferir un "martini."
49. No saber prepararla.
50. Prejuicio hacia lo rojo.
51. Por método.
52. Por principios.
53. Por tradición.
54. Por apuesta.
55. Por ser "watch-tower."
56. Estar en un lugar donde no se la conoce.
57. Vivir en un país donde está prohibida.
58. No tomar nada con el estómago vacío.
59. Ser daltónico y preferir la menta.
60. Prescripción médica.
61. Alergia.

## 143. Six or more reasons why some people have never played chess

1. No opportunity to learn.
2. Peer pressure.
3. Fear of failure.
4. Reputation of game.
5. Parents are good players.
6. Hard to learn.
7. Low popularity of game.
8. Low publicity for game.
9. Lack of an opponent.

10. Takes too much time to play.
11. Too busy to learn.
12. Think it's too hard to play.
13. Don't like sitting down.
14. Can't take silence.
15. Too friendly for conflict.
16. Don't like defeat.
17. Don't like men.
18. Lack of confidence.
19. Blindness.
20. Impatience.
21. Not aware chess exists.
22. No chess set.
23. Illiteracy.
24. Autism.
25. They're not interested in it.
26. They're too stupid to play.
27. It can get boring sometimes.
28. It doesn't take any physical strain.
29. They'd rather play checkers.
30. They have uncoordinated fingers.
31. They don't live in houses.
32. Evitar problemas con damas.
33. Muy jóven para aprenderlo.
34. Demasiado viejo para empezar.
35. No querer aprenderlo.
36. No sentirse computadora.
37. No sentirse programadora.
38. Daltonismo.
39. Lo dejan para mañana.
40. Lo consideran muy antiguo.
41. Les tiemblan las manos.
42. Pacifismo.
43. No querer perder.
44. No querer ganar.
45. No querer empatar (tablas).
46. No gustan usar peones.
47. No simpatizan con los reyes.
48. No saben hacer saltar los caballos.
49. No quieren saber nada con los Obispos (alfiles).
50. Les cuesta mover torres.
51. No saben qué es.
52. Vivieron antes de que se lo inventara.
53. Vivirán cuando ya no se lo use más.

---

144. Seven or more feelings you have when you see a policeman in your rearview mirror

1. Apprehension.
2. Why?
3. Disdain.
4. Dislike.
5. Trapped.
6. Appreciation.
7. Safety.
8. Comfort.
9. Sorry for lack of understanding.
10. Registration.
11. Pumped up.

12. Oppressed.
13. Wish for reallocation of police/law efforts.
14. Guilt.
15. It's someone I know.
16. My husband's dead.
17. Spouse locked himself out.
18. Trepidation.
19. Nails/glass on the road.
20. Accident ahead.
21. Will I be stopped?
22. Am I presentable?
23. Do I smell?
24. Am I speeding?
25. Is the vehicle alright?
26. Where's he going?
27. Driving license?
28. Insurance and tax?
29. He likes my car.
30. I'm in a one-way street.
31. He fancies me.
32. Pull over and smile.
33. Is he a policeman?
34. Victimisation?
35. Dwarfed.
36. Subdued.
37. Reluctant.
38. Submissive.
39. Wary.
40. Curious.
41. Dread.
42. Anticipation.
43. Frustration.
44. Anger.
45. Deviousness.
46. Sadness.
47. Perspiration.
48. Death.
49. Coldness of a jail.
50. Happiness.
51. Que está limpio el espejo.
52. Que llevo los anteojos.
53. Que se siguen cumpliendo las leyes de la Optica.
54. Que todavía puedo distinguir un policía.
55. Está detrás de mí.
56. Estoy delante de él.
57. Que estoy en un lugar público.
58. Simpatía.
59. Seguridad.
60. Confianza.
61. Que está colocado en el campo del espejo.
62. Que él también me vé.
63. Aprensión.
64. Que tengo espejismos.
65. Que no creo conocerlo.
66. Que lo conozco y viene a saludarme.
67. Curiosidad.
68. Animosidad.
69. Que suelo sufrir injusticias
70. Que tiene mal el reloj y viene a preguntar la hora.
71. Viene a avisarme que se me cayó algo.
72. Confusión.

---

145. Six or more places the sun never shines

1. Inside the earth and other planets.
2. Far reaches of universe.
3. Far side of some planets and other stars.
4. Inside fauna.
5. Inside some flora.
6. Deep caves/mines.
7. The world of blind people.
8. Some people's minds.
9. Parts of windowless buildings.
10. Certain laboratory experiments.
11. In a shadow.
12. Behind a rainbow.
13. Under a leaf.
14. Into my eyes.
15. In a larder.
16. Under the bed.
17. In the toes of my boots.
18. In a mousehole.
19. In an underground cavern.
20. Wall cavity of a house.
21. Eardrum.
22. Cellar.
23. Cinema screen.
24. Rabbit warren.
25. In a submarine.
26. Under the Arctic ice.
27. Under a windowsill.
28. Where bats hang out.
29. Under a cloud.
30. In an attic.
31. On a star.
32. In a coffin.
33. On an unborn baby.
34. Under posh sofas.
35. Round "the bend."
36. The sun.
37. Horizontal air duct.
38. Under a carpet.
39. Middle of a tunnel.
40. Ocean trench.
41. Your rectum and anal area.
42. The bottom of your feet.
43. In your mouth.
44. In a dark room.
45. In your nose.
46. The dark side of the earth.
47. In the shade.
48. En los núcleos atómicos.
49. Tan lejano que no las llegue su luz.
50. Dentro de un espejo.
51. En el núcleo del sol.
52. Dentro de un aro hueco.
53. Donde su longitud de onda no le permite.
54. Dentro de un tubo hermético.
55. Donde no hay éter.
56. Que se desplazan a más de 300,000 km/sg por delante de sus rayos.
57. En la superficie opuesta de los cuerpos celestes que no rotan.

58. Que existan cuando ya se haya apagado.
59. Que existieron cuando todavía no había sol.
60. En las zonas suficientemente profundas del mar.
61. En una película fotográfica que nunca se usa.
62. En una caverna suficientemente profunda.
63. Dentro de un objeto hueco cuya abertura es menor que la amplitud de sus ondas luminosas.
64. En un lugar donde el período (o la frecuencia) de sus ondas se quiebre.
65. Poco antes de un lugar donde un segundo valga infinito.
66. En un lugar que esté a menos de 300,000 km. de su emisión y al que se pueda llegar antes de un segundo.

---

146. Seven or more reasons why most paintings are more expensive than photographs

1. Take more time to make.
2. Older than photographs.
3. Societal values.
4. A bad photographer can come up with a good photograph; not so with painting.
5. Photography is easier to attempt.
6. More variety in paintings.
7. Style more apparent in paintings.
8. Talent more apparent in paintings.
9. Paintings have been a better investment historically.
10. Painting can depict the non-corporeal easier.
11. Paintings have a texture.
12. Painting has more identifiable "schools," etc.
13. Paintings can be more controversial.
14. Paintings are built piece by piece by a craftsman.
15. Photographs are too easily duplicated.
16. Photographs give the feeling: "I could have done that."
17. Paintings have history of showing creative urge and interpretation of life from cave days.
18. Materials cost more.
19. Need thinking about.
20. Have to find an artist.
21. Take longer to do.
22. Photos are usually smaller.
23. Show less insight.

24. Need less framing.
25. Taken by amateurs.
26. Painting is individual, unique.
27. Paintings capture person's aura.
28. Paintings require greater skill.
29. Paintings can leave out the bad parts of a portrait.
30. Paintings are rarer.
31. Paintings are potentially valuable.
32. Paintings are an expression of artistic thought.
33. Paintings are handmade.
34. Photographs are made by pushing a button.
35. Adelanto de la técnica.
36. Manufactura.
37. Irrepetibilidad.
38. Redimen la naturaleza.
39. Excentricidad.
40. Egocentrismo.
41. El arte (pese a su técnica) es más caro que la técnica (pese a su arte).
42. Tela y pintura valen más que papel fotográfico.
43. Se tarda más en pintar que en revelar.
44. No se pueden sacar copias idénticas.

---

### 147. Six or more reasons we use checks

1. Habit.
2. To keep from carrying cash.
3. To establish credit rating.
4. To have proof of payment.
5. Fear of electronic funds transfer.
6. To take advantage of "float."
7. To be able to cancel payment.
8. To make unexpected transactions possible.
9. To defraud.
10. To even cash flow (I'll cover it tomorrow).
11. To insure proper recipient (not a "bearer" instrument).
12. To make muggers look silly.
13. Keep banks in business.
14. Lighter than cash.
15. Instant availability.
16. Save trips to the bank.
17. Delay using money.
18. Avoid paying a bill.
19. Show I have my own income.
20. Prevent frittering.
21. Stop buying candybars.
22. Budget better.
23. Show where housekeeping goes.
24. Encourage shopping at one store.
25. Give shops my address.

26. Feeling important.
27. Spend large sums easier.
28. Taking on responsibility.
29. Showing trustworthiness.
30. Showing my credit's good.
31. Proving you can write.
32. Proving you live somewhere.
33. Paying bills by post.
34. Paying unexpected bills.
35. Talking to cashiers.
36. Borrowing pens.
37. Making people wait.
38. Purchasing on impulse.
39. To keep printers in business.
40. To look at the pictures.
41. They look good.
42. People like signing their names.
43. Checks can bounce.
44. People don't always have money on hand.
45. They're green like money.
46. They come in books.
47. People feel like they're making their own money.
48. Stolen checks aren't worth anything.
49. Higiene.
50. Poder estafar.
51. Poder ser estafados.
52. Evitar estafas.
53. Coleccionar talones (tickets).
54. Simplificar.
55. Unificar.
56. Variar.
57. Ver nuestro numbre en algo de valor.
58. Usar dinero sin tocarlo.
59. Concurrir a los bancos.
60. Hacer que se concurra a los bancos.
61. Firmar.
62. Gastar papel y tinta.
63. Hacer firmar.
64. Favorecer la inflación.
65. Favorecer la deflación.
66. Pagar.
67. Cobrar.
68. Hacer gastar papel y tinta.
69. Dar trabajo a los empleados bancarios.
70. Dar ganancia a los bancos.
71. Dar trabajo a los impresores de cheques.
72. Dar trabajo a los agentes de cambio.
73. Usar un mismo tamaño de papel para diversos valores monetarios.
74. Alergia al papel-moneda.
75. Ecología.
76. Economía de metales.
77. Emplear algo que los antepasados no podían.
78. Respeto excesivo a los próceres que aparencen en los billetes.
79. Antipatía a los próceres.
80. Coleccionar talonarios.
81. Tener cuentas corrientes.
82. No tener que contar dinero para transacciones.

---

### 148. Seven or more reasons for not using postage stamps

1. Labor intensive action for user.
2. Adds steps to mailing action.
3. Can be counterfeited.
4. Must be cancelled.
5. Could transfer bacteria if licked.
6. Could be used to poison licker.
7. They stick together in your wallet.
8. Difficult to determine correct postage to apply.
9. Can become detached while in transit.
10. They are fragile.
11. Once bought they are useless except for one use.
12. When you need one you don't have one and vice versa.
13. Won't stick.
14. Bankrupt post office.
15. Lose friends.
16. Preclude replies.
17. Confuse postman.
18. Ensure personal delivery by postman.
19. Meet a postman.
20. Leave a clean envelope.
21. Save saliva.
22. Freeport address.
23. Prepaid reply label.
24. Sent British Rail.
25. It's a telegram.
26. Hand delivered by sender.
27. Aerogram.
28. Franking machine.
29. Nowhere to send it.
30. Internal post.
31. To Father Christmas.
32. Xmas cards at school.
33. Make more phone calls.
34. Telex message.
35. Forget them.
36. Isolated—no post office.
37. Embossed envelope (with stamp design).
38. They're small.
39. They cost money.
40. They're a waste of paper.
41. They keep getting more and more expensive.
42. Decepcionar filatelistas.
43. Ahorrar saliva.
44. Ahorrar agua.
45. Ahorrar goma.
46. Ahorrar coleccionistas.
47. No enviar correspondencia.
48. Tener timbrofobia.
49. Tener mensajeros propios.
50. Haber vivido antes de 1840.
51. Imprimirlos en el sobre.
52. Usar aerogramas.
53. Por apuesta.
54. Por principios.
55. Ahorrar impresiones estatales.
56. Tener franqueo pagado.
57. Tener franqueo libre.
58. Vivir en un país donde no existen las estampillas.
59. Ser filatelista y guardar todos los que llegan a sus manos.

---

### 149. Six or more reasons for picture frames

1. To bring attention to picture.
2. To complement the room.
3. To cover ragged edges of picture.
4. To make picture look a certain way (elegant, clean . . .).
5. To identify pictures in a set.
6. To hide things like keys and secret papers.
7. To smuggle things.
8. To provide a way to hold and carry without harming painting.
9. To hold glass over picture.
10. To define boundaries of picture.
11. To protect picture.
12. To focus interest on picture.
13. To justify higher price.
14. To give look of completeness.
15. Habit.
16. To hang picture by.
17. Ease of handling.
18. Prevent wear on edges.
19. Prevent canvas shrinking.
20. Stop canvas flapping.
21. Woodwork training.
22. Keep moths from eating the picture.
23. Keep photos from curling.
24. To show a particularly cherished picture.
25. So visitors know the painting's finished.
26. To take a "donated by" plate.
27. Make dusting for me.
28. Catch cobwebs.
29. Make grandpa feel useful.
30. Match colour scheme.
31. To measure picture by.
32. To be valuable.
33. To reflect light.
34. Use as a substitute mirror.
35. Show manual ability in making.
36. Take small nails.
37. Use mitre joint.
38. They look good.
39. They offer a contrasting border to the picture.
40. They can be trimmed.
41. They're a sign of accomplishment.
42. You can draw on them.
43. Destacar los cuadros.
44. Protegerlos.

45. Usar vidrio.
46. Por agrandar.
47. Disimular bordes gastados.
48. Dar trabajo a quienes los hacen.
49. Disimular manchas en la pared.
50. Tapar huecos.
51. Haberlos recidido de regalo.
52. Haber comprado algunos, pensando que eran otra cosa.

## 150. Seven or more common things kept in most wallets

1. Credit cards.
2. Driver's license.
3. Business cards.
4. Membership cards.
5. Extra car key.
6. Telephone numbers.
7. Addresses.
8. Extra house key.
9. Stamps.
10. Paper money.
11. Cherished photo.
12. Union card.
13. Season ticket.
14. Scraps of paper.
15. Bankers card.
16. Cash card.
17. Loose change.
18. Bus tickets.
19. Insurance certificate.
20. Appointment cards.
21. Social club card.
22. Library tickets.
23. Theatre tickets.
24. Donor card.
25. Inoculation card.
26. Contact phone number.
27. Fingermarks.
28. Laundry tickets.
29. Deposit slips.
30. Stitching.
31. Lettering.
32. Business card (personal).
33. Receipts.
34. Lottery tickets.
35. Newspaper cutting.
36. Trading stamps.
37. Contraceptives.
38. I.D. cards.
39. Secret letters.
40. Metropolitan Museum of Art (MMA) buttons.
41. Chewing gum.
42. Chewing-gum wrappers.
43. Baseball cards.
44. Invitation.
45. Calendar.
46. Checkbook.
47. Doctor's prescription.
48. Coupons.
49. Subway tokens.
50. Circus tickets.
51. Band-Aids.
52. Buttons that fell off.
53. Note to self.
54. Directions.
55. Easter seals.
56. Rabbit's foot.
57. Algunas cerillas.
58. Piedras de encendedor.
59. Tarjetas de visita.
60. Entradas a espectáculos.
61. Fotografías.
62. Pequeños papeles con anotaciones.
63. Almanaques.
64. Documentos personales.
65. Estampillas postales.
66. Papel con tintura de tornesol.
67. Estampas religiosas.
68. Agujas.
69. Alfileres.
70. Imanes planos.
71. Hilo.
72. Transistores.
73. Botones.
74. Alambre.
75. Llaves pequeñas.
76. Pequeños clavos y tornillos.
77. Talones de cheques.
78. Señaladores de libros.
79. Pequeños sobres.
80. Tarjetas de apuestas.
81. Insignias pequeñas.
82. Semillas de muestra.
83. Papel higiénico.
84. Etiquetas.
85. Monedas.
86. Medallas.
87. Billetes de banco.
88. Cápsulas con algún medicamento.
89. Goma de borrar.
90. Goma de mascar.
91. Papel en blanco para anotar.
92. Pañuelos de papel.
93. Plumas para escribir.
94. Alguna pequeña regla de cálculo.
95. Piedras preciosas.
96. Cintas de goma.
97. Lentes de contacto.
98. Ganchitos (clips).

## 151. Seven or more things impossible to store in most airport lockers

1. A bowling alley.
2. A football field.
3. The key you lock it with.
4. Yourself.
5. A forest.
6. A highway.
7. The moon.
8. An airport.
9. Another locker.
10. Patience.
11. A rainbow.
12. Fresh food (goes off).
13. Love.
14. A palm tree.
15. A hot dinner.
16. Sunshine.
17. An echo.
18. A Land Rover.
19. My husband.
20. Time.
21. Rain.
22. A cloud.
23. Baby.
24. A mood.
25. A bath.
26. A shame.
27. A thought.
28. A dream.
29. Double bed.
30. A promise.
31. A lake.
32. A mountain.
33. Flying saucer.
34. The sun.
35. Piano.
36. Fridge.
37. Car.
38. Motorbike.
39. Elephants.
40. Houses.
41. Dogs.
42. Ice.
43. Basketball backboards, rims, nets, and poles.
44. Objetos de dimensiones mayores que ellos.
45. Fluídos sin recipiente.
46. Partículas elementales (electrones, neutrones, &).
47. Un enjambre sin colmena.
48. Una colonia de hormigas sin su hormiguero.
49. 172 moscas vivas, sin recipiente.
50. Un papel con un número primo par mayor que 3.
51. Una solución anotada, geométrica, del Problema de Delos.
52. Una solución al Problema de la trisección del ángulo, anotada, geométrica.
53. Una solucion al Problema de la cuadratura, anotada, geométrica.
54. Un tratado de Algebra escrito por Aristóteles.
55. Una larga serpiente con artritis deformante que le impide doblarse.
56. Un ejemplar de "Mental Jogging," antes de 1979.
57. Un haz de luz.

# JUNE

## Mental Calisthenic #6

Have a friend place in a shopping bag ten common objects. Close your eyes and reach into the bag and remove ONE object. Try to identify it. Touch it, feel its texture. Smell it. Get to "know" the object. Explore the object for about one minute. Replace it and remove another object. Repeat the exercise until all the objects have been explored. Open your eyes and re-examine each object. Go to a Mental Jogging exercise.

### 152. Eight or more reasons why three-month-old infants can't walk

| Response | Score |
|---|---|
| 1. _____ | 1 |
| 2. _____ | 1 |
| 3. _____ | 1 |
| 4. _____ | 1 |
| 5. _____ | 1 |
| 6. _____ | 1 |
| 7. _____ | 1 |
| 8. _____ | 1 |

**Bonus Responses**

| | |
|---|---|
| 9. _____ | 2 |
| 10. _____ | 2 |
| 11. _____ | 2 |
| 12. _____ | 2 |
| 13. _____ | 2 |
| 14. _____ | 2 |
| 15. _____ | 2 |
| 16. _____ | 2 |

Total ☐

### 153. Six or more non-dental uses of toothpaste

| Response | Score |
|---|---|
| 1. _____ | 1 |
| 2. _____ | 1 |
| 3. _____ | 1 |
| 4. _____ | 1 |
| 5. _____ | 1 |
| 6. _____ | 1 |

**Bonus Responses**

| | |
|---|---|
| 7. _____ | 2 |
| 8. _____ | 2 |
| 9. _____ | 2 |
| 10. _____ | 2 |
| 11. _____ | 2 |
| 12. _____ | 2 |
| 13. _____ | 2 |
| 14. _____ | 2 |
| 15. _____ | 2 |
| 16. _____ | 2 |

Total ☐

## 154. Seven or more things impossible to lasso

| Response | Score |
|---|---|
| 1. _____ | 1 |
| 2. _____ | 1 |
| 3. _____ | 1 |
| 4. _____ | 1 |
| 5. _____ | 1 |
| 6. _____ | 1 |
| 7. _____ | 1 |

Bonus Responses

| | |
|---|---|
| 8. _____ | 2 |
| 9. _____ | 2 |
| 10. _____ | 2 |
| 11. _____ | 2 |
| 12. _____ | 2 |
| 13. _____ | 2 |
| 14. _____ | 2 |
| 15. _____ | 2 |
| 16. _____ | 2 |

Total ☐

## 155. Six or more reasons why we have "baby teeth"

| Response | Score |
|---|---|
| 1. _____ | 1 |
| 2. _____ | 1 |
| 3. _____ | 1 |
| 4. _____ | 1 |
| 5. _____ | 1 |
| 6. _____ | 1 |

Bonus Responses

| | |
|---|---|
| 7. _____ | 2 |
| 8. _____ | 2 |
| 9. _____ | 2 |
| 10. _____ | 2 |
| 11. _____ | 2 |
| 12. _____ | 2 |
| 13. _____ | 2 |
| 14. _____ | 2 |
| 15. _____ | 2 |
| 16. _____ | 2 |

Total ☐

## 156. Seven or more reasons why policemen should not wear badges

| Response | Score |
|---|---|
| 1. _____ | 1 |
| 2. _____ | 1 |
| 3. _____ | 1 |
| 4. _____ | 1 |
| 5. _____ | 1 |
| 6. _____ | 1 |
| 7. _____ | 1 |

Bonus Responses

| | |
|---|---|
| 8. _____ | 2 |
| 9. _____ | 2 |
| 10. _____ | 2 |
| 11. _____ | 2 |
| 12. _____ | 2 |
| 13. _____ | 2 |
| 14. _____ | 2 |
| 15. _____ | 2 |
| 16. _____ | 2 |

Total ☐

## 157. Six or more places never to surfboard

| Response | Score |
|---|---|
| 1. _____ | 1 |
| 2. _____ | 1 |
| 3. _____ | 1 |
| 4. _____ | 1 |
| 5. _____ | 1 |
| 6. _____ | 1 |

Bonus Responses

| | |
|---|---|
| 7. _____ | 2 |
| 8. _____ | 2 |
| 9. _____ | 2 |
| 10. _____ | 2 |
| 11. _____ | 2 |
| 12. _____ | 2 |
| 13. _____ | 2 |
| 14. _____ | 2 |
| 15. _____ | 2 |
| 16. _____ | 2 |

Total ☐

## 158. Six or more non-military uses of radar

| Response | Score |
|---|---|
| 1. _____ | 1 |
| 2. _____ | 1 |
| 3. _____ | 1 |
| 4. _____ | 1 |
| 5. _____ | 1 |
| 6. _____ | 1 |

Bonus Responses

| | |
|---|---|
| 7. _____ | 2 |
| 8. _____ | 2 |
| 9. _____ | 2 |
| 10. _____ | 2 |
| 11. _____ | 2 |
| 12. _____ | 2 |
| 13. _____ | 2 |
| 14. _____ | 2 |
| 15. _____ | 2 |
| 16. _____ | 2 |

Total ☐

## 159. Seven or more reasons why living rooms are carpeted and kitchens are tiled

| Response | Score |
|---|---|
| 1. _____ | 1 |
| 2. _____ | 1 |
| 3. _____ | 1 |
| 4. _____ | 1 |
| 5. _____ | 1 |
| 6. _____ | 1 |
| 7. _____ | 1 |

Bonus Responses

| | |
|---|---|
| 8. _____ | 2 |
| 9. _____ | 2 |
| 10. _____ | 2 |
| 11. _____ | 2 |
| 12. _____ | 2 |
| 13. _____ | 2 |
| 14. _____ | 2 |
| 15. _____ | 2 |
| 16. _____ | 2 |

Total ☐

## 160. Six or more reasons for ethnic neighborhoods

| Response | Score |
|---|---|
| 1. _____ | 1 |
| 2. _____ | 1 |
| 3. _____ | 1 |
| 4. _____ | 1 |
| 5. _____ | 1 |
| 6. _____ | 1 |

Bonus Responses

| | |
|---|---|
| 7. _____ | 2 |
| 8. _____ | 2 |
| 9. _____ | 2 |
| 10. _____ | 2 |
| 11. _____ | 2 |
| 12. _____ | 2 |
| 13. _____ | 2 |
| 14. _____ | 2 |
| 15. _____ | 2 |
| 16. _____ | 2 |

Total ☐

## 161. Seven or more ways to eat dinner without utensils

| Response | Score |
|---|---|
| 1. _____ | 1 |
| 2. _____ | 1 |
| 3. _____ | 1 |
| 4. _____ | 1 |
| 5. _____ | 1 |
| 6. _____ | 1 |
| 7. _____ | 1 |

Bonus Responses

| | |
|---|---|
| 8. _____ | 2 |
| 9. _____ | 2 |
| 10. _____ | 2 |
| 11. _____ | 2 |
| 12. _____ | 2 |
| 13. _____ | 2 |
| 14. _____ | 2 |
| 15. _____ | 2 |
| 16. _____ | 2 |

Total ☐

## 162. Seven or more ways your life would change if you became blind

| Response | Score |
|---|---|
| 1. _____ | 1 |
| 2. _____ | 1 |
| 3. _____ | 1 |
| 4. _____ | 1 |
| 5. _____ | 1 |
| 6. _____ | 1 |
| 7. _____ | 1 |

**Bonus Responses**

| | |
|---|---|
| 8. _____ | 2 |
| 9. _____ | 2 |
| 10. _____ | 2 |
| 11. _____ | 2 |
| 12. _____ | 2 |
| 13. _____ | 2 |
| 14. _____ | 2 |
| 15. _____ | 2 |
| 16. _____ | 2 |

Total ☐

## 163. Seven or more ways to communicate with someone who doesn't speak your language

| Response | Score |
|---|---|
| 1. _____ | 1 |
| 2. _____ | 1 |
| 3. _____ | 1 |
| 4. _____ | 1 |
| 5. _____ | 1 |
| 6. _____ | 1 |
| 7. _____ | 1 |

**Bonus Responses**

| | |
|---|---|
| 8. _____ | 2 |
| 9. _____ | 2 |
| 10. _____ | 2 |
| 11. _____ | 2 |
| 12. _____ | 2 |
| 13. _____ | 2 |
| 14. _____ | 2 |
| 15. _____ | 2 |
| 16. _____ | 2 |

Total ☐

## 164. Seven or more things never to put in bread

| Response | Score |
|---|---|
| 1. _____ | 1 |
| 2. _____ | 1 |
| 3. _____ | 1 |
| 4. _____ | 1 |
| 5. _____ | 1 |
| 6. _____ | 1 |
| 7. _____ | 1 |

**Bonus Responses**

| | |
|---|---|
| 8. _____ | 2 |
| 9. _____ | 2 |
| 10. _____ | 2 |
| 11. _____ | 2 |
| 12. _____ | 2 |
| 13. _____ | 2 |
| 14. _____ | 2 |
| 15. _____ | 2 |
| 16. _____ | 2 |

Total ☐

## 165. Six or more reasons why blind people ski

| Response | Score |
|---|---|
| 1. _____ | 1 |
| 2. _____ | 1 |
| 3. _____ | 1 |
| 4. _____ | 1 |
| 5. _____ | 1 |
| 6. _____ | 1 |

**Bonus Responses**

| | |
|---|---|
| 7. _____ | 2 |
| 8. _____ | 2 |
| 9. _____ | 2 |
| 10. _____ | 2 |
| 11. _____ | 2 |
| 12. _____ | 2 |
| 13. _____ | 2 |
| 14. _____ | 2 |
| 15. _____ | 2 |
| 16. _____ | 2 |

Total ☐

## 166. Eight or more reasons for having teeth

| Response | Score |
|---|---|
| 1. _____ | 1 |
| 2. _____ | 1 |
| 3. _____ | 1 |
| 4. _____ | 1 |
| 5. _____ | 1 |
| 6. _____ | 1 |
| 7. _____ | 1 |
| 8. _____ | 1 |

**Bonus Responses**

| | |
|---|---|
| 9. _____ | 2 |
| 10. _____ | 2 |
| 11. _____ | 2 |
| 12. _____ | 2 |
| 13. _____ | 2 |
| 14. _____ | 2 |
| 15. _____ | 2 |
| 16. _____ | 2 |

Total ☐

## 167. Eight or more reasons why policemen wear guns

| Response | Score |
|---|---|
| 1. _____ | 1 |
| 2. _____ | 1 |
| 3. _____ | 1 |
| 4. _____ | 1 |
| 5. _____ | 1 |
| 6. _____ | 1 |
| 7. _____ | 1 |
| 8. _____ | 1 |

**Bonus Responses**

| | |
|---|---|
| 9. _____ | 2 |
| 10. _____ | 2 |
| 11. _____ | 2 |
| 12. _____ | 2 |
| 13. _____ | 2 |
| 14. _____ | 2 |
| 15. _____ | 2 |
| 16. _____ | 2 |

Total ☐

## 168. Nine or more reasons for getting married

| Response | Score |
|---|---|
| 1. _____ | 1 |
| 2. _____ | 1 |
| 3. _____ | 1 |
| 4. _____ | 1 |
| 5. _____ | 1 |
| 6. _____ | 1 |
| 7. _____ | 1 |
| 8. _____ | 1 |
| 9. _____ | 1 |

**Bonus Responses**

| | |
|---|---|
| 10. _____ | 2 |
| 11. _____ | 2 |
| 12. _____ | 2 |
| 13. _____ | 2 |
| 14. _____ | 2 |
| 15. _____ | 2 |
| 16. _____ | 2 |

Total ☐

## 169. Nine or more reasons for not getting married

| Response | Score |
|---|---|
| 1. _____ | 1 |
| 2. _____ | 1 |
| 3. _____ | 1 |
| 4. _____ | 1 |
| 5. _____ | 1 |
| 6. _____ | 1 |
| 7. _____ | 1 |
| 8. _____ | 1 |
| 9. _____ | 1 |

**Bonus Responses**

| | |
|---|---|
| 10. _____ | 2 |
| 11. _____ | 2 |
| 12. _____ | 2 |
| 13. _____ | 2 |
| 14. _____ | 2 |
| 15. _____ | 2 |
| 16. _____ | 2 |

Total ☐

## 170. Six or more reasons why we use envelopes

| Response | Score |
|---|---|
| 1. _____ | 1 |
| 2. _____ | 1 |
| 3. _____ | 1 |
| 4. _____ | 1 |
| 5. _____ | 1 |
| 6. _____ | 1 |

Bonus Responses

| | |
|---|---|
| 7. _____ | 2 |
| 8. _____ | 2 |
| 9. _____ | 2 |
| 10. _____ | 2 |
| 11. _____ | 2 |
| 12. _____ | 2 |
| 13. _____ | 2 |
| 14. _____ | 2 |
| 15. _____ | 2 |
| 16. _____ | 2 |

Total ☐

## 171. Seven or more things never to feed an elephant

| Response | Score |
|---|---|
| 1. _____ | 1 |
| 2. _____ | 1 |
| 3. _____ | 1 |
| 4. _____ | 1 |
| 5. _____ | 1 |
| 6. _____ | 1 |
| 7. _____ | 1 |

Bonus Responses

| | |
|---|---|
| 8. _____ | 2 |
| 9. _____ | 2 |
| 10. _____ | 2 |
| 11. _____ | 2 |
| 12. _____ | 2 |
| 13. _____ | 2 |
| 14. _____ | 2 |
| 15. _____ | 2 |
| 16. _____ | 2 |

Total ☐

## 172. Seven or more uses of a rolled-up sweat sock

| Response | Score |
|---|---|
| 1. _____ | 1 |
| 2. _____ | 1 |
| 3. _____ | 1 |
| 4. _____ | 1 |
| 5. _____ | 1 |
| 6. _____ | 1 |
| 7. _____ | 1 |

Bonus Responses

| | |
|---|---|
| 8. _____ | 2 |
| 9. _____ | 2 |
| 10. _____ | 2 |
| 11. _____ | 2 |
| 12. _____ | 2 |
| 13. _____ | 2 |
| 14. _____ | 2 |
| 15. _____ | 2 |
| 16. _____ | 2 |

Total ☐

## 173. Nine or more uses of newspaper

| Response | Score |
|---|---|
| 1. _____ | 1 |
| 2. _____ | 1 |
| 3. _____ | 1 |
| 4. _____ | 1 |
| 5. _____ | 1 |
| 6. _____ | 1 |
| 7. _____ | 1 |
| 8. _____ | 1 |
| 9. _____ | 1 |

Bonus Responses

| | |
|---|---|
| 10. _____ | 2 |
| 11. _____ | 2 |
| 12. _____ | 2 |
| 13. _____ | 2 |
| 14. _____ | 2 |
| 15. _____ | 2 |
| 16. _____ | 2 |

Total ☐

## 174. Six or more reasons why some men wear a mustache

| Response | Score |
|---|---|
| 1. _____ | 1 |
| 2. _____ | 1 |
| 3. _____ | 1 |
| 4. _____ | 1 |
| 5. _____ | 1 |
| 6. _____ | 1 |

Bonus Responses

| | |
|---|---|
| 7. _____ | 2 |
| 8. _____ | .2 |
| 9. _____ | 2 |
| 10. _____ | 2 |
| 11. _____ | 2 |
| 12. _____ | 2 |
| 13. _____ | 2 |
| 14. _____ | 2 |
| 15. _____ | 2 |
| 16. _____ | 2 |

Total ☐

## 175. Eight or more places never to scuba dive

| Response | Score |
|---|---|
| 1. _____ | 1 |
| 2. _____ | 1 |
| 3. _____ | 1 |
| 4. _____ | 1 |
| 5. _____ | 1 |
| 6. _____ | 1 |
| 7. _____ | 1 |
| 8. _____ | 1 |

Bonus Responses

| | |
|---|---|
| 9. _____ | 2 |
| 10. _____ | 2 |
| 11. _____ | 2 |
| 12. _____ | 2 |
| 13. _____ | 2 |
| 14. _____ | 2 |
| 15. _____ | 2 |
| 16. _____ | 2 |

Total ☐

## 176. Seven or more reasons why we don't eat porpoises

| Response | Score |
|---|---|
| 1. _____ | 1 |
| 2. _____ | 1 |
| 3. _____ | 1 |
| 4. _____ | 1 |
| 5. _____ | 1 |
| 6. _____ | 1 |
| 7. _____ | 1 |

Bonus Responses

| | |
|---|---|
| 8. _____ | 2 |
| 9. _____ | 2 |
| 10. _____ | 2 |
| 11. _____ | 2 |
| 12. _____ | 2 |
| 13. _____ | 2 |
| 14. _____ | 2 |
| 15. _____ | 2 |
| 16. _____ | 2 |

Total ☐

## 177. Eight or more reasons why some nationalities wear jewelry on their nose

| Response | Score |
|---|---|
| 1. _____ | 1 |
| 2. _____ | 1 |
| 3. _____ | 1 |
| 4. _____ | 1 |
| 5. _____ | 1 |
| 6. _____ | 1 |
| 7. _____ | 1 |
| 8. _____ | 1 |

Bonus Responses

| | |
|---|---|
| 9. _____ | 2 |
| 10. _____ | 2 |
| 11. _____ | 2 |
| 12. _____ | 2 |
| 13. _____ | 2 |
| 14. _____ | 2 |
| 15. _____ | 2 |
| 16. _____ | 2 |

Total ☐

## 178. Eight or more non-writing uses for a pencil

| Response | Score |
|---|---|
| 1. | 1 |
| 2. | 1 |
| 3. | 1 |
| 4. | 1 |
| 5. | 1 |
| 6. | 1 |
| 7. | 1 |
| 8. | 1 |

### Bonus Responses

| | |
|---|---|
| 9. | 2 |
| 10. | 2 |
| 11. | 2 |
| 12. | 2 |
| 13. | 2 |
| 14. | 2 |
| 15. | 2 |
| 16. | 2 |

Total ☐

## 179. Six or more reasons we eat tuna fish

| Response | Score |
|---|---|
| 1. | 1 |
| 2. | 1 |
| 3. | 1 |
| 4. | 1 |
| 5. | 1 |
| 6. | 1 |

### Bonus Responses

| | |
|---|---|
| 7. | 2 |
| 8. | 2 |
| 9. | 2 |
| 10. | 2 |
| 11. | 2 |
| 12. | 2 |
| 13. | 2 |
| 14. | 2 |
| 15. | 2 |
| 16. | 2 |

Total ☐

## 180. Seven or more reasons for not having a two-cent piece

| Response | Score |
|---|---|
| 1. | 1 |
| 2. | 1 |
| 3. | 1 |
| 4. | 1 |
| 5. | 1 |
| 6. | 1 |
| 7. | 1 |

### Bonus Responses

| | |
|---|---|
| 8. | 2 |
| 9. | 2 |
| 10. | 2 |
| 11. | 2 |
| 12. | 2 |
| 13. | 2 |
| 14. | 2 |
| 15. | 2 |
| 16. | 2 |

Total ☐

## 181. Seven or more ways how not to attract other men

| Response | Score |
|---|---|
| 1. | 1 |
| 2. | 1 |
| 3. | 1 |
| 4. | 1 |
| 5. | 1 |
| 6. | 1 |
| 7. | 1 |

### Bonus Responses

| | |
|---|---|
| 8. | 2 |
| 9. | 2 |
| 10. | 2 |
| 11. | 2 |
| 12. | 2 |
| 13. | 2 |
| 14. | 2 |
| 15. | 2 |
| 16. | 2 |

Total ☐

# CONTRIBUTORS' SAMPLE RESPONSES

## 152. Eight or more reasons why three-month-old infants can't walk

1. Lack of coordination.
2. Improper muscle development.
3. They haven't crawled yet.
4. They're not taught to walk.
5. They don't want to.
6. They would hurt themselves.
7. Their skeletons can't support them.
8. All their needs are met.
9. They're not expected to.
10. Disease.
11. Get dizzy.
12. Get tired.
13. Farther to fall.
14. No competitive spirit.
15. Can't balance on just two limbs.
16. Nowhere to go.
17. Too busy playing.
18. Wears out bootees.
19. People carry them.
20. Don't know about gravity.
21. Too busy growing.
22. Needs thought.
23. Makes arms redundant.
24. Mustn't show friends up.
25. Mustn't excite Mum or Dad.
26. Bump into things quicker.
27. Can't stop suddenly.
28. Two left feet.
29. Haven't learned to want things they can't reach.
30. Too much like hard work.
31. All fours develop more strength.
32. Don't want to be sociable.
33. Left on their own more.
34. Mimics pets.
35. Soft bones.
36. Toes for playing with.
37. Psychological block.
38. In a sleeping bag.
39. Too heavy.
40. Haven't realized walking is different from crawling.
41. Their feet aren't developed enough.
42. Their legs are too weak.
43. They're too stupid.
44. They drool too much.
45. They don't know how to.
46. They'd rather crawl.
47. They use the bathroom in their diapers too much.
48. They're too young.
49. No saban qué es pasear.
50. No les gusta.
51. No usan bastón.
52. Quieren guardar equilibrio.
53. No les gusta caer.
54. Prefieren que los paseen en brazos.
55. Prefieren ver pasear.
56. Se marean fácilmente.
57. Se cansan pronto.
58. No están seguros de poder volver.
59. Por llevar la contra.
60. No cambian costumbres.
61. Están esperando mejor ocasión.
62. Por apuesta.
63. Por principios.
64. Por falta de aprendizaje.
65. Por olvido.
66. Por distracción.
67. Por capricho.
68. Por dependencia.

## 153. Six or more non-dental uses of toothpaste

1. To clean tools, etc.
2. To create a design.
3. To squirt on someone.
4. To write a message.
5. To squirt under someone's door as a prank.
6. To make metal shine.
7. Cleaning chins.
8. Cleaning chipped enamel.
9. Breath freshener.
10. Source of fluoride (eaten).
11. Glue.
12. Substitute icing.
13. Abrasive.
14. Floor cleaner.
15. Small weight.
16. For measuring (tube).
17. White paint.
18. Lubricant.
19. Filling tubes with screw-on caps.
20. Keeping chemists busy.
21. Drawer/shelf filler.
22. Fill the hole by the brushes.
23. Something to put in a box.
24. Something to spin out.
25. To advertise.
26. To hoard.
27. To squeeze between your fingers.
28. As a healing rub for mosquito bites.
29. To suffocate bugs with.
30. To aliviar quemaduras.
31. Obturar huecos.
32. Pintar.
33. Como golosina.
34. Desodorante.
35. Irritar los ojos.
36. Formar espuma para afeitarse.
37. Cosmético.
38. Pegamento suave.
39. Dejar mensajes en el espejo.
40. Decorar tortas.
41. Extraer mentol casero.
42. Extraer flúor casero.
43. Trampa para ciertos insectos.
44. Amortiguador.
45. Sacar un objeto de un tubo.
46. Guardar un objeto en un tubo.
47. Urticante de la piel.
48. Como jabón.
49. Mentolar cigarrillos.
50. Moldear figuras.
51. Comparar viscosidades.
52. Aumentar la densidad de los líquidos.
53. Limpiar objetos metálicos.
54. Hacer gargarismos.
55. Afrodisíaco.
56. Condimento.
57. Dieléctrico.
58. Amagnético.
59. Hacer opaco lo transparente.
60. Hacer opaco lo translúcido.
61. Hacer translúcido lo transparente.
62. Lustrar zapatos.
63. Patinar.
64. Hacer caer a la gente.
65. No oir, tapando las orejas.
66. No ver, tapendo los ojos.
67. No oler, tapando la nariz.
68. Cauterizar heridas.
69. Secar las plantas.
70. Comparar olores.
71. Comparar sabores.
72. Sofocar combustiones.
73. Lubricante.
74. Combustible.
75. Hacer bromas pegajosas.
76. Atraer gusanos.

## 154. Seven or more things impossible to lasso

1. A line.
2. A canyon.
3. A star.
4. A noise.
5. A vacuum.
6. A fire.
7. Mercury (a liquid).
8. An electron.
9. Electricity (a lightning bolt).
10. A highway.
11. A dinosaur.
12. An albatross.
13. A Land Rover.
14. A whale.
15. The moon.
16. A ball.
17. Butterfly.
18. Motorbike.
19. Optical illusion.
20. Atom.
21. Snake.
22. Wind.
23. Echo.
24. Absolutely nothing.
25. Black Hole.
26. Bonfire.
27. Lake.
28. Shadow.
29. Mountain.
30. The Earth.
31. A cloud.
32. Rabbit warren.
33. House door (on its hinges).
34. Time.
35. A hole in the ground.
36. A path.
37. A staircase.
38. A gap.
39. Freedom.
40. Feelings.
41. Dreams.
42. A blackberry.
43. Change.
44. A dodo.
45. A Martian.
46. A Frisbee.
47. Dolly Parton.
48. A cheetah.
49. A vulture.
50. Air.
51. Water.
52. Popcorn.
53. A Mack truck.
54. The sun.
55. A dead bumblebee.
56. Your buttocks.
57. Vigas doblemente empotradas.
58. Aros o ruedas lubricadas.
59. Columnas de edificios.
60. Huecos.
61. Cables tendidos.
62. El aro del propio lazo.
63. Líquidos, sin recipiente.
64. Gases sin recipiente.
65. Sombras.
66. Un haz de luz.
67. Barrotes biempotrados.
68. Al que inventó enlazar, antes de su invención.
69. Raíces de árboles no desenterradas.
70. Objetos de díametro mayor que la lazada.
71. Objetos cargados con electricidad del mismo signo que el lazo.
72. Puertas y ventanas cerradas.
73. Cualquier objeto de 4ta. dimensión o dimensiónes superiores.
74. Un enjambre de abejas.
75. Una bandada de aves.
76. Cualquier objeto de mayor velocidad que el lazo.
77. Un cardumen de peces.

## 155. Six or more reasons why we have "baby teeth"

1. When young our mouths are too small for adult teeth.
2. They will decay and need to be replaced.
3. We are more prone to accidents while young and need replacements.

4. Baby and adult teeth have different chewing purposes.
5. Genetic habit.
6. We are less able to care for our teeth while young.
7. To teach babies about pain.
8. To use up excess calcium.
9. Adult teeth take longer to develop.
10. So we can chew sooner.
11. To study when they fall out.
12. To pull out ourselves.
13. For dentists to practice on.
14. So children can get a sweet tooth.
15. To earn sixpence.
16. To hide under pillows.
17. To keep as treasures.
18. To misuse.
19. To talk sooner.
20. To say "Daddy."
21. To say "tooth."
22. To grind in our sleep.
23. To look normal.
24. To use "Punch and Judy" toothpaste on.
25. To use "Mickey Mouse" toothpaste on.
26. Adult teeth need more attention.
27. Children care less about teeth.
28. To look good in baby photos.
29. Because we're babies.
30. Because they pave the way for grown-up teeth.
31. Why not?
32. To chew on.
33. To give to the tooth fairy.
34. To punch out.
35. Perderlos.
36. Transformar el calcio materno.
37. Acostumbrarnos.
38. Proteger las encías mutuamente.
39. Quedar agradables.
40. Hablar.
41. Morder.
42. Mostrarlos.
43. Esconderlos.
44. Transformar el calcio no-materno.
45. Hacerlos sonar.
46. Preparar las encías a los posteriores.
47. Aprender a intercambiar.
48. Para que se distinga la edad (cronológica).
49. Para poder visitar al dentista.
50. Para acostumbrarnos al dentista.
51. Para comenzar a detestar al dentista.
52. Para interesarnos por la odontología.
53. Para desinteresarnos por la odontología.
54. Par no apoyar vasos y tazas en las encías.
55. Para disfrutar del sonido que

hacen al cerrar las mandíbulas.
56. Para que la lengua verifique su presencia.
57. Para poder pronunciar ciertas letras.
58. Para usar pasta dental.
59. Para distinguir el color blanco.

### 156. Seven or more reasons why policemen should not wear badges

1. It shows they are policemen.
2. It damages the clothing.
3. It can reflect light at an inopportune moment.
4. It allows identification by number.
5. It promotes elitism.
6. It is a waste of metal.
7. It gives confidence to the observer that can be taken advantage of by an impostor.
8. As a symbol of authority, it instills fear.
9. It wastes time (donning, polishing. . . ).
10. Catch on seatbelts.
11. To get a girl.
12. To relax at home.
13. To travel incognito.
14. To avoid danger.
15. They're in a strange town.
16. They don't know the time.
17. They don't know the way.
18. They don't like guns.
19. To live longer.
20. To look normal.
21. To be friendly.
22. To not get involved.
23. Off duty.
24. Out for a drink.
25. Looking around.
26. To have fun.
27. Badges shine.
28. They show off.
29. They're pointy.
30. They can be duplicated.
31. They're visible at night.
32. Tener más coraje.
33. Ser populares.
34. Sorprender.
35. Ser sorprendidos.
36. Ahorrar insignias.
37. No parecer militares.
38. Ahorrar costumbres.
39. Sentirse policías secretos.
40. Salir de lo común.
41. Establecer nuevas costumbres.
42. Antitradicionalismo.
43. Para crear nuevas tradiciones.
44. Desechar viejas costumbres.
45. Igualitarismo.
46. Disimular las jerarquías.
47. Civilismo.

48. Para tranquilizar a los curas con clergyman.
49. Para no engancharse con los objetos salientes.
50. Recordar el tiempo en que no eran policías.
51. Conmemorar las épocas en que no había policías.
52. Usar ropa de un solo color.
53. Daltonismo.
54. Alergia a los metales.
55. Superstición.
56. Por apuesta.
57. Por principios.
58. Aprensión a las estrellas.
59. Para no perderlas.
60. Por humildad.
61. Para que no hagan ruido al caer.

### 157. Six or more places never to surfboard

1. In your bathtub.
2. In a fishing area.
3. In shipping lanes.
4. In shark-infested waters.
5. In front of a tidal wave.
6. In a hurricane.
7. In the middle of a speedboat race.
8. Near reefs.
9. Near cliffs.
10. Around boulders.
11. On an oil slick.
12. In whales' mating areas.
13. Near a drilling platform.
14. In freezing water.
15. Around ice floes.
16. Where there is no surf.
17. Down a railway line.
18. Off a mountain.
19. Down a house.
20. In the sink.
21. In the Arctic.
22. In a penguin pool.
23. In a goldfish bowl.
24. In a salt lake.
25. In a pond.
26. Sea of Tranquility.
27. Lake of Dreams.
28. Jovian Red Spot.
29. Gravesend, Kent, U.K.
30. Mineral pool.
31. Swimming pool.
32. Bermuda Triangle.
33. In the sand.
34. In the living room.
35. On a mountain.
36. In the sewer.
37. In a glass house.
38. In a shark's cage.
39. Dentro el agua.
40. En líquidos de menor densidad que la madera.
41. Delante de la lancha.
42. En una pileta de natación.
43. En el Mar de los Sargazos.
44. En el Triágulo de las Bermudas.
45. En las caídas del Niágara.

46. En el Maelstrom.
47. En las caídas del Iguazú.
48. En una corriente de ancho menor que la tabla.
49. En una corriente con curvas de radio incompatible.
50. En metal fundido.

### 158. Six or more non-military uses of radar

1. To guide airplanes.
2. To check speeders on the highway.
3. To gauge speed of a baseball.
4. By bats to fly.
5. To search for UFOs.
6. To map terrain.
7. To transmit messages.
8. Tracking meteorites.
9. Tracking satellites.
10. Tracking UFOs.
11. Traversing asteroid belt.
12. Navigation aid.
13. Finding a planet's distance.
14. Finding your way in fog.
15. Finding planet's rotation.
16. Finding your way in a blizzard.
17. For blind people.
18. To see in the dark.
19. To cook a dinner (slowly!).
20. To make cool signals.
21. To spell (R . . . A . . . D . . . A . . . R).
22. To say.
23. To give as a name for a character on "M*A*S*H."
24. To run through.
25. To look at.
26. To try to hear.
27. To ask questions about.
28. Mapas civiles.
29. Aterrizaje de aviones comerciales.
30. Caza de aves.
31. Evitar congestiones de tráfico.
32. Enseñanza del radar.
33. Pasear en la noche.
34. Cuando no hay faros en la costa.
35. Lugares sin aeropuerto.
36. Para no descarrilar los trenes.
37. Vehículos sin luz delantera.
38. Murciélagos.
39. Ciegos.
40. Caza de ballenas.

### 159. Seven or more reasons why living rooms are carpeted and kitchens are tiled

1. To give a warm, homey feeling.

2. Because things in the kitchen are messy.
3. Because tile looks clean.
4. Because tile is easy to clean.
5. So walking noise is muffled for talking, etc., in living room.
6. So the floor is warm when barefoot.
7. So visitors will think home is opulent.
8. Designs on tile hide stains and spots.
9. Pets are more often fed in kitchen.
10. Tile will not burn like carpeting.
11. Texture of carpeting complements furniture in living room.
12. Carpets are prettier.
13. Carpets don't reflect glare.
14. Carpets are softer to tread.
15. Carpets are nice to lie on.
16. Tiles are quicker drying.
17. Tiles are easier for casters.
18. Tiles dent less easily.
19. Tiles are easier to fit behind obstacles.
20. Tiles are next to back door.
21. Tiles are next to garden.
22. Tiles reflect more light.
23. Because God made it that way.
24. Because living rooms have furniture.
25. Because people are used to it that way.
26. Because. . . .
27. Because Tuesday comes before Friday.
28. Because the sun shines in the kitchen.
29. Because we wax kitchens and vacuum living rooms.
30. So the dog can dirty carpets.
31. Distinta categoría.
32. Costumbre tradicional.
33. Proteger piso y techo.
34. Buen gusto.
35. Mal gusto.
36. Estética.
37. Antiestética.
38. Economía.
39. Dar trabajo a fabricantes de alfombras y a techistas.
40. Gastar.

### 160. Six or more reasons for ethnic neighborhoods

1. To reinforce your beliefs.
2. More likely to meet a compatible mate.
3. To be around relatives.
4. To feel more secure.
5. To preserve culture.
6. To form political strength.
7. To gain concerted action.
8. To encourage ethnocentricism.
9. To reduce contact with "outside" differences.
10. To retard change.
11. To feel part of a group.
12. To interact with those of common interests.
13. To preserve family ties.
14. To preserve religious ties.
15. Reduces friction in the short term.
16. Services can be tailored to a group's particular needs.
17. Easy to rear children according to parents' own customs.
18. To satisfy Archie Bunker.
19. Because people are prejudiced.
20. Because people want to live with their own type.
21. To make jokes about.
22. To satisfy the laws of selection.
23. To throw bombs in.
24. As status symbols.
25. To have riots in.
26. To live in.
27. Puerza de raza.
28. Mejor entendimiento.
29. Mayor entendimiento.
30. Menor entendimiento.
31. Peor entendimiento.
32. Desentendimiento.
33. Tradiciones comunes.
34. Semejanza en las casas.
35. Su eliminación es más rápida.
36. Mejores estudios etnológicos.
37. Ventajas idiomáticas.
38. Conservación de tradiciones.
39. Buen entendimiento en la denominación de las calles.
40. Mejores estudios estadísticos.
41. Mejores estudios demográficos.
42. Mejores estudios históricos.
43. Mejores estudios sociológicos.
44. Mejores estudios psicológicos.
45. Mejores estudios folklóricos.
46. Mejores estudios económicos.
47. Mejores estudios ecológicos.
48. Predicciones probabilísticas.
49. Ecología.
50. Especialidades comerciales.
51. Especialidades industriales.
52. Modas uniformes.
53. Enseñanza más efectiva de niñez y juventud.

### 161. Seven or more ways to eat dinner without utensils

1. Licking.
2. Share a fish with an Eskimo.
3. Wiping with chunks of bread.
4. Soaking bread, rice, etc.
5. Stuffing into an edible envelope.
6. Sandwiching.
7. Biting off.
8. Gnawing.
9. Eat bread.
10. Eat fruit and vegetables straight from the tree/earth.
11. Wind spaghetti round one's fingers.
12. Messily!
13. Glucose drip in hospital.
14. Vitamin pills.
15. Live on love.
16. Eat hot dogs.
17. Bite your fingernails and swallow.
18. Lie under a chute and have someone pour food down it.
19. Be force-fed with a funnel.
20. Be force-fed by assault on nerve centers (e.g., in suffragette campaign).
21. Duck for apples (on Halloween).
22. Lift plate to mouth and push food in.
23. Have someone else feed you.
24. Spread the food over your body and absorb it through the skin.
25. Convert the food to liquid by a processor or blender, then drink it.
26. Enter an environment where you are weightless (i.e., no gravity). Eat the food as it floats by.
27. Levitate the food to your mouth, using mind-over-matter techniques.
28. Create a suction with your mouth that will pull the food off the plate.
29. Wait for the wind to blow the food to your mouth.
30. Finger food.
31. Poi.
32. Sloppily.
33. Carefully.
34. Bad-mannered.
35. Hungrily.
36. Eat chili with tortillas.
37. From a trough.
38. With your hands.
39. Graze.
40. Intravenously.
41. At McDonald's.
42. Eat with your cat.
43. Eat with Tom Jones.
44. Live on drumsticks (own handles).
45. Heat food until it becomes a gas—inhale.
46. Bathe in soup; recycle it (avoid cannibals).
47. Share an Eskimo Pie with a fish.
48. Shove food in toothpaste tube.
49. Become controversial and get a pie in your face.
50. Try to eat with a plastic fork; fail.
51. Be committed to mental ward; be classified "violent."
52. Join a tribe of baboons.
53. Become an aardvark.
54. Become a religious devotee of a fern.
55. Grow roots (easy for Capricorns).
56. Pick your nose.
57. Move to Poland.
58. Become a paraplegic.
59. By osmosis.
60. Become a vampire.
61. Eat the heads of chocolate bunnies.
62. Become a fruititarian.
63. Mash food into powder; snort it.
64. Nurse.
65. Enroll in survival training.
66. Smoke banana peels or lettuce cigarettes.
67. Have a friend chew for you.
68. Chew a friend.

### 162. Seven or more ways your life would change if you became blind

1. Couldn't paint/draw.
2. Couldn't take photographs.
3. Couldn't shave with a razor blade.
4. Couldn't bake a cake.
5. Couldn't go into a fashion show.
6. Couldn't be referee in a beauty contest.
7. Couldn't be a surgeon.
8. Couldn't walk on a rope across the Niagara.
9. Couldn't embroider.
10. No driving.
11. No colors.
12. No sightseeing.
13. No art appreciation.
14. Could not play sports.
15. Appearance would probably deteriorate.
16. Could not tell the time of day or night.
17. Would not need contact lenses anymore!
18. Would miss "body language" communication.
19. Could not read.
20. Could not watch TV.
21. Would be more dependent on friends.
22. Could spend more time on abstract thought.
23. Could not fill in mental jogging questionnaires.

24. Would not see girlfriends (tragic!).
25. Would not know any children and new acquaintances so well.
26. Total darkness.
27. Become more systematic.
28. Rely upon memory.
29. Take more precaution.
30. Increased sensitivity.
31. More respect for the handicapped.
32. Learn new skills.
33. Increased use of public transportation.
34. Dictate the rest of my answers.
35. Increase patronage to audio art forms (e.g., symphony).
36. Take up new recreational pursuits.
37. Appreciate many things now taken for granted.
38. Increased interest in technology for the handicapped.
39. Identify objects by sound, feel, taste.
40. New methods of mobility.
41. Have to retire.
42. Become hesitant.
43. Become fearful.
44. Have to change jobs.
45. Clothes hung in color combo order.
46. Furniture could never be moved.
47. Tape-record letters.
48. Never read junk mail.
49. Save dollars on magazine and newspaper subscriptions.
50. Work at night.
51. Beg on the side.
52. Never see people age.
53. Dirty house not a problem.
54. Learn to use radio, not TV.
55. Couldn't sew.
56. Become a pinball fanatic.
57. Laser light show in your mind.
58. Wouldn't run traffic lights.
59. Couldn't find red-light districts.
60. No peril in staring at eclipses.
61. Bump into people.
62. Buy a seeing-eye dog.
63. Hearing improves, hear dog-whistle.
64. Become adept at blindman's buff.
65. People have hard time reading your eyes.
66. Meet Boy Scouts on street corners.
67. Additional tax exemption.
68. Start "Blind Is Beautiful" campaign.
69. Play on people's sympathy.
70. Believe day is night and black is white.

71. Become movie star: Blind Bat Masterson.
72. Get a pet bat.
73. Learn sonar from a bat.
74. Become more introspective.
75. Join organization of blind and make toys.
76. Learn Braille.
77. Feel faces when meeting.
78. Buy cane.
79. Jaywalk a lot.
80. Test if I can see each morning as I wake.
81. Become religious.
82. Listen to music more.
83. Drink more.
84. Maladjust.
85. Become depressive.
86. Commit suicide.
87. Start skiing.
88. Can't see the forest *or* the trees.
89. Could be an executive.
90. Could be a judge.
91. Sing.
92. Might disregard traffic signs.
93. Might come late to work.
94. Could look straight into the sun.
95. Could work in a massage parlor.
96. Could tell others how it feels when one doesn't see.
97. Could be a wine/coffee/tea taster.
98. Could be a psychic.
99. Could be a sculptor.
100. I couldn't walk in the streets unattended.
101. Couldn't hunt and shoot.
102. Couldn't sail.
103. Couldn't buy a table.
104. Couldn't collect stamps.
105. Couldn't do shopping in an open-air market.
106. Couldn't be a shop assistant.
107. Couldn't ride a bike/ motorcycle.
108. Couldn't learn to read in a foreign language.
109. Couldn't take down notes in shorthand.
110. Couldn't use my home pharmacy.
111. Couldn't use a pocket calculator.
112. Couldn't work as a barber/ hairdresser.
113. Couldn't work as a physician.
114. Couldn't work as a librarian.
115. Couldn't be a computer operator.
116. Couldn't be a policeman or chimney boy.
117. Couldn't use my mirror.
118. Couldn't pick mushrooms.
119. Couldn't keep up my herbarium.
120. Couldn't collect jewels.

121. Couldn't be a cashier.
122. Couldn't harpoon a whale.
123. Couldn't be a watchmaker.

---

### 163. Seven or more ways to communicate with someone who doesn't speak your language

1. I could speak the other person's language.
2. I could use gestures.
3. I could wink.
4. I could draw.
5. I could use mind control.
6. I could use hypnotics.
7. I could use ESP.
8. I could show him phrases in a phrase book.
9. I could use Chinese characters.
10. I could use flowers (the language of love).
11. I could painstakingly look up words in a dictionary.
12. I could use an interpreter.
13. I could use international symbols.
14. I could write in my language.
15. I could write in his language.
16. I could write in a third language.
17. I could use a translating computer.
18. I could make love (if of opposite sex).
19. I could use sign language.
20. Shout.
21. Invent language converter.
22. Speak slowly.
23. Slap his face.
24. Morse code (e.g., CQ, etc.).
25. Music.
26. Semaphore (standard messages, e.g., SOS).
27. Wave.
28. Blow a kiss.
29. Eye contact.
30. Mime.
31. Card sharp's secret card-code.
32. Try to find a third language both can speak.
33. Speak English with a foreign accent.
34. Speak slowly in case there are common words the other person understands.
35. Use a combination of hand symbols and speech.
36. Sit back and listen. Many languages are pleasant to listen to.
37. Take a crash course at Berlitz.
38. Show them a picture (it'll save you 1,000 words).

39. Smile.
40. Math symbols.
41. Perhaps they *write* my language.
42. Charades.
43. Poorly.
44. Very poorly.
45. Across a void.
46. Wait for Earth to adopt a universal language.
47. Drop acid together.
48. Become a ventriloquist.
49. Star gazing.
50. Telepathically.
51. Empathically.
52. Watch foreign movie with subtitles; hit both languages.
53. Develop cosmic awareness.
54. Dancing.
55. With cats—pet them.
56. At a poker table.
57. Become a wino; don't notice different language.
58. Voice pitch emphasis.
59. Frown.
60. Flinch.
61. Shake hands—
62. —and then show your new karate move.
63. With Tarot cards.
64. Even more poorly.
65. Play.

---

### 164. Seven or more things never to put in bread

1. Screws.
2. Nuts.
3. Dentures.
4. Mouse.
5. Spectacles.
6. Money.
7. Dreams.
8. Toothbrush.
9. Dynamite.
10. Shoe cream.
11. Wedding ring.
12. Ice.
13. Chewing gum.
14. Keys.
15. Snuff.
16. Eraser.
17. Sawdust.
18. Plaster of paris.
19. Chemical preservatives.
20. Bread knife.
21. Birch bark.
22. Sliced cabbage.
23. Cornmeal.
24. Sand.
25. Tar.
26. Ball-pen.
27. Fish hooks.
28. Mouse trap.
29. Rosary.
30. Rubber sole.
31. Soap.
32. Tennis ball.
33. Steel.
34. Lava.

35. Bricks.
36. Elephant tusks.
37. Rubber chicken.
38. Pillows.
39. Metals.
40. Yeast toxins (unless you want it unleavened).
41. Railway sleepers.
42. Fruitbats.
43. Nihilists.
44. Driving licenses.
45. Stockbrokers.
46. Digital watches.
47. Power stations.
48. Asteroids.
49. Hemorrhoids.
50. Epicyclic gears.
51. A shoe.
52. Pair of skis.
53. Water.
54. Spam and anchovies.
55. Razor blades.
56. Plastic fruit.
57. Unpopped corn kernels.
58. Boeing 747.
59. Poisoned berries.
60. Bugs.
61. Rubber bands.
62. Ink.
63. Uranium.
64. Cleaning fluid.
65. Rocks.
66. Nails.
67. Glass.
68. Pictures.
69. Hair.
70. Mud.
71. Gravel.
72. Ticks.
73. Fly wings.
74. Cockroach parts.
75. Twice the yeast the recipe calls for.
76. Buffalo chips.
77. Poker chips.
78. Potato chips.
79. Chipmunks.
80. Monkey's vomit.
81. Scabs.
82. Puss.
83. Eagles' eyeballs.
84. Camel's snot.
85. Horses' goo.
86. Files.
87. Fortune cookies' fortunes.
88. Rat poison.
89. Cat litter.
90. Anything that builds strong bodies twelve ways.
91. Red dye.
92. Wasp eggs.
93. Guano.
94. Cow cuds.
95. Paraquat-treated wheat.
96. Napalm-treated rice.
97. Government taxes.
98. Empire State Building.
99. Moose aphrodisiacs.
100. Ant farms.
101. Rhode Island (but Connecticut is okay).
102. Mafia money

103. Virulent micro-organisms.
104. Belly-button lint.

## 165. Six or more reasons why blind people ski

1. To see the stars when they hit a tree.
2. To look tough.
3. To catch up with the wind.
4. Because they cannot play ice hockey.
5. They enjoy it.
6. Cannot be run over by a car on the slope.
7. To become the center of others' attention.
8. To train their ESP.
9. To learn how to see with their feet.
10. Because it's safer than rope walking.
11. Because it's in.
12. Snow is softer than the pavement.
13. They cannot afford flying.
14. It improves on their fitness.
15. They enjoy the après-ski socializing.
16. They have an excuse for taking a drink after skiing.
17. They expect to gain insight into sports.
18. To have something to talk about.
19. It is an unusual experience.
20. They are used to using a stick.
21. To be admired.
22. To compete with oneself.
23. To feel more competent than other people.
24. To enjoy the lift ride.
25. Cannot be horrified by the steepness of the slope.
26. They only live once.
27. To run into a life-partner.
28. Adventure.
29. Suspense.
30. Bravery.
31. Frustration.
32. Love of the sport.
33. To be outdoors.
34. Try something new.
35. Relieve boredom.
36. Listen to sound of skis on snow.
37. Develop new skills.
38. Plunge to the unknown.
39. To feel the snow.
40. To accompany sighted friends.
41. To win a bet.
42. To show off.
43. To get down the mountain.
44. Because they always have skied.
45. For a suicide.
46. They're wild and crazy guys.
47. For charity.

48. Through blatant stupidity.
49. Practice for Olympics.
50. Develop confidence.
51. To get to school in Sweden.
52. Won a vacation.
53. Fraternity initiation.
54. It's faster than walking.
55. As therapy.
56. To use the suntan lotion, "Ski & See."
57. Masochism.
58. To get in the news.
59. Excuse to go to ski lodge.
60. They're too handicapped to sky-dive.
61. To eat snow.
62. They can't see the forest or the trees.
63. To hide blindness.
64. To collect on insurance after accident.
65. To escape polar bears.
66. To test sonar.
67. Because their seeing-eye dog is a husky.
68. Employed as a trapper.
69. To get on *The David Susskind Show.*
70. They have a death wish.
71. To lose warts.
72. To catch a thief.
73. To escape pursuit.
74. To write a story.

## 166. Eight or more reasons for having teeth

1. Chewing.
2. Sign of beauty.
3. Source of pain.
4. Gold mine for dentists.
5. Something to worry about.
6. Sign of health.
7. Gold depository.
8. Bacteria farm.
9. Close-range weapon.
10. Source of ugliness.
11. Age indicator.
12. Base for jewels.
13. Personal nutcracker.
14. Substitute for dentures.
15. Object of daily oral hygiene.
16. For personal identification.
17. Container for drug smuggling.
18. Indicator of times, culture, and social status.
19. Pipe clencher.
20. God decided to give me them.
21. Not eating sugary foods.
22. Biting jugular veins.
23. To scare people.
24. A reason to visit a dentist you like.
25. Ease the strain on the rest of the digestive system.
26. Gripping a snorkel mouthpiece.

27. Smile looks nicer with teeth in it.
28. To bite carpets.
29. To chew pencils.
30. To strip electrical wire.
31. Tapping them with a pencil to make a tune.
32. Tongue biting (masochists only).
33. Can't afford dental treatment.
34. Eat with.
35. Talk.
36. Bite nails.
37. Chatter when cold.
38. To cut things.
39. Rip things open.
40. Something to put braces on.
41. Defense.
42. Whistling.
43. Speaking.
44. Keep your tongue from falling out.
45. Strain incoming liquids.
46. Show off, as in case of gold teeth.
47. Erotic to some people.
48. Assist in blowing bubblegum bubbles.
49. Serves as extra hand in certain applications (i.e., can hold things).
50. Replace knife.
51. Do impersonation of castanets.
52. Place to get a cavity.
53. To fill our mouths.
54. For better speech.
55. To scare people.
56. To strain bugs out of the water.
57. For pearly smiles.
58. Make fluoride useful.
59. Carry calcium around.
60. Saws don't work without teeth.
61. Hold cigars securely.
62. Make babies cry more.
63. Necessary for vampires.
64. To gnash and grind.
65. Help gears.
66. Change gears.
67. To gear up.
68. Avoid liquid diets.
69. To brush.
70. To meet the tooth fairy.
71. Braces on them help prevent premarital sex.
72. Compensate for no claws.
73. Protect tongue.
74. Hide ugly gums.
75. Bite the bullet.
76. Eat the poulet.
77. To spit broken ones in the toilet.
78. Break and look mean and nasty.
79. Bend nails.
80. Pulverize meat.
81. Trim fingernails.
82. To cap.
83. Make hickies.

110

## 167. Eight or more reasons why policemen wear guns

1. To look tough.
2. To warn culprits.
3. To shoot at fugitives and assailants.
4. Feel safe.
5. Deter perpetrators.
6. Use as an extra weight for slimming.
7. Impotent without them.
8. For the fun of it.
9. Out of tradition.
10. Because they do not want to carry a lance.
11. Feel frustrated.
12. To use for scratching on the back.
13. Americans are more violent than U.K. citizens.
14. Private gun ownership now uncontrollable.
15. Protect public.
16. More glamorous to wear guns.
17. Americans are richer, hence more robbery.
18. Human life seems cheaper today.
19. Killing poisonous snakes.
20. To fiddle with if they get bored.
21. Howitzers wouldn't fit in the holsters.
22. To shoot tyres (or rear windows) of cars being chased.
23. Impressing little children.
24. Something to put bullets in.
25. Trigger-happiness.
26. Holster replaces belt.
27. To look important.
28. To show people they can defend themselves.
29. To fill the holster.
30. To open up walnuts using the butt of the gun.
31. Impress criminals.
32. A Swiss army knife can't do everything.
33. Wearing a cannon is ridiculous.
34. Self-protection.
35. Uniform requirement.
36. Hold belt down.
37. For banging on doors with gun butts.
38. Scare people.
39. Show authority.
40. They have stock in the manufacturing company.
41. So you can tell them from firemen.
42. To capture criminals with.
43. To shoot three times for distress signal.
44. To start avalanches.
45. To open locked doors.
46. To demand more than is reasonable.
47. To kill (never just to disable).
48. Phallic symbol.
49. Pretend they're Roy Rogers.
50. Pretend they're Dale Evans.
51. To get respect from Trigger.
52. To get an imitation of respect from citizens.
53. Prevent armed organizing by others.
54. Protect the State.
55. So that they needn't stick to enforcing *just* laws.
56. To be macho.
57. To watch western movies.
58. To hunt (people).
59. Target practice.
60. Because there is a Kaiser Wilhelm III for every hole.
61. Makes a flashier uniform.
62. Hint: I fought the law and the law won.
63. Short nightstick to club people.
64. Win bar fights.
65. Holsters hold pants up.
66. So you don't think they're night watchmen.
67. To shoot cats out of trees.
68. To become known as "The Kid."
69. Overcome inferiority complex.
70. Fulfill childhood fantasy.
71. Helps in directing traffic.
72. Essential in writing tickets.
73. To prevent anyone doing it in the road.
74. To handle kids necking in cars.
75. To light cigarettes.

## 168. Nine or more reasons for getting married

1. Share home.
2. Beget children.
3. Avoid doing the dishes.
4. Have someone to care about.
5. Have someone to quarrel with.
6. Look forward to being single again.
7. Abandon poverty.
8. Change name.
9. Manage and subjugate the husband.
10. Share things.
11. Have a tennis partner.
12. Have a bed partner.
13. Have twice as many domestic chores to do.
14. Improve one's prospects in life.
15. Have someone to cater to.
16. Boost one's ego.
17. Enjoy tax advantages.
18. Justify the need for a bigger car.
19. Have a personal cook.
20. Have an intimate friend.
21. Have a bitter enemy.
22. Have a hobby partner.
23. Love.
24. Sexual desire.
25. To have money.
26. To change one's class (up or down).
27. For a bet.
28. Under obligation.
29. She won't have sex unless you do.
30. To emigrate/immigrate legally.
31. Mutual empathy.
32. To murder wife and inherit her money.
33. Both have very rare blood groups (can transfuse to each other).
34. To produce a super-race by marrying a fanatic specimen.
35. Desire to give children of previous marriage a home and mother.
36. Pregnancy.
37. Loneliness.
38. Children need two parents.
39. Unhappiness.
40. Religious reasons.
41. Companionship.
42. Live-in maid.
43. I don't know how to sew.
44. Someone to talk to.
45. Someone to play cribbage with.
46. Cooking is easier for two.
47. Appeases parents more than living together.
48. Legally sign in to a motel as Mr. and Mrs.
49. For wedding night.
50. Creates business for local merchants (e.g., purchasing anniversary gifts).
51. Protect estate for children.
52. To be supported.
53. Everyone else is married.
54. Someone to take care of me.
55. Title.
56. On rebound.
57. Avoid draft (army).
58. Gain property.
59. To collect insurance.
60. Shotgun at your head.
61. Support government with license fees.
62. Keep government files on you up to date.
63. Get presents.
64. To ensure that *all* your affairs are adulterous.
65. Rape without penalty.
66. Mate-beating without penalty.
67. To commit incest easier.
68. Disguise homosexuality.
69. For a gold ring.
70. To get divorced.
71. To join a swinger's club.
72. To get a leave from jail.
73. Get out an impulse.
74. Get Big Brother's approval of living together.
75. To throw a party.
76. To get extra "marriage" vacation days.
77. To have anniversaries.
78. As an experiment.
79. To use "Mrs."
80. To be a married bee.
81. For a cocktail party partner.
82. Must be to be a marriage counselor.
83. Apartment rule: can't have pets, so. . . .
84. To learn to tie a hitch knot.
85. Make a house into a home.
86. To find the key to the universe.

## 169. Nine or more reasons for not getting married

1. Enjoy independence.
2. Avoid quarrels.
3. Avoid boredom.
4. Decrease household expenses.
5. Feel safe.
6. Avoid disappointment.
7. Not to be betrayed.
8. Not to be deceived.
9. Save the legal costs of divorcement.
10. Not being abused.
11. Not to have to beget children.
12. Not to have to wash diapers.
13. Not to lose one's own personality.
14. Not to wait on someone else.
15. Save a lot of money.
16. Avoid listening to women's chatter.
17. Homosexual/lesbian.
18. Misogynist/misanthrope.
19. Shy.
20. Afraid you are not yet good enough.
21. Think you are too good.
22. Afraid of sexual inadequacy.
23. Afraid of sexual inadequacy on partner's part.
24. Promise to a spouse who has (e.g.) just died.
25. Being a hermaphrodite.
26. Being the last person in the world after A/H/N bomb detonation.
27. No priests left in the world.
28. Worried about overpopulation.
29. Like a bit on the side from many different women.
30. Don't want to share property money.
31. Don't like people "leaving the top off the toothpaste"!
32. Have VD and are a responsible person.

33. Frightened of catching VD.
34. Not liking sex.
35. Not in love.
36. Can't afford ring.
37. Parents do not approve.
38. Religion.
39. Solitaire is sometimes more exciting than cribbage.
40. Live like a slob without someone giving you a hard time.
41. Play the field.
42. Less guilt feelings.
43. Work late without being hassled.
44. Greater opportunity to meet people.
45. Less responsibility.
46. Love them all.
47. Stay with my mother (or father).
48. Keep my own property.
49. Might pass on disease or other—?
50. No one good enough.
51. Never long enough in one place.
52. Get two Social Security checks as singles.
53. No reason to get government approval for living arrangement.
54. Pay government enough without another license fee.
55. Avoid divorce.
56. Doing one's laundry is bad enough, let alone two's.
57. Have the fun without the responsibility.
58. Not know how.
59. Not have ring.
60. Mute: can't say "I do."
61. Fifty ways to leave a lover; only one way to leave a wife.
62. Not have anyone to marry.
63. Already intimate with an azalea bush.
64. Suspicious everyone else is a gold digger.
65. A radical, so waiting for Mr. Left.
66. Wishy-washy: waiting for Mr. Middle of the Road.
67. Neuter.
68. Pre-pubescent.
69. Employed as Pope.
70. In love with a married person.
71. In love with yourself.
72. Divorced and didn't like marriage.
73. Are married people like your parents?
74. Involved with a sheep.
75. Looking for Mr. Goodbar.
76. Looking for a Diane Keaton.
77. Dominated by mother.
78. Afraid to "pop the question."
79. In a coma.
80. Dead for two months.
81. Known as The Wanderer.
82. Too busy with this book.
83. Married to your work.

170. Six or more reasons why we use envelopes

1. Classification of clippings.
2. Keeping of photographs.
3. Metaphorically, in science and in mathematics.
4. Stop getting things lost in post.
5. Ease of handling by postal services (regular-shaped robust units).
6. To camouflage (e.g., brown plain wrapper).
7. For protection.
8. To stop money being discovered in transit and maybe being stolen.
9. To use up all the envelopes in the world.
10. To disguise letter bombs.
11. As jotting pads.
12. People enjoy guessing what the letter inside is about.
13. Formality.
14. To stop the scent escaping from scented notepaper.
15. Something to use tongue on.
16. Filing folders substitute.
17. Storage for small, flat objects.
18. To make paper airplanes with gummed wing.
19. Paycheck container.
20. Pink slip container.
21. Keeps object hidden.
22. Easier to steam open an envelope than a steel box.
23. Holder for used stamps.
24. To mail letters.
25. To put addresses on.
26. To wrap up tiny gifts.
27. To sort things.
28. And keep them separate.
29. For writing lists on.
30. Keep small parts.
31. Hold garden seeds.
32. Keep letters clean.
33. Postcards too small.
34. "Stuff envelopes in spare time for $100 weekly."
35. Have envelopeitus.
36. We like them.
37. Envelopes are an expression of our times.
38. Some envelopes smell neat.
39. They want to be used.
40. Because they're there.
41. Smuggle dope.
42. Part of our cultural heritage.
43. To store seeds.
44. As wallets.
45. As a use for paper pulp.
46. To line our shoes.
47. Stone tablets too heavy.
48. Passenger pigeons extinct.
49. Pony Express ponies smell.
50. As a stylistic tribute to "Cross Your Heart" bras.
51. Keep letters dry.
52. Biodegradable.
53. Because they're letter-retentive.
54. Because kicks keep getting harder to find.
55. No viable alternative.
56. We're poor at telepathy.
57. Telegraph inconvenient.
58. Telephone too costly.
59. Can't tap an envelope.
60. To collect fingerprints.
61. To save teardrops.

171. Seven or more things never to feed an elephant

1. Hedgehog.
2. Shoes.
3. Ice cream.
4. Spaghetti.
5. Cactus.
6. Fish bait.
7. Hand grenade.
8. Elephants
9. Squirrels.
10. Cascara!
11. Sneezing powder!
12. Growth hormone!
13. LSD.
14. His own trunk.
15. Space dust.
16. Forget-me-nots.
17. Brass wart.
18. Expectorants.
19. Magic mushrooms.
20. Calcium carbide.
21. Gasoline.
22. Prunes.
23. Acid.
24. Lye.
25. Mice.
26. Your best friend.
27. Your mother-in-law (it would give the elephant the runs).
28. Pointed objects.
29. Elephant jokes.
30. Peanut butter (it sticks to their tusks).
31. Peanuts still in the bag.
32. Cookies.
33. Butter.
34. Ice cubes.
35. Garlic.
36. Onions.
37. Beans.
38. Meat.
39. Hot dogs.
40. Alcohol.
41. Donut holes.
42. Caramels.
43. Elephant poison.
44. Plastic peanuts.
45. Fish hooks.
46. Cement.
47. Kerosene.
48. Cacao leaves.
49. Hemp.
50. Whale lard.
51. People parts.
52. Cat's meow.
53. Existentialism.
54. *New York Times*.
55. The "force."
56. Mr. Peanut.
57. Tom Thumb.
58. Laxative.
59. Zoo dope.
60. Cultures for venereal disease.
61. The Siberian fireball.
62. Bullshit.
63. Acid.
64. Beer.
65. *Jonathan Livingston Seagull*.
66. Jungle juice.
67. Sahib.
68. Seven blind men.
69. Hippos.
70. Munchkins.
71. Bicarbonate of soda.
72. Shaving cream.

172. Seven or more uses of a rolled-up sweat sock

1. Carrying tote.
2. Wind indicator.
3. Mousetrap.
4. Deterrent for unwelcome guests.
5. Windshield wiper.
6. Handkerchief.
7. Boxing glove.
8. Collecting bag.
9. Pennant.
10. Block a leak.
11. Play cricket in school classroom.
12. Breed germs on.
13. To clean a motorbike.
14. Padding out a bra.
15. As a gag.
16. To protect delicate china in transit.
17. To cover in petrol and use as tinder.
18. Put behind dartboard on a thin wall as padding.
19. Nitrating to produce explosive (guncotton, e.g.).
20. Throwing at a friend (in fun).
21. For hitting if very bad at karate.
22. To block a mousehole and kill them with the fumes.
23. Wash car.
24. Polish silverware.
25. Put on foot.
26. Wash windows.
27. Put in drawer.
28. Smell.
29. Put in wash.
30. Indoor baseball.
31. Non-violent weapon.
32. Cat toy.

33. Cushion.
34. Dust rag.
35. Scrub floor.
36. Blackjack.
37. Dog chewie.
38. Boot stuffer.
39. Door stop.
40. Sink stopper.
41. Badminton bird.
42. Skunk repellent.
43. Loser's trophy.
44. Soft softball.
45. Insulation.
46. Prop in a locker-room scene.
47. Shoe tree.
48. Napkin.
49. Washcloth.
50. Neutron bomb.
51. Horse's ear plug.
52. Soup spice.
53. Christmas stocking stuffer.
54. Sweet sanctuary.
55. Slingshot pellet.
56. Cannonball.
57. Soundproofing.
58. Plug tailpipe.
59. Sock for clubfoot.
60. July snowball.
61. An object in a scavenger hunt.
62. Ward off vampires.
63. But attract cheerleaders.
64. Joggers' coat of arms.
65. Membership card in Jock Club.
66. Fill a coin purse.
67. Bite on during conscious surgery.
68. Fly killer.
69. Earmuff.
70. Hockey puck.

---

### 173. Seven or more uses of newspaper

1. Clean kerosene lamp chimney.
2. Clean stove top.
3. Chink log cabin.
4. Start fire.
5. Use as wallpaper.
6. Use as rug padding.
7. Use as insulation.
8. Recycle.
9. Kill insects.
10. Protect clean floors.
11. Fill garbage cans.
12. Use as mulch.
13. Read.
14. Make paper hats.
15. Make paper airplanes.
16. Make papier-mâché.
17. Line footlockers.
18. Litter the subway.
19. Make confetti.
20. Save for paper drive.
21. Put on microfilm.
22. Use as blanket for bums.
23. Element in collage.

---

### 174. Six or more reasons why some men wear a mustache.

1. To look masculine.
2. Change identity.
3. Look older.
4. Imitate famous personalities.
5. Too lazy to shave.
6. Protection against cold.
7. Bacteria breeder.
8. To hide behind.
9. Lost the razor.
10. Scars on top lip.
11. To filter fizzy beer.
12. To look attractive.
13. To win "best mustache" competition.
14. To sing in barber-shop quartets.
15. To look machismo.
16. To cover sensitive skin.
17. For self-confidence.
18. Because "the boss" approves.
19. To create turbulent boundary layer around face and prevent boundary layer separation.
20. To make a mustache cup a worthwhile buy.
21. Shave off.
22. Show off.
23. Something to pull at.
24. Want to try it.
25. Cover a mole.
26. Cover a harelip.
27. Keep lip warm in winter.
28. Soup strainer.
29. Draw attention to his lip.
30. Impress girls.
31. Impress boys.
32. Keeps milk off your lip.
33. Less having to do.
34. Vanity.
35. Long upper lip.
36. Short upper lip.
37. Too shaky to shave.
38. Habit.
39. Because other men have mustaches.
40. Because no other men have any.
41. Savor food later.
42. Emulate Hitler.
43. Afraid to shave lip.
44. Don't own a mirror.
45. To look distinguished.
46. To chew on it as a nervous habit.
47. Hope a bird will nest in it.
48. Compensate for baldness.
49. Fodder for hair transplant.
50. Pass for eighteen (twenty-one) in a bar.
51. Look like an artist.
52. Needed in a theatrical part.
53. To gain weight.
54. They're mustachio nuts.
55. Because little hairs grow out of their face.
56. To catch dope they snort.
57. To dust their face.
58. Family tradition.
59. To tell them apart from twin sister.
60. To filter air they breathe.
61. To please themselves.
62. So you don't notice they only have one eye.
63. Save time in morning in preparation for work.
64. Eccentric.
65. Because they're hairy guys.
66. No arms to shave with.
67. To hide evidence.
68. As an appendage.

---

### 175. Eight or more places never to scuba dive

1. Bathtub.
2. Loch Ness.
3. Crater of a volcano.
4. Aquarium.
5. Outhouse.
6. Bermuda Triangle.
7. Pond in a public park.
8. Kettle of soup.
9. Empty swimming pool.
10. Underwater minefield.
11. Sewage works.
12. Mariana Trench (too deep).
13. Puddle.
14. Supermarket.
15. Oil well.
16. Sea of Tranquility.
17. Quicksand.
18. Slurry pit.
19. Recently mixed epoxy resin and hardener.
20. Proton accelerator.
21. Nuclear material storage pit.
22. In a block of ice.
23. Toilet bowl.
24. Septic tank.
25. Hudson River.
26. Any place near a factory.
27. Great Lakes (some parts).
28. Glass of water.
29. Dead Sea.
30. A wishing well.
31. Arctic Ocean.
32. Antarctic Ocean.
33. Water less than two feet deep.
34. Twenty thousand leagues under the sea.
35. Near Iberian oil tankers.
36. Sahara Desert.
37. Cesspool.
38. Fish tank.
39. Geysers.
40. Nebraska's creeks.
41. Platte River.
42. Horse tank.
43. Waterfalls.
44. Sargasso Sea.
45. Bering Strait.
46. On dry land.
47. In mercury.
48. In hydrochloric acid.
49. In a cauldron.
50. In dew.
51. Great Salt Lake.
52. Marineland.
53. Rice paddie.
54. In nuclear waste.
55. Hot Springs.
56. At a chemical plant.
57. In a vat of chocolate.
58. In champagne.
59. In a hurricane.
60. In Harlem.
61. In the Jordan River.
62. In a dormant volcano.
63. On top of Old Smokey.
64. In a "hot" fishing spot.
65. In a war zone.
66. Among five-foot frogs.
67. Among sharks.
68. Among sting rays.
69. Among Corvettes.
70. In the fat lady's underwear.
71. In a cyclotron.

---

### 176. Seven or more reasons why we don't eat porpoises

1. Not edible.
2. Man's best friend in the aquatic world.
3. We play with them.
4. Not commercially attractive.
5. Too big for the can.
6. Swim too fast.
7. Have tough flesh.
8. They look appealing.
9. They are too intelligent.
10. Convention says not to.
11. Are useful for other purposes, e.g., defense.
12. Fishermen don't deliberately aim to catch them.
13. They are worth a lot.
14. No good recipes yet developed.
15. Oven not big enough.
16. Not easy to catch a large number of them at once (nets not much use).
17. They might eat us in revenge!
18. Slimey.
19. Ugly.
20. Other things to eat.
21. Taste may not be good.
22. Too hard to raise.
23. Too hard to slaughter.
24. They don't eat us.
25. Reminds us of Flipper.
26. Not kosher.
27. No good wines to serve with it.
28. Not easily available in stores.
29. Believe it's wrong to eat porpoises.
30. Too expensive.
31. Too many bones.
32. Not hungry enough.
33. Can't eat a whole one.
34. Not canned.

35. Aren't at supermarket.
36. Madison Ave doesn't provide.
37. Can't find them.
38. Because we confuse them with dolphins.
39. Too large to fit in frying pan.
40. Too smart to bite fish hooks.
41. They talk.
42. P.R. campaign on about tuna fishermen catching them.
43. Turn rancid quickly.
44. They guide boats.
45. Fishermen hog porpoises for themselves to eat.
46. No tradition in it.
47. We have a treaty with them.
48. They work for the CIA.
49. They keep us informed on Atlantis.
50. If we did, Neptune would have our asses.
51. No purpose in porpoise eating.
52. They don't die; can't do things for immortal porpoises (Mann Act).
53. Too fattening.
54. Could become endangered species.
55. They don't grow on trees.
56. Vegetarian plot.
57. Porpoises are one with God.
58. They're coaches on USC swim team.
59. Brainwashing; i.e., Peter Piper picked pickled peppers, not porpoises.
60. Because porpoise poop is invaluable fertilizer.
61. Little demand for porpoise coats.
62. Because name starts with "P"; we don't eat penguins either.
63. If we did there'd be *porpoise* in life; we aren't ready for that.
64. Ignorance and indifference.
65. We rarely think: "Boy, I'd like to eat a porpoise."
66. They're good friends with an evil wizard.

## 177. Eight or more reasons why some nationalities wear jewelry on their nose

1. Have big-enough nose.
2. Have nothing else on in the head.
3. The glitter of the jewels indicates to them which way to go.
4. The jewels cannot be stolen.
5. It makes people more beautiful.
6. The jewels jingle nicely.
7. Good to have instead of a handkerchief.
8. To look attractive.
9. To distinguish between tribes.
10. Mark of fidelity.
11. Mark of marital status.
12. To prevent sunburn.
13. To ward off evil spirits.
14. To look ferocious.
15. To camouflage its size shape
16. To prevent nose-rubbing with other people.
17. To hang bats on (of the animal type).
18. To suppress sneezes.
19. To cure compulsive nose-picking.
20. As a weapon in head-butting.
21. To prevent broken noses when walking into trees.
22. To be seen at night or in dim light.
23. Religious belief.
24. To be "in."
25. To prove something about them.
26. They may be masochists.
27. They may be sadists.
28. Something to get their picture in *National Geographic*.
29. To play with.
30. Replacement for lost earring.
31. Group identification.
32. Caste separation.
33. Custom.
34. Habit.
35. Unwilling to change.
36. Culture.
37. Working women use hands—so no finger rings.
38. Easily seen in nose.
39. It's fun.
40. Show off wealth.
41. Fast-talking jewelry salesman.
42. No ears.
43. Can only afford one piece of jewelry so don't use earrings.
44. Will adorn anything.
45. Imitate bulls.
46. Hook noses when married.
47. Born with holes in nose.
48. Cover hereditary nose blemishes.
49. Advertise sexual proclivity.
50. Advertise availability.
51. Carry little menthol inhalators.
52. Substitute for belt buckles.
53. To get invited to Leonard Bernstein parties as "savages."
54. Carry their money.
55. To hook a carrot to.
56. To show national derring-do
57. Carry extra bullets into battle.
58. Who wants to be able to smell in an underdeveloped country?
59. Not hidden by hair.
60. Frighten enemy tribes.
61. Initiation into man woman-hood.
62. Carry poison.
63. Adornment styles are relative.
64. Their relatives do so.
65 As a joke.
66. To cure sleeping on one's face.
67. As a voodoo charm ("Who do?" "You do?" "Do what?" "Voodoo!" "Who do?". . . ).
68. Badge of slavery.
69. Look more colorful.
70. To scare Europeans.
71. As a gastronomical aid.
72. To follow noses easier.

## 178. Eight or more non-writing uses for a pencil

1. Nose poker.
2. Ear poker.
3. Head scratcher.
4. Ruler.
5. Can be used instead of a finger for dialing.
6. Killing worms and insects.
7. Tattooing.
8. Stir coffee tea with.
9. Drill.
10. For drawing.
11. Pointer.
12. Reel.
13. Bookmark.
14. Carbon electrode in an arc.
15. For (amateur) karate-chop practice.
16. Operating calculator with small keys.
17. Doing brass rubbing.
18. To blunt a pencil sharpener!
19. To stir epoxy glues (that have to be mixed).
20. Jamming a door open.
21. Letting down a bicycle tyre.
22. Use as a former for winding an electrical coil.
23 Rubbing a tape cassette mechanism to cut friction.
24. Burning for heat in a case of life and death.
25. Pulling a quartz crystal (i.e., altering resonant frequency).
26. To sharpen away for sawdust shavings production.
27. Erasing.
28. Breaking.
29. Sharpening.
30. Sticking behind ear.
31. Sticking in mouth.
32. Something to tap with.
33. Something to hit someone with.
34. Sharp weapon.
35. Mast for small ship.
36. Drumstick.
37. Javelin for fleas.
38. Battering ram for ants.
39. Eraser makes good pincushion.
40. If a good-looking girl in office has a sharpener, makes a good icebreaker.
41. Prop something up.
42. Ring doorbell.
43. Hold window open.
44. Shave it to start fire.
45. Advertising.
46. Chew for inspiration.
47. Goose friends.
48. Roll paper heads on it.
49. Tie bows around it.
50. Exercise fingers.
51. For arrowshaft.
52. Roll pincurls.
53. Icepick.
54. As large toothpick.
55. Practice thermometer.
56. As a dummy cigarette.
57. Baton.
58. Basketball needle.
59. Darning needle.
60. Record needle.
61. As a bolt.
62. To poison kids with the lead.
63. Mix paint.
64. Mix drinks.
65. Lock pick.
66. Dagger.
67. Paperweight.
68. Beginners in karate break them.
69. Tickle feet with.
70. In a stick-up as a fake gun.
71. Letter opener.
72. As a chopstick.
73. To stave off a predator.
74. To break light bulbs.
75. Bookmark.
76. Fondue fork.
77. Mix salads.
78. Put over ear to imitate an accountant.
79. As a small fence post.

## 179. Six or more reasons we eat tuna fish

1. Delicious.
2. Nutritious.
3. Abundant.
4. Makes simple meals palatable.
5. Conventional.
6. Can't drink it!
7. Does you good.
8. Of good consistent quality (in cans).
9. As a change.
10. Keeps tuna-fishing industry going.
11. Tuna is not (yet) endangered.
12. Parents force it into one when one is young.
13. Does not contain many toxins.

14. Lots of meat per unit bodyweight.
15. Hunger.
16. Goes with most wines.
17. May be eaten at any time of day.
18. Easy to store.
19. Requires no refrigeration.
20. It's canned.
21. Non-fattening.
22. Cheap.
23. Substitute for chicken in recipes.
24. Cultural habit.
25. Mixes with other foods well.
26. Quick to fix.
27. It's Friday.
28. Because we don't eat porpoise.
29. Propaganda by Charlie Tuna.
30. To emulate cats.
31. Low calories.
32. Goes well with beer.
33. The only fish sandwich in town.
34. We don't know any personally.
35. Mother makes me.
36. Fun to catch.
37. Extensive advertising.
38. Even some "vegetarians" eat tuna fish.
39. Army contract.
40. Doesn't make you fart.
41. Pets will eat the leftovers.
42. Goes with mayo.
43. Restaurants serve it.
44. There's too many fish in the sea.
45. For sea seasoning.
46. Masochism.
47. In a fit of passion.
48. In the throes of despair.
49. To attend a fish cookout.
50. Once you catch the tuna, what else would you do with it?
51. We'll eat anything.
52. Tastes like marinated frog legs.
53. Has protein.
54. Helps you to swim.
55. Jealousy—they breathe water, we don't.
56. To avoid killing a mockingbird.

---

### 180. Seven or more reasons for not having a two-cent piece

1. Doesn't exist.
2. Has no purchasing power.
3. I have no coin pouch.
4. I have two one-cent pieces.
5. Threw it into the Fontana di Trevi.
6. Had to use it as a washer.
7. Have lost it.
8. Have given it to a beggar.
9. Used it in a slot machine.
10. Just made long phone call.
11. In a nudist camp (i.e., no pockets).
12. Being in a foreign country.
13. Just been robbed.
14. Just given all your possessions to charity.
15. Just thrown it over the side of a ship at sea for good luck.
16. Just built a tower with all your coins.
17. Have holes in your pockets.
18. Allergic to the particular alloy.
19. Superstitious at having one.
20. Running in a marathon (i.e., to keep one's weight low).
21. Being dead.
22. Being a baby.
23. Being broke.
24. Being generous.
25. Most prices are not multiples of two.
26. Already have enough coins.
27. Every other coin is based on five, except for 1¢.
28. Waste of time.
29. No more designs.
30. We have an even amount of coins; with 2¢ it would be odd.
31. Seven is an unlucky number (seven coins).
32. Nothing costs two cents (not even a 2¢ plain).
33. Not enough drawers in cash register.
34. Government can spend money in better ways than minting a new coin.
35. Most items cost something + 9¢ (i.e., requires 1¢ change).
36. Would probably not be accepted by general public, like $2 bill.
37. If inflation continues, no coins will be needed.
38. Create in-fighting to determine whose portrait will be on it.
39. Name is too long.
40. Too hard to count by twos.
41. Won't fit coin machines.
42. Politics.
43. The old ones cost too much.
44. If you're given one you'd be on "Candid Camera."
45. Don't need another coin worth zip.
46. Confuse morons.
47. Confuse geniuses.
48. Can't eat them.
49. Can't drink them.
50. Not costly enough for government to make.
51. Government on a 1¢ standard.
52. They have holes in center or are too large.
53. You can't always get what you want.
54. Produce 100% gumball inflation.
55. No more penny candy.
56. Awkward to say "2¢ piece."
57. Wouldn't buy a banana.
58. Have to rewrite arithmetic texts.
59. Produce a trend for 3¢ pieces.
60. We tried it once; it failed.
61. Banks dislike new coins.
62. Produce inflation.
63. Metal is too expensive to make them.
64. Require remaking vending machines.
65. People would make too many poor jokes.
66. Poland already has it.
67. There are higher priorities.
68. Can't smoke them.
69. More coins to counterfeit.
70. Hard to accept.
71. No philosophical justification.

---

### 181. Seven or more ways how not to attract other men

1. Get a pet rattlesnake.
2. Speak with a nasal, singsong twang.
3. Eat at least two cloves of garlic daily.
4. Become an expert on everything.
5. Monopolize all conversation.
6. Buy clothes four sizes too large.
7. Forget all manners.
8. Do everything to excess.
9. Develop habits: crack knuckles, pick nose, etc.
10. Be a borrower.
11. Complain incessantly.
12. Grow dandelions in your hair.
13. Eat cockroaches.
14. Wear a Nazi uniform.
15. Never look anyone in the eye.
16. Never use a handkerchief—use the floor.
17. Never zip your fly.
18. Eat gaseous foods and pass it on.
19. Suck your thumb.
20. Tell them you are married.
21. Bring your homely sister with you.
22. Wear a "Vote for Bella Abzug" button.
23. Whistle at every woman who passes by.
24. Deck the first guy who looks sideways at you.
25. Tell people you work undercover for the vice squad.
26. Wear size-twelve construction boots and a hard hat.
27. Wear your karate black belt.
28. Panhandle.
29. Carry far-out religious literature prominently displayed.
30. Don't wiggle your rear end.
31. Don't wear nice clothes.
32. Don't wear tight pants.
33. Don't shower.
34. Don't clean your nails.
35. Don't brush your teeth.
36. Don't comb your hair.
37. Act gay.
38. Act like you're not gay.
39. Look mad.
40. Brag a lot.
41. Act crazy.
42. Act childish.
43. Cry.
44. Ignore them.
45. Don't wear perfume.
46. Don't wear women's clothes.
47. Be constantly escorted by a girl.
48. Don't go to public school.
49. Continually boast about your love of women.
50. Don't use deodorant.
51. Act like a stupid person.
52. Put yourself in a closet for no one to see.
53. Become a lousy dirty bum.
54. Hate anyone who comes near you and yell at them.
55. Murder all men who make passes at you.

### Mental Calisthenic #7

Pick one room in your house or apartment and carefully explore and examine its ceiling. Look for CRACKS, MODULATIONS IN TEXTURE, BUMPS, CREVICES, IMPERFECTIONS, COLORS, CONSISTENCIES. Proceed with other rooms during subsequent sessions. Go into a public place and repeat the exercise. Proceed with a Mental Jogging exercise.

## 182. Eight or more reasons why cars cost more than motorcycles

| Response | Score |
|---|---|
| 1. | 1 |
| 2. | 1 |
| 3. | 1 |
| 4. | 1 |
| 5. | 1 |
| 6. | 1 |
| 7. | 1 |
| 8. | 1 |
| **Bonus Responses** | |
| 9. | 2 |
| 10. | 2 |
| 11. | 2 |
| 12. | 2 |
| 13. | 2 |
| 14. | 2 |
| 15. | 2 |
| 16. | 2 |

Total ☐

## 183. Six or more reasons why the sky is blue

| Response | Score |
|---|---|
| 1. | 1 |
| 2. | 1 |
| 3. | 1 |
| 4. | 1 |
| 5. | 1 |
| 6. | 1 |
| **Bonus Responses** | |
| 7. | 2 |
| 8. | 2 |
| 9. | 2 |
| 10. | 2 |
| 11. | 2 |
| 12. | 2 |
| 13. | 2 |
| 14. | 2 |
| 15. | 2 |
| 16. | 2 |

Total ☐

## 184. Seven or more new names for children's cereal

| Response | Score |
|---|---|
| 1. _____ | 1 |
| 2. _____ | 1 |
| 3. _____ | 1 |
| 4. _____ | 1 |
| 5. _____ | 1 |
| 6. _____ | 1 |
| 7. _____ | 1 |

Bonus Responses

| | |
|---|---|
| 8. _____ | 2 |
| 9. _____ | 2 |
| 10. _____ | 2 |
| 11. _____ | 2 |
| 12. _____ | 2 |
| 13. _____ | 2 |
| 14. _____ | 2 |
| 15. _____ | 2 |
| 16. _____ | 2 |

Total ☐

## 185. Seven or more ways to drink liquor without becoming intoxicated

| Response | Score |
|---|---|
| 1. _____ | 1 |
| 2. _____ | 1 |
| 3. _____ | 1 |
| 4. _____ | 1 |
| 5. _____ | 1 |
| 6. _____ | 1 |
| 7. _____ | 1 |

Bonus Responses

| | |
|---|---|
| 8. _____ | 2 |
| 9. _____ | 2 |
| 10. _____ | 2 |
| 11. _____ | 2 |
| 12. _____ | 2 |
| 13. _____ | 2 |
| 14. _____ | 2 |
| 15. _____ | 2 |
| 16. _____ | 2 |

Total ☐

## 186. Six or more reasons why the government has more money than any one individual or corporation

| Response | Score |
|---|---|
| 1. _____ | 1 |
| 2. _____ | 1 |
| 3. _____ | 1 |
| 4. _____ | 1 |
| 5. _____ | 1 |
| 6. _____ | 1 |

Bonus Responses

| | |
|---|---|
| 7. _____ | 2 |
| 8. _____ | 2 |
| 9. _____ | 2 |
| 10. _____ | 2 |
| 11. _____ | 2 |
| 12. _____ | 2 |
| 13. _____ | 2 |
| 14. _____ | 2 |
| 15. _____ | 2 |
| 16. _____ | 2 |

Total ☐

## 187. Six things never to do while watching tennis on TV

| Response | Score |
|---|---|
| 1. _____ | 1 |
| 2. _____ | 1 |
| 3. _____ | 1 |
| 4. _____ | 1 |
| 5. _____ | 1 |
| 6. _____ | 1 |

Bonus Responses

| | |
|---|---|
| 7. _____ | 2 |
| 8. _____ | 2 |
| 9. _____ | 2 |
| 10. _____ | 2 |
| 11. _____ | 2 |
| 12. _____ | 2 |
| 13. _____ | 2 |
| 14. _____ | 2 |
| 15. _____ | 2 |
| 16. _____ | 2 |

Total ☐

## 188. Seven or more reasons why crickets sing

| Response | Score |
|---|---|
| 1. _____ | 1 |
| 2. _____ | 1 |
| 3. _____ | 1 |
| 4. _____ | 1 |
| 5. _____ | 1 |
| 6. _____ | 1 |
| 7. _____ | 1 |

**Bonus Responses**

| | |
|---|---|
| 8. _____ | 2 |
| 9. _____ | 2 |
| 10. _____ | 2 |
| 11. _____ | 2 |
| 12. _____ | 2 |
| 13. _____ | 2 |
| 14. _____ | 2 |
| 15. _____ | 2 |
| 16. _____ | 2 |

Total ☐

## 189. Eight or more common mistakes in ordering restaurant wines

| Response | Score |
|---|---|
| 1. _____ | 1 |
| 2. _____ | 1 |
| 3. _____ | 1 |
| 4. _____ | 1 |
| 5. _____ | 1 |
| 6. _____ | 1 |
| 7. _____ | 1 |
| 8. _____ | 1 |

**Bonus Responses**

| | |
|---|---|
| 9. _____ | 2 |
| 10. _____ | 2 |
| 11. _____ | 2 |
| 12. _____ | 2 |
| 13. _____ | 2 |
| 14. _____ | 2 |
| 15. _____ | 2 |
| 16. _____ | 2 |

Total ☐

## 190. Eight or more reasons for not taking drugs

| Response | Score |
|---|---|
| 1. _____ | 1 |
| 2. _____ | 1 |
| 3. _____ | 1 |
| 4. _____ | 1 |
| 5. _____ | 1 |
| 6. _____ | 1 |
| 7. _____ | 1 |
| 8. _____ | 1 |

**Bonus Responses**

| | |
|---|---|
| 9. _____ | 2 |
| 10. _____ | 2 |
| 11. _____ | 2 |
| 12. _____ | 2 |
| 13. _____ | 2 |
| 14. _____ | 2 |
| 15. _____ | 2 |
| 16. _____ | 2 |

Total ☐

## 191. Six or more things you always wanted to stop doing

| Response | Score |
|---|---|
| 1. _____ | 1 |
| 2. _____ | 1 |
| 3. _____ | 1 |
| 4. _____ | 1 |
| 5. _____ | 1 |
| 6. _____ | 1 |

**Bonus Responses**

| | |
|---|---|
| 7. _____ | 2 |
| 8. _____ | 2 |
| 9. _____ | 2 |
| 10. _____ | 2 |
| 11. _____ | 2 |
| 12. _____ | 2 |
| 13. _____ | 2 |
| 14. _____ | 2 |
| 15. _____ | 2 |
| 16. _____ | 2 |

Total ☐

## 192. Seven or more things never to say to a bartender

| Response | Score |
|---|---|
| 1. | 1 |
| 2. | 1 |
| 3. | 1 |
| 4. | 1 |
| 5. | 1 |
| 6. | 1 |
| 7. | 1 |

Bonus Responses

| | |
|---|---|
| 8. | 2 |
| 9. | 2 |
| 10. | 2 |
| 11. | 2 |
| 12. | 2 |
| 13. | 2 |
| 14. | 2 |
| 15. | 2 |
| 16. | 2 |

Total ☐

## 193. Seven or more reasons why most headaches stop after taking two aspirin

| Response | Score |
|---|---|
| 1. | 1 |
| 2. | 1 |
| 3. | 1 |
| 4. | 1 |
| 5. | 1 |
| 6. | 1 |
| 7. | 1 |

Bonus Responses

| | |
|---|---|
| 8. | 2 |
| 9. | 2 |
| 10. | 2 |
| 11. | 2 |
| 12. | 2 |
| 13. | 2 |
| 14. | 2 |
| 15. | 2 |
| 16. | 2 |

Total ☐

## 194. Eight or more house plants nobody wants

| Response | Score |
|---|---|
| 1. | 1 |
| 2. | 1 |
| 3. | 1 |
| 4. | 1 |
| 5. | 1 |
| 6. | 1 |
| 7. | 1 |
| 8. | 1 |

Bonus Responses

| | |
|---|---|
| 9. | 2 |
| 10. | 2 |
| 11. | 2 |
| 12. | 2 |
| 13. | 2 |
| 14. | 2 |
| 15. | 2 |
| 16. | 2 |

Total ☐

## 195. Eight or more things to think about while driving alone at night

| Response | Score |
|---|---|
| 1. | 1 |
| 2. | 1 |
| 3. | 1 |
| 4. | 1 |
| 5. | 1 |
| 6. | 1 |
| 7. | 1 |
| 8. | 1 |

Bonus Responses

| | |
|---|---|
| 9. | 2 |
| 10. | 2 |
| 11. | 2 |
| 12. | 2 |
| 13. | 2 |
| 14. | 2 |
| 15. | 2 |
| 16. | 2 |

Total ☐

## 196. Seven or more reasons for not brushing your teeth

| Response | Score |
|---|---|
| 1. _____ | 1 |
| 2. _____ | 1 |
| 3. _____ | 1 |
| 4. _____ | 1 |
| 5. _____ | 1 |
| 6. _____ | 1 |
| 7. _____ | 1 |

Bonus Responses

| | |
|---|---|
| 8. _____ | 2 |
| 9. _____ | 2 |
| 10. _____ | 2 |
| 11. _____ | 2 |
| 12. _____ | 2 |
| 13. _____ | 2 |
| 14. _____ | 2 |
| 15. _____ | 2 |
| 16. _____ | 2 |

Total ☐

## 197. Seven or more things about yourself not to admit to anybody

| Response | Score |
|---|---|
| 1. _____ | 1 |
| 2. _____ | 1 |
| 3. _____ | 1 |
| 4. _____ | 1 |
| 5. _____ | 1 |
| 6. _____ | 1 |
| 7. _____ | 1 |

Bonus Responses

| | |
|---|---|
| 8. _____ | 2 |
| 9. _____ | 2 |
| 10. _____ | 2 |
| 11. _____ | 2 |
| 12. _____ | 2 |
| 13. _____ | 2 |
| 14. _____ | 2 |
| 15. _____ | 2 |
| 16. _____ | 2 |

Total ☐

## 198. Seven or more things to do if you are thirsty but there is nothing to drink

| Response | Score |
|---|---|
| 1. _____ | 1 |
| 2. _____ | 1 |
| 3. _____ | 1 |
| 4. _____ | 1 |
| 5. _____ | 1 |
| 6. _____ | 1 |
| 7. _____ | 1 |

Bonus Responses

| | |
|---|---|
| 8. _____ | 2 |
| 9. _____ | 2 |
| 10. _____ | 2 |
| 11. _____ | 2 |
| 12. _____ | 2 |
| 13. _____ | 2 |
| 14. _____ | 2 |
| 15. _____ | 2 |
| 16. _____ | 2 |

Total ☐

## 199. Six or more reasons why jogging has become popular

| Response | Score |
|---|---|
| 1. _____ | 1 |
| 2. _____ | 1 |
| 3. _____ | 1 |
| 4. _____ | 1 |
| 5. _____ | 1 |
| 6. _____ | 1 |

Bonus Responses

| | |
|---|---|
| 7. _____ | 2 |
| 8. _____ | 2 |
| 9. _____ | 2 |
| 10. _____ | 2 |
| 11. _____ | 2 |
| 12. _____ | 2 |
| 13. _____ | 2 |
| 14. _____ | 2 |
| 15. _____ | 2 |
| 16. _____ | 2 |

Total ☐

## 200. Seven or more things to do if you are lonely and there is no one around

| Response | Score |
|---|---|
| 1. _____ | 1 |
| 2. _____ | 1 |
| 3. _____ | 1 |
| 4. _____ | 1 |
| 5. _____ | 1 |
| 6. _____ | 1 |
| 7. _____ | 1 |

**Bonus Responses**

| Response | Score |
|---|---|
| 8. _____ | 2 |
| 9. _____ | 2 |
| 10. _____ | 2 |
| 11. _____ | 2 |
| 12. _____ | 2 |
| 13. _____ | 2 |
| 14. _____ | 2 |
| 15. _____ | 2 |
| 16. _____ | 2 |

Total ☐

## 201. Six or more things to do if you are hungry, but there is nothing to eat

| Response | Score |
|---|---|
| 1. _____ | 1 |
| 2. _____ | 1 |
| 3. _____ | 1 |
| 4. _____ | 1 |
| 5. _____ | 1 |
| 6. _____ | 1 |

**Bonus Responses**

| Response | Score |
|---|---|
| 7. _____ | 2 |
| 8. _____ | 2 |
| 9. _____ | 2 |
| 10. _____ | 2 |
| 11. _____ | 2 |
| 12. _____ | 2 |
| 13. _____ | 2 |
| 14. _____ | 2 |
| 15. _____ | 2 |
| 16. _____ | 2 |

Total ☐

## 202. Seven or more reasons for having bar stools

| Response | Score |
|---|---|
| 1. _____ | 1 |
| 2. _____ | 1 |
| 3. _____ | 1 |
| 4. _____ | 1 |
| 5. _____ | 1 |
| 6. _____ | 1 |
| 7. _____ | 1 |

**Bonus Responses**

| Response | Score |
|---|---|
| 8. _____ | 2 |
| 9. _____ | 2 |
| 10. _____ | 2 |
| 11. _____ | 2 |
| 12. _____ | 2 |
| 13. _____ | 2 |
| 14. _____ | 2 |
| 15. _____ | 2 |
| 16. _____ | 2 |

Total ☐

## 203. Eight or more ways you prove that you are smart

| Response | Score |
|---|---|
| 1. _____ | 1 |
| 2. _____ | 1 |
| 3. _____ | 1 |
| 4. _____ | 1 |
| 5. _____ | 1 |
| 6. _____ | 1 |
| 7. _____ | 1 |
| 8. _____ | 1 |

**Bonus Responses**

| Response | Score |
|---|---|
| 9. _____ | 2 |
| 10. _____ | 2 |
| 11. _____ | 2 |
| 12. _____ | 2 |
| 13. _____ | 2 |
| 14. _____ | 2 |
| 15. _____ | 2 |
| 16. _____ | 2 |

Total ☐

## 204. Seven or more ways to get a waitress's attention

| Response | Score |
|---|---|
| 1. _____ | 1 |
| 2. _____ | 1 |
| 3. _____ | 1 |
| 4. _____ | 1 |
| 5. _____ | 1 |
| 6. _____ | 1 |
| 7. _____ | 1 |

**Bonus Responses**

| | Score |
|---|---|
| 8. _____ | 2 |
| 9. _____ | 2 |
| 10. _____ | 2 |
| 11. _____ | 2 |
| 12. _____ | 2 |
| 13. _____ | 2 |
| 14. _____ | 2 |
| 15. _____ | 2 |
| 16. _____ | 2 |

Total ☐

## 205. Seven or more ways to strike up a conversation with a farmer

| Response | Score |
|---|---|
| 1. _____ | 1 |
| 2. _____ | 1 |
| 3. _____ | 1 |
| 4. _____ | 1 |
| 5. _____ | 1 |
| 6. _____ | 1 |
| 7. _____ | 1 |

**Bonus Responses**

| | Score |
|---|---|
| 8. _____ | 2 |
| 9. _____ | 2 |
| 10. _____ | 2 |
| 11. _____ | 2 |
| 12. _____ | 2 |
| 13. _____ | 2 |
| 14. _____ | 2 |
| 15. _____ | 2 |
| 16. _____ | 2 |

Total ☐

## 206. Six or more reasons why some people are afraid to ride a roller coaster

| Response | Score |
|---|---|
| 1. _____ | 1 |
| 2. _____ | 1 |
| 3. _____ | 1 |
| 4. _____ | 1 |
| 5. _____ | 1 |
| 6. _____ | 1 |

**Bonus Responses**

| | Score |
|---|---|
| 7. _____ | 2 |
| 8. _____ | 2 |
| 9. _____ | 2 |
| 10. _____ | 2 |
| 11. _____ | 2 |
| 12. _____ | 2 |
| 13. _____ | 2 |
| 14. _____ | 2 |
| 15. _____ | 2 |
| 16. _____ | 2 |

Total ☐

## 207. Six or more famous people who have never been on television

| Response | Score |
|---|---|
| 1. _____ | 1 |
| 2. _____ | 1 |
| 3. _____ | 1 |
| 4. _____ | 1 |
| 5. _____ | 1 |
| 6. _____ | 1 |

**Bonus Responses**

| | Score |
|---|---|
| 7. _____ | 2 |
| 8. _____ | 2 |
| 9. _____ | 2 |
| 10. _____ | 2 |
| 11. _____ | 2 |
| 12. _____ | 2 |
| 13. _____ | 2 |
| 14. _____ | 2 |
| 15. _____ | 2 |
| 16. _____ | 2 |

Total ☐

## 208. Seven or more famous people whose initials are "A" and/or "T"

| Response | Score |
|---|---|
| 1. | 1 |
| 2. | 1 |
| 3. | 1 |
| 4. | 1 |
| 5. | 1 |
| 6. | 1 |
| 7. | 1 |

Bonus Responses

| | |
|---|---|
| 8. | 2 |
| 9. | 2 |
| 10. | 2 |
| 11. | 2 |
| 12. | 2 |
| 13. | 2 |
| 14. | 2 |
| 15. | 2 |
| 16. | 2 |

Total ☐

## 209. Six or more ways to look at yourself in the mirror

| Response | Score |
|---|---|
| 1. | 1 |
| 2. | 1 |
| 3. | 1 |
| 4. | 1 |
| 5. | 1 |
| 6. | 1 |

Bonus Responses

| | |
|---|---|
| 7. | 2 |
| 8. | 2 |
| 9. | 2 |
| 10. | 2 |
| 11. | 2 |
| 12. | 2 |
| 13. | 2 |
| 14. | 2 |
| 15. | 2 |
| 16. | 2 |

Total ☐

## 210. Seven or more ways to go to sleep when you are not tired

| Response | Score |
|---|---|
| 1. | 1 |
| 2. | 1 |
| 3. | 1 |
| 4. | 1 |
| 5. | 1 |
| 6. | 1 |
| 7. | 1 |

Bonus Responses

| | |
|---|---|
| 8. | 2 |
| 9. | 2 |
| 10. | 2 |
| 11. | 2 |
| 12. | 2 |
| 13. | 2 |
| 14. | 2 |
| 15. | 2 |
| 16. | 2 |

Total ☐

## 211. Seven or more ways to prevent shoplifting

| Response | Score |
|---|---|
| 1. | 1 |
| 2. | 1 |
| 3. | 1 |
| 4. | 1 |
| 5. | 1 |
| 6. | 1 |
| 7. | 1 |

Bonus Responses

| | |
|---|---|
| 8. | 2 |
| 9. | 2 |
| 10. | 2 |
| 11. | 2 |
| 12. | 2 |
| 13. | 2 |
| 14. | 2 |
| 15. | 2 |
| 16. | 2 |

Total ☐

## 212. Seven or more reasons why a bee sting hurts

| | Response | Score |
|---|---|---|
| 1. | _____ | 1 |
| 2. | _____ | 1 |
| 3. | _____ | 1 |
| 4. | _____ | 1 |
| 5. | _____ | 1 |
| 6. | _____ | 1 |
| 7. | _____ | 1 |

### Bonus Responses

| | | |
|---|---|---|
| 8. | _____ | 2 |
| 9. | _____ | 2 |
| 10. | _____ | 2 |
| 11. | _____ | 2 |
| 12. | _____ | 2 |
| 13. | _____ | 2 |
| 14. | _____ | 2 |
| 15. | _____ | 2 |
| 16. | _____ | 2 |

Total ☐

# CONTRIBUTORS' SAMPLE RESPONSES

### 182. Eight or more reasons why cars cost more than motorcycles

1. Cars have more tires, moving parts, weight and size, lights, passenger room, and ashtrays.
2. Can be used year round.
3. Are more in demand.
4. Are more comfortable.
5. Can be steered with one hand.
6. Have places for making out.
7. Have places for trailer hitch.
8. Have places for carrying pets, packages, garbage, etc.
9. Have spare tires.
10. Can kill more people per accident.
11. Have reverse gears.
12. Take up more room on highway.
13. Require more parking space.
14. Can be driven more easily by little old ladies.
15. Easier to keep upright.
16. Have places to hang window speaker at drive-in movies.
17. Have glove compartments.
18. Have cigarette lighters.
19. Have doors and windows that open and close.
20. Most cars are made by Americans and motorcycles by foreigners.
21. It is easier to charge more for something bigger.
22. Motorcycles appeal more to the young with less money—cars to the older with more money.
23. People like to brag how much they can afford to pay for something—if cars cost the same or less, they wouldn't have the same status or appeal.
24. People will pay more for a built-in bed.
25. A lot of people in Detroit would be out of work if cars cost less than motorcycles.
26. Four wheels cost more than two.
27. It costs more to raise the roof.
28. More labor to produce.
29. More dependable.
30. Can be driven in the snow.
31. They've been around longer.
32. Cars are a more established part of the American way of life.
33. Cars are considered a necessity.
34. It takes longer to put them together.
35. Their makers are on strike more often.
36. They have more horsepower.
37. They are safer.
38. The people don't want to get wet.
39. People like getting run over by four wheels, not one.

### 183. Six or more reasons why the sky is blue

1. For the poets—it rhymes better than orange.
2. If it were red we couldn't distinguish sunup and sundown.
3. If it were white we couldn't see the clouds.
4. If it were green we couldn't tell up from down.
5. If it were gray we couldn't see the pollution.
6. If it were yellow we couldn't see the lightning bolts.
7. If it were white we couldn't see the snowflakes falling.
8. If it were black we couldn't see the night fall.
9. Brown would be depressing.
10. It feels sad looking down at this polluted earth.
11. It isn't—it just looks blue to blue-eyed people.
12. Because "blue moon" sounds better than "shocking pink moon" and "blue sky" better than "chartreuse sky."
13. Because it's pretty.
14. Light reflects off the dust particles in the sky.
15. Blue is the favorite color of many people.
16. It's easy to look at.
17. It's better than black.
18. Because it's not any other color.
19. Because it is the complementary color of yellow, which is the color of the sun.
20. Blue is a synonym for depression. When God asked everything what color they wanted to be no one wanted to be blue, so there was a lot left over.
21. To match the oceans.
22. It matches the color of many famous people's eyes.
23. The rays of the sun: more blue rays than red rays filter through the atmosphere.
24. Because it's miserable.
25. It's the reflection of the sea!
26. Because someone told it that the moon was, too.
27. It's a royal colour.
28. God painted it like that.
29. Your eyes are on the blink.
30. Blue rocket ships cover the sky.
31. You are not watching the sky, but a blue bikini.
32. Someone popped a blue paint bottle in your face.

### 184. Seven or more new names for children's cereal

1. Ghost Toasties.
2. Corn Fancies.
3. Nuts 'n Oats.
4. Bran Major.
5. Tri-Umps.
6. Fancy Flakes.
7. Wholey-Oats.
8. Honey Wheats.
9. Mother Nature's.
10. Twice Rice.
11. Neat Wheats.
12. Bran New.
13. Super Sludge.
14. Superbran.
15. Shredded Feet.
16. Snap, Crackle & Slop.
17. Mush Mouth.
18. Corn Critters.
19. Scrapple Jacks.
20. Bunchy Munchies.
21. Goop Loops.
22. Slop Pops.
23. Good-n-Sweet.
24. Giddy-Ups.
25. Go-Go's.
26. Bully-Chips.
27. Hy-di Hoes.
28. Kiddy Krap.
29. Blinkies.
30. Crunchle.
31. Cracky.
32. Snackle.
33. Puffum.
34. Snapple.
35. Good Stuff.
36. Hector Bites.
37. Crunchola.
38. Mikie's.
39. Biteum's.
40. Biteables.
41. Munchies.
42. Cornsnips.
43. Snapdragon.
44. Crackeroats.
45. Morndew.
46. Babywheat.
47. Oatinales.
48. Crumblies.
49. Ergo Space Pimples.
50. Herbert's Happy Candy.
51. Larry's Lunar Lumps.
52. Freckles.
53. Goody Gilda-Gunk.
54. Oozy-Woozy Chips.
55. Harry's Homebaked Cereals.

### 185. Seven or more ways to drink liquor without becoming intoxicated

1. Eat well before drinking.
2. Don't mix drinks.
3. Keep on your feet and keep moving.
4. Don't get involved in deep conversations.
5. Drink from the backside of the glass.
6. Mix it with water.
7. Mix it with milk.
8. Choose a drink of low proof.
9. Avoid overheated rooms.
10. With a very small eyedropper.
11. Very-y-y slowly.
12. Taken half and half with knockout drop.
13. Taken half and half with an emetic.
14. Heat the liquor first so the alcohol burns off.
15. Run around the block three times between sips.
16. Drink standing on your head.
17. Eat a pound of butter before each drink.
18. Swallow a sponge on a string first and pull it up and wring it out between drinks.
19. Don't drink through a straw.
20. Don't drink a lot at one time.
21. Have only one drink.
22. Drink liquor that evaporates as soon as you drink it.
23. Drink liquor that combines with stomach acid to become marshmallows.
24. Eat seven pepperoni pizzas one hour before you start to drink.
25. Have a transfusion.
26. Drink through a straw with holes in the sides so that the drink never reaches you.
27. Drink only seven pints.
28. Alternate with coffee.
29. Pour down your shirt.
30. Drink only one glass of wine.
31. Fall asleep before you get drunk.
32. Act drunk but remain normal.
33. Make yourself think you're not drunk.
34. Drink a bottle of water labeled liquor.

## 186. Six or more reasons why the government has more money than any one individual or corporation

1. The government does not pay taxes.
2. The government does not pay rent.
3. The government does not have kids.
4. The government does not have to provide for retirement.
5. The government does not take holidays.
6. The government does not support bad habits (drinking, womanizing, etc.)
7. The government does not tithe.
8. The government does not celebrate births, weddings, anniversaries, etc.
9. The government does not drive a car.
10. The government does not own life insurance.
11. The government does not get sick.
12. The government does not maintain a wardrobe.
13. The government does not contend with federal regulations.
14. In times of crisis, it hires people at a dollar per year.
15. It can operate at a deficit indefinitely.
16. If it needs money, it prints some.
17. We all contribute to its welfare.
18. It makes the rules saying who gets what.
19. It has been around longer.
20. It can make you an offer you can't refuse.
21. It can come up with better reasons why it needs your money more than you need theirs.
22. It can bury its money deeper than you.
23. It has more people working for it than you.
24. It doesn't have to spend its capital but can use other people's.
25. It's greedier.
26. Graft.
27. Embezzlement.
28. Swiss bank accounts.
29. Federal Reserve System.
30. Income tax.
31. Shrewd lawyers.
32. They're the only ones allowed to print it.
33. They spend more.
34. They need more because they waste more.
35. They have the entire population as "shareholders."
36. They can never go bankrupt (it's called "inflation").
37. No one gets fired if they don't make a profit.
38. They inherit money from Uncle Sam.
39. They sell dead pigs to the market.
40. They sold President Nixon's tapes for money.
41. The tax goes up along with the government salaries.

## 187. Six things never to do while watching tennis on TV

1. Sympathize with the ball.
2. Try to count the spectators.
3. Become emotionally involved with the ball girls.
4. Worry about close calls.
5. Compare it with a less taxing sport, such as football.
6. Become sexually attracted to Chrissy Evert and/or Nasty Nastase.
7. Blink too often.
8. Practice your golf game.
9. Do pushups in sync.
10. Turn the sound off and listen to a wrestling match on radio.
11. Turn the sound off and listen to a soap opera.
12. Stand on your head.
13. Think of your pet cat being gutted to make cat-gut.
14. Criticize the people playing.
15. Talk during a point.
16. Change channels.
17. Turn the TV off.
18. Sit in front of others.
19. Throw stuff at the TV.
20. Shout obscenities at the line judges—they may be able to hear you.
21. Go back for an overhead smash.
22. Try to hit the ball.
23. Call the courts with advice.
24. Demonstrate *your* backhand.
25. Challenge the loser to a match.
26. Nod your head.
27. Call out "Goal!"
28. Smash the screen.
29. Throw your own tennis ball at the players.
30. Say "I'll expose this racquet."
31. Eat marshmallows.
32. Watch the ball bounce.
33. Pick a winner.
34. Leave the room during a serve.
35. Look for the name on the ball during a volley.

## 188. Seven or more reasons why crickets sing

1. To break the silence.
2. To help some people sleep.
3. To keep some people awake.
4. To attract a lover.
5. To exercise their front wings.
6. For the *shrill* of it.
7. To establish a territory.
8. To warn possible intruders.
9. To show happiness.
10. To signal distress.
11. Just for the hell of it.
12. To tell the temperature.
13. To avoid being stepped on in the dark.
14. Because they are happy they are not cockroaches.
15. Because they never learned how to whistle.
16. Because they never learned how to dance.
17. They are auditioning for a part in *Pinocchio.*
18. Someone just tickled them.
19. It sounds better than humming.
20. Because they're happy.
21. Because they can't talk.
22. To keep in practice.
23. They are poor hummers.
24. The money.
25. Their legs are cold.
26. They're hungry and singing for their supper.
27. Because they want to win the Eurovision song contest.
28. Because they're "bats."
29. To prove that they're not footballs.
30. They are almost always drunk.
31. They are worried and scared to be alone in the dark.
32. They want to audition for Arthur Fiedler.
33. They are nothing but show-offs.
34. They have sore throats.
35. The crickets want to scare off builders.
36. They are all drowning in puddles.
37. The cockroaches are having a gang war with them.

## 189. Eight or more common mistakes in ordering restaurant wines

1. Asking the waiter's advice.
2. Not asking the waiter's advice.
3. Pretending you know what you're doing.
4. Asking for it in a brown paper bag.
5. Asking the price.
6. Not asking the price.
7. Ordering it chilled.
8. Thinking you know what the hell you're talking about.
9. Thinking the wine steward knows that he's doing.
10. Thinking it will make any difference in what you actually get.
11. Thinking that the restaurant *has* anything in their wine cellars but three kegs of red, white, and rosé wines anyhow.
12. Thinking that paying more gets you a better wine.
13. Thinking that memorizing the name of a wine out of a James Bond book will impress the waiter.
14. Ditto your date—who hasn't even read James Bond.
15. Ordering wine in the first place when the beer is better and cheaper.
16. Wrong pronunciation.
17. Wrong color.
18. Wrong brand.
19. Ordering a wine that's too expensive.
20. Getting drunk.
21. Ordering a wine that turned sour.
22. Ordering red with fish.
23. Ordering white with meat.
24. Laughing when you see how skimpy the selection is.
25. Ordering Ripple.
26. Not ordering enough.
27. Ordering too much and finishing it.
28. Calling Chianti "*Chee*-anti."
29. Asking whether it's "vintage."
30. Not "tasting" the wine when it arrives.
31. Not returning wine, if bad, because one doesn't want "to make a fuss."
32. Not asking for the wine list.
33. Tearing off the labels from bottles.
34. Forgetting the name.
35. Spilling it when sampling.
36. You find out you're in the wrong restaurant.
37. Your wife doesn't agree with it.
38. You were one of the makers and you know it's deadly.

## 190. Eight or more reasons for not taking drugs

1. Drugs are expensive.
2. Drugs are addictive.
3. Drugs are immoral.
4. Drugs are illegal.
5. Drugs create mental problems.
6. Drugs may be harmful to your health.
7. Drugs don't mix with booze.
8. Drugs cause you to lose touch with reality.
9. Drugs can cause birth defects.
10. Money could be spent on other things.
11. It takes time to earn or steal the money.
12. Who knows what sort of reaction *you* will get—after all, you are better than anyone, therefore different, so you are sure not to have ordinary everyday reactions like the common herd.
13. Why admit you are not perfect as you are—that you need anything more?
14. Why not be different—and brag about your superiority?
15. You might not enjoy it—so why bother?
16. You might enjoy it—and then you might be hooked and go on to worse.
17. It's fattening because you don't feel like doing much when you take drugs—you just lie there.
18. Hinders learning.
19. Causes accidents.
20. Causes death.
21. Makes you look foolish.
22. Makes you lose friends.
23. You enjoy pain.
24. No money.
25. None available.
26. They all become legal.
27. Allergic reaction.
28. Social pressure.
29. They have a nasty taste.
30. They're not always readily available.
31. They are not at the breakfast table.
32. Life's too short.
33. You want to live a long life.
34. They taste funny.
35. They have ugly colors.
36. They are round and square only.
37. Mommy says not to.

## 191. Six or more things you always wanted to stop doing

1. Working.
2. Going through bad winters.
3. Getting included in projects such as this.
4. Suffering unwarranted guilt.
5. Trying to stop things.
6. Tolerating bores.
7. Making rash statements.
8. Asking stupid questions.
9. Watching TV.
10. Listening to other people's bad advice.
11. Giving other people bad advice.
12. Wasting time.
13. Shaving.
14. Eating liver.
15. Filling out questionnaires.
16. Getting junk mail.
17. Nail biting.
18. Exaggerating.
19. Playing with my hair.
20. School.
21. War.
22. Inflation.
23. Taking tests.
24. Reading junk mail.
25. Eating junk food.
26. Hiccuping.
27. Worrying.
28. Frowning.
29. Spending money.
30. Having to get up in the morning.
31. Paying taxes.
32. Paying bills.
33. Paying rent.
34. Getting F's in school.
35. Picking your nose.
36. Eating things that are gummy.
37. Smelling ugly smells.
38. Seeing people get hit by trucks.
39. Falling out of airplanes.

## 192. Seven or more things never to say to a bartender

1. "Do you know how to make—?"
2. "I'd like to start a bar tab."
3. "What do you have to do to get a little service here?"
4. "Can you break a hundred?"
5. "This glass is dirty."
6. "Can you cash a personal check?"
7. "That was a twenty I gave you, not a single."
8. "This booze has been watered."
9. "Could you change channels on that TV?"
10. "I ordered a *dry* martini."
11. "Could you lend me ten till payday?"
12. "Boy have you got it made—booze, broads, easy work—"
13. "I got a little problem. . . ."
14. "Do you have to know much to do that?"
15. "It doesn't taste the way my mother used to make it."
16. "What are you doing after work, Big Boy?"
17. "Get your dirty thumb out of my drink."
18. "Personally, I don't believe in tipping."
19. "My name is Carry Nation."
20. "Would you like to take an ad in the *Women's Christian Temperance Union* magazine?"
21. "Give me another and this time put some alcohol in it."
22. "What's a nice guy like you doing in a place like this?"
23. "Say, this reminds me—my battery acid is getting low."
24. "My wife doesn't understand me——"
25. "I'm not here to buy."
26. "You don't know how to mix drinks."
27. "Your water stinks."
28. "You have body odor."
29. "Your hair is greasy."
30. "Your bar is filthy."
31. "Your drinks make me sick."
32. "Give me anything."
33. "Give me the specialty of the house."
34. "Heard any good jokes lately?"
35. "Did you raise the prices again?"
36. "They make better drinks across the street."
37. "That waitress sure is ugly."
38. "Where can I find a girl?"
39. "Fill 'er up."
40. "I could mix it better."
41. "So you think *you've* got trouble—!"
42. "How about one on the house?"
43. "How long have you been a bartender?"
44. "Has anyone ever called you a 'bar steward'?"
45. "The bar is too small."
46. His customers are lower than he.
47. His place will be wrecked if he doesn't pay you back.
48. He is gay.
49. The bar is not in a great location.
50. His wife is seeing someone.

## 193. Seven or more reasons why most headaches stop after taking two aspirin

1. Because the commercials say it will.
2. Because you think it will.
3. Headaches are afraid of aspirin.
4. Two of anything is better than one.
5. The challenge of trying to remove a childproof bottle cap will make you forget the headache.
6. Two is a magic number.
7. Aspirin may cause a stomach pain that will negate the head pain.
8. Because if it doesn't you may fear that there is something seriously wrong.
9. They were imaginary in the first place.
10. The power of suggestion.
11. You really had a two-aspirin headache and the two aspirin cured it.
12. You forget you had a headache, so it doesn't last.
13. Your headache stops because you tell yourself it will and if it didn't you might have to face the thought that you might have a brain tumor and your mind can't face that, so you program yourself to believe it will go away after taking two aspirin.
14. You felt you deserved the headache and after paying the appropriate penalty (two aspirin) and waiting the appropriate time it would go away.
15. After two aspirin you could care less about a headache.
16. You are so happy that you don't have to pay a doctor, your headache goes away.
17. Aspirin contains pain killers.
18. Most headaches aren't that bad.
19. The aspirins are very effective.
20. Because aspirin works better than Rolaids.
21. Because ten aspirin would kill you.
22. Because one aspirin isn't strong enough.
23. Coincidence.
24. They've seen the commercials, too, and feel that it must be the thing to do.
25. It is a good, effective pain reliever.

26. Your body will do anything to prevent you from taking any more of those miserable pills.
27. Maximum headache duration = thirty min. without help.
28. Headache self-inflicted—same as cure.
29. Water is the cure.
30. Aspirin may really work.
31. Because mother always said so.
32. Because nothing else has the same psychological effect.
33. Because after two aspirin, your head falls off!
34. It is mind over matter.
35. The aspirin made you pass out.
36. Because they have the special formula.

### 194. Eight or more house plants nobody wants

1. African Rubber Plant—unless you're too timid to ask the druggist.
2. Maidenhair Fern—your friends would probably rape it.
3. Christmas Pepper—it comes only once a year.
4. Mum—it probably won't keep.
5. Sensitive Plant—can't stand abuse.
6. Alpine Violet—shrinks at low altitudes.
7. Shrimp Plant—can cause botulism.
8. Zebra Plant—may kill all your derelict friends.
9. Venus Fly Trap—may develop a taste for you.
10. Cactus.
11. Pot Plants.
12. Dandelions.
13. Sticker Bushes.
14. Poison Ivy.
15. Poison Oak.
16. Sumac (Poison).
17. Crab Grass.
18. Ones that gossip.
19. Ones that fart.
20. Ones that insult your guests.
21. Ones that laugh at you when you're doing your exercises.
22. Ones that breathe all your air instead of $CO_2$.
23. Ones that eat your television.
24. Ones that eat your pets.
25. Ones that stick their heads out the window without bothering to open it, to get more sun.
26. Ones that won't tell you

when they're hungry or thirsty, they just die on you.
27. Spider Plant.
28. "Bizzy Lizzy."
29. Aspidistra.
30. Holly.
31. Plastic plants.
32. Smellious Cheapious.
33. Crokus Lumpus.
34. Goofy Glumper.
35. Deadly Dumplings.
36. Smelling Planters.

### 195. Eight or more things to think about while driving alone at night

1. Your driving.
2. The new broad at work.
3. Your future.
4. How nice it would be to quit your boring job.
5. A new invention.
6. Marilyn Monroe.
7. How you would spend ten million, if you had it.
8. Having a sex-change operation.
9. Having sex.
10. How the universe happened.
11. What's on the outside of the universe.
12. What you could be talking about if you had your girlfriend with you.
13. What you could be doing if you were home with your girlfriend.
14. How you can organize your time so you won't be stuck driving alone at night again.
15. Think about stopping to eat.
16. Think about stopping to drink.
17. Think about stopping to sleep.
18. Think about your sins.
19. Make New Year's resolutions in advance.
20. Count your blessings.
21. Count your enemies.
22. The car that's about to hit you.
23. Your speed.
24. Where you are going.
25. The place you just came from.
26. Making sure you don't have an accident.
27. Making sure your headlights are on.
28. Making sure you have enough gas.
29. What kind of shape are my tires in?
30. When was the last vampire reported in this neighborhood?
31. Is there really a bogey man?

32. What if the sandman finds me now?
33. Do men ever get raped?
34. What do the police cars look like at night?
35. Will Broderick Crawford really save me if I get into trouble?
36. Staying on the right road.
37. Keeping one's eyes off other vehicles' headlights.
38. Traveling hopefully to arrive.
39. What to do at one's destination.
40. Whether to *have* a destination.
41. What would happen if I went the other way?
42. Have I forgotten my home address?
43. What to run into.
44. Who will jump out?
45. Will Big Foot attack?
46. Shall I fall asleep at the wheel?
47. Who did I just run over?
48. At what speed shall I jump out and live?
49. What's crawling up my leg?
50. Count the miles going by.

### 196. Seven or more reasons for not brushing your teeth

1. It's boring.
2. May erode the enamel.
3. May cause cancer in laboratory rats.
4. May cause tennis elbow.
5. Animals don't and they don't go to dentists.
6. It takes time.
7. Another expense.
8. Tends to wake you up.
9. It's not sexually stimulating.
10. Your teeth may not like being brushed.
11. Your hair may become jealous of the time spent on your teeth—and fall out.
12. Or your teeth may grow hair.
13. You don't have any.
14. You don't want to have any.
15. You have better things to do.
16. You are allergic to toothpaste.
17. You are in love with your dentist.
18. You were frightened by a toothbrush when you were a child.
19. Someone told you false teeth are sexy.
20. You are in love with the tooth fairy.
21. You need the nickel the tooth fairy will bring you.

22. So you don't scratch your teeth.
23. You're allergic to water.
24. You wear dentures.
25. You don't have a mouth.
26. Your breath is naturally sweet.
27. No toothbrush.
28. You're a member of the Crest control group.
29. Save water.
30. Save energy (your own).
31. You prefer using a cloth.
32. You reckon bad breath will frighten your old girlfriend away.
33. You're feeling down in the mouth.
34. You have a toothache.
35. Watch the nice yellow color appear.
36. Save money not buying toothpaste or brush.
37. Brag about the teeth rotting.
38. Chew on the rotting fallen-out teeth.
39. So you can bite on things to loosen bent and ugly teeth.
40. Pay the dentist a lot of nice green money for drilling.
41. So you can go the way of the dentist's office to get high on the gas.
42. Watch the dentist's evil smile when he sees your teeth.

### 197. Seven or more things about yourself not to admit to anybody

1. That you are not so self-confident as you seem.
2. You drink too much.
3. You are afraid.
4. You masturbate.
5. You occasionally have homosexual fantasies.
6. You are impotent.
7. You really don't like people.
8. You are financially overextended.
9. You were born a bastard.
10. You abuse your children.
11. You wear women's clothes at home (if a man).
12. You've joined a lonely hearts club.
13. Your age.
14. Your ambitions.
15. Your fears.
16. Your pet aversions.
17. Your sins.
18. Your vital statistics.
19. Your salary.
20. Your bank balance.
21. Your sexual inclinations.
22. Your religious beliefs.
23. Your real political beliefs.
24. Your racial prejudices.

25. My pre-license driving experience.
26. My experience with a shrink.
27. My camp days.
28. My sophomore year in high school.
29. Christmas, 1976.
30. I'm not perfect.
31. I used to have acne.
32. I am probably not the world's greatest lover.
33. I'm greedy.
34. My teeth are crooked.
35. I lied about my height.
36. You have bad breath.
37. You're a secret lemonade drinker.
38. You take drugs.
39. You've just committed a murder.
40. You're just about to commit a murder.
41. You are a secret agent.
42. You are the President of the United States.
43. That you like toy soldiers at age twenty-five.
44. That you enjoy taking baths in the toilet.
45. That you hate life and want to die.
46. That you are a compulsive nose picker.
47. That you get kicks starting fires all the time.
48. That your dog leaves droppings in the cabinet.

---

198. **Seven or more things to do if you are thirsty but there is nothing to drink**

1. Chew on a stone.
2. Don't spit.
3. Think intently on something else.
4. Suck your thumb.
5. Chew gum.
6. Eat something sour.
7. Keep your mouth closed.
8. Sleep.
9. Take a fast-acting sleeping pill.
10. Eat a watermelon.
11. Go where there is something to drink.
12. Sublimate.
13. Hypnotize yourself into thinking you are not thirsty.
14. Hypnotize yourself into thinking you are drinking.
15. Wrap yourself head-to-toe in Saran wrap to preserve yourself from losing water by sweat.
16. Shoot yourself.
17. Don't think about water.
18. Salivate.
19. Don't eat pretzels.

20. Have sex.
21. Watch TV.
22. Read a book.
23. Keep from talking.
24. Pray for rain.
25. Crush a coconut.
26. Cut open a cactus like they do in the movies.
27. Drink the water out of your radiator.
28. Look for a St. Bernard.
29. Dig a well.
30. Use a divining rod to find water.
31. Fly to Alaska and melt a small glacier.
32. Bite on an ice cube.
33. Eat oranges.
34. Have an apple.
35. Scrape the walls and melt the paint so you can drink it.
36. Drink water out of the toilet bowl.
37. Suck on a leaf.
38. Suck on candy.
39. Chew on branches.

---

199. **Six or more reasons why jogging has become popular**

1. It's purportedly healthy.
2. Fashionable.
3. Chance to meet people.
4. Makes your legs happy.
5. Chance to sweat without working.
6. It's so nice when you stop.
7. You don't need a ticket.
8. You don't have to stand in line.
9. You don't need a partner.
10. There are no age requirements.
11. Requires no skill.
12. Is sexually stimulating.
13. It gets you out of the house.
14. It gets you away from your wife.
15. It gets you away from TV.
16. It gets you away from your kids.
17. It gets you away from housework.
18. It gets you away from homework.
19. It gets you away from washing dishes.
20. It gives you an excuse to chase girls.
21. It gives you an excuse to chase boys.
22. It gives you an excuse to wear dirty old clothes.
23. It gives you an excuse to be too tired to do anything you don't want to do.
24. It gives you something to brag about.
25. It gives you something to

feel superior about.
26. It's fun.
27. It keeps you in shape for other sports.
28. It beats smoking.
29. It's faster than walking.
30. It gives people an opportunity to buy those cute little gym shorts.
31. It's cheap.
32. It can be done in almost any kind of weather.
33. Your parents can't do it.
34. Publicity about health problems—heart disease in particular.
35. More visible than many activities because it's not confined to certain areas, unlike tennis, basketball, etc.
36. Because it's not as fast as running.
37. Because it shakes up your medicine if you forgot to shake the bottle.
38. Because doctors say it's bad for the heart.
39. Because other people do it.
40. Because it's something to do when you've nothing else to waste your time on.
41. Because people like to fall.
42. People are sick of obesity.
43. People are always running from something.
44. So people can act like sportsmen.
45. So others think they are strong.
46. So you get in shape for sleeping.

---

200. **Seven or more things to do if you are lonely and there is no one around**

1. Use the phone.
2. Write letters.
3. Masturbate.
4. Fantasize.
5. Work.
6. Sleep.
7. Get stoned.
8. Tell yourself your life story.
9. Have a little talk with God.
10. Invent an imaginary companion.
11. Think about all the people you would enjoy being with.
12. Think about all the people you would not enjoy being with and be grateful you are not stuck with them.
13. Do all the things you would be embarrassed to do with someone around.
14. Make indecent phone calls.
15. Read about boring parties.
16. Watch a documentary about

urban overcrowding.
17. Write your uncensored memoirs.
18. Write a love letter to someone you wished to were in love with.
19. Write your will.
20. Spend an imaginary fortune before you write your will.
21. Pretend you are a Mafia chieftain and make a "hit list" of all your enemies.
22. Pretend you are Pope.
23. Imagine you are irresistible and have only to lift your finger for the phone to summon anyone you want.
24. Sing.
25. Watch TV.
26. Read a book.
27. Listen to the radio.
28. Talk to yourself.
29. Listen to a record.
30. Play solitaire.
31. Talk to your pets.
32. Talk to your plants.
33. Talk to your house.
34. Go somewhere else.
35. Call the operator.
36. Call up several friends.
37. Crash a party.
38. Visit your neighbour.
39. Call up a "phone-in" programme.
40. Shoot others' windows out.
41. Plant bombs in the bathroom.
42. Do your homework.
43. Chew on a breadstick.
44. Talk to the rug.
45. Exercise.
46. Construct a telephone.
47. Read the Bible.
48. Clean the oven.
49. Take a walk.
50. Call an elderly person and ask if there's anything they need.
51. Clean anything.
52. Go through drawers and closets.
53. Take discards to church.
54. Put scrapbook mementos in scrapbook.
55. Play the piano.
56. Draw or sketch.
57. Shop.
58. Catch up on magazines.

---

201. **Six or more things to do if you are hungry, but there is nothing to eat**

1. Cook.
2. Go to a restaurant.
3. Invite yourself over to a friend's for a meal.
4. Call a friend on the phone.
5. Read.

129

6. Sleep.
7. Listen to music.
8. Drink water.
9. Exercise.
10. Go to supermarket.
11. Watch TV.
12. Listen to radio.
13. Mow grass.
14. Build snowman.
15. Clean refrigerator.
16. Clean oven.
17. Clean house.
18. Write a book.
19. Write letters.
20. Bird watch.
21. Star gaze.
22. Paint a picture.
23. Paint the house.
24. Brush the cat.
25. Go for a drive.
26. Go skiing.
27. Go shopping.
28. Go window shopping.
29. File nails.
30. Wash hair.
31. Take a bath.
32. Rake leaves.
33. Do needlework.
34. Knit.
35. Sew.
36. Dance.
37. Sing.
38. Play musical instrument.
39. Visit friends.
40. Pray.
41. Go to church.
42. Take photographs.
43. Fix car.
44. Swim.
45. Hang pictures.
46. Water plants.
47. Wax floors.
48. Do laundry.
49. Iron.
50. Ride a bicycle.
51. Ride a horse.
52. Sharpen pencils.
53. Wind clocks.
54. Inventory your possessions.
55. Fantasize.
56. Play games.
57. Shave.
58. Cut hair.
59. Manicure.
60. Pedicure.
61. Get a tattoo.
62. Whistle.
63. Plan a trip.
64. Garden.
65. Wash the dog.
66. Plan a menu.
67. Exercise.
68. Work puzzles.
69. Go to sleep.
70. Engage in controversy.
71. Build or repair something.
72. Chain smoke until you feel unwell.
73. Go for a long drive.
74. Try to obtain food by fishing or hunting.

75. Chew anything chewable.
76. Try to eat things not usually considered food—that is, get *something* into your stomach.
77. Eat things (e.g., tobacco) likely to make you sick.
78. Swallow paper and then drink water or something else to make it swell.
79. Do something painful.
80. Do something sexual.
81. Make rhyming poetry or verse or limericks.
82. Practice self-hypnosis to kill hunger pangs.
83. Meditate.
84. Try to remember lyrics to old songs.
85. Use the telephone to order food.
86. Smoke pot.
87. Get drunk.
88. Take uppers.
89. Take downers.
90. Do yoga breathing exercises.
91. Bake some cookies.
92. Go see your parents.
93. Check the strawberry patch.
94. Ride a bike.
95. Run a mile.
96. Think about food.
97. Take your mind off of being hungry.
98. Suck on some pebbles.
99. Suffer with the hunger.
100. Ignore the hunger until it passes.

---

### 202. Seven or more reasons for having bar stools

1. To sit on.
2. As interior decoration.
3. As conversation piece.
4. As an excuse for having a bar.
5. To make a room look less empty.
6. To impress friends.
7. To make people feel taller.
8. To use as a step stool.
9. To use in barroom brawls.
10. As a prop for posing art subjects.
11. They were on sale.
12. To fall off.
13. To use, with a crosspiece, as table legs.
14. To use as spare chairs.
15. To use as small tables.
16. To use as room dividers.
17. To use as saw horses.
18. For children to use as playhouses.
19. To furnish a barroom.
20. To train animals (lion tamers' use of chair).
21. To use in conjunction with model railroads and toy racing car sets.
22. To use as seats at a work or lab bench.
23. Shorten legs and use as seats and/or tables for children.
24. Turn upside down and use as umbrella stand.
25. Wire together (or tie) and use as playpen.
26. Use as TV stand.
27. Use as easily portable stands for stereo speakers, microphones, lights for still and moving pictures, projectors.
28. To use in B&D sexual activity.
29. So that you can't lean back on it.
30. More comfortable than standing.
31. They look nice.
32. Better to drink sitting.
33. They're fun to spin around in.
34. They take up space in front of the bar.
35. So short people can reach the bar.
36. So tall people don't have to bend down to the bar.
37. To steady a wobbly butt.
38. To swivel around on.
39. To feel like you are in the bartender's psychological realm.
40. To put a plant on.
41. To give height for a child to sit at a table.
42. To stand on to change a light bulb.

---

### 203. Eight or more ways you can prove that you are smart

1. I.Q. tests.
2. Educational degrees.
3. Games of skill.
4. Memberships in groups like Mensa.
5. Shopping for the lowest prices without compromising quality.
6. Holding intelligent conversations with specialists in different subjects.
7. By moderation in the use of drugs.
8. By eating a balanced diet.
9. Organising time wisely.
10. Making money from creative efforts.
11. Never throwing away anything that might be of value.
12. Living life fully.
13. Not letting others run my life.

14. Being skeptical unless provided with ample proof.
15. Thinking things out for myself.
16. Cultivating good connections.
17. Wise investments.
18. Consulting experts when necessary.
19. By not watching too much TV.
20. By taking advantage of unexpected opportunities.
21. By doing as little work as possible.
22. Avoiding excess responsibility.
23. Keeping your mouth shut on subjects about which you are ignorant.
24. Not overstaying welcome.
25. Employing foodtaster.
26. Buying insurance.
27. Writing a will early.
28. Being tactful.
29. Keep up with broad areas of knowledge.
30. Keeping an open mind.
31. Fail (score low) on an I.Q. test on purpose.
32. Consistently solve problems that have stumped others in your peer group.
33. Devise new and easier ways of doing established routine tasks.
34. Be accepted as one of a group of known intellectuals.
35. Keep insisting you're stupid.
36. Limit your associates to those who are less intelligent than you are.
37. In public, do only what you can do well.
38. Devise a workable plan to convince others that you're smart.
39. Know your limits and never exceed them.
40. Let others do it for you.
41. Offer but refuse to execute ingenious ideas.
42. Look at a report card.
43. Ask a teacher.
44. Ask your mother.
45. Get the principal's recommendation.
46. Make the dean's list.
47. Solve an equation.
48. Exam scores.
49. School grades.
50. Enter an elite profession.
51. How much money you have.
52. Place of residence.
53. The intelligence of your friends.
54. The intelligence of your parents/children.
55. Listen.
56. Publish written works.
57. Speak or lecture to a group in your major field.

58. Display common sense.
59. Be rational—cool and calm.
60. Be in an administrative position.
61. Invent something.

---

204. **Seven or more ways to get a waitress's attention**

---

1. Snap fingers.
2. Call out,"Miss!"
3. Call out, "Ma'am!"
4. Call out, "Excuse me!"
5. Drop utensil.
6. Drop dish.
7. Walk up to her.
8. Do something unconventional, like undressing.
9. Tap on glass.
10. Bang on table.
11. Shout, "Hey you!"
12. Ask maître d' to get waitress.
13. Ask busboy to get waitress.
14. Whistle.
15. Scream, "There's a fly in my soup!"
16. Dance on the table.
17. Throw something at her.
18. Call out, "Waitress!"
19. Trip her.
20. Bar her way.
21. Wave money in her face.
22. Pinch her.
23. Snap her rear.
24. Grab her.
25. Talk loudly.
26. Spill something.
27. Clap hands.
28. Hiss (as in Latin America).
29. Tap fork on plate.
30. Wave menu.
31. Stand up and wave or signal with hand or menu.
32. Start to leave without getting check or paying bill.
33. Start altercation with neighboring table.
34. Tell busboy you want to see manager.
35. Start toward kitchen with menu in hand.
36. Throw hard roll.
37. Discuss her appearance so she can just catch some of what you say.
38. Sit on table.
39. Obstruct service-way between tables.
40. Seat pet at table with napkin around neck.
41. Walk to waitress and ask if this is a self-service restaurant.
42. Bring loud bell (electric) to table and let it ring (e.g., alarm clock).
43. Shine flashlight in her face.
44. Knock over a glass of water.
45. Throw a temper tantrum.
46. Knock over your table.
47. Cough loudly and have your friend summon waitress for water.
48. Put your head on your place setting and don't move.
49. Feign a faint.
50. Feign a convulsive attack.

---

205. **Seven or more ways to strike up a conversation with a farmer**

---

1. Talk about weather.
2. Talk about government price supports.
3. Mention inflation.
4. Ask him what he raises.
5. Talk about the price of gasoline.
6. Mention taxes.
7. Compliment him on crops or livestock.
8. Ask him for road directions.
9. Ask him about pests.
10. Talk about the "simple life."
11. Ask his advice on growing things or raising livestock.
12. Ask how his crops or livestock are doing this year.
13. Ask if rain will hurt the rhubarb.
14. Ask any stupid question about a farm.
15. Ask for any information within his presumed field of knowledge.
16. Ask why food prices are so high.
17. Inquire as to price of land.
18. Praise or condemn government farm policies.
19. Ask about local politics.
20. Discuss labor situation.
21. Discuss migrant labor living conditions.
22. Discuss unicorns.
23. Discuss animal husbandry.
24. Ask why he is a farmer.
25. Ask about eating places in nearest town.
26. Ask him to explain rationale behind farm subsidies— especially payment for *not* planting.
27. Ask if he believes in something for nothing.
28. Talk about tractors.
29. Ask to use his phone.
30. Break into his house.
31. Drive through his house.
32. Burn his fields.
33. Shoot his livestock.
34. Cross-pollinate your crops with his.
35. Run a tractor through his barn.
36. Burn down his grain silo.
37. Send your rooster into his hen house.
38. Knock down his fence.
39. Sell him a tractor.
40. Buy a cow from him.
41. Attend the same church.
42. Ask him where he purchased his overalls.
43. Ask a question about how rain (or lack of it) is affecting his crops.
44. Pay attention to his spouse.
45. Just walk up and say "hi."

---

206. **Six or more reasons why some people are afraid to ride a roller coaster**

---

1. Dizziness.
2. Nausea.
3. Falling off.
4. High speed.
5. Sudden turns.
6. Lack of control over own movements.
7. Fear of accident.
8. Fear of heights.
9. Seems childish.
10. Inability to breathe while wind is rushing into one's face.
11. Rubber knees.
12. Fear of flying.
13. Gives them bad dreams.
14. Have no control over the machine.
15. Don't like being locked in.
16. Don't like noise.
17. Don't like to show distress before others.
18. Feel such a ride is catering to a death wish.
19. Fear of appearing afraid.
20. Fear of incontinence.
21. Fear of loss of face.
22. Fear of loss of dignity.
23. Fear of appearing foolish.
24. Fear of hysteria.
25. Fear of fear.
26. Hate going up and down.
27. Do not like riding in anything.
28. Do not like returning to the place that they started from.
29. Lose your last meal.
30. Have persons sitting around you lose their meal.
31. The coaster car jumping off its track.
32. They may faint.
33. Friend or spouse may suffer circulation difficulties from you holding on too tight.
34. Wig may fall off.
35. May lose valuables.
36. May become hoarse from screaming.
37. May have a heart attack.

---

207. **Six or more famous people who have never been on television**

---

1. George Washington.
2. Richard Strauss.
3. Julius Caesar.
4. Archimedes.
5. James Monroe.
6. A representative of the silent majority.
7. Andrew Jackson.
8. Franklin Pierce.
9. Abraham Lincoln.
10. Ulysses S. Grant.
11. Andrew Johnson.
12. General Burgoyne.
13. Le Marquis de Lafayette.
14. John Alden.
15. Miles Standish.
16. Betsy Ross.
17. Thomas Paine.
18. Alexander Hamilton.
19. Benjamin Franklin.
20. Aaron Burr.
21. Queen Victoria.
22. Peter the Great.
23. Tutankhamen.
24. Anne Boleyn.
25. John Milton.
26. William Shakespeare.
27. Miguel de Cervantes.
28. Dante Alighieri.
29. Henry Fielding.
30. Daniel Defoe.
31. Jonathan Swift.
32. H. G. Wells.
33. Anonymous.
34. Victor Hugo.
35. Alexandre Dumas.
36. Daniel Boone.
37. Davy Crockett.
38. Jesus of Nazareth.
39. Saint Paul.
40. Aristotle.
41. Marquis de Sade.
42. Louis XVI.
43. Marie Antoinette.
44. Charles Dickens.
45. Benjamin Disraeli.
46. Patrick Henry.
47. Rudyard Kipling.
48. Mark Twain.

---

208. **Seven or more famous people whose initials are "A" and/or "T"**

---

1. Arnold Toynbee.
2. Alvin Toffler.
3. Alfred Lord Tennyson.
4. Alice B. Toklas.
5. Arturo Toscanini.
6. Arthur Treacher.
7. Ann Todd.
8. Akim Tamiroff.
9. Alan Arkin.

10. Arthur Ashe.
11. Agnes Ayres.
12. Tiny Tim.
13. Tom Tryon.
14. Thomas Tallis.
15. Alan Alda.

### 209. Six or more ways to look at yourself in the mirror

1. Straight on.
2. Indirectly, using other mirrors.
3. Sideways.
4. Upside down.
5. Cross-eyed.
6. Through a camera.
7. Dressed.
8. Undressed.
9. With makeup.
10. Without makeup.
11. With someone else.
12. Alone.
13. With pleasure.
14. With discipline.
15. While dressing.
16. While applying makeup.
17. With suspicion.
18. To see if I'm sick.
19. To check my teeth.
20. To check my skin.
21. While doing my hair.
22. To check for gray hairs.
23. Various types clothing.
24. Sober.
25. Drunk.
26. When you first get up (still sleepy).
27. Just before bed (sleepy).
28. Smiling.
29. Scowling.
30. Laughing.
31. Angry.
32. Surprised.
33. Critically.
34. Smugly.
35. Full face.
36. In profile.
37. From behind.
38. Various costumes (clown, pirate, etc.).
39. Sneak glance.
40. Long study.

41. Making love.
42. Exercising.
43. Shaving.
44. With disgust.
45. With a funny face.
46. In a funny suit.
47. Lying down.
48. Stand on head and turn head to the right.
49. Perform yoga "fish" position and look.

### 210. Seven or more ways to go to sleep when you are not tired

1. Sleeping pills.
2. Warm drink.
3. Liquor.
4. Read a boring book.
5. Watch a boring TV show.
6. Put on relaxing music.
7. Hypnosis.
8. Force of will.
9. Overheat room.
10. Turn out lights.
11. Take a warm bath.
12. Get drunk.
13. Relax totally.
14. Lie down in small warm room with poor ventilation.
15. Read a book printed in the 1800s.
16. Get tired.
17. Lie in bed.
18. Inhale chloroform.
19. Hit yourself with a hammer.
20. Fall down the stairs.
21. Jump out the window.
22. Shoot yourself.
23. Watch Johnny Carson.
24. Make love excessively.
25. Do 100 push-ups.
26. Take a hot shower.
27. Do yoga breathing exercises.
28. Count sheep.
29. Count number of specks in ceiling.

### 211. Seven or more ways to prevent shoplifting

1. "Fish-eye" mirrors.
2. Cameras.
3. Security guards.
4. Tight security at exits.
5. Behavior modification.
6. Fines.
7. Public ostracism.
8. Public censure.
9. Public corporal punishment.
10. Public humiliation.
11. Have enough personnel to wait on customers instead of using self-service.
12. Fasten all display goods to counter or rack.
13. Have customers wear mittens that can only be removed by store personnel.
14. Have customers wear jump suits without pockets and fastened by zippers that can only be unfastened by store personnel.
15. Have all portable merchandise in glass cases to which only store personnel have key.
16. Conduct random spot searches of customers throughout store and at checkout or exits.
17. Notify customers that portable display merchandise is mildly radioactive—only harmful over a period of time—say two or three days—or if ingested.
18. Notify customers that merchandise on display is unsaleable because it is defective.
19. Establish a shop policy that any customer or employee who reports a shoplifter will be paid one-half the sales price of the goods recovered and that all apprehended shoplifters will be charged and prosecuted.
20. Don't have any merchandise worth shoplifting.

21. Only have nonportable merchandise.
22. Go out of business.
23. Give away products.
24. Watch everyone.
25. Don't open store.
26. Lock up the most valuable merchandise.
27. Label all articles with coded tape that activates a beeping device in all store exits.
28. Have small items on counter closely watched by salespeople.
29. Put valuables under glass.

### 212. Seven or more reasons why a bee sting hurts

1. Skin is broken.
2. Barbs in skin.
3. Expectation.
4. Blood rushes to it.
5. To warn body of foreign matter invading.
6. Affects nervous system.
7. Swelling.
8. Fear of bee sting.
9. Penetration of skin by stinger.
10. Because the bee wants it to.
11. The purpose of the sting is protective, hence it's designed to hurt.
12. The human system is allergic to bee venom.
13. To make us appreciate honey more.
14. To protect the beehive from aliens.
15. To protect the queen and larvae within the hive.
16. Bees are unsociable and wish to hurt intruders.
17. Bees don't like interference.
18. Bees are sadists and like to inflict pain.
19. What good would it be if it didn't hurt?
20. Bee was moving fast.
21. Allergic to honey.
22. Sensitive skin.
23. Bee is mad.

# AUGUST

Mental Calisthenic #8

Sit quietly in an area free of noise and distractions. Keep your eyes open. Multiply 11 × 14 in your head. What is the answer? Now subtract 6 from 200, then 6 from 194, etc., until you reach 0. Now multiply 189 × 567 in your head. What is the answer? During these calculations did you look right or left? Proceed with a Mental Jogging exercise.

## 213. Seven or more reasons to fake fainting

| Response | Score |
|---|---|
| 1. | 1 |
| 2. | 1 |
| 3. | 1 |
| 4. | 1 |
| 5. | 1 |
| 6. | 1 |
| 7. | 1 |

Bonus Responses

| | |
|---|---|
| 8. | 2 |
| 9. | 2 |
| 10. | 2 |
| 11. | 2 |
| 12. | 2 |
| 13. | 2 |
| 14. | 2 |
| 15. | 2 |
| 16. | 2 |

Total ☐

## 214. Six or more reasons why someone would want to become President of the United States

| Response | Score |
|---|---|
| 1. | 1 |
| 2. | 1 |
| 3. | 1 |
| 4. | 1 |
| 5. | 1 |
| 6. | 1 |

Bonus Responses

| | |
|---|---|
| 7. | 2 |
| 8. | 2 |
| 9. | 2 |
| 10. | 2 |
| 11. | 2 |
| 12. | 2 |
| 13. | 2 |
| 14. | 2 |
| 15. | 2 |
| 16. | 2 |

Total ☐

## 215. Six or more reasons for inflation

| Response | Score |
|---|---|
| 1. _____ | 1 |
| 2. _____ | 1 |
| 3. _____ | 1 |
| 4. _____ | 1 |
| 5. _____ | 1 |
| 6. _____ | 1 |

**Bonus Responses**

| | |
|---|---|
| 7. _____ | 2 |
| 8. _____ | 2 |
| 9. _____ | 2 |
| 10. _____ | 2 |
| 11. _____ | 2 |
| 12. _____ | 2 |
| 13. _____ | 2 |
| 14. _____ | 2 |
| 15. _____ | 2 |
| 16. _____ | 2 |

Total ☐

## 216. Seven or more ways to get a bus driver's attention

| Response | Score |
|---|---|
| 1. _____ | 1 |
| 2. _____ | 1 |
| 3. _____ | 1 |
| 4. _____ | 1 |
| 5. _____ | 1 |
| 6. _____ | 1 |
| 7. _____ | 1 |

**Bonus Responses**

| | |
|---|---|
| 8. _____ | 2 |
| 9. _____ | 2 |
| 10. _____ | 2 |
| 11. _____ | 2 |
| 12. _____ | 2 |
| 13. _____ | 2 |
| 14. _____ | 2 |
| 15. _____ | 2 |
| 16. _____ | 2 |

Total ☐

## 217. Seven or more ways to make yourself less attractive

| Response | Score |
|---|---|
| 1. _____ | 1 |
| 2. _____ | 1 |
| 3. _____ | 1 |
| 4. _____ | 1 |
| 5. _____ | 1 |
| 6. _____ | 1 |
| 7. _____ | 1 |

**Bonus Responses**

| | |
|---|---|
| 8. _____ | 2 |
| 9. _____ | 2 |
| 10. _____ | 2 |
| 11. _____ | 2 |
| 12. _____ | 2 |
| 13. _____ | 2 |
| 14. _____ | 2 |
| 15. _____ | 2 |
| 16. _____ | 2 |

Total ☐

## 218. Eight or more ways to make yourself physically stronger

| Response | Score |
|---|---|
| 1. _____ | 1 |
| 2. _____ | 1 |
| 3. _____ | 1 |
| 4. _____ | 1 |
| 5. _____ | 1 |
| 6. _____ | 1 |
| 7. _____ | 1 |
| 8. _____ | 1 |

**Bonus Responses**

| | |
|---|---|
| 9. _____ | 2 |
| 10. _____ | 2 |
| 11. _____ | 2 |
| 12. _____ | 2 |
| 13. _____ | 2 |
| 14. _____ | 2 |
| 15. _____ | 2 |
| 16. _____ | 2 |

Total ☐

## 219. Six or more things you've always wanted to say to your mother-in-law

| Response | Score |
|---|---|
| 1. _____ | 1 |
| 2. _____ | 1 |
| 3. _____ | 1 |
| 4. _____ | 1 |
| 5. _____ | 1 |
| 6. _____ | 1 |

Bonus Responses

| | |
|---|---|
| 7. _____ | 2 |
| 8. _____ | 2 |
| 9. _____ | 2 |
| 10. _____ | 2 |
| 11. _____ | 2 |
| 12. _____ | 2 |
| 13. _____ | 2 |
| 14. _____ | 2 |
| 15. _____ | 2 |
| 16. _____ | 2 |

Total ☐

## 220. Six or more reasons why fish don't talk

| Response | Score |
|---|---|
| 1. _____ | 1 |
| 2. _____ | 1 |
| 3. _____ | 1 |
| 4. _____ | 1 |
| 5. _____ | 1 |
| 6. _____ | 1 |

Bonus Responses

| | |
|---|---|
| 7. _____ | 2 |
| 8. _____ | 2 |
| 9. _____ | 2 |
| 10. _____ | 2 |
| 11. _____ | 2 |
| 12. _____ | 2 |
| 13. _____ | 2 |
| 14. _____ | 2 |
| 15. _____ | 2 |
| 16. _____ | 2 |

Total ☐

## 221. Nine or more reasons why some married women prefer to be called "Ms."

| Response | Score |
|---|---|
| 1. _____ | 1 |
| 2. _____ | 1 |
| 3. _____ | 1 |
| 4. _____ | 1 |
| 5. _____ | 1 |
| 6. _____ | 1 |
| 7. _____ | 1 |
| 8. _____ | 1 |
| 9. _____ | 1 |

Bonus Responses

| | |
|---|---|
| 10. _____ | 2 |
| 11. _____ | 2 |
| 12. _____ | 2 |
| 13. _____ | 2 |
| 14. _____ | 2 |
| 15. _____ | 2 |
| 16. _____ | 2 |

Total ☐

## 222. Six or more reasons not to pluck feathers from a chicken

| Response | Score |
|---|---|
| 1. _____ | 1 |
| 2. _____ | 1 |
| 3. _____ | 1 |
| 4. _____ | 1 |
| 5. _____ | 1 |
| 6. _____ | 1 |

Bonus Responses

| | |
|---|---|
| 7. _____ | 2 |
| 8. _____ | 2 |
| 9. _____ | 2 |
| 10. _____ | 2 |
| 11. _____ | 2 |
| 12. _____ | 2 |
| 13. _____ | 2 |
| 14. _____ | 2 |
| 15. _____ | 2 |
| 16. _____ | 2 |

Total ☐

## 223. Seven or more reasons for not wearing a tie

| Response | Score |
|---|---|
| 1. _____ | 1 |
| 2. _____ | 1 |
| 3. _____ | 1 |
| 4. _____ | 1 |
| 5. _____ | 1 |
| 6. _____ | 1 |
| 7. _____ | 1 |

**Bonus Responses**

| | |
|---|---|
| 8. _____ | 2 |
| 9. _____ | 2 |
| 10. _____ | 2 |
| 11. _____ | 2 |
| 12. _____ | 2 |
| 13. _____ | 2 |
| 14. _____ | 2 |
| 15. _____ | 2 |
| 16. _____ | 2 |

Total ☐

## 224. Six or more reasons why some restaurants are more popular than others

| Response | Score |
|---|---|
| 1. _____ | 1 |
| 2. _____ | 1 |
| 3. _____ | 1 |
| 4. _____ | 1 |
| 5. _____ | 1 |
| 6. _____ | 1 |

**Bonus Responses**

| | |
|---|---|
| 7. _____ | 2 |
| 8. _____ | 2 |
| 9. _____ | 2 |
| 10. _____ | 2 |
| 11. _____ | 2 |
| 12. _____ | 2 |
| 13. _____ | 2 |
| 14. _____ | 2 |
| 15. _____ | 2 |
| 16. _____ | 2 |

Total ☐

## 225. Eight or more words in any language spelled the same backwards as forwards

| Response | Score |
|---|---|
| 1. _____ | 1 |
| 2. _____ | 1 |
| 3. _____ | 1 |
| 4. _____ | 1 |
| 5. _____ | 1 |
| 6. _____ | 1 |
| 7. _____ | 1 |
| 8. _____ | 1 |

**Bonus Responses**

| | |
|---|---|
| 9. _____ | 2 |
| 10. _____ | 2 |
| 11. _____ | 2 |
| 12. _____ | 2 |
| 13. _____ | 2 |
| 14. _____ | 2 |
| 15. _____ | 2 |
| 16. _____ | 2 |

Total ☐

## 226. Seven or more reasons for not visiting a physician

| Response | Score |
|---|---|
| 1. _____ | 1 |
| 2. _____ | 1 |
| 3. _____ | 1 |
| 4. _____ | 1 |
| 5. _____ | 1 |
| 6. _____ | 1 |
| 7. _____ | 1 |

**Bonus Responses**

| | |
|---|---|
| 8. _____ | 2 |
| 9. _____ | 2 |
| 10. _____ | 2 |
| 11. _____ | 2 |
| 12. _____ | 2 |
| 13. _____ | 2 |
| 14. _____ | 2 |
| 15. _____ | 2 |
| 16. _____ | 2 |

Total ☐

## 227. Six or more consequences of doing away with waiting rooms

| Response | Score |
|---|---|
| 1. _____ | 1 |
| 2. _____ | 1 |
| 3. _____ | 1 |
| 4. _____ | 1 |
| 5. _____ | 1 |
| 6. _____ | 1 |

**Bonus Responses**

| | |
|---|---|
| 7. _____ | 2 |
| 8. _____ | 2 |
| 9. _____ | 2 |
| 10. _____ | 2 |
| 11. _____ | 2 |
| 12. _____ | 2 |
| 13. _____ | 2 |
| 14. _____ | 2 |
| 15. _____ | 2 |
| 16. _____ | 2 |

Total ☐

## 228. Seven or more reasons why church bells are allowed to chime at all hours of the night

| Response | Score |
|---|---|
| 1. _____ | 1 |
| 2. _____ | 1 |
| 3. _____ | 1 |
| 4. _____ | 1 |
| 5. _____ | 1 |
| 6. _____ | 1 |
| 7. _____ | 1 |

**Bonus Responses**

| | |
|---|---|
| 8. _____ | 2 |
| 9. _____ | 2 |
| 10. _____ | 2 |
| 11. _____ | 2 |
| 12. _____ | 2 |
| 13. _____ | 2 |
| 14. _____ | 2 |
| 15. _____ | 2 |
| 16. _____ | 2 |

Total ☐

## 229. Seven or more reasons for being turned down for a bank loan

| Response | Score |
|---|---|
| 1. _____ | 1 |
| 2. _____ | 1 |
| 3. _____ | 1 |
| 4. _____ | 1 |
| 5. _____ | 1 |
| 6. _____ | 1 |
| 7. _____ | 1 |

**Bonus Responses**

| | |
|---|---|
| 8. _____ | 2 |
| 9. _____ | 2 |
| 10. _____ | 2 |
| 11. _____ | 2 |
| 12. _____ | 2 |
| 13. _____ | 2 |
| 14. _____ | 2 |
| 15. _____ | 2 |
| 16. _____ | 2 |

Total ☐

## 230. Six or more reasons why titles are not important

| Response | Score |
|---|---|
| 1. _____ | 1 |
| 2. _____ | 1 |
| 3. _____ | 1 |
| 4. _____ | 1 |
| 5. _____ | 1 |
| 6. _____ | 1 |

**Bonus Responses**

| | |
|---|---|
| 7. _____ | 2 |
| 8. _____ | 2 |
| 9. _____ | 2 |
| 10. _____ | 2 |
| 11. _____ | 2 |
| 12. _____ | 2 |
| 13. _____ | 2 |
| 14. _____ | 2 |
| 15. _____ | 2 |
| 16. _____ | 2 |

Total ☐

## 231. Six or more reasons why some children become scared at night

| Response | Score |
|---|---|
| 1. | 1 |
| 2. | 1 |
| 3. | 1 |
| 4. | 1 |
| 5. | 1 |
| 6. | 1 |

**Bonus Responses**

| | |
|---|---|
| 7. | 2 |
| 8. | 2 |
| 9. | 2 |
| 10. | 2 |
| 11. | 2 |
| 12. | 2 |
| 13. | 2 |
| 14. | 2 |
| 15. | 2 |
| 16. | 2 |

Total ☐

## 232. Seven or more ways to keep a license plate clean

| Response | Score |
|---|---|
| 1. | 1 |
| 2. | 1 |
| 3. | 1 |
| 4. | 1 |
| 5. | 1 |
| 6. | 1 |
| 7. | 1 |

**Bonus Responses**

| | |
|---|---|
| 8. | 2 |
| 9. | 2 |
| 10. | 2 |
| 11. | 2 |
| 12. | 2 |
| 13. | 2 |
| 14. | 2 |
| 15. | 2 |
| 16. | 2 |

Total ☐

## 233. Eight or more ways to tell whether your car brake lights are on

| Response | Score |
|---|---|
| 1. | 1 |
| 2. | 1 |
| 3. | 1 |
| 4. | 1 |
| 5. | 1 |
| 6. | 1 |
| 7. | 1 |
| 8. | 1 |

**Bonus Responses**

| | |
|---|---|
| 9. | 2 |
| 10. | 2 |
| 11. | 2 |
| 12. | 2 |
| 13. | 2 |
| 14. | 2 |
| 15. | 2 |
| 16. | 2 |

Total ☐

## 234. Six or more reasons why *Roots* was the most popular TV show of its day

| Response | Score |
|---|---|
| 1. | 1 |
| 2. | 1 |
| 3. | 1 |
| 4. | 1 |
| 5. | 1 |
| 6. | 1 |

**Bonus Responses**

| | |
|---|---|
| 7. | 2 |
| 8. | 2 |
| 9. | 2 |
| 10. | 2 |
| 11. | 2 |
| 12. | 2 |
| 13. | 2 |
| 14. | 2 |
| 15. | 2 |
| 16. | 2 |

Total ☐

## 235. Seven or more reasons for not watching daytime TV

| Response | Score |
|---|---|
| 1. | 1 |
| 2. | 1 |
| 3. | 1 |
| 4. | 1 |
| 5. | 1 |
| 6. | 1 |
| 7. | 1 |

Bonus Responses

| | |
|---|---|
| 8. | 2 |
| 9. | 2 |
| 10. | 2 |
| 11. | 2 |
| 12. | 2 |
| 13. | 2 |
| 14. | 2 |
| 15. | 2 |
| 16. | 2 |

Total ☐

## 236. Six or more reasons for not having a telephone answering service

| Response | Score |
|---|---|
| 1. | 1 |
| 2. | 1 |
| 3. | 1 |
| 4. | 1 |
| 5. | 1 |
| 6. | 1 |

Bonus Responses

| | |
|---|---|
| 7. | 2 |
| 8. | 2 |
| 9. | 2 |
| 10. | 2 |
| 11. | 2 |
| 12. | 2 |
| 13. | 2 |
| 14. | 2 |
| 15. | 2 |
| 16. | 2 |

Total ☐

## 237. Eight or more reasons not to chlorinate a YMCA swimming pool

| Response | Score |
|---|---|
| 1. | 1 |
| 2. | 1 |
| 3. | 1 |
| 4. | 1 |
| 5. | 1 |
| 6. | 1 |
| 7. | 1 |
| 8. | 1 |

Bonus Responses

| | |
|---|---|
| 9. | 2 |
| 10. | 2 |
| 11. | 2 |
| 12. | 2 |
| 13. | 2 |
| 14. | 2 |
| 15. | 2 |
| 16. | 2 |

Total ☐

## 238. Six or more reasons why some newspapers do not publish on Saturday

| Response | Score |
|---|---|
| 1. | 1 |
| 2. | 1 |
| 3. | 1 |
| 4. | 1 |
| 5. | 1 |
| 6. | 1 |

Bonus Responses

| | |
|---|---|
| 7. | 2 |
| 8. | 2 |
| 9. | 2 |
| 10. | 2 |
| 11. | 2 |
| 12. | 2 |
| 13. | 2 |
| 14. | 2 |
| 15. | 2 |
| 16. | 2 |

Total ☐

## 239. Eight or more reasons for not subscribing to *The Wall Street Journal*

| Response | Score |
|---|---|
| 1. _____ | 1 |
| 2. _____ | 1 |
| 3. _____ | 1 |
| 4. _____ | 1 |
| 5. _____ | 1 |
| 6. _____ | 1 |
| 7. _____ | 1 |
| 8. _____ | 1 |

Bonus Responses

| | |
|---|---|
| 9. _____ | 2 |
| 10. _____ | 2 |
| 11. _____ | 2 |
| 12. _____ | 2 |
| 13. _____ | 2 |
| 14. _____ | 2 |
| 15. _____ | 2 |
| 16. _____ | 2 |

Total ☐

## 240. Seven or more reasons for desk blotters

| Response | Score |
|---|---|
| 1. _____ | 1 |
| 2. _____ | 1 |
| 3. _____ | 1 |
| 4. _____ | 1 |
| 5. _____ | 1 |
| 6. _____ | 1 |
| 7. _____ | 1 |

Bonus Responses

| | |
|---|---|
| 8. _____ | 2 |
| 9. _____ | 2 |
| 10. _____ | 2 |
| 11. _____ | 2 |
| 12. _____ | 2 |
| 13. _____ | 2 |
| 14. _____ | 2 |
| 15. _____ | 2 |
| 16. _____ | 2 |

Total ☐

## 241. Six or more reasons why there were not more signers of the Declaration of Independence

| Response | Score |
|---|---|
| 1. _____ | 1 |
| 2. _____ | 1 |
| 3. _____ | 1 |
| 4. _____ | 1 |
| 5. _____ | 1 |
| 6. _____ | 1 |

Bonus Responses

| | |
|---|---|
| 7. _____ | 2 |
| 8. _____ | 2 |
| 9. _____ | 2 |
| 10. _____ | 2 |
| 11. _____ | 2 |
| 12. _____ | 2 |
| 13. _____ | 2 |
| 14. _____ | 2 |
| 15. _____ | 2 |
| 16. _____ | 2 |

Total ☐

## 242. Six or more reasons for not having leap year

| Response | Score |
|---|---|
| 1. _____ | 1 |
| 2. _____ | 1 |
| 3. _____ | 1 |
| 4. _____ | 1 |
| 5. _____ | 1 |
| 6. _____ | 1 |

Bonus Responses

| | |
|---|---|
| 7. _____ | 2 |
| 8. _____ | 2 |
| 9. _____ | 2 |
| 10. _____ | 2 |
| 11. _____ | 2 |
| 12. _____ | 2 |
| 13. _____ | 2 |
| 14. _____ | 2 |
| 15. _____ | 2 |
| 16. _____ | 2 |

Total ☐

## 243. Seven or more reasons why most people prefer freshly brewed instead of instant coffee

| Response | Score |
|---|---|
| 1. _____ | 1 |
| 2. _____ | 1 |
| 3. _____ | 1 |
| 4. _____ | 1 |
| 5. _____ | 1 |
| 6. _____ | 1 |
| 7. _____ | 1 |

**Bonus Responses**

| | |
|---|---|
| 8. _____ | 2 |
| 9. _____ | 2 |
| 10. _____ | 2 |
| 11. _____ | 2 |
| 12. _____ | 2 |
| 13. _____ | 2 |
| 14. _____ | 2 |
| 15. _____ | 2 |
| 16. _____ | 2 |

Total ☐

# CONTRIBUTORS' SAMPLE RESPONSES

### 213. Seven or more reasons to fake fainting

1. To eavesdrop on conversations.
2. To get out of working.
3. To get out of an unpleasant social situation.
4. To get attention.
5. In order to be pampered.
6. To create a disturbance.
7. For a play.
8. To pose for an artist.
9. For a movie.
10. As a decoy.
11. To gain sympathy.
12. To get out of playing charades.
13. To feign illness for any reason.
14. To pretend shock.
15. To get one's way.
16. To gain a favor.
17. To make others sorry for something done or not done.
18. Because you're tired of waiting at the clinic or doctor's office.
19. Because you're tired of standing up.
20. Because you like smelling salts.
21. Because you want a drink.
22. Get out of class.
23. To ride in an ambulance.
24. To see the nurse.
25. To see a doctor.
26. Burglar approaches you.
27. To get a waitress's attention.
28. To get to the front of a line.
29. Hearing that someone you don't like has passed away.
30. You catch your spouse in the act of adultery.
31. A bill collector approaches you.

### 214. Six or more reasons why someone would want to become President of the United States

1. To meet other famous people.
2. So wife will be First Lady.
3. To be first woman President.
4. To be first black President.
5. To be first atheist President.
6. To be first Oriental President.
7. To be first Libertarian President.
8. Power.
9. Salary.
10. Perquisites.
11. Retirement benefits.
12. Honor.
13. Fame.
14. Travel.
15. Get even with enemies.
16. Do favors for friends.
17. Boost one's ego.
18. Rob the public (taxpayer) blind.
19. Make one's fortune—aside from salary and allowances.
20. Indulge one's hobbies.
21. Direct the country's destiny.
22. Interfere in the government of other countries.
23. Throw one's weight around.
24. Get TV and radio time on demand.
25. Entertain in White House.
26. Have airplane #U.S.1 at personal disposition.
27. Become elder statesman.
28. Possibly do something beneficial for country.
29. Enjoy pomp and circumstance—both music and fact.
30. Live in Washington, D.C., for free.
31. Get free postage.
32. Change course of history.
33. Test one's theories of government.
34. Like the job.
35. To be called "Mr. President."
36. To have guards.
37. To go to war.
38. Work for needed reforms.
39. Promote personal business interests.

### 215. Six or more reasons for inflation

1. Lack of faith in economy.
2. Growth of economy.
3. Rising wages.
4. Speculation.
5. Poor balance of trade.
6. Scarcity of goods.
7. Large demand for goods.
8. Monopolies.
9. Constant improvements in products and services.
10. Growing taxes.
11. Too much money for too little production.
12. Supply and demand out of proportion.
13. Excessive issuing of token money with no material backing.
14. Excessive spending by government on non-productive operations.
15. Artificial raising of prices by limiting import of less expensive foreign products.
16. Too much regulation of business by government.
17. Unions wielding too much power both political and economic.
18. Too much waste of money through careless and/or criminal handling at all levels of government.
19. Efforts of government to be all things to all men.
20. Too many people seeking and obtaining something for nothing.
21. A feeling that no one is responsible for his own support but that the government is responsible for everyone.
22. Higher prices.
23. Bad crops.
24. Greedy people.
25. Cold winter.
26. Not enough oil.
27. Uncle Sam washed the dollar in hot water.

### 216. Seven or more ways to get a bus driver's attention

1. Tap him/her on shoulder.
2. Speak to him/her.
3. Throw something.
4. Shout.
5. Create a disturbance.
6. Break a window.
7. Stand in front of bus.
8. Kick him/her.
9. Pull on his/her arm.
10. Annoy other passengers.
11. Jump out of bus.
12. Drive into bus.
13. Block path of bus.
14. Pass a note.
15. Give him/her money.
16. Have "accident" on bus.
17. Play musical instrument.
18. Eat something with a strong smell.
19. Pop a balloon or air-filled bag.
20. Start singing very loud.
21. Get near driver and pull emergency brake.
22. Pretend to faint.
23. Make loud speech (orate) to other passengers on any subject at all.
24. Sham illness.
25. Pretend offensive drunkenness.
26. Climb on and over seats.
27. Fall on knees in center aisle and pray aloud.
28. Bang on seats.
29. Trip on steps.
30. Hijack the bus.
31. Hit him/her.
32. Wink at him/her.
33. Kiss him/her.
34. Take his/her hat, etc.
35. Vomit.

### 217. Seven or more ways to make yourself less attractive

1. Wear no makeup.
2. Wear too much makeup.
3. Apply makeup badly.
4. Don't wash.
5. Mistreat your hair.
6. Bite nails.
7. Don't iron clothes.
8. Wear badly matching clothing.
9. Don't comb hair.
10. Wear unflattering glasses.
11. Wear toe-pinching shoes that ruin your walk.
12. Chew gum.
13. Smoke.
14. Speak ungrammatically.
15. Use a lot of four-letter words.
16. Spit in public.
17. Pick at teeth.
18. Pick nose.
19. Rub eyes until they become bloodshot.
20. Pick at pimples.
21. Wear torn clothing.
22. Bruise yourself in obvious places.
23. Wear gaudy jewelry.
24. Wear mismatched jewelry.
25. Don't brush teeth.
26. Don't use mouthwash.
27. Don't clean shoes.
28. Don't keep shoes in repair.
29. Wear clothes too tight.
30. Wear cheap perfume.
31. Eat garlic.
32. Don't wash clothes.
33. Gum up hair with hairspray.
34. Don't use deodorant.
35. Get dirty.
36. Get drunk.
37. Muss your hair.
38. Black out one or more teeth.
39. Sneer at everything that's said.
40. Be argumentative.
41. Monopolize conversation.
42. Be rude.
43. Make faces.
44. Dress sloppily.
45. Criticize everything.
46. Gossip.
47. Tell tales.
48. Lie habitually.
49. Be a troublemaker.
50. Try to turn friends against each other.

51. Cheat.
52. Be ungrateful.
53. Be selfish.
54. Be conceited.
55. Be vain.
56. Be inconsiderate.
57. Be abusive.
58. Be untrustworthy.
59. Don't do your share.
60. Be dishonest.
61. Become very fat.
62. Get sick.
63. Don't sleep.
64. Walk in mud.
65. Wear clothes too big.

## 218. Eight or more ways to make yourself physically stronger

1. Get more sleep.
2. Eat well.
3. Take vitamins.
4. Minimize use of drugs.
5. Breathe properly.
6. Talk yourself into it.
7. Get massages.
8. Lift weights.
9. Swim.
10. Do hard physical labor.
11. Follow prescribed course of body building.
12. Study some form of martial arts.
13. Take up wrestling.
14. Take up gymnastics.
15. Take up rowing.
16. Run.
17. Pushups.
18. Pullups.
19. Sports.
20. Jumping jacks.
21. Jump rope.
22. Chinups.
23. Jog.
24. Walk briskly.
25. Move heavy furniture.
26. Do isometric exercises.
27. Practice Hatha Yoga.

## 219. Six or more things you've always wanted to say to your mother-in-law

1. Shut up.
2. Mind your own business.
3. We don't want you here.
4. We don't need your advice.
5. Who cares what you think?
6. You have bad breath.
7. You have terrible taste in clothes.
8. He isn't your "baby" anymore.
9. You don't know anything, do you?
10. What would you know about music?
11. Your peasant upbringing is showing through.
12. If you can't say anything intelligent, don't say anything.
13. I don't like your cooking.
14. Your perfume smells cheap.
15. Your taste in jewelry is really provincial.
16. Your child-raising methods belong in the Dark Ages.
17. You're looking really rundown.
18. You shouldn't wear makeup in such an obvious way.
19. What would you know about art?
20. Do you think anyone is interested in what an old woman thinks?
21. Don't you think it's time you stepped aside for a younger generation?
22. If you want grandchildren, adopt them.
23. Don't try to run *my* life.
24. You're the worst mother-in-law anyone ever had.
25. No one wants to hear about your medical problems.
26. No one wants to hear about your charity work.
27. You're ugly.
28. You have an irritating nose.
29. Don't nag me.
30. Stop pestering me.
31. Mothers-in-law should be seen and not heard.
32. I don't like you.
33. Leave me alone.
34. Go bother someone else.
35. Up yours.
36. Get lost.
37. Drop dead.
38. Voulez-vous coucher avec moi?
39. I married your daughter, not you.
40. Did you ever have any girl children?
41. Where did you learn to raise kids? In a zoo?
42. Now I know how your daughter got so sexy.
43. Come on over for dinner—bring the food.
44. When you first saw my wife did it inspire you to give up drinking?
45. After I got to know you I realized why my wife was so eager to get married.
46. Did your husband allow you the run of the house or were you usually confined to your cage?
47. Don't you have a home of your own?
48. After knowing you I often wonder how my wife turned out to be such a nice person.
49. They say to see how a girl will be in later life, look at her mother. I hope they're wrong.
50. Good night, dear mother. Parting is such great delight.
51. You're stupid.
52. You talk too much.
53. You're overweight.
54. You're in the way.
55. I love you.
56. I miss you.
57. I know your sons have been a disappointment to you.
58. Relax.
59. Don't sing.
60. You're amazing.
61. You're a great cook.
62. You're a hard act to follow.

## 220. Six or more reasons why fish don't talk

1. Too stupid.
2. Too smart.
3. Nothing to say.
4. Water gets in way.
5. They are mouth breathers.
6. No vocal cords.
7. They use body language.
8. Did you ever try to talk and drink at the same time?
9. Who could bear them?
10. They travel in schools and everyone knows talking in class isn't allowed.
11. Whales (not fish) talk, and look where they are—almost extinct.
12. Submarines are known as "the silent service"—why not fish, too?
13. Who'd listen?
14. Who could hear?
15. They have no ears.
16. They have more sense.
17. They swore a vow of silence in return for the ability to swim well and live underwater where it's quiet.
18. They spend their time in deep thought and meditation.
19. They're too busy evolving so they can live on land.
20. They're not on speaking terms with each other.
21. They're so bad tempered they won't even talk to themselves.
22. Don't speak English.
23. They're innately shy.
24. We just can't hear them.
25. Fishermen might be able to hear them.
26. They wouldn't be able to understand each other.
27. They might scare away their food.

## 221. Nine or more reasons why some married women prefer to be called "Ms"

1. To get dates if they're married.
2. So they won't be marked as a married woman.
3. To be with the times.
4. It's shorter to write than Miss or Mrs.
5. They like the sound the word makes when spoken.
6. To be like Billie Jean King.
7. It makes them feel proud.
8. When H&R Block says "Ms," people listen.
9. To be mysterious.
10. Maintain self-identity.
11. Membership in Mensa.
12. Maintain unmarried feeling.
13. It's easier to spell.
14. To express solidarity with their sisters, married or not.
15. To express independence from their husbands.
16. To irritate (or please) their mother-in-law.
17. To irritate their husbands.
18. It's a fad.
19. To qualify for membership in NOW.
20. To intrigue male friends.
21. They can't remember if they're married or not.
22. They are too lazy to use the extra "r."
23. Because they are jealous that men only use two letters in their title, "Mr."
24. They are trying to get attention.
25. So she doesn't get attached to flying saucers.
26. To prevent forest fires.
27. So she's not called "Mrs."
28. So they won't catch a cold.
29. To try to get a job.
30. Because it's easier to write.
31. To signify their liberation.
32. For women with a poor vocabulary.
33. To confuse men.
34. To aggravate men.
35. "Mrs." sounds old-fashioned.
36. Ashamed they're married.
37. Helps them forget about their husbands.
38. Want to identify with professional women.
39. May need to hide the fact that they're married for professional reasons.
40. Employer may discriminate against married women (Mrs.).
41. Because "Ms." is used in magazines.

42. Will encourage people to use their Christian name (difficult to pronounce Ms.).
43. Their friends use "Ms."
44. Their husbands prefer "Ms."
45. To shock society.
46. Doesn't write "r"'s well.
47. Ashamed of being married.
48. Sounds better.
49. Conversation subject.
50. They think it is sexier.
51. It beats being called Esmerelda.

---

## 222. Six or more reasons not to pluck feathers from a chicken

1. Chicken won't like it.
2. Chicken may bite your finger.
3. You may be accused of cruelty to chickens.
4. May be allergic to chicken feathers.
5. Chickens look prettier with their feathers on.
6. You could get attacked by angry cockerel.
7. You could get attacked by angry farmer.
8. Chicken may refuse to lay eggs afterwards.
9. It's hard work.
10. Feathers will fall all over floor.
11. No available chicken.
12. Don't like hurting chicken.
13. Afraid of chickens.
14. Feathers will stick to your clothes.
15. May have more exotic bird to pluck (e.g., peacock).
16. Not a social activity.
17. Have more exciting things to do.
18. Never occurred to you to pluck feathers.
19. Pillows now are mostly synthetics.
20. It's better than plucking chickens from a feather.
21. Because there would be too many sick chickens.
22. There are already an overabundance of pillows.
23. Someone might pluck the wrong thing.
24. Some people like to eat feathery chickens.
25. It's to be mounted by a taxidermist.
26. The machinery for plucking is broken.
27. The chicken is still alive.
28. It's to be plucked commercially.
29. The chicken has not yet been prepared for plucking.

30. Because he's wearing boxing gloves.
31. It may peck you.
32. Plucking feathers is boring.
33. The chicken will get cold.
34. Chickens cannot fly without feathers.
35. Chickens need feathers to hatch eggs.
36. It will embarrass the chicken to be naked.
37. How would you like a big chicken to pluck you?
38. Feathers taste good when they're cooked.
39. Live chickens make good pillows.
40. You can get feather stains on your hands.
41. The other chickens will laugh at it.
42. You may hurt your fingers.
43. Bald chickens develop acne.
44. You may find you are attracted to nude chickens.

---

## 223. Seven or more reasons for not wearing a tie

1. Ties feel uncomfortable.
2. To shock the boss.
3. To appear nonconformist.
4. To be fashionable.
5. Wearing a sweater.
6. Can't find tie.
7. Too much effort.
8. Feel overdressed.
9. In bed.
10. In the bath.
11. In theatrical costume.
12. Playing football.
13. You're an animal.
14. Relaxing.
15. Not allowed to.
16. Not part of uniform.
17. Can't afford to buy tie.
18. All your ties have been stolen.
19. All ties have been burned in a house fire.
20. Possible strangulation.
21. When working on the roof.
22. When the tie is polka-dots.
23. Gets wet when you indulge in a drinking fountain.
24. On windy days, it whips you in the face.
25. When going to a beach.
26. When going to a nudist colony.
27. To give your neck a rest.
28. To show off your neckline.
29. So you can leave for where you are going ten minutes earlier.
30. Maybe if you're lucky, someone will call you "Ms."
31. For safety reasons around rotating machinery.
32. For comfort in hot weather.

33. Wearing a clerical collar.
34. Can't find one to match.
35. Doing a messy job.
36. Wearing a T-shirt.
37. Wearing military fatigues.
38. Shirt being worn does not have proper kind of collar.
39. Can't stand tightness around neck.
40. Reminiscent of hanged ancestor.
41. Not proper for a woman.
42. Too young.
43. Railroad ties are too heavy to wear.
44. A tie is an absurd convention.
45. A tie may restrict blood flow to the brain.
46. A burning tie creates great danger.
47. It is frustrating to knot a tie.
48. So you can't get into fancy restaurants.
49. It gives people the idea that you don't want any more ties for presents.
50. To send the tie companies out of business.
51. To boycott expensive, colorful ties.
52. If you get it caught in a door, it's possible to hang yourself.
53. If the tie happens to be eight feet long.
54. No one can cut it off.
55. You don't have to match your shirt.
56. No one else is going to wear one.
57. I am going fishing.
58. They give me a neck rash.
59. All I own is narrow ties.
60. The casual look is in.
61. I look sexy with my collar open.
62. I spilled tomato sauce on it yesterday.

---

## 224. Six or more reasons why some restaurants are more popular than others

1. Proprietor has good connections.
2. Some restaurants publicized in food reviews.
3. Good music.
4. People want to show they can afford it.
5. Informal atmosphere.
6. Luxurious surroundings.
7. Don't have difficult French menus.
8. Has historical connection.
9. Said to be haunted.
10. Famous owner.
11. Fewer flies.

12. Fewer vermin.
13. Cigarette and then vending machines.
14. Beautiful workers.
15. Fast food.
16. They pluck the feathers from the chicken.
17. They don't have roaches.
18. They have more comfortable seats.
19. They have a better atmosphere.
20. They are inexpensive.
21. They are expensive.
22. They serve ethnic foods.
23. Well-known chef.
24. The hostess greets guests by name.
25. They have children's menu.
26. Facilities for the handicapped.
27. Offer free seconds.
28. Honor credit cards.
29. Free salad bar.
30. Good wine selection.
31. Happy hour drink prices.
32. Cafeteria style—no tipping.
33. Easy access from highway and return.
34. Luncheon specials.
35. Generous portions.
36. Pleasant waitresses/waiters.
37. Affable bartender.
38. They give a patron a blank receipt to fill in for an expense account.
39. Physically attractive menu.
40. Good entertainment.
41. Allow dancing.
42. Kitchen open to inspection.
43. Spotless restrooms.
44. Prohibit smoking.
45. Twenty-four hour service.
46. Offer meeting facilities.
47. Air-conditioned.
48. Owned by prominent politician.
49. Near the office.
50. Intimate.
51. Pleasantly landscaped.
52. Give favors to children.
53. Complimentary wine.
54. Near theater.
55. Topless waitresses.
56. Bottomless waitresses.
57. Have stomach pump available.
58. Attached to casino.
59. Truckers' stop.
60. Protected by Mob.
61. Offer disco lessons.
62. Celebrities eat there.
63. Serve fresh vegetables.
64. Specialize in seafood.
65. Unlimited dessert bar.
66. Strolling musicians.
67. Good prices.
68. Expansive menu.
69. Specialty foods.
70. Exceptional service.
71. Unique location.
72. Outstanding cuisine.

73. Fast service.
74. They might happen to serve that rare substance called good food.
75. Waiters are more careful about sticking their thumbs on your food.
76. The good ones are not located next to a slaughterhouse.
77. They have the placemats with games on them.
78. The eating utensils are washed every other year.
79. They have doggie bags.
80. You can tell the good ones because all good restaurants don't have enough light to see what you're eating.
81. Better drinks.
82. Better advertising.
83. Good cocktail lounge.

---

### 225. Eight or more words in any language spelled the same backward as forward

1. Radar (English).
2. Ala (Spanish).
3. Elle (French).
4. Ara (Latin).
5. Minim (English, musical).
6. Dad (English, colloquial).
7. Pop (English).
8. Tot (English).
9. Peep (English).
10. Acá (Spanish).
11. Allá (Spanish).
12. Apa (Spanish-Mexican).
13. Ojo (Spanish).
14. Ama (Spanish).
15. Ése (Spanish).
16. Deed (English).
17. Noon (English).
18. Poop (English).
19. Gag (English).
20. Gig (English).
21. Pip (English).
22. Pep (English).
23. Eté (French).
24. Rajar (Spanish).
25. Rallar (Spanish).
26. Did (English).
27. Nadan (From verb "nadar," Spanish).
28. Ama (from verb amore, Latin).
29. Toot (English).
30. Tôt (French).
31. Ibi (Latin).
32. Ici (French).
33. Tit (English).
34. Tat (English).
35. Nun (English).
36. Eye (English).
37. Ecce (Latin).
38. Bib (English).
39. Kook (English).
40. Oho (English).
41. I.
42. A.
43. Gog (English).
44. Mam (English).
45. Mom (English).
46. Non.
47. Boob (English).
48. Hah (English).
49. Heh (English).
50. Ibi.
51. Idi.
52. Oro (Spanish).
53. Bob (English).
54. Ere.
55. Abba.
56. Wow (English, slang).
57. Dud.
58. Mum (English, colloquial).
59. Mom (English, colloquial).
60. Pup (English).
61. Pap (English).
62. Sis (English, colloquial).
63. Tut (English, colloquial).

---

### 226. Seven or more reasons for not visiting a physician

1. Feeling well.
2. Can't spare time.
3. Don't like doctor.
4. Doctors make you feel ill.
5. Can't afford it.
6. Doctor lives too far away.
7. Afraid to go.
8. Don't want to waste doctor's time.
9. Doctor is unpleasant.
10. Doctor said to be quack.
11. Have better things to do.
12. People may say you're hypochondriac.
13. Doctor will recommend you go on diet.
14. Doctor will tell you to rest more.
15. Doctor will tell you to stop drinking.
16. Your family will worry you're ill.
17. Insurance company monitors your trips to doctor's.
18. Hate examinations.
19. Faint if he takes blood pressure.
20. Have no doctor.
21. Never heard of doctors.
22. Your witch doctor will kill you if you go.
23. Don't want people at work to know—they'll think you're cracking under strain.
24. When he's caught for malpractice.
25. When he charges more dollars for seconds he spends with you.
26. When you have a toothache.
27. You've got to go someplace else.
28. You're afraid of the sight of needles.
29. Beyond medical help.
30. Cannot make an appointment.
31. Christian Scientist.
32. No medical insurance.
33. Isolated from civilization.
34. Being stubborn.
35. Being negligent.
36. Can't get out of work during office hours.
37. Remission.
38. Recovery from illness.
39. High mortality rate of physician.
40. Cancelled appointment.
41. Too sick to get to the office.
42. Lack of adequate transportation.
43. You're already dead.
44. They just happen to be playing golf.
45. Your physician is in the hospital for getting hit with a golf club.
46. He will put me in the hospital.
47. He never does any good.
48. Sit in his office for an hour to spend ten minutes with him?
49. I don't like his nurse.
50. All he wants is my money.
51. Once I start he keeps me coming back.
52. He has cold hands.
53. He is too young.
54. He is too old.
55. No place to park.
56. He will give me a shot.
57. I'll go when I have to go.
58. He is always on vacation.

---

### 227. Six or more consequences of doing away with waiting rooms

1. No one would have to wait.
2. Next we could do away with doctors' offices.
3. We couldn't read while we waited.
4. We'd have to wait out in the street.
5. There would be thousands of homeless magazines.
6. Receptionists' lobbies would be cold during the winter.
7. You couldn't ban smoking.
8. No one would go to the doctor's anymore.
9. With the current slow service in doctors' offices, business offices, etc. line-ups have become acute and waiting rooms are too small. Waiting auditoria are being constructed as an improvement.
10. Rooms cost money and are now too expensive; patients and other "waiters" will be requested to wait in the street.
11. Reduced infections and disease in children, contracted from other children in doctors' waiting rooms, would result.
12. There would be an immediate glut on the market of ten-year-old *Reader's Digests*.
13. Dental patients would have less opportunity to get nervous listening to the dulcet screams of other patients.
14. There would be an increase in the number of loitering citations as patients wait in the streets.
15. Doctors may not be so apt to overbook their patients if there were no place to put them.
16. There would arise a mass movement for the preservation of that hallowed institution, the waiting room.
17. After a brief period without waiting rooms, doctors, dentists, etc., would try to surreptitiously have rooms with euphemistic names, like "ready room" or "sojourning salon."
18. Secret waiting rooms would spring up like speakeasies during Prohibition (perhaps these rooms would serve liquor) and the patients might have to knock three times and say, "Sidney sent me."

---

### 228. Seven or more reasons why church bells are allowed to chime at all hours of the night

1. They aren't.
2. People like it.
3. To wake us up.
4. To tell the world they're happy.
5. What else can they do?
6. To make sure they're working.
7. To tell us it's ringing.
8. That's what they were made for.
9. They like to.
10. The parishioners can't tell time.
11. People need to go to midnight mass.
12. Because people are allowed

to pull their cords at all hours of the night.
13. To signal danger.
14. To scare us.
15. Churches are a sacred cow—they pay no taxes, make their own rules (canon law), so it's no wonder that they are allowed to ring bells all night.
16. Bell chiming protects the community from werewolves, vampires, and wookies.
17. The campanologist must get his practice sometime.
18. It's for the good of the public; the bells are an indispensable ingredient of exorcisms.
19. They are needed for effective faith-healing.
20. The bells are used by a faithful and religious public, to apprise them of their hourly prayers to Mecca.
21. The bell ringing tends to drown out the water hammer of the region's water main system. The cost of repair would be prohibitive and the population would prefer to drown out the noise with bells.
22. The bells mask the screams of human sacrificial victims in the church, and that saves long-drawn explanations to the neighborhood children.
23. The bells, like Tibetan prayer wheels, are used for votive veneration of St. Barbara, the patron saint of toothache. The local dental association is getting a little upset about this, because it seems to work too well.
24. It keeps the bats from roosting in the (a) belfry, (b) campanile, or (c) bells.
25. It's a splendid way to make sure that they are still working.
26. It keeps them from freezing up in the winter.
27. It discourages stray cats from mating in the sacristy.
28. It reminds the faithful to attend the daily divine service.
29. It serves as a beacon for ships lost in the fog, and for the Boy Scouts in the woods.
30. It provides a market for ear plug manufacturers (who donate substantial sums to the church).
31. It reassures those who have an irrational fear of going deaf that they can still hear.

## 229. Seven or more reasons for being turned down for a bank loan

1. Can't fill in loan application.
2. Have robbed that bank previously.
3. Want money for risky investment.
4. Bank manager nervous—you're his first applicant.
5. Wearing smelly shoes.
6. Smoking a cigar.
7. Not brushing your teeth.
8. Having eight or more children.
9. Earning minimum wage.
10. Caught once before for embezzling.
11. No collateral.
12. No bank.
13. You don't need the loan.
14. You arrived in a flying saucer.
15. You need the money to hire the Mafia.
16. Because you killed the bank president.
17. No established credit rating.
18. The bank doesn't make the kind of loan needed.
19. Unable to produce a co-signer.
20. Unsatisfactory reason for needing loan.
21. Demanding a low interest rate.
22. Proposing too slow a repayment schedule.
23. No steady income.
24. Criminal record.
25. Too old.
26. Too young.
27. Poor health.
28. Intoxicated when applying.
29. High when applying.
30. Poorly dressed.
31. Can't speak English.
32. Used obscenities.
33. Acted strange.
34. Officer of bank.
35. Lives in motel.
36. In mental hospital.
37. Bad credit.
38. No account with the bank.
39. Lack of income.
40. Surfeit of previous debits.
41. Pending bankruptcy.
42. Borrower mentally incompetent.
43. Bank has no money.
44. Never applied for one.
45. Your application was for a million dollars.
46. You openly admit that you never plan to pay them back.
47. You're not a member of a minority group.
48. You are on welfare.
49. You skipped to California after your last loan.
50. Your mother-in-law is president of the bank.
51. You are just out of jail for bank robbery.
52. You're just out of college and you want the money to go bumming around the country.
53. You want the money to elope with the loan manager's daughter.
54. You are the town drunk.

## 230. Six or more reasons why titles are not important

1. We don't live in England.
2. You can't tell a book by its cover.
3. Titles are for selling bonds.
4. I thought *Jaws* was a book on dentistry.
5. I just look at the pictures.
6. Even Count Dracula had a title.
7. I have a dog named Duke.
8. You can't judge a title by its cover—or something like that.
9. The "title" family was never really important.
10. Titles discriminate.
11. Dogs don't like titles.
12. They waste ink.
13. Does the mind have a title?
14. Movement toward a class society.
15. Titles are now easily purchased.
16. The content of the book is what counts.
17. The rich men make the rules.
18. We no longer live in a feudal system.
19. The play's the thing.
20. Have no legal status in U.S.
21. Some movie titles have little relevance to the story.
22. Book titles are secondary to author's name.
23. They are sometimes ridiculed.
24. They have no practical use.
25. Car titles can be forged.
26. Alienate friends.
27. Forbidden by military service.
28. It is the person, not the title, that counts.
29. They have no value.
30. They get lost very easily.
31. Not important when signing your name.
32. Not important because you are always being looked at.
33. Not important when you're a sanitation engineer.
34. Not important because takes too long to write.
35. Not important because people don't care.
36. Not important because hardly ever used.
37. Democratic world.
38. Too many titled people—getting common.
39. Money speaks louder than titles.
40. No one knows whether titles are inherited or assumed.
41. Titles mean little abroad.
42. Titles can't buy love.
43. Titles can't buy happiness.
44. Titles do not mean you are clever or talented.
45. Titles can be a worry.

## 231. Six or more reasons why some children become scared at night

1. The boogie man.
2. Thoughtless parents think it's funny and add to the problem.
3. They sleep alone.
4. They are too young to dream about sex.
5. T.V. influence (it gets blamed for everything).
6. Parents don't allow the dog to sleep with them.
7. Noises outside.
8. They live in the slums.
9. Bet-wetters are always scared.
10. If your mother's name was Tondalayo you might be scared, too.
11. Their parents have garlic breath.
12. Active imaginations.
13. Horror movies.
14. Disorientation in the dark.
15. Stimulus deprivation.
16. Parental suggestions.
17. Presence of evil spirits.
18. Infantile neurosis.
19. Fear of darkness is a human trait.
20. Some bedtime stories have fear of darkness as main theme.
21. Sounds are more frightening when their origins cannot be seen.
22. Peer pressure.
23. They see adults fear the dark.
24. Get their parents' sympathy.
25. They think they should.
26. Excuse to stay up late.
27. Because they become scared at night.
28. They don't feel protected.
29. They want their mommy.

30. Because of bad dreams.
31. When mother threatens the youngster to go to bed or else.
32. When they forgot to do their homework.
33. Afraid of witches and goblins from fairy stories.
34. Sleep in haunted room.
35. Afraid of burglars.
36. Use Ouija boards—afraid of device.
37. Live in lonely, windswept houses.
38. Afraid house may catch fire.
39. Worry about problems at school.
40. Worry about problems at home.
41. Under the threat of kidnapping.
42. Afraid they'll die.

## 232. Seven or more ways to keep a license plate clean

1. In a car wash.
2. Spit on it.
3. Drive through puddles.
4. Ask your wife to do it.
5. Drive in the rain.
6. Drive behind a truck without mud flaps.
7. Ask attendant at full service island to clean it.
8. Put it in the dishwasher.
9. Lose it and get a clean one from motor vehicle department.
10. Wipe it with your pants leg.
11. Never drive.
12. Put plastic baggies on them.
13. Buy it its own windshield wiper.
14. Only drive underwater.
15. Only drive in soap.
16. Don't drive in New York.
17. Put it in your desk drawer.
18. Wash it daily.
19. Cover it with plastic.
20. Give it to a friend.
21. Put it in the refrigerator.
22. Put it in a suitcase.
23. Put it in a special box.
24. Encase it in paraffin.
25. Hang it on a wall in a collection.
26. Don't drive in wet weather.
27. Don't follow another vehicle closely.
28. Make it a weekly chore for a child.
29. Keep the car in a garage.
30. Display it through the rear window.
31. Keep it in the envelope it came in.
32. Display it on a wall at place of business.
33. Keep it in your house.
34. Keep it in your car.
35. Lay some plucked chicken feathers over it.
36. By not writing bad words on it.
37. By not stealing one.
38. Get on your knees and scrub it.
39. By getting a new car every year.
40. Owning a hearse.
41. Fit automatic license plate cleaner to car.
42. Employ servant to clean license plate.
43. Send car to be display car in dealer's window—will always be kept clean.
44. Spray plate with dust repellent.
45. Move to country where air is cleaner.
46. Change engine from petrol consuming to electric—less fumes.
47. Put exhaust pipe on side of car—less fumes near plate.
48. Fit plate washers (like windscreen washers) onto back bumper.
49. Fit spring covered with dust cloth inside luggage compartment. Every time compartment opens, spring pops out and wipes plate.
50. Drive car through clean, shallow river.

## 233. Eight or more ways to tell whether your car brake lights are on

1. Put a meter in circuit and watch for increase in power flow.
2. Put a big mirror on the front of your trailer.
3. You will find out at the next state inspection.
4. Back into something; then there is no doubt.
5. A good samaritan will tell you if something is wrong sooner or later.
6. Trade the car—then it doesn't matter.
7. Ask a teacher.
8. Check the manual.
9. Guess.
10. Stand in back while a friend puts on brakes.
11. Put on brakes with the car's tail to a wall.
12. Mount a mirror on each rear fender.
13. Ride in a car behind your own.
14. Have a friend stand in back when you brake.
15. Watch your rearview mirror when you press the pedal.
16. Have a friend ride in the trunk of your car.
17. Maneuver in front of a police car and apply brakes.
18. Back up to a show window and look through rearview mirror.
19. Back up to a puddle of water and look at reflection.
20. Take car for a safety inspection.
21. Hold brakes down with a weight and get out and look.
22. In fog, look for glow in water droplets.
23. Work brakes and immediately feel if bulbs are warm.
24. Stop your car and go to look at it.
25. Don't stop your car and go out to look.
26. Use your C.B. and ask someone behind you.
27. If your car won't move.
28. If your brake light is on.
29. If the car behind you is far behind.
30. If the car behind you is honking at you.
31. If your car battery goes dead.
32. Wait for night and see if the light is on.
33. If the car behind hits you at night.
34. When you brake.
35. Get a mechanic to check it out.
36. Ask someone who is not blind.
37. Look at dashboard—have sensor light fitted.
38. Watch reactions of driver behind—does he slow when you do?
39. Fit mirror onto front of car parked behind you.
40. Use periscope out of side window.

## 234. Six or more reasons why *Roots* was the most popular TV show of its day

1. All the blacks watched it.
2. What else was there to watch?
3. It showed how to make the most of very poor conditions.
4. Curiosity.
5. There was no Monday night football that week.
6. It was a struggle for dignity.
7. Once you turned it on, it kept your interest.
8. Everybody was talking about it.
9. You felt you would miss something if you didn't watch.
10. Good network advertising.
11. The commercials were great.
12. It was so short.
13. *Laverne and Shirley* were off that week.
14. Some show had to be the best.
15. The actors were well chosen.
16. It spoke to a national concern.
17. It was part of our history.
18. It was a unique format.
19. Sensationalistic exploitation.
20. It was on prime time TV.
21. It was heavily promoted.
22. It was tied in with sale of the book.
23. The author was widely interviewed in media.
24. It gave blacks a sense of pride in their heritage.
25. It was on an unusually large number of TV stations.
26. Its TV competition was relatively weak.
27. Its theme was innovative.
28. It was a well-written and researched story.
29. It had a large cast with whom the audience could empathize.
30. Its serial format was suspenseful.
31. It was unusually attractive to and supported by major advertisers.
32. It had many story lines.
33. It set a precedent.
34. Because people were interested in the way of life back in that time.
35. To be able to see Alex Haley's background.
36. People like shows about plants.
37. People like ethnic shows.
38. Because of so many plants in America.
39. Some people want to own slaves.
40. Over 35,000,000 blacks in the country.
41. Over 150,000,000 whites in country.
42. Over 220,000,000 people in the U.S.
43. Primitive scenes and good acting.
44. America's favorite past-time.
45. People had read book.
46. Alex Haley has lots of friends.
47. Good storyline.
48. Serial-audience had to watch next episode.
49. Good cast.

50. Shown at peak viewing hours.
51. Large black population to watch show.
52. Family histories popular.
53. Story of success.
54. People watched it so they could talk about it with their friends.
55. First show of its kind—long-term black history.

236. **Six or more reasons for not having a telephone answering service**

1. Cheaper to have your wife do it.
2. Only bill collectors would use it.
3. If it's important enough, I can be reached.
4. Most calls can wait.
5. I would have to pay for long distance calls that I returned.
6. You don't have a phone in the first place.
7. You're deaf.
8. You get an average of one call per month.
9. You have no friends.
10. You're too cheap.
11. You have bad breath.
12. It depersonalizes the communication situation.
13. Messages get transmitted incorrectly.
14. Often calls are answered rudely.
15. Poor handling of emergency calls.
16. Wasteful of toll calls.
17. Messages are sometimes garbled.
18. Intrusion of privacy.
19. Impossible to deny receipt of call.
20. Required information might not be provided correctly.
21. Could cause third party misunderstanding.
22. Hours of available service may not be adequate.
23. You like to answer the telephone.
24. Being home all day.
25. Having a secretary.
26. Expensive.
27. People will phone back in any case.
28. Unnerving for friends who call.
29. Can't be bothered to listen to tape when you get in.
30. Can't be bothered to leave messages on tape when you go out.
31. Get few telephone calls.
32. Gives opportunity for unwanted callers to talk for hours on tape.
33. Service staff may tap your phone.
34. No available answering service.
35. Don't know what answering service is.

39. Watching TV makes you fat.
40. TV makes you a boring person.
41. Have friends in.
42. Too many news bulletins in the day.
43. Too many children's programs.

235. **Seven or more reasons for not watching daytime TV**

1. Too many commercials.
2. Just watch them once—that's all the reason anyone would want.
3. I might get my wife interested.
4. You sleep during the day.
5. You're dead.
6. You'd rather sort socks.
7. There are better things to do.
8. It is intellectually dissipating.
9. Boss will fire you for having a TV at work.
10. Television is too fluid a medium.
11. It wastes electricity.
12. There is no longer a "Gong Show."
13. Limited types of shows.
14. Interferes with household duties.
15. Reception is inferior to that at night.
16. The children take it over.
17. Best time for grocery shopping.
18. Too many reruns.
19. Because you would rather be plucking chickens.
20. Because you're in school.
21. Because it's not nighttime TV.
22. Because you don't like soap operas.
23. Because I am playing mental jogging.
24. Boring and routine.
25. Not to get aggravated.
26. Not to become sad.
27. TV on the fritz.
28. Have no TV.
29. Blind (can't see).
30. Deaf.
31. Bad for eyesight.
32. Gives you headaches.
33. Prefer radio/records.
34. TV too noisy.
35. TV kills conversation.
36. Not allowed to (e.g. child being punished).
37. Weather is too nice—go out instead.
38. Get stiff sitting down too long.

237. **Eight or more reasons not to chlorinate a YMCA swimming pool**

1. It turns the water green.
2. The kids don't like it.
3. Maybe it will turn the kids green.
4. It will make the water hard, so someone could get hurt.
5. More people would use the pool.
6. There's no water in the pool.
7. Little kiddies will counteract the cleansing.
8. It's wintertime and the pool is now an ice rink.
9. You belong to the YMHA.
10. You can't swim anyway.
11. You happen to love filth and scum.
12. Just for spite.
13. YMCA members are naturally clean.
14. Too much will kill the fish.
15. It could be too expensive.
16. If everyone showers, none will be needed.
17. Goldfish could keep the pool clean.
18. Excess chlorine might bleach the hair.
19. Other ways of achieving the same results.
20. It's cheaper to change the water.
21. Chlorine tastes bad.
22. It's harmful to swimclothes.
23. I don't own a YMCA swimming pool.
24. Can't afford the chlorine.
25. The store was out of chlorine.
26. If you want it polluted.
27. A boycott on chlorine.
28. Not working for YMCA.
29. Outdoor pool in the wintertime.
30. Living in Alaska.
31. Chlorine stings eyes.
32. Chlorine pollutes water.
33. People may not use pool.
34. Some people allergic to chlorine.
35. Chlorine bad for hair.
36. Chlorine bad for skin.

238. **Six or more reasons why some newspapers do not publish on Saturday**

1. Rest the presses.
2. More to put in Sunday paper.
3. People go out Saturday night, so no time to read it.
4. Blue Laws.
5. No news ever happens on Saturday.
6. Always honor the Sabbath.
7. They're prejudiced against Saturday.
8. Every Saturday the papers seem to run out of ink.
9. No one buys them.
10. To get a day off.
11. Preparation for the Sunday edition.
12. Jewish publishers.
13. Newspaper published weekly on Sunday.
14. Low advertising activity on Saturdays.
15. Readership interest is lowest.
16. Union rules would require overtime pay.
17. Mailed copies would receive slow delivery.
18. Paperboys have other activities on Saturdays.
19. Saturday is the Sabbath in its area.
20. It is a day of rest.
21. They can't afford it.
22. They use the rest of their paper for a bonfire.
23. Too much competition from other papers.
24. Because of the paperboys' contract.
25. Paper shortage.
26. Labor expensive at weekend
27. People may not buy Saturday paper.
28. Journalists want day off.
29. Less government news at weekends.
30. Presses may be used at weekend for Sunday papers.
31. May not be able to distribute on Saturdays.

239. **Eight or more reasons not to subscribe to *The Wall Street Journal***

1. Market too depressing.
2. Expensive.
3. You can always read someone else's.
4. No time to read it.
5. I like to leave business at work when I leave.

6. Most radio stations give market news summaries.
7. Non-market news is the same as other local papers carry.
8. Market news is a day late.
9. What do you do with the old papers?
10. You have a subscription to the *Floor Street Journal*.
11. You don't own stocks or care to.
12. You print that filth.
13. You live on Elm Street, not Wall Street.
14. You hate money (very rare).
15. Just plain ole "you just don't want to."
16. You hate the editor.
17. No interest in stock market.
18. No concern for news of any kind.
19. No mailing address.
20. Hatred of capitalism.
21. Paranoid fear of New York publications.
22. Not knowing what an outstanding publication it is.
23. Not having the time to devote to adequately read it daily.
24. Not agreeing with its editorial policy.
25. Adequate information from other business publications.
26. Employer refuses to subsidize the subscription.
27. It does not relate to some persons' spheres of interest.
28. More convenient to pick it up at a newspaper store.
29. Live in a country where it is forbidden.
30. Blind.
31. No way of getting it delivered.
32. You don't believe in the stock market.
33. You're two years old.
34. There aren't any pictures.
35. You're not having a paper drive.
36. Living through the Depression.
37. Disliking ups and downs.
38. Living in Alaska as an Eskimo.
39. Find it boring.
40. Find it incomprehensible.
41. Can't read.
42. Not interested in business.
43. Don't speak English.
44. Can't afford it.
45. Have no money to invest.
46. Think its information unsound.
47. Depressing—reminds you of work.
48. Your company subscribes to it already.
49. Small print bad for eyes.
50. Live out of America—it takes weeks to arrive.
51. You work for *Wall Street Journal*—get free copy.
52. Bad for health—people get heart attacks reading it.
53. Prefer to make up own mind on financial matters.
54. Think it misleads investors.
55. Think it represents conservative views.
56. Your dog would chew it to bits as it dropped through letterbox.
57. Your wife might suspect you were speculating with her money.
58. Your left-wing children wouldn't approve.
59. Newsagent has never heard of it—won't order it.
60. Don't want to be reminded how shaky your investments are.

## 240. Seven or more reasons for desk blotters

1. To keep coffee cup ring off desk.
2. To hide scratches on desk.
3. To prevent more scratches on desk.
4. It is soft to write on.
5. To blot ink.
6. To absorb coffee spills.
7. To impress other people.
8. In case you run out of scrap paper.
9. To cover tunafish stains.
10. They taste good with white wine.
11. To bloot or blott.
12. Better to put on desks than on toilet seats.
13. Fancy smancy.
14. They're fuzzy.
15. Runny desks.
16. Traditional desk set.
17. For throwing at unruly office people.
18. Killing bugs on the desk.
19. To jot down easily-referred-to notes.
20. For doodling.
21. To add to the color scheme of an office.
22. As a status symbol in an office.
23. To enhance the appearance of the furniture.
24. Add a nostalgic touch.
25. Easily renewable surface.
26. Convenient for hiding small papers underneath.
27. Can be cut up for craft work.
28. Serve as a hot plate.
29. Reason for buying liquid cleaner.
30. Excuse to beat children.
31. Help the carpet cleaning business.
32. Stimulate the economy.
33. Fuel for a pen.
34. Owning cartridge pens.
35. To give the professional touch to your desk.
36. Something to lean on.
37. All executives on TV shows have them.
38. Book rest.
39. Elbow rest.
40. Can slip reminder notes under leather frame.
41. Could play "drop darts."
42. Soak up rain coming in from window.
43. To keep your desk clean.
44. To give you a place to write on.
45. To cover an ugly desk.
46. In case you spill your desk.

## 241. Six or more reasons why there were not more signers of the Declaration of Independence

1. No one else wanted to.
2. John Hancock's signature took up too much room.
3. People feared reprisals from England.
4. Those who did were the only ones present who knew how to write their names.
5. They didn't think of women as signers.
6. They didn't want to share the limelight for posterity.
7. No one else could write.
8. The number who signed were considered sufficient.
9. There were no more present.
10. A line had to be drawn.
11. Only those signed who helped in draughting.
12. Done late, got dark, had no light, and couldn't see anymore.
13. Harry's watch stopped.
14. There was a sudden threat of trouble and everybody scattered.
15. Others forgot to sign.
16. It was not bilingual.
17. Didn't want to get involved.
18. Signed on legal holiday; everyone had gone to the lake.
19. Everyone else liked the King.
20. Broke the point on the quill.
21. Ran out of ink.
22. All the names that were legally required.
23. Only union members were allowed to sign.
24. No one else could read.
25. No one else liked John Hancock.
26. Happy hour started at the local pub.
27. Five o'clock whistle blew.
28. Someone spilled coffee on the other sheets of signatures.
29. Everyone else was intimidated by King's men.
30. Ran out of room on paper.
31. J.W. Shwartz dropped dead at the last minute.
32. Harvey missed the connecting flight to Philadelphia.
33. Due to the energy crisis, several horses conked out.
34. Someone thought they said "New York."
35. The party was by invitation only.
36. The men in red picked up Joe at the corner.
37. It was raining.
38. Somebody forgot his name.
39. Arthritis.

## 242. Six or more reasons for not having leap year

1. It screws up digital watches.
2. Who cares what day it is anyway?
3. It gives us another day in February and it's too cold a month.
4. Save paper on those tear-off-each-day calendars.
5. It is a repeated reminder of an irregularity somewhere.
6. It carries undertones of disorder.
7. Centuries cannot all be off the same length.
8. It is a problem to explain to children at first.
9. It is uninteresting.
10. It can be confusing when unexpected.
11. Because the assigning of an additional day to February seems to have been haphazard.
12. Because one has to work an extra day.
13. Because it is even more assymetrical than any other year.
14. It is grossly offensive to the sensibilities.
15. Easier on bachelors: no Sadie Hawkins Day.
16. Eliminate people having birthdays only every fourth year.
17. Standardize February.

149

18. Makes it harder for kids to learn the calendar.
19. So February could have exactly four weeks every year.
20. So February and March will always start on the same day of the week.
21. 29 is a prime number.
22. 29 is an unlucky number.
23. Too tired to jump every four years.
24. Because if everyone jumps on the 29th we could have an earthquake.
25. You might die on the 29th.
26. Too confusing.

---

**243. Seven or more reasons why most people prefer freshly brewed instead of instant coffee**

1. To avoid chemicals.
2. To avoid the "luxury loving," "convenience food" trend in society.
3. A reason to use that coffee pot you got as a gift.
4. It's fun to watch it perk in the glass top.
5. Because instant coffee manufacturers automatically include in their product a substance deliberately intended to be repellent to the tastebuds.
6. Because someone sneaked into the factories of the instant coffee manufacturers and dosed all their coffee with a substance which causes an outbreak of eczema on the eyeballs of anyone who drinks it.
7. Because they let astrologers make their preferences.
8. Because they like drinking coffee, but using instant coffee seems to suggest they're always in a great hurry, when in fact they always aren't.
9. They prefer the former because they just love to do that little bit more work involved in preparing a cup.
10. Because fresh-brewed coffee helps conquer inferiority complexes.
11. Because fresh-brewed coffee is intoxicating.
12. Because fresh-brewed coffee is not intoxicating.
13. Because it is addictive.
14. Mrs. Olsen says it's better.
15. Help Juan Valdez sell his beans.
16. Enjoy the smell of a freshly opened can of ground coffee.
17. Just old fashioned.
18. You can use the coffee cans for paint buckets.
19. Tastes better, not bitter.
20. Instant stains on dentures.
21. Fresh is fresher.
22. Takes longer to make.
23. Costs less.
24. Don't need spoons.
25. Can smell aroma while brewing.

# SEPTEMBER

### Mental Calisthenic #9

Scribble on a plain white piece of paper, using blue ink. Now repeat the procedure using RED, YELLOW, BROWN, and PURPLE ink (or felt-tip pens). Choose the color that you are most comfortable with. Spend about five minutes with the exercise. Use only ONE color next time, in subsequent sessions. What do your doodles "look like"? Proceed with Mental Jogging exercise.

## 244. Eight or more reasons for not becoming a United States Senator

| Response | Score |
|---|---|
| 1. | 1 |
| 2. | 1 |
| 3. | 1 |
| 4. | 1 |
| 5. | 1 |
| 6. | 1 |
| 7. | 1 |
| 8. | 1 |

**Bonus Responses**

| | |
|---|---|
| 9. | 2 |
| 10. | 2 |
| 11. | 2 |
| 12. | 2 |
| 13. | 2 |
| 14. | 2 |
| 15. | 2 |
| 16. | 2 |
| Total | |

## 245. Eight or more consequences of an eight-foot blizzard

| Response | Score |
|---|---|
| 1. | 1 |
| 2. | 1 |
| 3. | 1 |
| 4. | 1 |
| 5. | 1 |
| 6. | 1 |
| 7. | 1 |
| 8. | 1 |

**Bonus Responses**

| | |
|---|---|
| 9. | 2 |
| 10. | 2 |
| 11. | 2 |
| 12. | 2 |
| 13. | 2 |
| 14. | 2 |
| 15. | 2 |
| 16. | 2 |
| Total | |

## 246. Seven or more reasons for buying stale bread

| Response | Score |
|---|---|
| 1. _____ | 1 |
| 2. _____ | 1 |
| 3. _____ | 1 |
| 4. _____ | 1 |
| 5. _____ | 1 |
| 6. _____ | 1 |
| 7. _____ | 1 |

**Bonus Responses**

| | |
|---|---|
| 8. _____ | 2 |
| 9. _____ | 2 |
| 10. _____ | 2 |
| 11. _____ | 2 |
| 12. _____ | 2 |
| 13. _____ | 2 |
| 14. _____ | 2 |
| 15. _____ | 2 |
| 16. _____ | 2 |

Total ☐

## 247. Seven or more reasons why Detroit changes car models every year

| Response | Score |
|---|---|
| 1. _____ | 1 |
| 2. _____ | 1 |
| 3. _____ | 1 |
| 4. _____ | 1 |
| 5. _____ | 1 |
| 6. _____ | 1 |
| 7. _____ | 1 |

**Bonus Responses**

| | |
|---|---|
| 8. _____ | 2 |
| 9. _____ | 2 |
| 10. _____ | 2 |
| 11. _____ | 2 |
| 12. _____ | 2 |
| 13. _____ | 2 |
| 14. _____ | 2 |
| 15. _____ | 2 |
| 16. _____ | 2 |

Total ☐

## 248. Six or more reasons not to attend the funeral of a close friend

| Response | Score |
|---|---|
| 1. _____ | 1 |
| 2. _____ | 1 |
| 3. _____ | 1 |
| 4. _____ | 1 |
| 5. _____ | 1 |
| 6. _____ | 1 |

**Bonus Responses**

| | |
|---|---|
| 7. _____ | 2 |
| 8. _____ | 2 |
| 9. _____ | 2 |
| 10. _____ | 2 |
| 11. _____ | 2 |
| 12. _____ | 2 |
| 13. _____ | 2 |
| 14. _____ | 2 |
| 15. _____ | 2 |
| 16. _____ | 2 |

Total ☐

## 249. Six or more reasons not to buy life insurance

| Response | Score |
|---|---|
| 1. _____ | 1 |
| 2. _____ | 1 |
| 3. _____ | 1 |
| 4. _____ | 1 |
| 5. _____ | 1 |
| 6. _____ | 1 |

**Bonus Responses**

| | |
|---|---|
| 7. _____ | 2 |
| 8. _____ | 2 |
| 9. _____ | 2 |
| 10. _____ | 2 |
| 11. _____ | 2 |
| 12. _____ | 2 |
| 13. _____ | 2 |
| 14. _____ | 2 |
| 15. _____ | 2 |
| 16. _____ | 2 |

Total ☐

## 250. Seven or more reasons why there is usually more than one "best picture" every year

| Response | Score |
|---|---|
| 1. _____ | 1 |
| 2. _____ | 1 |
| 3. _____ | 1 |
| 4. _____ | 1 |
| 5. _____ | 1 |
| 6. _____ | 1 |
| 7. _____ | 1 |

Bonus Responses

| | |
|---|---|
| 8. _____ | 2 |
| 9. _____ | 2 |
| 10. _____ | 2 |
| 11. _____ | 2 |
| 12. _____ | 2 |
| 13. _____ | 2 |
| 14. _____ | 2 |
| 15. _____ | 2 |
| 16. _____ | 2 |

Total ☐

## 251. Seven or more characteristics of your ideal space monster

| Response | Score |
|---|---|
| 1. _____ | 1 |
| 2. _____ | 1 |
| 3. _____ | 1 |
| 4. _____ | 1 |
| 5. _____ | 1 |
| 6. _____ | 1 |
| 7. _____ | 1 |

Bonus Responses

| | |
|---|---|
| 8. _____ | 2 |
| 9. _____ | 2 |
| 10. _____ | 2 |
| 11. _____ | 2 |
| 12. _____ | 2 |
| 13. _____ | 2 |
| 14. _____ | 2 |
| 15. _____ | 2 |
| 16. _____ | 2 |

Total ☐

## 252. Eight or more things never to store in closets

| Response | Score |
|---|---|
| 1. _____ | 1 |
| 2. _____ | 1 |
| 3. _____ | 1 |
| 4. _____ | 1 |
| 5. _____ | 1 |
| 6. _____ | 1 |
| 7. _____ | 1 |
| 8. _____ | 1 |

Bonus Responses

| | |
|---|---|
| 9. _____ | 2 |
| 10. _____ | 2 |
| 11. _____ | 2 |
| 12. _____ | 2 |
| 13. _____ | 2 |
| 14. _____ | 2 |
| 15. _____ | 2 |
| 16. _____ | 2 |

Total ☐

## 253. Seven or more reasons why legal pads are yellow

| Response | Score |
|---|---|
| 1. _____ | 1 |
| 2. _____ | 1 |
| 3. _____ | 1 |
| 4. _____ | 1 |
| 5. _____ | 1 |
| 6. _____ | 1 |
| 7. _____ | 1 |

Bonus Responses

| | |
|---|---|
| 8. _____ | 2 |
| 9. _____ | 2 |
| 10. _____ | 2 |
| 11. _____ | 2 |
| 12. _____ | 2 |
| 13. _____ | 2 |
| 14. _____ | 2 |
| 15. _____ | 2 |
| 16. _____ | 2 |

Total ☐

## 254. Six or more reasons for not owning a calendar

| Response | Score |
|---|---|
| 1. | 1 |
| 2. | 1 |
| 3. | 1 |
| 4. | 1 |
| 5. | 1 |
| 6. | 1 |
| **Bonus Responses** | |
| 7. | 2 |
| 8. | 2 |
| 9. | 2 |
| 10. | 2 |
| 11. | 2 |
| 12. | 2 |
| 13. | 2 |
| 14. | 2 |
| 15. | 2 |
| 16. | 2 |
| Total ☐ | |

## 255. Seven or more reasons for postponing a vacation

| Response | Score |
|---|---|
| 1. | 1 |
| 2. | 1 |
| 3. | 1 |
| 4. | 1 |
| 5. | 1 |
| 6. | 1 |
| 7. | 1 |
| **Bonus Responses** | |
| 8. | 2 |
| 9. | 2 |
| 10. | 2 |
| 11. | 2 |
| 12. | 2 |
| 13. | 2 |
| 14. | 2 |
| 15. | 2 |
| 16. | 2 |
| Total ☐ | |

## 256. Eight or more reasons why some taxpayers never pay any taxes

| Response | Score |
|---|---|
| 1. | 1 |
| 2. | 1 |
| 3. | 1 |
| 4. | 1 |
| 5. | 1 |
| 6. | 1 |
| 7. | 1 |
| 8. | 1 |
| **Bonus Responses** | |
| 9. | 2 |
| 10. | 2 |
| 11. | 2 |
| 12. | 2 |
| 13. | 2 |
| 14. | 2 |
| 15. | 2 |
| 16. | 2 |
| Total ☐ | |

## 257. Seven or more reasons for government grants

| Response | Score |
|---|---|
| 1. | 1 |
| 2. | 1 |
| 3. | 1 |
| 4. | 1 |
| 5. | 1 |
| 6. | 1 |
| 7. | 1 |
| **Bonus Responses** | |
| 8. | 2 |
| 9. | 2 |
| 10. | 2 |
| 11. | 2 |
| 12. | 2 |
| 13. | 2 |
| 14. | 2 |
| 15. | 2 |
| 16. | 2 |
| Total ☐ | |

## 258. Six or more reasons for not having fashion designers

| Response | Score |
|---|---|
| 1. _____ | 1 |
| 2. _____ | 1 |
| 3. _____ | 1 |
| 4. _____ | 1 |
| 5. _____ | 1 |
| 6. _____ | 1 |

Bonus Responses

| | |
|---|---|
| 7. _____ | 2 |
| 8. _____ | 2 |
| 9. _____ | 2 |
| 10. _____ | 2 |
| 11. _____ | 2 |
| 12. _____ | 2 |
| 13. _____ | 2 |
| 14. _____ | 2 |
| 15. _____ | 2 |
| 16. _____ | 2 |

Total ☐

## 259. Seven or more reasons why out-of-state students pay more tuition than in-state students

| Response | Score |
|---|---|
| 1. _____ | 1 |
| 2. _____ | 1 |
| 3. _____ | 1 |
| 4. _____ | 1 |
| 5. _____ | 1 |
| 6. _____ | 1 |
| 7. _____ | 1 |

Bonus Responses

| | |
|---|---|
| 8. _____ | 2 |
| 9. _____ | 2 |
| 10. _____ | 2 |
| 11. _____ | 2 |
| 12. _____ | 2 |
| 13. _____ | 2 |
| 14. _____ | 2 |
| 15. _____ | 2 |
| 16. _____ | 2 |

Total ☐

## 260. Six or more reasons why some college faculty never obtain tenure

| Response | Score |
|---|---|
| 1. _____ | 1 |
| 2. _____ | 1 |
| 3. _____ | 1 |
| 4. _____ | 1 |
| 5. _____ | 1 |
| 6. _____ | 1 |

Bonus Responses

| | |
|---|---|
| 7. _____ | 2 |
| 8. _____ | 2 |
| 9. _____ | 2 |
| 10. _____ | 2 |
| 11. _____ | 2 |
| 12. _____ | 2 |
| 13. _____ | 2 |
| 14. _____ | 2 |
| 15. _____ | 2 |
| 16. _____ | 2 |

Total ☐

## 261. Six or more reasons why Harvard's tuition is more expensive than Brown's

| Response | Score |
|---|---|
| 1. _____ | 1 |
| 2. _____ | 1 |
| 3. _____ | 1 |
| 4. _____ | 1 |
| 5. _____ | 1 |
| 6. _____ | 1 |

Bonus Responses

| | |
|---|---|
| 7. _____ | 2 |
| 8. _____ | 2 |
| 9. _____ | 2 |
| 10. _____ | 2 |
| 11. _____ | 2 |
| 12. _____ | 2 |
| 13. _____ | 2 |
| 14. _____ | 2 |
| 15. _____ | 2 |
| 16. _____ | 2 |

Total ☐

## 262. Eight or more reasons for not awarding the Nobel Prize

| Response | Score |
|---|---|
| 1. | 1 |
| 2. | 1 |
| 3. | 1 |
| 4. | 1 |
| 5. | 1 |
| 6. | 1 |
| 7. | 1 |
| 8. | 1 |

Bonus Responses

| | Score |
|---|---|
| 9. | 2 |
| 10. | 2 |
| 11. | 2 |
| 12. | 2 |
| 13. | 2 |
| 14. | 2 |
| 15. | 2 |
| 16. | 2 |

Total ☐

## 263. Seven or more novel uses of a large rubber band

| Response | Score |
|---|---|
| 1. | 1 |
| 2. | 1 |
| 3. | 1 |
| 4. | 1 |
| 5. | 1 |
| 6. | 1 |
| 7. | 1 |

Bonus Responses

| | Score |
|---|---|
| 8. | 2 |
| 9. | 2 |
| 10. | 2 |
| 11. | 2 |
| 12. | 2 |
| 13. | 2 |
| 14. | 2 |
| 15. | 2 |
| 16. | 2 |

Total ☐

## 264. Eight or more differences between a barber and hair stylist

| Response | Score |
|---|---|
| 1. | 1 |
| 2. | 1 |
| 3. | 1 |
| 4. | 1 |
| 5. | 1 |
| 6. | 1 |
| 7. | 1 |
| 8. | 1 |

Bonus Responses

| | Score |
|---|---|
| 9. | 2 |
| 10. | 2 |
| 11. | 2 |
| 12. | 2 |
| 13. | 2 |
| 14. | 2 |
| 15. | 2 |
| 16. | 2 |

Total ☐

## 265. Six or more reasons for not awarding diplomas

| Response | Score |
|---|---|
| 1. | 1 |
| 2. | 1 |
| 3. | 1 |
| 4. | 1 |
| 5. | 1 |
| 6. | 1 |

Bonus Responses

| | Score |
|---|---|
| 7. | 2 |
| 8. | 2 |
| 9. | 2 |
| 10. | 2 |
| 11. | 2 |
| 12. | 2 |
| 13. | 2 |
| 14. | 2 |
| 15. | 2 |
| 16. | 2 |

Total ☐

156

## 266. Seven or more reasons why some college professors earn less than plumbers

| Response | Score |
|---|---|
| 1. | 1 |
| 2. | 1 |
| 3. | 1 |
| 4. | 1 |
| 5. | 1 |
| 6. | 1 |
| 7. | 1 |

**Bonus Responses**

| | |
|---|---|
| 8. | 2 |
| 9. | 2 |
| 10. | 2 |
| 11. | 2 |
| 12. | 2 |
| 13. | 2 |
| 14. | 2 |
| 15. | 2 |
| 16. | 2 |

Total ☐

## 267. Eight or more reasons for not having a World Heavyweight Boxing Champion

| Response | Score |
|---|---|
| 1. | 1 |
| 2. | 1 |
| 3. | 1 |
| 4. | 1 |
| 5. | 1 |
| 6. | 1 |
| 7. | 1 |
| 8. | 1 |

**Bonus Responses**

| | |
|---|---|
| 9. | 2 |
| 10. | 2 |
| 11. | 2 |
| 12. | 2 |
| 13. | 2 |
| 14. | 2 |
| 15. | 2 |
| 16. | 2 |

Total ☐

## 268. Seven or more reasons for having prime time

| Response | Score |
|---|---|
| 1. | 1 |
| 2. | 1 |
| 3. | 1 |
| 4. | 1 |
| 5. | 1 |
| 6. | 1 |
| 7. | 1 |

**Bonus Responses**

| | |
|---|---|
| 8. | 2 |
| 9. | 2 |
| 10. | 2 |
| 11. | 2 |
| 12. | 2 |
| 13. | 2 |
| 14. | 2 |
| 15. | 2 |
| 16. | 2 |

Total ☐

## 269. Seven or more reasons to want to grow old

| Response | Score |
|---|---|
| 1. | 1 |
| 2. | 1 |
| 3. | 1 |
| 4. | 1 |
| 5. | 1 |
| 6. | 1 |
| 7. | 1 |

**Bonus Responses**

| | |
|---|---|
| 8. | 2 |
| 9. | 2 |
| 10. | 2 |
| 11. | 2 |
| 12. | 2 |
| 13. | 2 |
| 14. | 2 |
| 15. | 2 |
| 16. | 2 |

Total ☐

## 270. Six or more new uses for yellow Jell-O

| Response | Score |
|---|---|
| 1. _____ | 1 |
| 2. _____ | 1 |
| 3. _____ | 1 |
| 4. _____ | 1 |
| 5. _____ | 1 |
| 6. _____ | 1 |

Bonus Responses

| | |
|---|---|
| 7. _____ | 2 |
| 8. _____ | 2 |
| 9. _____ | 2 |
| 10. _____ | 2 |
| 11. _____ | 2 |
| 12. _____ | 2 |
| 13. _____ | 2 |
| 14. _____ | 2 |
| 15. _____ | 2 |
| 16. _____ | 2 |

Total ☐

## 271. Eight or more reasons for not having a Best Seller List

| Response | Score |
|---|---|
| 1. _____ | 1 |
| 2. _____ | 1 |
| 3. _____ | 1 |
| 4. _____ | 1 |
| 5. _____ | 1 |
| 6. _____ | 1 |
| 7. _____ | 1 |
| 8. _____ | 1 |

Bonus Responses

| | |
|---|---|
| 9. _____ | 2 |
| 10. _____ | 2 |
| 11. _____ | 2 |
| 12. _____ | 2 |
| 13. _____ | 2 |
| 14. _____ | 2 |
| 15. _____ | 2 |
| 16. _____ | 2 |

Total ☐

## 272. Nine or more reasons why the president of General Motors earns more than the President of the United States

| Response | Score |
|---|---|
| 1. _____ | 1 |
| 2. _____ | 1 |
| 3. _____ | 1 |
| 4. _____ | 1 |
| 5. _____ | 1 |
| 6. _____ | 1 |
| 7. _____ | 1 |
| 8. _____ | 1 |
| 9. _____ | 1 |

Bonus Responses

| | |
|---|---|
| 10. _____ | 2 |
| 11. _____ | 2 |
| 12. _____ | 2 |
| 13. _____ | 2 |
| 14. _____ | 2 |
| 15. _____ | 2 |
| 16. _____ | 2 |

Total ☐

## 273. Six or more interpretations of "All's fair in love and war"

| Response | Score |
|---|---|
| 1. _____ | 1 |
| 2. _____ | 1 |
| 3. _____ | 1 |
| 4. _____ | 1 |
| 5. _____ | 1 |
| 6. _____ | 1 |

Bonus Responses

| | |
|---|---|
| 7. _____ | 2 |
| 8. _____ | 2 |
| 9. _____ | 2 |
| 10. _____ | 2 |
| 11. _____ | 2 |
| 12. _____ | 2 |
| 13. _____ | 2 |
| 14. _____ | 2 |
| 15. _____ | 2 |
| 16. _____ | 2 |

Total ☐

# CONTRIBUTORS' SAMPLE RESPONSES

---

### 244. Eight or more reasons for not becoming a United States Senator

1. Politics is not currently a prestigious profession.
2. Your job security is limited as you have to continually run for reelection.
3. Your life would be too public.
4. You have to pay attention to a lot of noisy pressure groups.
5. You'd have to live in (ugh) Washington, D.C.
6. If you're not a millionaire you'll feel inferior.
7. You like your present job.
8. You'd have to kiss babies.
9. Because there are quite enough already.
10. Because there are no more vacancies.
11. Because you're an active person and have no wish to sit on your butt all day and night doing nothing.
12. Because you wouldn't like to be seen in *that* company.
13. You've no ambition to be.
14. Because you're a lethargic person and have never been able to summon the energy needed to try for the office.
15. Because you're a procrastinator and you'll become one next time.
16. Because you've good reason to stay out of the public eye.
17. Because you're not an American and don't live in the U.S.
18. Because being a senator is the highest aspiration of the lowest strata of society and you know that you don't belong among those types.
19. Because you're afraid you might be expected to do some work for once.
20. You weren't elected.
21. Because the challenge presented by the office is too insignificant for your superabundant talent and elevated abilities.
22. You're a dropout from society.
23. Too many headaches.
24. Want to be President or nothing.
25. Can't stand rejection.
26. Too shy.
27. Can't lie with a straight face.
28. Dislike travelling.
29. Don't like Koreans.
30. Unable to refuse a bribe.
31. Too much paperwork.
32. Hours are too long.
33. You can make more friends in the House.
34. You can make more enemies in the House.
35. Not enough room for advancement.
36. You can't write a complaint to your Senator.
37. Too expensive to campaign.
38. Too expensive to entertain.
39. Destroys family life.
40. Disrupts love life.
41. You can be impeached.
42. Tax evasion is more difficult.
43. You are honest.
44. Infidelity is more difficult.

---

### 245. Eight or more consequences of an eight-foot blizzard

1. Increases sales of shovels and snowplows.
2. School and stores shut down.
3. Increased traffic accidents.
4. Increases business on the ski slopes.
5. Many pretty photos could be taken.
6. Sliding and sledding would be good for kids.
7. Boy! Have you got problems!—if you're in it, that is.
8. A lot of people who don't mean it saying, "What a tragedy!"
9. Absolutely no problems if it occurs in an area mankind doesn't use.
10. To obscure, albeit temporarily, an unsightly landscape.
11. Destruction of life.
12. A reminder to man that he is subordinate to the forces of nature.
13. Calm—after the force is spent.
14. Knowledge that others will follow, in time.
15. Potential damage to property.
16. Frozen pipes.
17. High heating bills.
18. Frostbite.
19. Inability to locate five-foot-high car.
20. Loss of electricity, due to downed lines.
21. Transportation standstill.
22. Collapsed roofs.
23. Unable to exit single-story houses.
24. Day off from work.
25. Overtime for people stranded at work.
26. School holidays.
27. Mothers with nervous breakdowns.
28. Loss of livestock.
29. Fish won't bite.
30. Beautiful crystal-clear air.
31. Give everyone topic of conversation for years.
32. Cars get stuck.
33. Supermarket shelves become empty.
34. People die of heart attacks shoveling driveways.
35. People die of heart attacks waiting for their driveway to be shovelled.
36. Homes disappear with the flood.
37. The dirty snow will last longer.
38. Snow blocks windows.
39. Plants die.
40. Snow covers the grass.
41. Can't spy on neighbors.
42. Hard to get to store.
43. Snowmobile would sink.

---

### 246. Seven or more reasons for buying stale bread

1. If you're not fussy, it's OK for you.
2. Similarly, it's less likely to be crushed in the grocery bag.
3. It prepares you for how it's going to be after the revolution.
4. Requires less time to toast.
5. To help the baker reduce his stock.
6. To use it in any application where stale bread can be used.
7. To spend some money.
8. To get something to throw while in a tantrum instead of plates and dishes.
9. Something to play with.
10. Something to grow yeast on.
11. To possess something worthless.
12. To conduct experiments with it.
13. To bait with poison to get rid of pests.
14. Cheaper.
15. Healthier.
16. Makes better toast.
17. Won't tear as easily when spreading peanut butter.
18. Birds like it better.
19. Tastes better.
20. Floats longer (for feeding ducks).
21. Makes better turkey stuffing.
22. Never have to worry about it going stale.
23. Can't tell when you burn it.
24. Not soft and squishy.
25. Easy to break crust off.
26. Good for bread crumbs.
27. Makes better french toast.
28. Gives healthier molds (penicillin easier to make).

---

### 247. Seven or more reasons why Detroit changes car models every year

1. For whimsy of head executive.
2. To give designers work.
3. To supply junkyards.
4. Because Dallas can't.
5. Too expensive to change them twice a year.
6. Americans get bored easily.
7. Because they're trying to impress the world and show everybody how clever they are.
8. Because people want to be fashionable and don't want to be seen driving last year's or any other year's model except this year's.
9. Because it's the best way yet discovered to get people to spend money and get nothing of value in return.
10. Because they're determined beyond reason to waste every resource they can lay their hands on.
11. Because they're on an ego-trip.
12. Because they've nothing better to do to keep themselves occupied.
13. Because planned obsolescence is the creed by which they live.
14. Because they believe there's nothing quite like promoting your own interests.
15. The profit motive.
16. To spatter advertising time and space.
17. To serve as a constant reminder of the kitsch man is capable of producing.
18. To do their share in covering the planet with junk.
19. To uphold capitalism's finest traditions.
20. Habit.
21. To keep ahead of competition.
22. To drive body shop and auto parts dealers crazy trying to keep up.
23. People tire of the old model quickly.
24. To give beautiful women something to lean on while

159

being photographed.
25. To avoid interchangeable parts.
26. To keep people employed.
27. To confuse people.
28. So people can't lie about the age of their cars.
29. So they can sell next year's cars this year.
30. Trying to get it right.
31. To keep up with the Japanese Joneses.
32. To make life interesting.

---

### 248. Six or more reasons not to attend the funeral of a close friend

1. He doesn't care anymore and won't know.
2. You don't have a dark suit.
3. You do have a dark suit but only sneakers to wear with it.
4. Funerals depress you.
5. You knew he didn't want to have a funeral and you're annoyed that they're having one anyway.
6. You want to remember him as he was, not in a casket.
7. Organ music drives you up a wall.
8. It's in a church and you're an atheist.
9. He died in Latvia and you're in Albuquerque, New Mexico.
10. There's a one-time-only showing of your favorite foreign movie and you liked your friend *but* . . .
11. You were always your own closest friend.
12. Because you had enemies who were gunning for you and your pal. They got him and you're scared they'll be waiting for you at the funeral.
13. Because you were bad friends with your friend's relatives and they're sure to be there in force.
14. Because a funeral is too much a reminder of death; and your fear of it exceeds even the bond that existed between you and your friend.
15. Because you made a pact that neither would attend the funeral of the other.
16. Because you both died at the same moment.
17. Because you're ill and are therefore unable.
18. Because you do not believe there is such a thing as death; so far as you're

concerned your friend is still alive.
19. You were far away and only heard about it too late.
20. Because you had two close friends; both died at the same time in different places and their funerals were held in locations far apart. It was a toss-up, and you went to the other one.
21. Unable to cope emotionally with the situation.
22. Unable to cry.
23. Allergic to flowers.
24. Funeral conflicts with the Game of the Week.
25. Can't stand the color black.
26. Car headlights don't work (for procession).
27. Afraid you'll be the only one there.
28. You might catch the bouquet.
29. Death could be contagious.
30. The World Series.
31. He/she owed you money.
32. The car died.
33. Your mascara might run (females only).
34. Nothing to do with the black clothes afterwards.
35. Your close friend can't accompany you.
36. Boring.
37. You murdered him/her.
38. Might drown in tears.

---

### 249. Six or more reasons not to buy life insurance

1. They only insure those with least risk.
2. It's "forced savings" and you can do better by investing yourself.
3. You live for today since we could all be gone tomorrow.
4. Because there's no way of insuring yourself against dying.
5. Because insurance companies too often try to wriggle out of their obligation to pay.
6. No one to name as beneficiary.
7. Poor investment.
8. Found a way to take it all with you.
9. Costs too much.
10. Peace of mind.
11. Death wish.
12. Won't help you when you are dead.
13. Wastes time filling out papers, etc.
14. Your life isn't worth much.
15. You are worth only three dollars.
16. Admission of mortality.

17. You won't be able to collect.
18. Salesmen are pushy.

---

### 250. Seven or more reasons why there is usually more than one "best picture" every year

1. They're all so bad, nobody could decide.
2. They make more money if they're billed that way.
3. Different critics make up different lists.
4. Someone has a bizarre sense of humor.
5. They were all exceptionally good.
6. Nobody would go if they were labeled "worst pictures."
7. Nobody cares.
8. Because they're *all* of the same mediocre standard, consequently they're all "best pictures."
9. Because there's more than one film company and each claims a "best picture."
10. Because the critics' tastes differ and each labels a picture "best" according to his/her taste.
11. Because every critic, if sufficiently bribed, will label any picture "best."
12. Because there are as many tastes as there are tasters.
13. Because pictures are in different categories and each category is likely to have its "best."
14. Because certain artists get a high rating, regardless of their merit, and if they appear in more than one picture a year, each of those pictures will likely get a "best" rating.
15. The judges were all female.
16. People are indecisive.
17. Common plots.
18. All budget pictures.
19. Producers bribe judges.
20. The contests are fixed.
21. To cause audience excitement.
22. People can't remember the morning after.

---

### 251. Seven or more characteristics of your ideal space monster

1. Non-humanoid in appearance, e.g., Richard Nixon-like.
2. Evil incarnate.

3. Main diet—human flesh.
4. Supernatural powers.
5. Advanced technology at his command.
6. Exudes a distinctive odor when he has passed by.
7. It doesn't land in Japan and is given a Japanese name.
8. It wouldn't rust.
9. It would not be able to sing out of tune.
10. It would enjoy writing limericks.
11. It would be apolitical.
12. It would not be a capitalist.
13. It would not suffer from halitosis.
14. It would be able to amuse itself when bored.
15. It wouldn't seek to demonetize gold.
16. It wouldn't be a Bible thumper.
17. It wouldn't be a door-to-door salesman.
18. It would not always insist on a scientific explanation for everything.
19. It would deflate the pompous.
20. It wouldn't have a double-barrelled name.
21. It wouldn't try to sell me insurance.
22. It would communicate in English.
23. It wouldn't go out of fashion.
24. It wouldn't be the life and soul of the party.
25. Huge.
26. Multi-legged.
27. Multi-eyed.
28. Drools a lot.
29. Makes hideous noises.
30. Strong enough to beat King Kong or Godzilla.
31. Green.
32. Intelligent.
33. Prefers to attack Tokyo.
34. Naturally curly hair.
35. Eleven toes.
36. Three and a half eyes.
37. Clear complexion.
38. Body odor.
39. Claws on every other hand.
40. Size 15 feet.
41. Handlebar mustache.
42. Three jaws.
43. Must dislike Captain Kirk.
44. Must be illogical.
45. Speaks Spanish.
46. Left feet webbed.

---

### 252. Eight or more things never to store in closets

1. Omelets.
2. Fruit.

3. Woolen garments without mothballs.
4. Solar heating panels.
5. Inflated weather balloons.
6. Spies.
7. Brothers-in-law.
8. Books.
9. Infectious diseases.
10. Recollections.
11. Rhinoceroses.
12. Fire.
13. Ideas.
14. Highways.
15. Relatives.
16. Homosexuals.
17. Elephants (they can't fit on the hangers).
18. Flammables.
19. Pets.
20. Perishable foods.
21. Car.
22. Bus.
23. '64 Chevies.
24. Closet door keys.
25. Younger brothers.
26. Road signs.
27. Women.
28. Closet doors.
29. Eggs.
30. Potted plants.
31. Unpotted plants.
32. Noses.
33. Skeletons.
34. Used five-day deodorant pads.
35. Stale bread.
36. U.S. Senator.
37. Dead friends.
38. This book.

### 253. Seven or more reasons why legal pads are yellow

1. They've always been that way.
2. Looks better than brown.
3. The law is a cowardly profession.
4. The paper is old.
5. To make them stand out in the store from other pads.
6. It goes with any color ink.
7. Easier to read.
8. Any other color is illegal.
9. Because the sky is blue.
10. Cheaper quality paper.
11. Red lines show up better.
12. Better visibility in dim moonlight.
13. To make them different from regular pads.
14. To allow them to be called "legal pads."
15. White is monotonous.
16. To confuse young law students.
17. White paper has been found to cause cancer in laboratory animals.

18. Beer stains don't show up as much.
19. To reduce glare.
20. Senators like them better.
21. Yellow goes well at funerals.
22. Yellow means 14 inches.

### 254. Six or more reasons for not owning a calendar

1. Conserve paper.
2. You can't be blamed for missing anniversaries, etc.
3. It's an arbitrary division of time anyway so why should you care.
4. No space to hang it.
5. Their presence is irritating.
6. They recall a past you'd sooner forget.
7. They point to a future you'd rather not face.
8. You can't read.
9. Life is complicated enough already.
10. Because of an unpleasant experience in childhood.
11. You'll always have an excuse for missing an appointment.
12. Never have to see your birthday coming.
13. Don't like calendar girls.
14. Don't have a bank account (free calendars from banks).
15. Save money.
16. Won't look forward to trouble tomorrow will bring.
17. Spent too much money on yellow legal pads.
18. Untimely demise.
19. Time is irrelevant.
20. Known to cause cancer in rats.
21. So won't know when weeks start or end.
22. Can always say your calendar is full.
23. Won't know when bills are due.

### 255. Seven or more reasons for postponing a vacation

1. Your companion can't get away at the same time.
2. The boss won't let you.
3. You prefer work to vacation.
4. The next vacation you take *has* to be to your mother-in-law's.
5. You just took one.
6. Because you're sick.
7. Because you want to.
8. Because the holiday resort you were going to go to has been destroyed in a catastrophe.

9. Because you've been told there's no place for you anywhere.
10. Your wife has a domineering personality and she says not now.
11. An emergency has been declared and all vacation leave cancelled.
12. You've died and have to await your rebirth.
13. Because you've suddenly gone bankrupt and can't afford it.
14. Because your car has broken down.
15. Because you are a foreigner in this land and can't speak the language and won't be able to make yourself understood.
16. The chance of a big business deal that you've been waiting for all along has arrived at last.
17. Because you don't believe in them.
18. Bad weather.
19. Because you're afraid of having your home burgled while you're away.
20. Because there has been a tremendous cataclysm and everything has been destroyed and everybody killed but you.
21. Because your mother-in-law has threatened to come with you.
22. Light has suddenly ceased to exist and your sight has not yet adjusted to the darkness.
23. Because it's suddenly been decided to change the money and you're right at the tail end of the queue and won't be able to get your new supply in time.
24. Mysterious spikes have suddenly appeared on all roads, highways, and airport landing strips.
25. An unexplained force restrains you.
26. You're apprehended.
27. You're injured.
28. It's been so frightfully hot that you've melted and must wait for it to cool down so you can solidify again.
29. Can't decide where to go.
30. Because you haven't been circumcised and your foreskin has grown so long that you keep tripping over it and you must wait for the doctor to return from *his* vacation to have it trimmed again.
31. Can't take time from work.
32. Illness in family.
33. Nowhere to go.

34. Illness.
35. Airline strike.
36. Political upheaval in country of vacation.
37. Mother-in-law decides not to visit after all.
38. Lack of money.
39. No vacancies.
40. To earn more vacation time.
41. Car broke down.
42. Had to attend funeral of a close friend.
43. To campaign to become senator.

### 256. Eight or more reasons why some taxpayers never pay any taxes

1. They forget.
2. They're trying to cheat.
3. They're wealthy enough to get into the loopholes.
4. They're protesting use of the money (Vietnam War, etc.).
5. If they don't pay taxes, they're not taxpayers.
6. They give all that money to charity.
7. Because they're called taxpayers when, in fact, they aren't.
8. Because they're smart enough to stay one jump ahead of the taxman.
9. Because they were winners in a lottery in which the prizes were exemption from taxes.
10. Because the only obligation to pay taxes is a moral one.
11. Because they have a rich maiden aunt who pays their taxes for them.
12. Because they fall into a category which the government has decided to exempt from paying taxes.
13. Because they know of a couple of Elizabeth Rays hiding away in the taxman's cupboard and he knows that they know.
14. Because they've hit on a way to bamboozle the taxman's computer into not assessing them.
15. Because they know how to hide their income.
16. Because they are members of the class that levies the taxes: quite obviously they don't tax themselves.
17. Underage.
18. Smart lawyers and accountants.
19. Too many children.
20. Excessive medical expenses.
21. Made too much money.

161

22. Made too little money.
23. Untimely demise.
24. Made money illegally.
25. Paid off IRS.
26. Proposition 13.
27. They spent all their money.
28. Loopholes.
29. Don't want to.
30. Ignorance.
31. Illegal aliens.
32. Don't care.

## 257. Seven or more reasons for government grants

1. To support worthy causes.
2. To support unworthy causes.
3. To spend the taxpayers' money.
4. To give the bureaucrats something to do.
5. To give newspaper editors something to rail at.
6. To help struggling artists and scientists keep busy.
7. It's the American way to throw money at problems.
8. Because the government is noted for its generosity.
9. Because they're satisfied that if they give something away today, they'll have a solid reason for taking back a good deal more tomorrow.
10. To finance research into pet projects.
11. To keep on improving the war machine.
12. If you've got access to them, to use to keep your own Elizabeth Ray nice and happy and nice and hot.
13. To keep the plumbers in business.
14. Research.
15. To keep white rat industry solvent.
16. To study bisexual frogs.
17. To see tricycles tip over.
18. To study effect of African pygmy breath on jungle ecology.
19. To determine if life exists on Mars.
20. To determine if anyone cares if life exists on Mars.
21. To determine if intelligent life exists on Earth.
22. To keep government employees busy.
23. To keep the paper industry employed.
24. Need money for yellow legal pads.
25. Sex.
26. Natural disasters.
27. Birth defects.
28. To educate college students.
29. To avoid surplus of government funds.

## 258. Six or more reasons for not having fashion designers

1. They're not necessary.
2. They increase the expense of clothing.
3. People should dress to *their* taste and not that of a designer.
4. They mark up clothing with their names and initials.
5. Most are French so they upset the balance of trade.
6. We wouldn't have to look at their silly photo displays in magazines.
7. To give one an opportunity to save some money for a change.
8. People don't wear clothes anymore.
9. Fashion has become unfashionable.
10. Because fashion designing is done by computers now.
11. Because they were ever demanding higher wages and have now priced themselves right out of employment.
12. Eliminate fashion cycles.
13. Save U.S. husbands untold millions of dollars.
14. Save models embarrassment of having to wear ridiculous-looking clothes.
15. Slobs.
16. To save sheep and cotton plants.
17. Limits freedom of choice.
18. They cause undue psychological stress.
19. People don't care what other people wear.
20. Decreases availability of librarians and hairdressers.

## 259. Seven or more reasons why out-of-state students pay more tuition than in-state students

1. Out-of-state students will probably move and take their skills out of state.
2. If they can afford to travel out of state, they can afford higher tuition.
3. To be perverse.
4. To subsidize the in-state students.
5. To keep the number of such students to a minimum.
6. Because they are foolish enough to admit that they're from out-of-state.
7. Because no good argument can be advanced why taxpayers in a state should be obliged to subsidize outsiders.
8. Because the state administration wants more money, but having already skinned up every taxpayer, it now needs to look elsewhere. This is a source of funds.
9. Because out-of-state students are renowned for their generosity and they always insist on paying more.
10. They pay more to compensate for medical attention which they get for nothing.
11. Because out-of-state students are always duller than in-state students, thus require more attention and, of course, must pay.
12. Because it has been established that out-of-state students always transmit mildly contagious diseases; more tuition is levied to act as a disincentive.
13. Because the fees are higher.
14. Gives parents feeling of status.
15. Because for reasons better known to themselves, states try to keep their knowledge within their borders and charge higher tuition in an endeavor to discourage those they feel might be tempted to take it away from them.
16. Because every student is a disguised Pied Piper of Hamelin and leads all the rats out of his state and into the host state. Higher tuition is charged in order to raise funds to combat the pests.
17. Commuting expenses.
18. Prejudice.
19. Discrimination.
20. In-staters paid taxes to state.
21. To keep students in the state.
22. Expense of learning a foreign language.
23. Because they support the Dodgers.
24. Because it costs more for out-of-state students.
25. To make them study more.
26. To bring more money into the state.

## 260. Six or more reasons why some college faculty never obtain tenure

1. They don't want it.
2. They're not good enough.
3. They don't play politics.
4. The college has limited funds.
5. They're women.
6. They lack credentials (i.e., right degrees).
7. Find better paying positions.
8. Can't stand kids.
9. Fired.
10. Marry and give up work.
11. Nervous breakdown.
12. The Super Bowl.
13. Incompetence.
14. Sex.
15. Poor evaluations.
16. Discriminating administrations.
17. Retirement.
18. Untimely demise.
19. Illness.
20. 'Cause they quit after ninure.
21. School closes down.
22. They don't **know** what it means.
23. Can't speek English.
24. Can't speak properly.
25. They give too many "A"s.

## 261. Six or more reasons why Harvard's tuition is more expensive than Brown's

1. The Dean of Harvard wants a new Mercedes, yacht, mansion . . .
2. The all-star jocks go to Harvard.
3. Harvard isn't as common a name as Brown's.
4. Harvard has a quicker and more elaborate mass production of brainy people.
5. Harvard's tuition is more because even though it deflates your wallet, it inflates your ego.
6. Harvard is for equality; it doesn't discriminate against rich people.
7. Harvard employs more professors.
8. Harvard grants more scholarships.
9. Harvard supports more research.
10. Harvard has greater prestige.
11. Harvard is older and thus has had more time to raise prices.
12. They charge by the letter and Harvard has two more letters in its name than Brown.
13. Harvard buys better equipment.
14. Harvard's purchasing officer was once employed by the GSA.
15. Harvard has higher building

maintenance costs.
16. Dormitory rooms are more luxurious.
17. Cafeteria serves better food.
18. Harvard has a bigger library.
19. Harvard does a better job of bribing the local cops so they don't bust too many students.
20. Harvard does a better job of bribing the local cops so they don't bust too many professors.
21. Harvard has a more expensive football team.
22. Harvard has more pressure on it to keep up with Yale than Brown does.
23. Harvard has a bigger computer.
24. Harvard makes more long distance phone calls.
25. Better teachers, staff.
26. Better reputation.
27. Higher standards.
28. Snob appeal.

### 262. Eight or more reasons for not awarding the Nobel Prize

1. The minority never gets its choice.
2. It's depressing and humiliating if you don't get one.
3. Students are stuck reading the books which received Nobel Prizes.
4. It becomes an obsession to the authors.
5. It's not fair to judge a book by its cover.
6. Well-written books without Nobel Prizes get left behind and go to waste.
7. There are so many prizes and awards that it gets monotonous.
8. No one was qualified.
9. The judges couldn't agree.
10. The trust fund went broke.
11. Someone just discovered that gunpowder causes cancer.
12. Two of last year's award winners were caught in bed together the night of the awards and no one wants to dredge up the memory of scandal.
13. The awards were to be run on TV opposite *The Muppets* and everyone was worried about bad ratings.
14. Someone tried to fix the nominations.
15. Norway invaded Sweden.
16. All of last year's winners came down with

Legionnaire's Disease.
17. Two of the judges were discovered to be KGB spies.
18. IT&T is negotiating to buy out the Nobel organization.
19. One of the judges was killed in a duel by one of the nominees.
20. They were worried about sufficient coverage since the New York *Times* is on strike.
21. All the ballots were eaten by someone's pet goat.
22. There's a big argument over whether to add a swimsuit competition.
23. The judge's handwriting is so bad that no one can read the ballots.
24. They were accused of racism and are trying to work out an affirmative action plan.
25. Creates tension among nations and individuals.
26. Unfair to differentiate between great and small achievements.
27. No one in the field achieves a high-enough standard.
28. Encourages excessive competition for notoriety.
29. Prize money could be better applied elsewhere.
30. Currency transfer frozen.
31. Chosen recipient couldn't accept prize in Sweden.
32. Often doesn't go to the *de facto* greatest contributor in a field.
33. May not even recognize the *recipient's* greatest achievement.

### 263. Seven or more novel uses of a large rubber band

1. To knock over a giant.
2. As a girdle.
3. To make a large ponytail.
4. To make little bundles of people.
5. Use it as an exerciser.
6. Stretch it from one end of a street to the other to block off traffic.
7. To hold the shoulder pad on my violin.
8. As a weapon in skirmishes with clerks on the other side of the room.
9. To provide a good grip on a tight jar lid.
10. To hold the car door shut when the lock freezes.
11. To clamp together glued objects.
12. To mark which coffee cup is yours.
13. To label flower pots.
14. To suspend a mobile.

15. To mark your place in a book.
16. To use instead of cord when tie-dying.
17. Temporary replacement for a broken sewing machine belt.
18. To hold the fabric in place if you only have one embroidery hoop.
19. Power a motor boat.
20. Substitute for chewing gum.
21. Make a slingshot.
22. Make a musical instrument.
23. Secure bundled clothing.
24. Hold a sandwich together.
25. Hold rolled newspapers together.
26. Insulate electrical contacts.
27. Paint *red*—use for person's *lips* in collage.
28. Use for puppet strings.
29. Mend broken vase or pot.
30. Make into a *snake*, or snake's tongue.
31. To keep your head attached to the rest of you.

### 264. Eight or more differences between a barber and hair stylist

1. A barber gives a crew cut no matter what you say.
2. Hair stylist gives the "in" look.
3. A hair stylist has plants and flowers.
4. A barber is old-fashioned.
5. A hair stylist gets you ready for disco.
6. A barber doesn't get customers like John Travolta.
7. You'll never catch a hair stylist without a blow dryer and curling iron.
8. Barber charges less.
9. For a hair stylist you need an appointment.
10. When you see a barber, you end up with shorter hair.
11. A hair stylist is younger.
12. A barber is usually married.
13. A hair stylist has a diploma.
14. A barber doesn't make you feel guilty for wearing pigtails.
15. A barber knows more local gossip.
16. Hair stylists don't have red and white striped poles.
17. No hair stylist has ever bled a person.
18. No hair stylist has ever pulled teeth.
19. A hair stylist sweeps up after each customer.
20. A hair stylist's shampoo is perfumed.
21. A hair stylist has a lot more

pictures of fancy hairdos around the shop.
22. Barbers serve *men* mainly— stylists both men and women.
23. Barbers do *shaves* as well as haircuts.
24. Barbers will trim hair in nose and ears.
25. Stylists do more *fashionable* work.
26. Reputations as to sexual preferences.
27. Barbers work at one chair— stylists at various stations.
28. Stylists do more shampooing and other beauty treatments.
29. Stylists generally work in a more prestigious atmosphere.

### 265. Six or more reasons for not awarding diplomas

1. Anyone can get a diploma.
2. It would be one less thing to clutter my room with.
3. The few people that don't get one feel worthless.
4. They don't tell you much about the person.
5. Save trees.
6. Save the cost of your rental.
7. Most kids go out and get drunk after graduation anyhow.
8. They can be purchased for $15.00 mail-order.
9. Grade devaluation in the past 10 years has made them nearly meaningless.
10. No one can read Latin anymore.
11. With all the current government programs for the disadvantaged, it's harder to get a job if you have a diploma.
12. Saves an elderly school board member the embarrassment of trying to pronounce all the seniors' names.
13. Relieves several kids of the suffering involved in preparing and delivering speeches.
14. Creates unfair advantages.
15. Creates unrealistic expectations.
16. Makes graduates feel their education is "complete."
17. Meaningless, useless.
18. Person may have failed to complete requirements or skipped graduation.
19. Hard to read and understand.
20. Artificial symbol of achievement.
21. Needed only for display.

### 266. Seven or more reasons why some college professors earn less than plumbers

1. Their philosophies won't hold water.
2. Plumbers do practical, necessary work.
3. Cost of overhead higher for universities.
4. Professors enjoy better working conditions.
5. Professors may do more research than teaching.
6. Greater need and demand for plumbers' services.
7. Professors may specialize in subject of interest to few people other than themselves.
8. Plumbers must endure discomfort and irregular hours.
9. Professors have greater "psychic income."
10. Plumbers are unionized.
11. Indoor plumbing is required by zoning regulations.
12. More people have sinks and toilets than have college degrees.
13. More people *want* sinks and toilets than want college degrees.
14. Plumbers have to make house calls.
15. Plumbers have to get physically dirty in their jobs.
16. College professors are more likely to perceive rewards other than monetary ones as being important.
17. Teachers are traditionally low paid to emphasize their altruism.
18. Plumbers are self-employed generally and just carry their own health insurance, social security, etc.
19. After spending a night listening to a drippy faucet, most people are willing to spend anything to get it repaired.
20. College professors must sit all day.
21. Plumbers have to use all of their physical strength.
22. College professors don't work.
23. Plumbers have to deal with rough and tough men.
24. College professors just babysit.
25. A plumber could get his finger stuck in a pipe.

### 267. Eight or more reasons for not having a World Heavyweight Boxing Champion

1. It would decrease the number of fat people in the world.
2. Fatness would not be considered an asset.
3. Fewer boxing gloves would have to be made.
4. Fewer people would get grossed out.
5. The World Featherweight Boxing Champion would get more attention.
6. Less blood would be shed.
7. There wouldn't be as many bullies.
8. The would-be Heavyweight Champions could do something more constructive.
9. The candy bar tastes awful.
10. It's not a true world title anyhow.
11. As political repression of Ali.
12. To divert the millions of dollars spent on championship matches to charity.
13. To save potential champions from corruption.
14. To eliminate an aggressive hero-figure.
15. To encourage physically strong young men to use their abilities for something useful to society.
16. It's a basically sexist enterprise.
17. To eliminate traffic jams around training camps.
18. Boxing is barbarous.
19. None of the contenders deserves the title.
20. Confusion as to how the "world" champ chosen.
21. Encourages gambling, corruption.
22. Encourages some youth to develop bodies versus minds.
23. Weight classifications are unfair.
24. Judging standards are arbitrary, unfair.
25. Economically indefensible.

### 268. Seven or more reasons for having prime time

1. So the whole family can watch TV together.
2. To make the shows seem better at that time.
3. So the stations can make more money.
4. So the advertisers can get everyone at the same time.
5. It adds to our system of categorizing everything.
6. So everyone has a chance to watch the popular shows.
7. Provides outlets for people with little to do.
8. Concentrates best programs in time most people can watch TV.
9. Ensures *news* programs available.
10. So people enjoy watching TV when they have time.
11. Provide acceptable programs for family viewing.
12. Foster competition among TV networks, stations.
13. Increase ad revenues.
14. Allow more efficient transmission of propaganda.

### 269. Seven or more reasons to want to grow old

1. To retire from work.
2. So you can collect social security checks.
3. To be able to just sit in a rocking chair and do nothing.
4. To be able to go on free senior citizen trips.
5. To change your status from a parent to a grandparent.
6. To look different than you look now.
7. To be able to say, "I'm a century old."
8. One lives in a society where age is revered.
9. So my parents quit hassling me about when am I getting married.
10. Needn't tolerate children.
11. To have other people work for me instead of my working for them.
12. To watch my hair get gray.
13. To gain the wisdom and experience which come with age.
14. So I'm not always the youngest in situations.
15. So other people stop thinking I'm weird to prefer Bach to rock.
16. To appear more dignified.
17. To have allowances made for eccentric behavior.
18. Attain maturity.
19. Finish life's pleasures and miseries.
20. See your children have problems with *their* kids.
21. Live off your children.
22. See parents and enemies die.
23. Learn more.
24. Understand life.
25. Eliminate hazards of sexual fertility.

### 270. Six or more new uses for yellow Jell-O

1. To shock your guests at dinner.
2. To brighten up a rainy day.
3. To lighten blonde hair.
4. It could come in handy if your doctor wants a urine specimen and you can't go to the bathroom.
5. To wax the floors with.
6. To fingerpaint with.
7. As a spotlight gel.
8. As a traffic signal.
9. As a "hi-liter" for cue cards.
10. For people who want an extra-firm water bed.
11. To fill glass jars as decoration.
12. (Unmixed) As the filler in an hour glass.
13. (Unmixed) Sprinkle in patterns over the icing of a cake.
14. Colored optical filters.
15. Use in crab salad.
16. Use in pumpkin pie.
17. Use as glaze on roast duck.
18. Use as title and subject for a poem.
19. Make non-flammable candles.
20. Make slime for aquariums.
21. Make a ski run.
22. Make a bobsled course.
23. Freeze into ice cubes for lemonade.
24. Cover roads to stop tanks, other military vehicles.
25. To blend in with the new yellow carpet.

### 271. Eight or more reasons for not having a Best Seller list

1. It restricts extent of people's reading.
2. The people that pick the best seller lists don't even buy the books.
3. It's impossible to find one of those books in a library.
4. Schools don't purchase best seller books because they're not suited for teenagers.
5. There's always a mad rush for these books at the bookstand.
6. It strangles open-mindedness and individuality.

7. They're usually made into movies and ruined.
8. The authors become filthy rich.
9. It's a self-fulfilling prophecy.
10. To slow down the economy by putting out of work those persons who compile the lists.
11. Save space in newspapers and magazines.
12. Give unsuccessful writers less to worry about.
13. Give successful writers one less reason to be arrogant.
14. They aren't terribly accurate anyway.
15. Readers should choose books by quality, not popularity.
16. Unfair to new authors—those with previous best sellers get most contracts and sales.
17. Causes authors to try to write books like those, which has a self-homogenizing effect.
18. Allows heavy advertising of mediocre books.
19. Books should compete on their merits, rather than ad budget.
20. Caters to mob psychology.
21. Draws excess attention to the mediocre tastes of the mob.
22. Encourages more people to read poorer books.
23. Tends to force libraries to stock extra copies of books without lasting value.

---

272. Nine or more reasons why the President of General Motors earns more than the President of the United States

1. The President of the U.S. gets everyone in trouble.
2. The President of General Motors doesn't get as many trips and vacations.
3. The President of the U.S. gets a big house with every room a different color.
4. Cars are in the greatest demand.
5. The President of General Motors doesn't get as many benefits, such as bodyguards.
6. A lot of money has to go to all of the helpers to the President of the U.S.
7. We don't need a President of the U.S., he's just there for status purposes.
8. The President of General Motor is in charge of production and the President of the U.S. is in charge of destruction.
9. Fewer people elect the President of General Motors.
10. The private sector traditionally pays better than government.
11. President of the U.S. is

supposed to have a certain altruistic motivation.
12. General Motors usually runs a profit; the U.S. always runs a loss.
13. Fewer people have reason to resent the President of General Motors.
14. Fewer people have any say in setting the salary for the President of General Motors.
15. Life is unfair.
16. President of General Motors probably had to do some actual productive work to gain his position.
17. President of U.S. has better fringe benefits.
18. Corporations requires presidents with *profit* motive.
19. President of General Motors has greater *direct* responsibilities.
20. President of U.S. is a "public servant."
21. President of U.S. is an elected official.
22. President of U.S. has guaranteed term.
23. President of U.S. has greater public popularity and regard.
24. Because no one ever went broke underestimating the taste of the American public.
25. President of General Motors can *bargain* for his salary.
26. President of General Motors has a piece of the action—stock ownership.
27. Americans are prejudiced

against wealthy politicians.

---

273. Six or more interpretations of "All's fair in love and war"

1. In time of war, you can kill anyone.
2. You can love or make love to more than one person.
3. If someone gets mad, you can take any steps to get revenge.
4. You can get away with anything if you say, "I did it for love."
5. Only blondes fight and have sex.
6. When one makes love or fights, one thinks the sun is always shining.
7. In L or W, no tactic may be labeled "unfair."
8. People in love, like people at war, are totally unscrupulous in achieving their ends.
9. When stakes are high, standards get low.
10. *Winning* is top priority in both cases.
11. There can be no bounds on love or hate.
12. Vanquish the opposition at all costs!
13. Surprise and deception may win the day.
14. In love, all is fair and delightful; in war, all *tactics* are permitted.

# OCTOBER

### Mental Calisthenic #10

Sit alone quietly in an area free of distractions. Close your eyes and focus on the space between your nostrils. Experience the air being inhaled and becoming part of you. Experience the exhaled air leaving your body. Then refocus on the rising and falling of your belly, as you breathe in and out. Breathe slowly and become aware of what your body is telling you. Proceed with a Mental Jogging exercise.

## 274. Eight or more reasons for not having IQ tests

| Response | Score |
|---|---|
| 1. | 1 |
| 2. | 1 |
| 3. | 1 |
| 4. | 1 |
| 5. | 1 |
| 6. | 1 |
| 7. | 1 |
| 8. | 1 |

Bonus Responses

| | |
|---|---|
| 9. | 2 |
| 10. | 2 |
| 11. | 2 |
| 12. | 2 |
| 13. | 2 |
| 14. | 2 |
| 15. | 2 |
| 16. | 2 |

Total ☐

## 275. Six or more languages you've never heard or read

| Response | Score |
|---|---|
| 1. | 1 |
| 2. | 1 |
| 3. | 1 |
| 4. | 1 |
| 5. | 1 |
| 6. | 1 |

Bonus Responses

| | |
|---|---|
| 7. | 2 |
| 8. | 2 |
| 9. | 2 |
| 10. | 2 |
| 11. | 2 |
| 12. | 2 |
| 13. | 2 |
| 14. | 2 |
| 15. | 2 |
| 16. | 2 |

Total ☐

## 276. Seven or more reasons to burn white toast

| Response | Score |
|---|---|
| 1. | 1 |
| 2. | 1 |
| 3. | 1 |
| 4. | 1 |
| 5. | 1 |
| 6. | 1 |
| 7. | 1 |

Bonus Responses

| | |
|---|---|
| 8. | 2 |
| 9. | 2 |
| 10. | 2 |
| 11. | 2 |
| 12. | 2 |
| 13. | 2 |
| 14. | 2 |
| 15. | 2 |
| 16. | 2 |

Total ☐

## 277. Eight or more reasons for not having filing cabinets

| Response | Score |
|---|---|
| 1. | 1 |
| 2. | 1 |
| 3. | 1 |
| 4. | 1 |
| 5. | 1 |
| 6. | 1 |
| 7. | 1 |
| 8. | 1 |

Bonus Responses

| | |
|---|---|
| 9. | 2 |
| 10. | 2 |
| 11. | 2 |
| 12. | 2 |
| 13. | 2 |
| 14. | 2 |
| 15. | 2 |
| 16. | 2 |

Total ☐

## 278. Seven or more thoughts that come to mind when you read the word "shell"

| Response | Score |
|---|---|
| 1. | 1 |
| 2. | 1 |
| 3. | 1 |
| 4. | 1 |
| 5. | 1 |
| 6. | 1 |
| 7. | 1 |

Bonus Responses

| | |
|---|---|
| 8. | 2 |
| 9. | 2 |
| 10. | 2 |
| 11. | 2 |
| 12. | 2 |
| 13. | 2 |
| 14. | 2 |
| 15. | 2 |
| 16. | 2 |

Total ☐

## 279. Six or more reasons why it should be legal to be married to more than one person at a time

| Response | Score |
|---|---|
| 1. | 1 |
| 2. | 1 |
| 3. | 1 |
| 4. | 1 |
| 5. | 1 |
| 6. | 1 |

Bonus Responses

| | |
|---|---|
| 7. | 2 |
| 8. | 2 |
| 9. | 2 |
| 10. | 2 |
| 11. | 2 |
| 12. | 2 |
| 13. | 2 |
| 14. | 2 |
| 15. | 2 |
| 16. | 2 |

Total ☐

## 280. Eight or more reasons for not having alimony

| | Response | Score |
|---|---|---|
| 1. | _____ | 1 |
| 2. | _____ | 1 |
| 3. | _____ | 1 |
| 4. | _____ | 1 |
| 5. | _____ | 1 |
| 6. | _____ | 1 |
| 7. | _____ | 1 |
| 8. | _____ | 1 |

**Bonus Responses**

| 9. | _____ | 2 |
|---|---|---|
| 10. | _____ | 2 |
| 11. | _____ | 2 |
| 12. | _____ | 2 |
| 13. | _____ | 2 |
| 14. | _____ | 2 |
| 15. | _____ | 2 |
| 16. | _____ | 2 |

Total ☐

## 281. Seven or more reasons for not having car insurance

| | Response | Score |
|---|---|---|
| 1. | _____ | 1 |
| 2. | _____ | 1 |
| 3. | _____ | 1 |
| 4. | _____ | 1 |
| 5. | _____ | 1 |
| 6. | _____ | 1 |
| 7. | _____ | 1 |

**Bonus Responses**

| 8. | _____ | 2 |
|---|---|---|
| 9. | _____ | 2 |
| 10. | _____ | 2 |
| 11. | _____ | 2 |
| 12. | _____ | 2 |
| 13. | _____ | 2 |
| 14. | _____ | 2 |
| 15. | _____ | 2 |
| 16. | _____ | 2 |

Total ☐

## 282. Eight or more reasons for not having a pencil sharpener

| | Response | Score |
|---|---|---|
| 1. | _____ | 1 |
| 2. | _____ | 1 |
| 3. | _____ | 1 |
| 4. | _____ | 1 |
| 5. | _____ | 1 |
| 6. | _____ | 1 |
| 7. | _____ | 1 |
| 8. | _____ | 1 |

**Bonus Responses**

| 9. | _____ | 2 |
|---|---|---|
| 10. | _____ | 2 |
| 11. | _____ | 2 |
| 12. | _____ | 2 |
| 13. | _____ | 2 |
| 14. | _____ | 2 |
| 15. | _____ | 2 |
| 16. | _____ | 2 |

Total ☐

## 283. Seven or more reasons why some people get sick after visiting a foreign country

| | Response | Score |
|---|---|---|
| 1. | _____ | 1 |
| 2. | _____ | 1 |
| 3. | _____ | 1 |
| 4. | _____ | 1 |
| 5. | _____ | 1 |
| 6. | _____ | 1 |
| 7. | _____ | 1 |

**Bonus Responses**

| 8. | _____ | 2 |
|---|---|---|
| 9. | _____ | 2 |
| 10. | _____ | 2 |
| 11. | _____ | 2 |
| 12. | _____ | 2 |
| 13. | _____ | 2 |
| 14. | _____ | 2 |
| 15. | _____ | 2 |
| 16. | _____ | 2 |

Total ☐

## 284. Seven or more reasons for not flying a kite

| Response | Score |
|---|---|
| 1. _____ | 1 |
| 2. _____ | 1 |
| 3. _____ | 1 |
| 4. _____ | 1 |
| 5. _____ | 1 |
| 6. _____ | 1 |
| 7. _____ | 1 |

Bonus Responses

| | |
|---|---|
| 8. _____ | 2 |
| 9. _____ | 2 |
| 10. _____ | 2 |
| 11. _____ | 2 |
| 12. _____ | 2 |
| 13. _____ | 2 |
| 14. _____ | 2 |
| 15. _____ | 2 |
| 16. _____ | 2 |

Total [ ]

## 285. Eight or more reasons for having more than one religion

| Response | Score |
|---|---|
| 1. _____ | 1 |
| 2. _____ | 1 |
| 3. _____ | 1 |
| 4. _____ | 1 |
| 5. _____ | 1 |
| 6. _____ | 1 |
| 7. _____ | 1 |
| 8. _____ | 1 |

Bonus Responses

| | |
|---|---|
| 9. _____ | 2 |
| 10. _____ | 2 |
| 11. _____ | 2 |
| 12. _____ | 2 |
| 13. _____ | 2 |
| 14. _____ | 2 |
| 15. _____ | 2 |
| 16. _____ | 2 |

Total [ ]

## 286. Six or more reasons why a live dinosaur will never appear in Central Park, New York City

| Response | Score |
|---|---|
| 1. _____ | 1 |
| 2. _____ | 1 |
| 3. _____ | 1 |
| 4. _____ | 1 |
| 5. _____ | 1 |
| 6. _____ | 1 |

Bonus Responses

| | |
|---|---|
| 7. _____ | 2 |
| 8. _____ | 2 |
| 9. _____ | 2 |
| 10. _____ | 2 |
| 11. _____ | 2 |
| 12. _____ | 2 |
| 13. _____ | 2 |
| 14. _____ | 2 |
| 15. _____ | 2 |
| 16. _____ | 2 |

Total [ ]

## 287. Seven or more reasons to have one brand of lager beer

| Response | Score |
|---|---|
| 1. _____ | 1 |
| 2. _____ | 1 |
| 3. _____ | 1 |
| 4. _____ | 1 |
| 5. _____ | 1 |
| 6. _____ | 1 |
| 7. _____ | 1 |

Bonus Responses

| | |
|---|---|
| 8. _____ | 2 |
| 9. _____ | 2 |
| 10. _____ | 2 |
| 11. _____ | 2 |
| 12. _____ | 2 |
| 13. _____ | 2 |
| 14. _____ | 2 |
| 15. _____ | 2 |
| 16. _____ | 2 |

Total [ ]

## 288. Six or more reasons for not having tow trucks

| Response | Score |
|---|---|
| 1. _____ | 1 |
| 2. _____ | 1 |
| 3. _____ | 1 |
| 4. _____ | 1 |
| 5. _____ | 1 |
| 6. _____ | 1 |

Bonus Responses

| | |
|---|---|
| 7. _____ | 2 |
| 8. _____ | 2 |
| 9. _____ | 2 |
| 10. _____ | 2 |
| 11. _____ | 2 |
| 12. _____ | 2 |
| 13. _____ | 2 |
| 14. _____ | 2 |
| 15. _____ | 2 |
| 16. _____ | 2 |

Total ☐

## 289. Seven or more reasons why some people lie all the time

| Response | Score |
|---|---|
| 1. _____ | 1 |
| 2. _____ | 1 |
| 3. _____ | 1 |
| 4. _____ | 1 |
| 5. _____ | 1 |
| 6. _____ | 1 |
| 7. _____ | 1 |

Bonus Responses

| | |
|---|---|
| 8. _____ | 2 |
| 9. _____ | 2 |
| 10. _____ | 2 |
| 11. _____ | 2 |
| 12. _____ | 2 |
| 13. _____ | 2 |
| 14. _____ | 2 |
| 15. _____ | 2 |
| 16. _____ | 2 |

Total ☐

## 290. Eight or more reasons for not having curtains

| Response | Score |
|---|---|
| 1. _____ | 1 |
| 2. _____ | 1 |
| 3. _____ | 1 |
| 4. _____ | 1 |
| 5. _____ | 1 |
| 6. _____ | 1 |
| 7. _____ | 1 |
| 8. _____ | 1 |

Bonus Responses

| | |
|---|---|
| 9. _____ | 2 |
| 10. _____ | 2 |
| 11. _____ | 2 |
| 12. _____ | 2 |
| 13. _____ | 2 |
| 14. _____ | 2 |
| 15. _____ | 2 |
| 16. _____ | 2 |

Total ☐

## 291. Eight or more reasons for not wanting to be a sports reporter

| Response | Score |
|---|---|
| 1. _____ | 1 |
| 2. _____ | 1 |
| 3. _____ | 1 |
| 4. _____ | 1 |
| 5. _____ | 1 |
| 6. _____ | 1 |
| 7. _____ | 1 |
| 8. _____ | 1 |

Bonus Responses

| | |
|---|---|
| 9. _____ | 2 |
| 10. _____ | 2 |
| 11. _____ | 2 |
| 12. _____ | 2 |
| 13. _____ | 2 |
| 14. _____ | 2 |
| 15. _____ | 2 |
| 16. _____ | 2 |

Total ☐

## 292. Seven or more reasons why the number of foreign correspondents has dramatically decreased since World War II

| Response | Score |
|---|---|
| 1. _____ | 1 |
| 2. _____ | 1 |
| 3. _____ | 1 |
| 4. _____ | 1 |
| 5. _____ | 1 |
| 6. _____ | 1 |
| 7. _____ | 1 |

Bonus Responses

| | |
|---|---|
| 8. _____ | 2 |
| 9. _____ | 2 |
| 10. _____ | 2 |
| 11. _____ | 2 |
| 12. _____ | 2 |
| 13. _____ | 2 |
| 14. _____ | 2 |
| 15. _____ | 2 |
| 16. _____ | 2 |

Total ☐

## 293. Eight or more reasons why many small newspapers are jealous of the *New York Times*

| Response | Score |
|---|---|
| 1. _____ | 1 |
| 2. _____ | 1 |
| 3. _____ | 1 |
| 4. _____ | 1 |
| 5. _____ | 1 |
| 6. _____ | 1 |
| 7. _____ | 1 |
| 8. _____ | 1 |

Bonus Responses

| | |
|---|---|
| 9. _____ | 2 |
| 10. _____ | 2 |
| 11. _____ | 2 |
| 12. _____ | 2 |
| 13. _____ | 2 |
| 14. _____ | 2 |
| 15. _____ | 2 |
| 16. _____ | 2 |

Total ☐

## 294. Six or more reasons for not having unions

| Response | Score |
|---|---|
| 1. _____ | 1 |
| 2. _____ | 1 |
| 3. _____ | 1 |
| 4. _____ | 1 |
| 5. _____ | 1 |
| 6. _____ | 1 |

Bonus Responses

| | |
|---|---|
| 7. _____ | 2 |
| 8. _____ | 2 |
| 9. _____ | 2 |
| 10. _____ | 2 |
| 11. _____ | 2 |
| 12. _____ | 2 |
| 13. _____ | 2 |
| 14. _____ | 2 |
| 15. _____ | 2 |
| 16. _____ | 2 |

Total ☐

## 295. Eight or more reasons to do away with late night talk shows

| Response | Score |
|---|---|
| 1. _____ | 1 |
| 2. _____ | 1 |
| 3. _____ | 1 |
| 4. _____ | 1 |
| 5. _____ | 1 |
| 6. _____ | 1 |
| 7. _____ | 1 |
| 8. _____ | 1 |

Bonus Responses

| | |
|---|---|
| 9. _____ | 2 |
| 10. _____ | 2 |
| 11. _____ | 2 |
| 12. _____ | 2 |
| 13. _____ | 2 |
| 14. _____ | 2 |
| 15. _____ | 2 |
| 16. _____ | 2 |

Total ☐

## 296. Seven or more reasons for not practicing birth control

| Response | Score |
|---|---|
| 1. | 1 |
| 2. | 1 |
| 3. | 1 |
| 4. | 1 |
| 5. | 1 |
| 6. | 1 |
| 7. | 1 |

**Bonus Responses**

| | |
|---|---|
| 8. | 2 |
| 9. | 2 |
| 10. | 2 |
| 11. | 2 |
| 12. | 2 |
| 13. | 2 |
| 14. | 2 |
| 15. | 2 |
| 16. | 2 |

Total ☐

## 297. Eight or more reasons for never attending a lecture

| Response | Score |
|---|---|
| 1. | 1 |
| 2. | 1 |
| 3. | 1 |
| 4. | 1 |
| 5. | 1 |
| 6. | 1 |
| 7. | 1 |
| 8. | 1 |

**Bonus Responses**

| | |
|---|---|
| 9. | 2 |
| 10. | 2 |
| 11. | 2 |
| 12. | 2 |
| 13. | 2 |
| 14. | 2 |
| 15. | 2 |
| 16. | 2 |

Total ☐

## 298. Eight or more reasons for being outside during a hailstorm

| Response | Score |
|---|---|
| 1. | 1 |
| 2. | 1 |
| 3. | 1 |
| 4. | 1 |
| 5. | 1 |
| 6. | 1 |
| 7. | 1 |
| 8. | 1 |

**Bonus Responses**

| | |
|---|---|
| 9. | 2 |
| 10. | 2 |
| 11. | 2 |
| 12. | 2 |
| 13. | 2 |
| 14. | 2 |
| 15. | 2 |
| 16. | 2 |

Total ☐

## 299. Seven or more reasons why most adults do not drink milk

| Response | Score |
|---|---|
| 1. | 1 |
| 2. | 1 |
| 3. | 1 |
| 4. | 1 |
| 5. | 1 |
| 6. | 1 |
| 7. | 1 |

**Bonus Responses**

| | |
|---|---|
| 8. | 2 |
| 9. | 2 |
| 10. | 2 |
| 11. | 2 |
| 12. | 2 |
| 13. | 2 |
| 14. | 2 |
| 15. | 2 |
| 16. | 2 |

Total ☐

## 300. Seven or more reasons for not becoming a forensic pathologist

| Response | Score |
|---|---|
| 1. _____ | 1 |
| 2. _____ | 1 |
| 3. _____ | 1 |
| 4. _____ | 1 |
| 5. _____ | 1 |
| 6. _____ | 1 |
| 7. _____ | 1 |

Bonus Responses

| | |
|---|---|
| 8. _____ | 2 |
| 9. _____ | 2 |
| 10. _____ | 2 |
| 11. _____ | 2 |
| 12. _____ | 2 |
| 13. _____ | 2 |
| 14. _____ | 2 |
| 15. _____ | 2 |
| 16. _____ | 2 |

Total ☐

## 301. Six or more reasons for not attending a Walt Disney movie

| Response | Score |
|---|---|
| 1. _____ | 1 |
| 2. _____ | 1 |
| 3. _____ | 1 |
| 4. _____ | 1 |
| 5. _____ | 1 |
| 6. _____ | 1 |

Bonus Responses

| | |
|---|---|
| 7. _____ | 2 |
| 8. _____ | 2 |
| 9. _____ | 2 |
| 10. _____ | 2 |
| 11. _____ | 2 |
| 12. _____ | 2 |
| 13. _____ | 2 |
| 14. _____ | 2 |
| 15. _____ | 2 |
| 16. _____ | 2 |

Total ☐

## 302. Seven or more reasons why most food labels are colorful

| Response | Score |
|---|---|
| 1. _____ | 1 |
| 2. _____ | 1 |
| 3. _____ | 1 |
| 4. _____ | 1 |
| 5. _____ | 1 |
| 6. _____ | 1 |
| 7. _____ | 1 |

Bonus Responses

| | |
|---|---|
| 8. _____ | 2 |
| 9. _____ | 2 |
| 10. _____ | 2 |
| 11. _____ | 2 |
| 12. _____ | 2 |
| 13. _____ | 2 |
| 14. _____ | 2 |
| 15. _____ | 2 |
| 16. _____ | 2 |

Total ☐

## 303. Six or more reasons why baseball tickets usually cost less than football tickets

| Response | Score |
|---|---|
| 1. _____ | 1 |
| 2. _____ | 1 |
| 3. _____ | 1 |
| 4. _____ | 1 |
| 5. _____ | 1 |
| 6. _____ | 1 |

Bonus Responses

| | |
|---|---|
| 7. _____ | 2 |
| 8. _____ | 2 |
| 9. _____ | 2 |
| 10. _____ | 2 |
| 11. _____ | 2 |
| 12. _____ | 2 |
| 13. _____ | 2 |
| 14. _____ | 2 |
| 15. _____ | 2 |
| 16. _____ | 2 |

Total ☐

## 304. Seven or more new rules of baseball if there were five bases

| Response | Score |
|---|---|
| 1. _____ | 1 |
| 2. _____ | 1 |
| 3. _____ | 1 |
| 4. _____ | 1 |
| 5. _____ | 1 |
| 6. _____ | 1 |
| 7. _____ | 1 |

**Bonus Responses**

| | |
|---|---|
| 8. _____ | 2 |
| 9. _____ | 2 |
| 10. _____ | 2 |
| 11. _____ | 2 |
| 12. _____ | 2 |
| 13. _____ | 2 |
| 14. _____ | 2 |
| 15. _____ | 2 |
| 16. _____ | 2 |

Total ☐

# CONTRIBUTORS' SAMPLE RESPONSES

## 274. Eight or more reasons for not having IQ tests

1. It adds to the reasons for committing suicide.
2. There're too many tests already.
3. They might take over and we'll all have numbers instead of names.
4. It wears out your brain.
5. It gives conceited people something else to brag about.
6. It increases our need for computers.
7. They waste class time.
8. They are culturally biased.
9. They don't test creativity.
10. They primarily tell who is good and who is not good at taking standardized tests.
11. They discourage less bright children.
12. It would drive MENSA crazy.
13. They discriminate against the other 24 letters of the alphabet.
14. Their results influence teachers who pre-judge students' ability to learn.
15. Save paper.
16. They perpetuate the class structure.
17. Unfair to those not verbally oriented.
18. Creates "labels," strata of potential abilities.
19. Creates lasting ideas of superiority or inadequacy.
20. Inefficient means of assessing potential.
21. Creates mental stress.
22. Results have undue influence on teachers, etc.
23. Measure only some aspects of "intelligence"—and those perhaps not too well.
24. Overlook common sense, other good attributes.
25. Creates an IQ "meritocracy."
26. Puts excessive pressure on students.
27. Creates different, sometimes unfair grading standards.
28. Create social pressures.
29. Allow employee selection to be based on arbitrary standards often unrelated to job qualifications or performance.

## 275. Six or more languages you've never heard or read

1. Body language.
2. Sign language.
3. Animal language.
4. Caveman language.
5. Outerspace language.
6. Plant language.
7. Swahili.
8. Basque.
9. Flemish.
10. Finnish.
11. Arabic.
12. Hottentot.
13. Afrikaans.
14. Tagalog.
15. Persian.
16. Sanskrit.
17. Tibetan.
18. Cambodian.
19. Cajun.
20. Yiddish.
21. Hebrew.
22. Hindi.
23. Serbo-Croatian.
24. Russian.
25. Swedish.
26. Gaelic.
27. Welsh.
28. Coptic.

## 276. Seven or more reasons to burn white toast

1. As a poison antidote.
2. Out of spite because you wanted whole wheat bread.
3. Too busy reading to watch the toaster.
4. The spring in a pop-up toaster stopped functioning.
5. To go with the leathery eggs.
6. As markers for hop-scotch.
7. To make charcoal which can be used to scrawl a message on the tablecloth.
8. For temporary roofing tiles.
9. So you can't be accused of being prejudiced.
10. To give the bread a nice dark tan.
11. To spite someone you're mad at.
12. If you've never seen what burnt toast looks like.
13. To make it into pumpernickel.
14. So nobody ever asks you to make toast again.
15. For a change of pace.
16. Produces charcoal, good for the stomach.
17. Test your smoke alarms.
18. Good excuse for painting the kitchen.
19. Good expression of opinion as to such products.

20. Ethnically satisfying.
21. Saves buttering.
22. Disguise it as black bread.

## 277. Eight or more reasons for not having filing cabinets

1. There is nothing to file.
2. It's easier just to keep piles on your desk.
3. Your company is too cheap to purchase office equipment.
4. You're redecorating and the old ones were sold before the new ones arrived.
5. All records are on microfilm.
6. You prefer open shelving.
7. It's too crowded in a coal mine.
8. Carousel horses don't fit in drawers anymore.
9. They're eyesores.
10. They're hard to operate.
11. "Out of sight, out of mind."
12. They look out of sight in modern offices.
13. They waste metal.
14. They waste floor space.
15. Secretaries hate them.
16. They tend to accumulate useless files.
17. So you don't have to put things in alphabetical order.
18. To save your money and buy something else.
19. I'm sure you could find something better to do with your time instead of setting up a filing cabinet.
20. Once you get a filing cabinet, it usually leads to other things, like a secretary.
21. It's no fun having everything perfect.
22. It causes a lot of extra walking, if you didn't have one you could throw your stuff anywhere.
23. People won't go through your papers if they're too sloppy and hard to find.
24. You'll throw more things away instead of keeping unnecessary junk.

## 278. Seven or more thoughts that come to mind when you read the word "shell"

1. Vietnam.
2. Pasta.
3. Quilts.
4. Crocheted afghans and sweaters.
5. Bob's grandmother.
6. Burned-out building.
7. Peas.
8. Turtles.
9. Summer band concerts.
10. Boat races.
11. Paying for something unwillingly.
12. Bonnie's science fair project.
13. Lobsters.
14. Clams.
15. Nuclear reactors.
16. Civil disobedience.
17. Lima beans.
18. Sleeveless sweaters.
19. Oysters.
20. Beetles.
21. Grasshoppers.
22. Pearls.
23. A fancy marble-topped vanity with a shell-shaped sink.
24. Shyness.
25. Baptism.
26. Gas stations.
27. Gunfire.
28. Petroleum.
29. Snails.
30. Games of chance.
31. A fly caught in a spider's web.
32. Artillery.
33. Eggs.
34. Hawaiian necklaces.
35. Closed in.
36. Eating seafood.
37. The ocean and sand.
38. Echoes.
39. Loneliness.
40. Things hard, cracked, and weathered.

## 279. Six or more reasons why it should be legal to be married to more than one person at a time

1. Government shouldn't interfere in a person's private life.
2. No one person can fulfill all the needs of another.
3. There is frequently a greater number of one sex than the other in a locale, so it would make it possible for everyone to be married who wants to be.
4. Larger economic base for the household.
5. Better genetic mix in offspring.
6. Children who would otherwise be illegitimate.
7. Few men or women find a single spouse who can meet all their needs.
8. Create more efficient economic units.
9. Provide alternate households for children.

10. Provide increased sexual, emotional outlets.
11. People differ too much to be restricted to one legal spouse.
12. Might restrain some adultery.
13. Correct imbalances in male-female populations.
14. Permit sailors and other travelers a legal girl in every port.
15. Survival of the fittest.
16. To prevent boredom.
17. To cut down on the divorce rate.
18. To get to know all kinds of people.
19. To prolong the weddings and honeymoons.
20. To spread your love around instead of confining it to one person.
21. To get more money and diamond wedding rings.
22. To have children that all look different.
23. To be able to use a variety of names.
24. To satisfy any sexual fantasy.

## 280. Eight or more reasons for not having alimony

1. A person shouldn't be rewarded for getting divorced.
2. It is not imposed equitably.
3. It promotes parasitism.
4. Eliminate financial incentives for wives to divorce.
5. Provide incentives for women to keep their husbands pleased.
6. Creates more legal and tax problems than benefits.
7. Excessive state interference with marital relations.
8. Many divorcees don't deserve it.
9. Excessive burden on husband and his new family.
10. Creates non-productive family units.
11. Recipients reluctant to remarry promptly, for reasons mainly financial.
12. It costs too much.
13. It's unfair to men.
14. Men would be able to get divorces easier.
15. Women would treat their husbands better.
16. There would be fewer fights.
17. To stay out of court.
18. So the husband can have more fun after the divorce.
19. To prevent lawyers from becoming so rich.

## 281. Seven or more reasons for not having car insurance

1. Waste of money.
2. Expensive in the long run, especially if you are a careful driver.
3. Makes your windscreen look dirty with an insurance sticker on it.
4. Less tension on the brain—you don't have to remember when your insurance runs out.
5. One less file for filing all the insurance papers and receipts.
6. Drivers will be more careful if the money they have to pay for banging someone's car comes from their own pocket.
7. The police wouldn't have to be called as a witness for the insurance agent during an accident. The two parties would settle the dispute amongst themselves.
8. One less bill (or reminder) to pay your dues for insurance.
9. No car.
10. No money.
11. Too mean.
12. Don't believe in insurance.
13. Forgot to buy it.
14. Not eligible.
15. Driving with a license anyway.
16. My car doesn't have insurance on me.
17. The car is covered under my zeppelin policy.
18. I live alone on a desert island.
19. I drive a truck, not a car.
20. Nothing ever happens to my car, but my policy was stolen twice.
21. My grandfather had life insurance and he died, so obviously insurance doesn't work.

## 282. Eight or more reasons for not having a pencil sharpener

1. Rarely use a pencil.
2. Razor blades accomplish the same thing.
3. A penknife does the same work.
4. To make the tip of the pencil sharp, you can rub it (the tip) on rough ground in a slanting position.
5. Saves money.
6. Really cumbersome and annoying looking for a sharpener. Can never find it when I want it.
7. If a sharpener is right beside you on the table, you'll feel your pencil tip is not as sharp as it should be and you'll want to sharpen it. It will become blunt fast (the tip). This trait is noticed especially amongst children. This way the pencil becomes smaller and you'll have to buy a new pencil. If the sharpener isn't around you will make do with your slightly blunt tip of the pencil.
8. Don't have to turn your pencil round and round.
9. To discourage pencil sharpener manufacturers.
10. To discourage pencil users.
11. To discourage pencil manufacturers.
12. No pencils.
13. Lost them.
14. Misplaced them.
15. Threw them out.
16. They were stolen.
17. They were all freed by the Emancipation Proclamation.
18. I didn't know what to feed mine and they died.
19. I'd rather be blunt.
20. I couldn't stand the way the pencils screamed when I cranked the handle.
21. If God had wanted man to sharpen pencils, she wouldn't have invented the felt tip pen.
22. Whittling a new point with a knife is more in keeping with the frontier spirit of America.
23. I already have a gerbil who gnaws new points on my pencils.
24. I didn't know they existed—I just thought you threw pencils away if the tip broke.

## 283. Seven or more reasons why some people get sick after visiting a foreign country

1. Eating too much.
2. Trying out new dishes—often undigestible ones.
3. Not having proper rest.
4. Sleeping on strange beds.
5. Travel sickness.
6. The sickness is the body's revolt against work. It (the body) has gotten used to the open air, getting up late, fun, etc., and therefore does not want to be confined to an office and have to get up early in time for office.
7. Travelling is often strenuous.
8. Different climatic conditions. Body has to adjust.
9. To be able to boast of your delicate body (in being not able to sustain hardship on the tiredness of the journey).
10. Body resistance goes down after travelling and hence more prone to sickness.
11. They need an excuse for a rest.
12. Too much excitement.
13. Too much booze or drugs.
14. Ate poisonous plants.
15. Made love to an infected person.
16. Got bit by an infected animal.
17. Got bit by an infected insect.
18. They remember what it's like at home.
19. They remember how much the trip cost.
20. They would have gotten sick no matter where they had been.
21. They drink the water when they get home.
22. They thought disease was part of their special tour package (like home movies).
23. At the end of their visit, they realize that someone has stolen their passport and wallet and they can never leave.
24. Jet lag.
25. They never find their luggage when they get back.
26. The foreign island they visited was the leper colony at Molokai.

## 284. Seven or more reasons for not flying a kite

1. Too much effort.
2. Makes you sad when you lose it.
3. Gets entangled with electricity wires.
4. It is a bit childish.
5. You can't fly it anytime you want to—the weather is the determining factor.
6. Bad kites are not fun to fly and good ones are expensive.
7. Only possible to fly on top of a building.
8. Skyscrapers obstruct the kite.
9. Need plenty of string.
10. Have to have the know-how.
11. The thread can get cut by other kites.
12. Don't know how.
13. Don't like to.

14. Don't like kites.
15. Raining too hard.
16. Too dark.
17. Don't have a kite.
18. Have something else to do.
19. They want to live a life with no strings attached.
20. An osprey is easier to catch than a kite.
21. No wind.
22. They live underground.
23. I only weigh six ounces and a kite would drag me away.
24. My twin brother flies kites and I never do anything he does.
25. Due to Eustachian tube disorders, I can't look up and kites are no fun if you can't watch 'em.

---

24. If one existed that made sense, we'd *all* join it.
25. To maintain holier-than-thou attitude.
26. More excused absences at work for religious feast days.
27. I'm trying to find out if God can hit a moving target.
28. For the same reason that Baskin-Robbins has thirty-seven flavors of ice cream—one flavor gets boring after a while.
29. I'm actually Jewish but I also joined the Catholic church because I love bingo.
30. I need the tax break.
31. I'm anti-logic, anti-facts, and anti-common sense—where better to turn than religion?
32. I want to be able to fight on both sides in Ireland, the Middle East, the next crusade, and other holy wars.

---

### 285. Eight or more reasons for having more than one religion

1. You can go and pray whenever you like.
2. You can pray wherever you like.
3. You can turn to another god if you feel one is not listening to your prayers.
4. You can pick up the best parts of the religion and leave out the part you don't like.
5. You can have more religious holidays.
6. Less restrictions.
7. Sense of satisfaction.
8. Meet more people.
9. Can have more than one holy book by your bedside.
10. Many festivals.
11. Many celebrations.
12. Can receive more gifts.
13. Your children can also have a choice.
14. You can talk with strangers when attending service.
15. Can compare religions.
16. The more the merrier.
17. If one is good, eight are better.
18. Each adds to the other.
19. Spiritual insurance.
20. Easier assimilation in a foreign place.
21. To marry the person of your dreams.
22. To spy in a different place.
23. I'm half of a set of Siamese twins and I always disagree with me.

---

### 286. Six or more reasons why a live dinosaur will never appear in Central Park, New York City

1. No living person on this earth has ever seen one (live).
2. For centuries, no one has heard about one being born.
3. It can't suddenly appear. It can end up there if at all.
4. Not enough food there.
5. Gates are guarded.
6. It would die if it fell from the sky—as it can't fly.
7. The police would not let it enter.
8. The gates are not wide enough for it to enter.
9. Wrong era.
10. Bad climate.
11. Not enough room.
12. Bears would eat it.
13. Police would arrest it.
14. Children would get frightened.
15. Because they are all under exclusive contract with Madison Square Garden.
16. Central Park is extinct.
17. The last time they appeared there, they were heckled and booed and they vowed never to return.
18. New York State law bars dinosaurs from urban areas.
19. Dinosaurs do not exist east of the Mississippi River.

---

20. They are not allowed on N. Y. subways, can never get a cab when they need one and, hence, can't get to Central Park.
21. They are all busy working on signs in Sinclair gas stations.
22. They fear their natural enemy—the mugger.

---

### 287. Seven or more reasons to have one brand of lager beer

1. The waiter does not have to ask you "which brand?" when you say "Beer!"
2. Easy work for the waiter. During the rush hour, he doesn't have to remember who ordered what.
3. Won't have to drink the expensive brand (in spite of the horrible taste) just to be with the Joneses.
4. Fewer problems when planning to give a party and having to think how much of each brand to order.
5. Don't have to keep in stock different brands to suit all your friend's choices when they drop in for a visit.
6. Cuts down cost of advertising.
7. Less rivalry amongst producers.
8. People who don't like that particular brand will eventually stop drinking.
9. One person won't feel the odd man out if he likes drinking some other brand. That sort of problem will not arise.
10. Prefer it.
11. Cheaper price.
12. Higher price.
13. Nothing else available.
14. Like the color.
15. Doesn't make you throw up.
16. Too unimaginative to try some other brand.
17. Easier inventory control for liquor store.
18. Only have to print one kind of label.
19. Nobody can tell the difference between brands anyway.
20. All beers are brewed in the same brewery anyway—so why kid ourselves with different brands.

---

21. Cut down on people carrying Coors back from Denver to the East.
22. Just have one brand but let it come in different colors.

---

### 288. Six or more reasons for not having tow trucks

1. Occupy a lot of space when parked.
2. Occupy space on roads.
3. You can't see the car in front of it if you are behind it.
4. You can't see the traffic lights if it is in front of your car.
5. In an accident, your car gets the most damage while the truck—very little.
6. The truck drivers are not very careful drivers.
7. They are expensive.
8. Often cause more accidents.
9. It would be difficult to tow a broken-down tow truck.
10. Don't need them.
11. Car is in garage.
12. Pushing instead of towing.
13. Not available.
14. Disposable cars (if they break, leave them).
15. Save towing charges.
16. I'm afraid of big metal hooks.
17. They aren't pretty.
18. God helps **cars** who help themselves.
19. I don't have one so nobody should have one.
20. They are a menace to the highway.

---

### 289. Seven or more reasons why some people lie all the time

1. Have been brought up that way.
2. Enjoy fooling people.
3. Have to tell many lies to cover up one single lie and then it becomes a habit.
4. Not bold enough to tell the truth (cowards).
5. Like to tell lies.
6. They believe that "a few lies a day keep trouble at bay."

7. Necessity.
8. Have superiority complex.
9. To keep up a pretense.
10. Of boastful nature and hence like to boast a lot—thereby telling a lot of lies.
11. Fear.
12. Dishonesty.
13. Everyone else around them does.
14. Want to be something they aren't.
15. Pretentious.
16. Snobs.
17. The truth isn't pretty.
18. It gives them something to talk about in the confessional.
19. They're tired of standing.
20. It's fun.
21. It's creative.
22. Any dolt can tell the truth.
23. To stay out of jail.
24. To stay in jail.
25. So people can make up games that start:
    Mr. X always lies—
    Mr. Y always tells the truth . . .

## 290. Eight or more reasons for not having curtains

1. You have to wash them—hence waste of soap, water, energy, etc.
2. Can have fresh air without having to open them.
3. Can look out any time without having to open them.
4. More light during the daytime if there are no curtains.
5. An extra strong reason if one is an exhibitionist.
6. You can look into other people's houses if they, too, do not have curtains.
7. You save money. Good curtain material is expensive.
8. You don't have to buy new ones when you change the colour of the room.
9. Don't have to have special fixtures for the curtains, e.g., things like curtain boxes, wire, hooks, etc.
10. Can't afford them.
11. Have blinds instead.
12. No windows.
13. Obstruct light.
14. No one can see in anyway.
15. Don't like them.
16. Don't want to wash and keep them up.
17. Fire hazard.
18. To let the light out.

19. To provide voyeurs with some entertainment.
20. Don't have to clean 'em if you don't own 'em.
21. Prefer shades.
22. So the cat can't climb them.
23. Don't want to spoil the view.
24. Live on a mountain top.
25. Prefer drapes.
26. Remind me of death ("It's curtains for you!").

## 291. Eight or more reasons for not wanting to be a sports reporter

1. It is a boring job.
2. It is a tiring job.
3. You have got to be interested in sports.
4. You should be quick in writing.
5. You should be quick in reporting.
6. You have to attend all the sport activities.
7. You have to know a lot of people.
8. You have to be a good photographer.
9. You don't always get a good seat and hence bear the discomfort.
10. You have to go in spite of the cold and snow.
11. You have to attend in spite of the heat and snow.
12. Don't like sports.
13. Have another job.
14. Don't want to travel.
15. Don't like public speaking.
16. Can't stand crowds.
17. Think it's a waste of time.
18. Not enough money in it.
19. Too few opportunities.
20. Don't like reporters.
21. Can't write.
22. Can't dictate.
23. Allergic to pigskin and horsehide.
24. I get so engrossed in sports action that I would forget to record what's happening.
25. Against my religion.
26. Prefer to participate rather than observe sports.

## 292. Seven or more reasons why the number of foreign correspondents has dramatically decreased since World War II

1. It is easier to telephone.
2. It is faster to telephone.

3. Travelling has become easier and faster.
4. People visit each other more.
5. The world population went down after World War II.
6. Because the British empire became smaller and smaller.
7. Postage rates have gone up.
8. Fewer spies sending reports to their country.
9. Travelling has become expensive and so not many people travel and, hence, less correspondence.
10. Prices of letters, postcards, envelopes have gone up.
11. It is easier and faster to send telegrams.
12. Not enough wars to cover.
13. Nothing's happening in foreign countries.
14. Too dangerous.
15. Readers not interested.
16. Asking publishers for too many benefits.
17. Isn't considered glamorous anymore.
18. Too many were shot.
19. Fewer papers exist today.
20. Fewer countries to report on.
21. Iron Curtain limits news flow.
22. People are tired of reading about the ills of the world.
23. Job doesn't pay enough.
24. TV covers the same events visually, eliminating the need for reporters.
25. The number really hasn't decreased, they've just been miscounted.

## 293. Eight or more reasons why many small newspapers are jealous of *The New York Times*

1. Because it is so big.
2. Because they are small.
3. It receives news of the world faster.
4. Their offices are better.
5. Their printing machines are of a better quality.
6. They use a better quality of paper.
7. They have better journalists.
8. They pay higher salaries to their employees.
9. It is sold in many countries.
10. Many people put ads into it.
11. They can earn more money by advertising other people's needs and merchandise.
12. *Times* has bigger circulation.
13. *Times* has more resources available.

14. *Times* has better reputation.
15. They don't appreciate themselves.
16. There's no news left over for them that's "Fit to Print."
17. They aren't on strike.
18. Common avarice.
19. They don't weigh as much.
20. They didn't get the Pentagon papers.
21. They have to publish smaller pictures.
22. The *Times* has better crossword puzzles.
23. If you lived in Minot, N.D. and published a paper, you'd be jealous of the *Times*, too.
24. In America, bigger is better.

## 294. Six or more reasons for not having unions

1. In order as not to have to attend meetings.
2. It's pointless.
3. So that they wouldn't ask for higher pay.
4. The union leader will be big headed.
5. It is a waste of time.
6. A union can bend the employer against his will. If no unions—no bending.
7. To have fewer strikes.
8. Less false propaganda against the employer.
9. More peace.
10. You can dismiss a worker whenever you like—even without a particular reason—if there are no unions to support the worker and to fight back.
11. Like less money.
12. Their lack of intelligence.
13. Their lack of ability to cooperate with others.
14. See themselves as more important than others.
15. Have faith in the fairness of management.
16. Too much like Communism.
17. I might be elected president and end up like Jimmy Hoffa.
18. Can't afford the dues.
19. Don't like organizations of any kind; won't even join the Kiwanis.
20. They're all corrupt.
21. Nobody ever asks *me* to join.

22. I like sweatshops.
23. Enforced child labor is more fun.

---

### 295. Eight or more reasons to do away with late night talk shows

1. They are boring.
2. Don't see the need for them.
3. Majority of the people don't see them.
4. Make people fat by eating while watching.
5. Strain on the eyes.
6. Strain on the brain.
7. Only boring people see them.
8. Oversleep and be late for work in the morning.
9. Give a headache.
10. They are not worth missing your sleep for.
11. Have to find some other way to fall asleep.
12. Would go to sleep earlier.
13. Might stay in the bars at night.
14. Would talk to other people in the family.
15. Would have a lot more fights.
16. Sales of tranquilizers would increase.
17. Charo would have to get a real job.
18. Merv Griffin would have to admit that he has no talent.
19. The same movies would rerun four times a year instead of the three times we see them now.
20. Johnny Carson would successfully run for the U.S. Senate to fill his empty hours.
21. Eighteen million kilowatts a year would be saved.
22. Nobody would ever again hear of Monte Rock III.
23. Utilization of libraries would go up.

---

### 296. Seven or more reasons for not practicing birth control

1. It's more enjoyable if you don't use a condom.
2. Most methods aren't 100% effective.
3. To increase the population.
4. Have to have a regular supply of condoms or pill or have to have a checkup to see if the loop or diaphragm is in its place.

---

5. Don't have to ask, "Have you taken precautions?"
6. Don't have to interrupt your love play or petting to put on a condom.
7. The I.U.D. can have serious effects on the body.
8. Can have lots of babies.
9. Too lazy.
10. Can't get pregnant.
11. Don't believe in birth control.
12. Against one's religion.
13. Don't know how.
14. Think "it" can't happen to me.
15. No sex anyway.
16. Like big families.
17. Trying to match India's birth rate.
18. Fear of underpopulation.
19. Catholicism.
20. Practice didn't make perfect anyway.
21. Never could decide between foam and jelly.
22. Want to keep 'em barefoot and pregnant.

---

### 297. Eight or more reasons for never attending a lecture

1. They are usually boring.
2. Take too much of your time.
3. Can't sit that long in a chair.
4. Most of the times, you can't get anything out of it.
5. Makes you sleepy.
6. You can't talk for fear of disturbing others.
7. Can't eat.
8. Can't drink.
9. Can't switch off the sound if you feel like having a nap.
10. Can't reduce the volume of the speaker if too loud.
11. Often too far away from home.
12. You have to push and fight to get out of the hall when it's over.
13. Rarely to the point.
14. Not interested.
15. Don't know there are such things.
16. Not available in your neighborhood.
17. Not available in your language.
18. Can't stand listening to other people.
19. Not interested in what others have to say.
20. Can't afford tickets.
21. Deafness.
22. Can't find one to attend.
23. The book was better.
24. Couldn't afford a ticket.
25. Always have to sit in the back.

---

26. Don't like crowds.
27. Never been invited to give one.
28. Everybody else does it and I like to be different.

---

### 298. Eight or more reasons for being outside during a hailstorm

1. You get a free shower.
2. The cold shower refreshes you.
3. Feel the water on your face.
4. Get little knocks on your head.
5. Can play at catching ice-pieces.
6. It is a beautiful sight.
7. Because no one else is around during the storm.
8. Get soaked.
9. Get knocked out.
10. Meet other people who also like to be out during one.
11. Overcome fear of touching cold things.
12. Catch a cold.
13. Bring down your body temperature.
14. It is tremendous fun.
15. To be able to feel part of nature.
16. Gives you an excuse to drink brandy or other alcoholic drinks.
17. Gives you an excuse to have a hot drink.
18. To show off that you are not a coward.
19. Like to be out in hailstorms.
20. Making a scientific analysis.
21. Want to see what hail feels like.
22. Can't find key to get inside.
23. Don't know you're supposed to be.
24. I'm a masochist.
25. To test my new football helmet.
26. Never seen one from the middle.
27. Can't get inside.
28. Got caught by surprise.
29. Trying to dodge hail stones.
30. Testing theory of probability.
31. To see if wind will hurt.
32. To collect hail stones.
33. Looks like fun.

---

### 299. Seven or more reasons why most adults do not drink milk

1. Milk is associated with children and many adults unconsciously think drinking milk is childish.

---

2. Adults often tease people (other adults) who drink milk by saying that "The baby must have a glass of milk every day."
3. You have so much of it as a child that you get fed up with it and that is why many people like having black tea or coffee.
4. Some think it is fattening.
5. After having got used to beer or other drinks like Coke or alcoholic drinks, you have no taste for it.
6. Milk does not go with any food.
7. It does not have the ability to keep you awake (unlike coffee or tea).
8. Some don't like the smell.
9. Some don't like the white colour.
10. The poor can't afford it.
11. Because people generally don't like what is good for them—and milk gives the idea of being medicinal.
12. Habit.
13. Indigestible.
14. Fattening.
15. Stupidity.
16. Prefer booze.
17. Not available.
18. Tastes bad mixed with beer.
19. They disliked their mothers intensely.
20. Don't think it looks grown-up.
21. Scared of Strontium 90.
22. Tastes bad with cigars.
23. Ashamed to buy Bosco to drink it with.
24. Stupidity.
25. The kids drink it all before the adults get up.

---

### 300. Seven or more reasons for not becoming a forensic pathologist

1. It is a dirty job.
2. Everything stinks (all the samples).
3. You have to be extremely careful when doing the blood grouping from the clothes and weapons, as another person's life depends on it. The outcome (result) can decide whether a man is guilty or innocent.
4. If a murderer knows you are the forensic pathologist, he might threaten you and force you to give out the analytical report in his favour.
5. You have to go to the court to give evidence and, hence, often be cross-examined

harshly by the defence counsel, who would try to confuse you.

6. It is a tedious job being confined to the laboratory.
7. You do not meet any new people.
8. Very few people know the importance of your work.
9. Your job keeps you so busy that you do not have the time and energy to do any research work.
10. You can't drink coffee or eat a sandwich in the room where you work (it stinks and is unhygienic).
11. You can't smoke.
12. No one likes to visit you in your room.
13. It is a lousy job if you are superstitious—touching a dead person's things.
14. Too much work.
15. Too much responsibility.
16. Too much hocus pocus.
17. Don't have enough ego.
18. Don't have the "right" disposition.
19. Don't have the "right" motivation.
20. Too much stress.
21. Too much pretense.
22. Patients never open wide and say "Aah."
23. It's cold work.
24. Patients refuse to answer questions.
25. If you find a patient you enjoy—you still can't socialize with 'em.
26. Patients never do what you ask them to do.

---

### 301. Six or more reasons for not attending a Walt Disney movie

1. I might think I was Mickey Mouse.
2. I might think I was the one hundred and second Dalmatian.
3. Have already seen it once.
4. Have already seen it twice.
5. Have already seen it three times.
6. To attend a Claudia Cardinale picture (she is so pretty!).
7. To attend a Jane Fonda picture.

8. Prefer westerns.
9. Prefer detective films.
10. Prefer porno films.
11. Too expensive.
12. Don't like cartoons.
13. Weak plots.
14. Prefer R-rated movies.
15. I'm blind.
16. Can't stand smell of popcorn.
17. I'm color blind, and the ghastly colors just sicken me.
18. The violence level is not high enough.
19. I don't like gum on my feet.
20. The people behind me can't see.
21. Children have trouble climbing over my legs.
22. They don't serve mixed drinks.
23. My dog can't go.
24. There's too much violence and sex.
25. I can see it on TV in a few years.

---

### 302. Seven or more reasons why most food labels are colourful

1. Food enters through eyes.
2. Food is not black and white.
3. Food manufacturers can charge more for colour labels than for black and white ones.
4. More and more people have already got a colour TV set.
5. This way food labels match colourful lady clothes.
6. Food manufacturers are not interested in our reading these labels: if they are colourful we cannot confound them with a newspaper text.
7. Coca-Cola publicity is colourful.
8. This way you think food taste is much better.
9. The first food advertisement in history (the apple offered to Adam) was a coloured one.
10. Customer eye appeal.
11. Brand recognition.
12. Label designers are frustrated artists.
13. Aesthetics.
14. For fun.

15. The label-makers are colour blind.
16. Manufacturer runs out of black and white dye.
17. Subliminal advertising.
18. To hide the contents.
19. Diversionary factor to redirect concentration about contents.
20. So we'll know it's not real food.
21. To cheer up grocery clerks.
22. To give jobs to advertising artists.
23. To help retard spoilage.
24. To frighten cockroaches.
25. The colors are a secret code known only by the FDA.
26. To help spot shoplifters.
27. To attract the attention of the children riding in the carts.

---

### 303. Six or more reasons why baseball tickets usually cost less than football tickets

1. Because of the law of supply and demand.
2. President Carter prefers baseball to football.
3. Football players earn much more money than baseball ones.
4. Football teams are made up with more players than baseball ones.
5. Football was imported from Europe.
6. Baseball is a "basic" food to America.
7. Fewer players to pay.
8. Equipment cheaper.
9. More games per season.
10. Residuals from TV higher.
11. Advertisement billboards in ballparks but not stadiums.
12. Medical insurance cheaper.
13. Field maintenance easier.
14. Baseball players can make more money on kickbacks than football players (thus lower wage demands).
15. Easier game to play (more competition).
16. More people watch baseball than football.
17. Don't have to pay cheerleaders.
18. Seventh inning stretches are *much* cheaper than half-times.

19. Football fans are bigger than baseball fans.
20. You might catch a ball at a baseball game.
21. There's more violence at a football game.
22. Football players are bigger eaters.
23. The seats at football stadiums are more comfortable than at baseball games.
24. Footballs are bigger and easier to see than baseballs.

---

### 304. Seven or more new rules of baseball if there were five bases

1. Teams would be eleven players each.
2. Five balls to walk a man.
3. Innings would be *seven* instead of nine.
4. All games should be played in *the* Pentagon.
5. If you score a home-run you are granted a position in the Pentagon.
6. In case of equal, players can ride a bicycle to continue the match.
7. Four outs per side each inning.
8. Require another baseman.
9. Not necessary to tag bases in order.
10. Field larger.
11. Stealing bases not allowed.
12. Pitcher not allowed to bat.
13. Pitched ball hitting a batter scores point, rather than automatic walk.
14. Fifth baseman cannot wear glove.
15. Ball is made of super-bounce rubber.
16. Two or more bases must be covered by a woman.
17. One or more bases must be covered by a Native American.
18. Four strikes to strike a player out.
19. No more shortstop. We add a fourth baseman.
20. Fourth base may not be stolen.
21. Player hitting ball out of park must stop at fourth base.

# NOVEMBER

### Mental Calisthenic #11

Talk a walk with a friend. Take turns with each other, walking with eyes closed while the other person leads. Listen to the sound of nature or of the city. Explore common outdoor objects with your eyes closed. Feel the texture, temperature, size. Discuss the experience with your friend. Repeat the exercise with a youngster, an elderly person, and with both sexes. Were the experiences different? Proceed with a Mental Jogging exercise.

---

**305. Seven or more new rules of football if there were six downs**

| Response | Score |
|---|---|
| 1. _____ | 1 |
| 2. _____ | 1 |
| 3. _____ | 1 |
| 4. _____ | 1 |
| 5. _____ | 1 |
| 6. _____ | 1 |
| 7. _____ | 1 |

Bonus Responses

| | |
|---|---|
| 8. _____ | 2 |
| 9. _____ | 2 |
| 10. _____ | 2 |
| 11. _____ | 2 |
| 12. _____ | 2 |
| 13. _____ | 2 |
| 14. _____ | 2 |
| 15. _____ | 2 |
| 16. _____ | 2 |

Total ☐

**306. Six or more new rules of basketball if there were two balls in play simultaneously**

| Response | Score |
|---|---|
| 1. _____ | 1 |
| 2. _____ | 1 |
| 3. _____ | 1 |
| 4. _____ | 1 |
| 5. _____ | 1 |
| 6. _____ | 1 |

Bonus Responses

| | |
|---|---|
| 7. _____ | 2 |
| 8. _____ | 2 |
| 9. _____ | 2 |
| 10. _____ | 2 |
| 11. _____ | 2 |
| 12. _____ | 2 |
| 13. _____ | 2 |
| 14. _____ | 2 |
| 15. _____ | 2 |
| 16. _____ | 2 |

Total ☐

## 307. Seven or more rules of soccer if there were two goalies in each goal

| Response | Score |
|---|---|
| 1. | 1 |
| 2. | 1 |
| 3. | 1 |
| 4. | 1 |
| 5. | 1 |
| 6. | 1 |
| 7. | 1 |

**Bonus Responses**

| | |
|---|---|
| 8. | 2 |
| 9. | 2 |
| 10. | 2 |
| 11. | 2 |
| 12. | 2 |
| 13. | 2 |
| 14. | 2 |
| 15. | 2 |
| 16. | 2 |

Total ☐

## 308. Eight or more new rules of Monopoly if one player began with $3,000 instead of the usual $1,500

| Response | Score |
|---|---|
| 1. | 1 |
| 2. | 1 |
| 3. | 1 |
| 4. | 1 |
| 5. | 1 |
| 6. | 1 |
| 7. | 1 |
| 8. | 1 |

**Bonus Responses**

| | |
|---|---|
| 9. | 2 |
| 10. | 2 |
| 11. | 2 |
| 12. | 2 |
| 13. | 2 |
| 14. | 2 |
| 15. | 2 |
| 16. | 2 |

Total ☐

## 309. Seven or more new rules of singles tennis if the service line were moved forward six feet

| Response | Score |
|---|---|
| 1. | 1 |
| 2. | 1 |
| 3. | 1 |
| 4. | 1 |
| 5. | 1 |
| 6. | 1 |
| 7. | 1 |

**Bonus Responses**

| | |
|---|---|
| 8. | 2 |
| 9. | 2 |
| 10. | 2 |
| 11. | 2 |
| 12. | 2 |
| 13. | 2 |
| 14. | 2 |
| 15. | 2 |
| 16. | 2 |

Total ☐

## 310. Eight or more new rules of ice hockey if offsides was never called

| Response | Score |
|---|---|
| 1. | 1 |
| 2. | 1 |
| 3. | 1 |
| 4. | 1 |
| 5. | 1 |
| 6. | 1 |
| 7. | 1 |
| 8. | 1 |

**Bonus Responses**

| | |
|---|---|
| 9. | 2 |
| 10. | 2 |
| 11. | 2 |
| 12. | 2 |
| 13. | 2 |
| 14. | 2 |
| 15. | 2 |
| 16. | 2 |

Total ☐

## 311. Eight or more reasons why most of us have never been to the 21 Club in Manhattan

| Response | Score |
|---|---|
| 1. _____ | 1 |
| 2. _____ | 1 |
| 3. _____ | 1 |
| 4. _____ | 1 |
| 5. _____ | 1 |
| 6. _____ | 1 |
| 7. _____ | 1 |
| 8. _____ | 1 |

Bonus Responses

| | |
|---|---|
| 9. _____ | 2 |
| 10. _____ | 2 |
| 11. _____ | 2 |
| 12. _____ | 2 |
| 13. _____ | 2 |
| 14. _____ | 2 |
| 15. _____ | 2 |
| 16. _____ | 2 |

Total ☐

## 312. Seven or more consequences of not having a reserved seat at the Metropolitan Opera

| Response | Score |
|---|---|
| 1. _____ | 1 |
| 2. _____ | 1 |
| 3. _____ | 1 |
| 4. _____ | 1 |
| 5. _____ | 1 |
| 6. _____ | 1 |
| 7. _____ | 1 |

Bonus Responses

| | |
|---|---|
| 8. _____ | 2 |
| 9. _____ | 2 |
| 10. _____ | 2 |
| 11. _____ | 2 |
| 12. _____ | 2 |
| 13. _____ | 2 |
| 14. _____ | 2 |
| 15. _____ | 2 |
| 16. _____ | 2 |

Total ☐

## 313. Seven or more new rules of horse racing if only win bets were allowed

| Response | Score |
|---|---|
| 1. _____ | 1 |
| 2. _____ | 1 |
| 3. _____ | 1 |
| 4. _____ | 1 |
| 5. _____ | 1 |
| 6. _____ | 1 |
| 7. _____ | 1 |

Bonus Responses

| | |
|---|---|
| 8. _____ | 2 |
| 9. _____ | 2 |
| 10. _____ | 2 |
| 11. _____ | 2 |
| 12. _____ | 2 |
| 13. _____ | 2 |
| 14. _____ | 2 |
| 15. _____ | 2 |
| 16. _____ | 2 |

Total ☐

## 314. Seven or more consequences of forcing a blackjack dealer to stick at 12

| Response | Score |
|---|---|
| 1. _____ | 1 |
| 2. _____ | 1 |
| 3. _____ | 1 |
| 4. _____ | 1 |
| 5. _____ | 1 |
| 6. _____ | 1 |
| 7. _____ | 1 |

Bonus Responses

| | |
|---|---|
| 8. _____ | 2 |
| 9. _____ | 2 |
| 10. _____ | 2 |
| 11. _____ | 2 |
| 12. _____ | 2 |
| 13. _____ | 2 |
| 14. _____ | 2 |
| 15. _____ | 2 |
| 16. _____ | 2 |

Total ☐

## 315. Eight or more reasons why the Toronto Bluejays will never win a pennant before the year 2000

| Response | Score |
|---|---|
| 1. | 1 |
| 2. | 1 |
| 3. | 1 |
| 4. | 1 |
| 5. | 1 |
| 6. | 1 |
| 7. | 1 |
| 8. | 1 |

**Bonus Responses**

| | Score |
|---|---|
| 9. | 2 |
| 10. | 2 |
| 11. | 2 |
| 12. | 2 |
| 13. | 2 |
| 14. | 2 |
| 15. | 2 |
| 16. | 2 |

Total ☐

## 316. Eight or more ways to spend one billion dollars in exactly twenty-four hours

| Response | Score |
|---|---|
| 1. | 1 |
| 2. | 1 |
| 3. | 1 |
| 4. | 1 |
| 5. | 1 |
| 6. | 1 |
| 7. | 1 |
| 8. | 1 |

**Bonus Responses**

| | Score |
|---|---|
| 9. | 2 |
| 10. | 2 |
| 11. | 2 |
| 12. | 2 |
| 13. | 2 |
| 14. | 2 |
| 15. | 2 |
| 16. | 2 |

Total ☐

## 317. Seven or more reasons for doing away with cushions

| Response | Score |
|---|---|
| 1. | 1 |
| 2. | 1 |
| 3. | 1 |
| 4. | 1 |
| 5. | 1 |
| 6. | 1 |
| 7. | 1 |

**Bonus Responses**

| | Score |
|---|---|
| 8. | 2 |
| 9. | 2 |
| 10. | 2 |
| 11. | 2 |
| 12. | 2 |
| 13. | 2 |
| 14. | 2 |
| 15. | 2 |
| 16. | 2 |

Total ☐

## 318. Seven or more reasons for not believing in ESP

| Response | Score |
|---|---|
| 1. | 1 |
| 2. | 1 |
| 3. | 1 |
| 4. | 1 |
| 5. | 1 |
| 6. | 1 |
| 7. | 1 |

**Bonus Responses**

| | Score |
|---|---|
| 8. | 2 |
| 9. | 2 |
| 10. | 2 |
| 11. | 2 |
| 12. | 2 |
| 13. | 2 |
| 14. | 2 |
| 15. | 2 |
| 16. | 2 |

Total ☐

## 319. Seven or more reasons for more lost ads than found ads

| Response | Score |
|---|---|
| 1. _____ | 1 |
| 2. _____ | 1 |
| 3. _____ | 1 |
| 4. _____ | 1 |
| 5. _____ | 1 |
| 6. _____ | 1 |
| 7. _____ | 1 |

Bonus Responses

| | |
|---|---|
| 8. _____ | 2 |
| 9. _____ | 2 |
| 10. _____ | 2 |
| 11. _____ | 2 |
| 12. _____ | 2 |
| 13. _____ | 2 |
| 14. _____ | 2 |
| 15. _____ | 2 |
| 16. _____ | 2 |

Total ☐

## 320. Eight or more reasons why the Dallas Cowboys will not win the 1988 Super Bowl

| Response | Score |
|---|---|
| 1. _____ | 1 |
| 2. _____ | 1 |
| 3. _____ | 1 |
| 4. _____ | 1 |
| 5. _____ | 1 |
| 6. _____ | 1 |
| 7. _____ | 1 |
| 8. _____ | 1 |

Bonus Responses

| | |
|---|---|
| 9. _____ | 2 |
| 10. _____ | 2 |
| 11. _____ | 2 |
| 12. _____ | 2 |
| 13. _____ | 2 |
| 14. _____ | 2 |
| 15. _____ | 2 |
| 16. _____ | 2 |

Total ☐

## 321. Six or more reasons why Chile has never had a soccer team in the finals of the World Cup

| Response | Score |
|---|---|
| 1. _____ | 1 |
| 2. _____ | 1 |
| 3. _____ | 1 |
| 4. _____ | 1 |
| 5. _____ | 1 |
| 6. _____ | 1 |

Bonus Responses

| | |
|---|---|
| 7. _____ | 2 |
| 8. _____ | 2 |
| 9. _____ | 2 |
| 10. _____ | 2 |
| 11. _____ | 2 |
| 12. _____ | 2 |
| 13. _____ | 2 |
| 14. _____ | 2 |
| 15. _____ | 2 |
| 16. _____ | 2 |

Total ☐

## 322. Seven or more new rules of volleyball if there were fifteen persons on a side

| Response | Score |
|---|---|
| 1. _____ | 1 |
| 2. _____ | 1 |
| 3. _____ | 1 |
| 4. _____ | 1 |
| 5. _____ | 1 |
| 6. _____ | 1 |
| 7. _____ | 1 |

Bonus Responses

| | |
|---|---|
| 8. _____ | 2 |
| 9. _____ | 2 |
| 10. _____ | 2 |
| 11. _____ | 2 |
| 12. _____ | 2 |
| 13. _____ | 2 |
| 14. _____ | 2 |
| 15. _____ | 2 |
| 16. _____ | 2 |

Total ☐

## 323. Eight or more reasons for not having bookends

| Response | Score |
|---|---|
| 1. _____ | 1 |
| 2. _____ | 1 |
| 3. _____ | 1 |
| 4. _____ | 1 |
| 5. _____ | 1 |
| 6. _____ | 1 |
| 7. _____ | 1 |
| 8. _____ | 1 |

**Bonus Responses**

| | |
|---|---|
| 9. _____ | 2 |
| 10. _____ | 2 |
| 11. _____ | 2 |
| 12. _____ | 2 |
| 13. _____ | 2 |
| 14. _____ | 2 |
| 15. _____ | 2 |
| 16. _____ | 2 |

Total ☐

## 324. Nine or more petty annoyances that everybody experiences

| Response | Score |
|---|---|
| 1. _____ | 1 |
| 2. _____ | 1 |
| 3. _____ | 1 |
| 4. _____ | 1 |
| 5. _____ | 1 |
| 6. _____ | 1 |
| 7. _____ | 1 |
| 8. _____ | 1 |
| 9. _____ | 1 |

**Bonus Responses**

| | |
|---|---|
| 10. _____ | 2 |
| 11. _____ | 2 |
| 12. _____ | 2 |
| 13. _____ | 2 |
| 14. _____ | 2 |
| 15. _____ | 2 |
| 16. _____ | 2 |

Total ☐

## 325. Seven or more reasons for not being superstitious

| Response | Score |
|---|---|
| . _____ | 1 |
| 2. _____ | 1 |
| 3. _____ | 1 |
| 4. _____ | 1 |
| 5. _____ | 1 |
| 6. _____ | 1 |
| 7. _____ | 1 |

**Bonus Responses**

| | |
|---|---|
| 8. _____ | 2 |
| 9. _____ | 2 |
| 10. _____ | 2 |
| 11. _____ | 2 |
| 12. _____ | 2 |
| 13. _____ | 2 |
| 14. _____ | 2 |
| 15. _____ | 2 |
| 16. _____ | 2 |

Total ☐

## 326. Eight or more consequences of being the first baby born in the new calendar year in the United States

| Response | Score |
|---|---|
| 1. _____ | 1 |
| 2. _____ | 1 |
| 3. _____ | 1 |
| 4. _____ | 1 |
| 5. _____ | 1 |
| 6. _____ | 1 |
| 7. _____ | 1 |
| 8. _____ | 1 |

**Bonus Responses**

| | |
|---|---|
| 9. _____ | 2 |
| 10. _____ | 2 |
| 11. _____ | 2 |
| 12. _____ | 2 |
| 13. _____ | 2 |
| 14. _____ | 2 |
| 15. _____ | 2 |
| 16. _____ | 2 |

Total ☐

## 327. Seven or more novel uses of crushed ice

| Response | Score |
|---|---|
| 1. _____ | 1 |
| 2. _____ | 1 |
| 3. _____ | 1 |
| 4. _____ | 1 |
| 5. _____ | 1 |
| 6. _____ | 1 |
| 7. _____ | 1 |

Bonus Responses

| | |
|---|---|
| 8. _____ | 2 |
| 9. _____ | 2 |
| 10. _____ | 2 |
| 11. _____ | 2 |
| 12. _____ | 2 |
| 13. _____ | 2 |
| 14. _____ | 2 |
| 15. _____ | 2 |
| 16. _____ | 2 |

Total ☐

## 328. Nine or more reasons why European trains are profitable whereas most American trains are in the red

| Response | Score |
|---|---|
| 1. _____ | 1 |
| 2. _____ | 1 |
| 3. _____ | 1 |
| 4. _____ | 1 |
| 5. _____ | 1 |
| 6. _____ | 1 |
| 7. _____ | 1 |
| 8. _____ | 1 |
| 9. _____ | 1 |

Bonus Responses

| | |
|---|---|
| 10. _____ | 2 |
| 11. _____ | 2 |
| 12. _____ | 2 |
| 13. _____ | 2 |
| 14. _____ | 2 |
| 15. _____ | 2 |
| 16. _____ | 2 |

Total ☐

## 329. Seven or more reasons for issuing a $3 bill

| Response | Score |
|---|---|
| 1. _____ | 1 |
| 2. _____ | 1 |
| 3. _____ | 1 |
| 4. _____ | 1 |
| 5. _____ | 1 |
| 6. _____ | 1 |
| 7. _____ | 1 |

Bonus Responses

| | |
|---|---|
| 8. _____ | 2 |
| 9. _____ | 2 |
| 10. _____ | 2 |
| 11. _____ | 2 |
| 12. _____ | 2 |
| 13. _____ | 2 |
| 14. _____ | 2 |
| 15. _____ | 2 |
| 16. _____ | 2 |

Total ☐

## 330. Eight or more reasons why only one woman is pictured on our national currency

| Response | Score |
|---|---|
| 1. _____ | 1 |
| 2. _____ | 1 |
| 3. _____ | 1 |
| 4. _____ | 1 |
| 5. _____ | 1 |
| 6. _____ | 1 |
| 7. _____ | 1 |
| 8. _____ | 1 |

Bonus Responses

| | |
|---|---|
| 9. _____ | 2 |
| 10. _____ | 2 |
| 11. _____ | 2 |
| 12. _____ | 2 |
| 13. _____ | 2 |
| 14. _____ | 2 |
| 15. _____ | 2 |
| 16. _____ | 2 |

Total ☐

## 331. Seven or more reasons for not using a .22 long bullet as a tie clasp

Response      Score

1. _____ 1
2. _____ 1
3. _____ 1
4. _____ 1
5. _____ 1
6. _____ 1
7. _____ 1

Bonus Responses

8. _____ 2
9. _____ 2
10. _____ 2
11. _____ 2
12. _____ 2
13. _____ 2
14. _____ 2
15. _____ 2
16. _____ 2

Total ☐

## 332. Eight or more reasons for not running five or more miles per day

Response      Score

1. _____ 1
2. _____ 1
3. _____ 1
4. _____ 1
5. _____ 1
6. _____ 1
7. _____ 1
8. _____ 1

Bonus Responses

9. _____ 2
10. _____ 2
11. _____ 2
12. _____ 2
13. _____ 2
14. _____ 2
15. _____ 2
16. _____ 2

Total ☐

## 333. Seven or more reasons why some combinations of letters are illegal on license plates

Response      Score

1. _____ 1
2. _____ 1
3. _____ 1
4. _____ 1
5. _____ 1
6. _____ 1
7. _____ 1

Bonus Responses

8. _____ 2
9. _____ 2
10. _____ 2
11. _____ 2
12. _____ 2
13. _____ 2
14. _____ 2
15. _____ 2
16. _____ 2

Total ☐

## 334. Nine or more reasons for not having patents

Response      Score

1. _____ 1
2. _____ 1
3. _____ 1
4. _____ 1
5. _____ 1
6. _____ 1
7. _____ 1
8. _____ 1
9. _____ 1

Bonus Responses

10. _____ 2
11. _____ 2
12. _____ 2
13. _____ 2
14. _____ 2
15. _____ 2
16. _____ 2

Total ☐

# CONTRIBUTOR'S SAMPLE RESPONSES

## 305. Seven or more new rules of football if there were six downs

1. Field 150 yards long
2. Only nine players per side.
3. Must gain twenty yards for first down.
4. Game lasts for 1½ hours.
5. No substitutions during quarter.
6. Interceptions gain one point.
7. Football is larger.
8. No time-outs allowed.
9. German shepherds get to attack on the 6th down.
10. Up to five man-sized obstacles may be placed on the field by the defense.
11. Players must be barefoot.
12. Cheerleaders must be over 5'6" tall.
13. Play does not stop during halftime activities.
14. Band members and song leaders must carry Blue Cross.
15. No games may be played when the moon is in Taurus.
16. All tackles must weigh less than 200 lbs. dressed for play.
17. Band members and song leaders must wear protective padding.

## 306. Six or more new rules of basketball if there were two balls in play simultaneously

1. Each team has seven players on the floor and ten as a maximum on the bench.
2. The match consists of two parts of twenty-five minutes each plus a rest of ten and another of five.
3. Each coach can ask for *three* "dead times" on each part of the match.
4. Size of courts would be 40 x 15 as a maximum and 35 x 13 as a minimum.
5. Each of the two judges will be an auxiliary one.
6. Each judge will be responsible for one half of the ground.
7. Two players per team will be able to jump to get the two balls on game (on occasion of neutral launchments).
8. No player can handle two balls simultaneously.
9. Six players per side.
10. Dribbling not necessary.
11. Court triangular with three baskets.
12. Fouls punished by loss of points.
13. Balls heavier.
14. Tackling allowed.
15. Court consists of wet mud.
16. If 1st free throw is successful, 2nd ball may be thrown also.
17. If a player's shoelaces become untied, he must sit out the rest of the game.
18. A ball held by the defense may be thrown and used to block a shot being made with the other ball.
19. Play does not stop when one ball goes out of bounds. Play continues until second ball is taken care of.
20. We do away with the Center position and add one Forward and one Guard to each team.

## 307. Seven or more rules of soccer if there were two goalies in each goal

1. Each team will be of thirteen players.
2. Offside rule would be limited to penalty area.
3. Corners are launched from the point where the ball went out.
4. Size of grounds would be 60 x 60 as a minimum and 100 x 100 as a maximum.
5. Every three corner kicks would be equal to a goal.
6. Every two corner kicks cause a five-minute retreat of the player who made the second of them even if he is a goalkeeper.
7. Goalies are not allowed to use hands.
8. Field is circular.
9. Off-side rule cancelled.
10. Ball smaller.
11. Penalties require player to leave field.
12. One goalie not permitted to use head for ball deflection.
13. Defense must wear eye-patches.
14. Goal is wider.
15. Goalies must hold hands.
16. One goalie must be a woman.
17. Players with vasectomies cannot be goalies.
18. Goalies may retire to dressing room when ball is not in play.
19. Right wingers cannot play left wing.
20. Left wing must wear a red bandanna.
21. The Center must be the tallest player on his team.

## 308. Eight or more new rules of Monopoly if one player began with $3,000 instead of the usual $1,500

1. He must lose every fifth turn.
2. Only other(s) may buy Boardwalk and Park Place.
3. He receives only $150 for passing Go.
4. He pays double when landing on utilities.
5. He must always pay to get out of jail.
6. He forfeits half of the money if landing on Free Parking.
7. He pays double for property during first six trips around the board.
8. Others pay only half the rent when landing on his property.
9. When landing on railroads, all players move halfway around board (to railroad across board).
10. Three dice are used.
11. Some of the money is counterfeit.
12. Pay 28% interest on loans.
13. Any player throwing two 4's must give $1,000 to every other player.
14. Any player visiting another player in jail must slip him $50.
15. Player starting with $3,000 is the banker.
16. Player starting with $3,000 must pay double whenever he has a tax of any kind to pay.
17. Player with $3,000 must move last at start of game.
18. Dice thrown at start of game to decide who gets the $1,500 additional. Second highest throw gets first move. Third highest—second move, etc.
19. Player with $3,000 at start of game may not buy utilities unless and until they should go bankrupt.
20. Player starting with $3,000 gets only $100 when passing Go.

## 309. Seven or more new rules of singles tennis if the service line were moved forward six feet

1. Ground size should be 25, 58 × 7, 57 mts.
2. Ball diameter should be 7 cms.
3. Ball weight should be 58, 45 gms. as a minimum and 62.4 gms. as a maximum.
4. The player who gets four games scores the set.
5. Each player can make up to three attempts to put the ball on his contrary ground.
6. It does not matter if the ball reaches the contrary ground at the same side from which the service is made or not.
7. The player who is expecting a service can be in movement along his service line.
8. Service to be underhanded.
9. Shorter racquet handles.
10. Less bounce for ball.
11. Players may not come closer than five feet to net.
12. Three serves per point instead of two.
13. Only people under 5'8" may play.
14. Bonus point(s) for scoring on first serve.
15. Net is 3 inches lower.
16. Play may only begin during rain.
17. Karate is legal if other player within range (but *not* with racquet).
18. Players must be barefoot.
19. Racquet must be held with both hands at all times.
20. Net is to be moved down six inches.
21. Diameter of balls reduced by ⅜".
22. Court to be widened by 4 feet.
23. Balls are made of Silly Putty.
24. Racquets used will be 40" long, same size head.

## 310. Eight or more new rules of ice hockey if offsides was never called

1. Maximum length of rink should be 55 mts; minimum, 51.
2. Goal width should be 1.65 mts.
3. Maximum of substitutes per team could be eleven.
4. A match consists of three parts of twenty minutes each

189

plus a fourth one of ten minutes.

5. Changes of position should be made at the end of the first three parts of match.
6. The goalkeeper can touch the ball with his feet while sitting on the ground.
7. It is forbidden to charge against an opponent.
8. There should be a penalty-corner as in grass hockey.
9. Offense may not approach goal closer than ten feet.
10. Goalie has two sticks.
11. Net is smaller.
12. Extra defense player.
13. Field is twenty feet longer.
14. Puck is ball-shaped.
15. Goals change after each point.
16. "Body-checking" not penalized.
17. One skate is ice skate, the other is roller skate.
18. Suits are made of mail.
19. Referees are fair play for attack.
20. Players with long hair must wear hair nets under their helmets.
21. No ice fishing allowed during game.
22. No tied games will stand—they must be replayed immediately.
23. All goalies must wear an iron vest.
24. No assists allowed.
25. Former Defence men shall be called Defence persons.
26. Players with broken hockey sticks must sit out remainder of game.
27. Goalie on team that is ahead must wear a patch over one eye.

---

### 311. Eight or more reasons why most of us have never been to the 21 Club in Manhattan

1. Nobody knows what country Manhattan is in.
2. Manhattan belongs to the Indians and people are afraid of being scalped.
3. Nobody is 21.
4. They can't fit into the glass.
5. We can't find it.
6. We can't afford it.
7. We don't want to.
8. It's too elite.
9. We don't have proper attire.
10. I was never invited.
11. I've never heard of it.
12. I can't afford to go to Manhattan.
13. I don't dance.
14. I don't drink.
15. Clubs turn me off.
16. The 21 Club only takes Saudi Arabian rials for payment of their cover charge and rials are hard to come by.
17. Inflation has forced the club to change its name to the 31 Club and cabbies don't know it. The city directory has not caught up to it. When everyone learns of the change, the club will have been renamed the 41 Club.
18. It's closed. Together with the rest of New York City it could not meet its mortgage. Abdullah Akhbar Magoub has bought the club at the foreclosure sale and renamed it "The Dubai Deli."
19. The recently instituted $1,000 cover charge is just too prohibitive for us peons.
20. It's next to impossible to afford to stay in New York, and you have to run the gauntlet of twenty street gangs and enraged Black, Chinese, Puerto Rican, and Swedish equal rights zealots. Survivors are usually rushed to Bleecker Hospital's intensive care ward, if they make it to the front door of the 21 Club.
21. I'm over 21 years of age.
22. The 21 Club has just been bought by William Randolph Hearst and turned into an SLA soup kitchen.

---

### 312. Seven or more consequences of not having a reserved seat at the Metropolitan Opera

1. Not be able to attend an opera sung by Pilar Lorengar.
2. Idem by Montserrat Caballé.
3. Not be able to applaud Teresa Berganza tonight.
4. Not be able to applaud Victoria de los Angeles.
5. Not appear in the photographs taken that night at the opera.
6. Have to pay an "extra" price to the re-sellers if you do attend an opera.
7. Have to go to dance with your wife.
8. Have to go to dinner with your secretary.
9. Not be able to talk about the opera, next day, with your colleagues.
10. Not be able to talk about the opera with your boss.
11. Not be able to practice the Italian you learnt thanks to the Assimil method.
12. Save the cost of hiring a car to go there.
13. Save the cost of a babysitter.
14. Having to stand.
15. Not attending.
16. Bribe usher.
17. Mingle with orchestra.
18. Appear onstage.
19. Date drops you.
20. Get to see Walt Disney movie instead.
21. Can turn off hearing aid without consequence.
22. Save money on opera ticket.
23. "No-score" with usherettes at after-event festivities.
24. Intimidate someone with reserved seat into allowing you to have his.
25. Might have to sit on someone's lap.
26. Have an excuse to stay home.
27. Might stand in line with the peons.
28. Might go to a rock concert instead.
29. Will have something to gripe about.
30. Something to tell your psychiatrist.

---

### 313. Seven or more new rules of horse racing if only win bets were allowed

1. All races should be handicap type.
2. Maximum bet allowed would be $20.
3. Races should be limited to many who should act more changeably.
4. Races should be limited to ponies (it would be thrilling, I suppose).
5. A horse, winner in a race, could not take part in the three following ones.
6. Horses should take part without a cavalier riding on them.
7. Those people betting on the horse arriving in the last place should bet next time for the same horse free of charge.
8. Track would be zigzag.
9. Photofinish races would be rerun.
10. Use of whips disallowed.
11. Jockeys must be 50 years or older.
12. All horses under one year old.
13. Blindfolds required on all horses.
14. Maces allowed for jockeys; points for hitting other jockeys, negative points for hitting opponents' horses.
15. Daily-doubles cancelled.
16. Horses may not be drugged, but jockeys can be.
17. Races only run in the rain.
18. The horse with the most bets placed on him must carry two jockeys.
19. Horses winning over $1,000,000 must be retired.
20. No drugs for two-year-olds.
21. Birth control mandatory for three-year-olds.
22. Jockeys weighing over 120 lbs. undressed must wear their birthday suits.
23. No individual may make more than one bet per race.
24. Jockeys with long hair must wear hairnets.

---

### 314. Seven or more consequences of forcing a blackjack dealer to stick at 12

1. Dealer will order a double martini.
2. Dealer will let you deal.
3. A streak of good luck.
4. Dealer will become ill.
5. Dealer will move to change a few rules.
6. Dealer will do a very slow shuffle.
7. Dealer will find a loophole.
8. Odds would change.
9. Cheating would increase.
10. Customers may not return after winning.
11. Darker lights required by proprietors.
12. Deck of cards certified by players.
13. Holograms substituted for cards by dishonest dealers.
14. Stakes lighter (minimum $40).
15. Stiffer drinks (served free) to customers.
16. He would lose a lot of money.
17. He would lose a little money.
18. He would lose nothing.
19. He would be terribly nervous until knowing the points of the others.
20. He would look at the faces of the others, trying to guess their cards.

### 315. Eight or more reasons why the Toronto Bluejays will never win a pennant before the year 2000

1. They haven't the motivation.
2. They won't learn to tie their shoelaces until then.
3. They don't eat their Wheaties.
4. Because they're good sports.
5. They can't keep a straight face.
6. They're not aggressive enough.
7. They're not playing up to their potential.
8. They're the Toronto Bluejays and not the Toronto Bighorns.
9. Bad Karma.
10. They haven't enough Frenchmen on their team.
11. They delight in losing.
12. They are being paid off.
13. The coach is a masochist.
14. Only cripples are players.
15. Umpires have it in for the team.
16. Team can't afford to practice.
17. The world will come to an end next year.
18. The team will disband.
19. The owner uses them as a tax write-off.
20. Sponsor decides to shift allegiance to a girl's badminton team.
21. Age limit for team members reduced to under twenty years of age.
22. Coed manning of team distracts player.
23. Toronto ceases to exist after 1994.
24. Players were trained with incorrect rules.
25. They have already disappeared.
26. They become the Toronto Redjays.
27. They moved to Quebec and became the Quebec Bluejays.
28. Pennants are no longer offered as a prize.
29. We are in the year 2001.
30. The Toronto Bluejays have not yet been formed as a team.
31. They became a pop group.
32. They entered the Cosmos football team looking for millions of dollars.
33. They were menaced to death if still in competition.
34. They are not to compete for a pennant.
35. They are all writing books on creativity after seeing their name in this one.
36. All pennants up to year 2000 will be won either by Dallas Cowboys or unknown team.

### 316. Eight or more ways to spend one billion dollars in exactly twenty-four hours

1. Simply announce that you intend to do so.
2. Call someone on the moon person to person.
3. Invest it in U. S. savings bonds.
4. Feed it to the hungry bears at Yosemite.
5. Hand it out at a rate of $694,444.43 per minute.
6. Make papier mâché Christmas tree ornaments with the cash.
7. Buy a used spaceship.
8. Buy a President.
9. Establish fund for scholarships.
10. Buy stocks and bonds.
11. Create one thousand millionaires.
12. Buy Samoa (plus or minus a few islands).
13. Feed India for one day.
14. Irrigate the Sahara.
15. Prepay 10,000 mercenaries and capture Kuwait.
16. Buy one-half of a nuclear aircraft carrier.
17. Sell out to jewel conglomerate.
18. Donate funds to the Mafia.
19. Be first person on earth to *burn* one billion dollars in cash.
20. Create chaos on the Finnish stock market.
21. Automate Montana.
22. Civilize Alabama.
23. Corner the market on coal production.
24. Bribe influential politicians.
25. Buy airlines around the world until one billion is spent.
26. Buy all petrol ships under the different flags in the world.
27. Fill them up with petrol.
28. Order all arms production of the principal countries in this field.
29. Offer this billion dollars to those countries prepared to accept you as their President.
30. Open a Giant Museum after acquiring the best pieces in the Louvre, El Prado, L'Hermitage, etc.
31. Contract for a harem all women who were prepared to serve such a super-rich master.
32. Order all shares offered in the principal stock exchanges in the world.
33. Pay so that all people in the world who have neither food nor houses are immediately supplied with the best available (you need much more money).
34. Ask an expert in creativity to look for other ways to spend the billion dollars and put into practice his suggestions.

### 317. Seven or more reasons for doing away with cushions

1. Discourage unwelcome guests.
2. To get closer to the ground.
3. To encourage standing.
4. To bring big fannies into fashion.
5. To discourage UFO landings.
6. To prevent cushion fights.
7. To do away with cushioned comfort.
8. They foster bad posture.
9. The price of down is up.
10. Would drive masochists buggy (a plus for sadists).
11. Eliminate source of income for the international cushion conspiracy.
12. Would reduce allergies in certain people.
13. Cushions are too materialistic.
14. The cat gets loose hair all over them anyway.
15. Sleeping without cushions eliminates the risk of snoring.
16. Doctors consider cushions are not a natural help to good sleep.
17. Without cushioning the risk of shoulder aches is smaller.
18. You can earn some money selling cushions.
19. You can make two car cushions out of each bed cushion.
20. Your wife will sleep badly without cushions.
21. Cushions are not necessary if you can embrace your wife.
22. Cushions are too expensive now.
23. Beds with cushions provoke "bad" thoughts in men because cushions have curves like women.

### 318. Seven or more reasons for not believing in ESP

1. You won't know the worst.
2. You can have secrets.
3. I haven't the ability.
4. I like surprises.
5. I'm not a Pisces.
6. I don't want to.
7. I don't like finding scarabs in my yogurt.
8. My mother does believe in ESP.
9. It causes nightmares for believers.
10. Will be declared illegal.
11. Cannot be proven.
12. My subsconscious says it's not true.
13. One would need special antennae.
14. Spirits from nether world say its BS.
15. Have *you* ever seen an *ASP*, let alone an *ESP*?
16. To have seen Uri Geller through TV.
17. To have read what his detractors have written about him.
18. To have contacted, without success, a foreteller.
19. To be a Ph.D.
20. To be too conservative in beliefs.
21. To be surprised by sudden events all the time.
22. Not to have heard about ESP.
23. If you cannot communicate with your neighbor, how can you translate your thoughts to anybody far in space?
24. To be a priest of a traditional faith.

### 319. Seven or more reasons for more lost ads than found ads

1. Many found items are assumed to be abandoned.
2. It's gotta be lost before it can be found.
3. There are many losers in this world.
4. Many "lost" items were really taken.
5. Many "lost" items really ran away.
6. Losers believe that perseverance furthers.
7. Finders keepers losers weepers.
8. Finders can't be sure of previous owners.
9. A lot of phonies expect gains.

10. Losers forget they've lost things.
11. Ad writers call in to claim "found" items.
12. Everyone sympathizes with losers, but finders? . . .
13. More things get lost than found.
14. You are not so worried when finding anything.
15. Newspapers used to title this column as "lost" ads.
16. You risk losing the cost of ad if the loser of the thing you found does not contact you.
17. Some people who keep for themselves what they found are not interested in announcing it.
18. People who lose something find those who found it before they can place an ad.
19. Lost Object offices are open to everybody but they make no publicity of their "stock" or, at least, they do not put their lists under the "lost" ad column.
20. People only place a found ad if they hope to get a reward.

---

### 320. Eight or more reasons why the Dallas Cowboys will not win the 1988 Super Bowl

1. The San Francisco 49ers.
2. The 1988 Super Bowl will be cancelled due to the high cost of beef.
3. Texas will be annexed to Mexico.
4. They'll lose.
5. Their drug contract won't come through.
6. Spiderman will intervene for the opposition.
7. They'll be too tired by then.
8. They don't eat their spinach.
9. Football will be banned in Texas.
10. Team killed in plane trip.
11. Owner refuses to comply with rules.
12. Team quits en masse.
13. Team goes coed and loses because line-backers have morning sickness.
14. Court order prohibits Cowboys' participation.
15. 1988 Super Bowl cancelled due to World War III.
16. Team disbanded due to cowardice.
17. Dallas is unincorporated.
18. Name changed to Dallas "Hopped-Up Weirdos" or the "Dallas Daffodils."
19. They have already disappeared.

20. They will disappear in 1987.
21. They will disappear next year.
22. The Super Bowl is no longer a current competition.
23. World will end in 1987.
24. World will end next year.
25. They will become a pop group sooner than 1988.
26. They will enter the Cosmos football team.
27. They are menaced to death if still in competition.
28. They are not to compete for the 1988 Super Bowl.
29. The 1988 Super Bowl will be won by the Toronto Bluejays.

---

### 321. Six or more reasons why Chile has never had a soccer team in the finals of the World Cup

1. Whoever runs the World Cup games hates Chile.
2. Whoever runs the World Cup games doesn't know Chile has a soccer team.
3. Chile is too busy having coups.
4. No one in Chile knows the real rules so no one can coach.
5. Chile is too poor to buy soccer balls for kids to practice with.
6. Chile needs a soccer coach.
7. Chilean soccer players don't use their heads.
8. Chilean forwards aren't straight shooters.
9. Chile never has a winning team.
10. The World Cup won't invite Chile to play.
11. Chile has no soccer team.
12. Finals are too decisive for Chilean temperament.
13. Chileans are just learning soccer.
14. Soccer balls don't go as far or as straight in the Andes.
15. Chile never won the soccer semifinals.
16. Other countries always beat Chile before the finals.
17. Chile can't afford to send a team.
18. Chile can't stay hot or "Chile's not hot."
19. The U. S. hires all their good players.
20. It's not whether you won or lose, it's . . .
21. Chile is a pepper of a soup.
22. Soccer isn't easy!
23. They don't play soccer.
24. Too much competition.
25. Chile's not consistent.

26. High altitude results in formation of wrong type of bodies for soccer playing.
27. Political situation too unstable for funding of athletes.
28. Political situation too unstable for athletes to concentrate on their game.
29. Mountainous regions unsuitable for playing soccer as balls too apt to roll away; if people run after them they fall over the edge, so the soccer-playing "aptitude" is a maladaptive one and is genetically selected out.
30. The aliens from outer space who built the landing fields in the Andes inserted pre-programmed instructions into the Incas never to win soccer games, which have been passed on from generation to generation via plasmids.
31. The people on the Chilean soccer teams were warned that they would be bombed if they won, by mobsters who had bet on opposing teams.
32. Pure chance.
33. Not enough money available to train athletes.
34. Mothers in Chile don't regard soccer as a suitable endeavor for their sons.
35. Feet too big.
36. Too close to the sun.
37. Air too thin.
38. Teams trying to look bad to attract bets against them; suddenly they will win and make a bundle of $.
39. They know they will not be allowed to leave country, so they don't try.
40. God so wills it.
41. The athletes aren't good enough.
42. They have been hypnotized.
43. The athletes have been poisoned on greed.
44. The other teams are made of supermen.
45. They only win in years divisible by 1,000.
46. Food kills off star athletes.
47. Players unused to foreign food and get sick.

---

### 322. Seven or more new rules of volleyball if there were fifteen persons on a side

1. More referees to keep an eye on all the extra players.
2. Higher net.
3. Smaller balls.

4. Rotate servers with every serve, don't let one server serve the ball until the other team gains possession of it.
5. New court size.
6. No "personal space" allowed.
7. At least three people have to touch the ball before return over the net.
8. Allow shin guards, elbow pads, and face masks.
9. Raise the net.
10. No spiking.
11. No more than seven in front "wall."
12. Limit substitution.
13. Coach cannot call plays from the bench.
14. Create injury time outs.
15. Use two or more balls.
16. Increase player participation.
17. No fraternization.
18. Abolish rules.
19. Abolish volleyballs and marathon dance instead.
20. Provide each player with their own ball and net.
21. Forbid drinking.
22. Demand absolute silence.
23. Larger ball.
24. Add two referees and a social director.
25. Huddle between plays.
26. Go to "2 platoon" system for offense/defense.
27. Court must be expended from this ⊞ size to this ⊞⊞ size.
28. Seven people sit on the sides on each team, and rotate in and out at serving time one by one.
29. The game will be played with two balls, each a different color, simultaneously—one ball for each team to score with.
30. The field could be expanded in depth: ▤
31. Serving would be allowed one assist from person in inert part of field.
32. The game would be played like tennis doubles: ⊡ Ball would have to go along arrows to court.
33. With expanded field, ball could be altered so that it would travel farther on one push than the present ball.
34. With expanded field, six assists would be allowed to return ball instead of three.
35. Field could be set up with three nets, arranged in layers. For A to score, ball would have to reach farthest team B area and vice versa.

36. "Extra" players would have to join hands and *be* the net, each net working for its own team, trying to stop opposing tennis balls from going over it.
37. Players must play with only one arm.
38. Players not allowed to move feet.
39. Alternate players only allowed to use head to hit ball.
40. Alternate players face sideways.
41. "Extra" players stand out of bounds and prevent ball from grounding out.
42. "Extra" players heckle opposing team.
43. Ball must be greased.

## 323. Eight or more reasons for not having bookends

1. They might get knocked over and broken.
2. If you have bookends you're obligated to keep your shelf neat.
3. Some minds blossom among profusions.
4. Often bookends are stupid/ ugly/gaudy/tacky/ ostentatious.
5. Don't have books.
6. Fill shelves so walls hold up books.
7. You don't know what they are.
8. Use rocks or heavy trinkets/ keepsakes.
9. Borrow books from friends (and return when through).
10. Borrow books from library (and return or pay fines).
11. Remain functionally illiterate.
12. Can't afford them.
13. You don't know how to get any.
14. Going to sell books.
15. Can't decide on decor.
16. I'm blind and can't read Braille.
17. Just moving out.
18. Just moved in.
19. Saving for an expensive set.
20. My mother promised me a set for Christmas.
21. All books have end(ing)s.
22. Termites ate them.
23. Only use books for paperweights.
24. You want to show a kid how to balance things.
25. They squash the books.
26. They cost money you could spend on more books.
27. They take up room you could use for more books.
28. They could fall on your toe when you push in another book.
29. Your grandmother didn't have any so you won't either.
30. Your bookends were stolen.
31. You can turn end books on their side so you don't read them.
32. You store all your books in bags.
33. You store all your books on microfilm.
34. You have a separate niche for each book on your walls, for decoration.
35. Bookends could be used as weapons by an intruder.
36. Bookends don't blend with your decor.
37. All your bookshelves have closed sides and are full.
38. All your books are too large to fit bookends.
39. All your books are too small to fit bookends.
40. All your books are on scrolls.
41. All your books are written on stones.
42. Your books are used as furniture.
43. Your Aunt Matilda was killed by a bookend.
44. You have a phobia about bookends.
45. It pleases your esthetic sense to see books slouching over.
46. You think bookends were an invention of the devil.
47. If your books stand up vertically your pet turtle won't be able to crawl up them into his container on top of them.
48. Picking up books gives you exercise.
49. You're a sadist and you use masochists to hold up your books.
50. You hate neatness.
51. You can't pull the books out without ruining the binding.
52. Bookends ruin the finish on the bookshelves.
53. You never put your books away.
54. You're trying to show everyone you're a Bohemian.
55. You can't bear to see anything restrained.
56. Spiders build webs on them.
57. You're trying to see how many books can fit in a given space.
58. You have an aversion to the letter "B" and all that begins with it.
59. A fortune-teller told you to beware of bookends.
60. Your father made you use them and now you refuse out of spite.

## 324. Nine or more petty annoyances that everybody experiences

1. Getting a skip in a favorite record.
2. LOUD neighbors.
3. Waiting for late trains and buses.
4. Missing early trains and buses.
5. Being splashed when trucks drive through mud puddles.
6. Breaking shoestrings when already in a hurry.
7. Not being able to find a pencil to take telephone messages.
8. Receiving torn magazines.
9. Long lines at supermarket checkouts.
10. Seeing checker close line once you get there.
11. Bitchy phone operators.
12. People who talk during concerts.
13. Being kept waiting for appointments.
14. No change for parking meters.
15. Stamps that fall off.
16. Being caught in storm without an umbrella or raincoat.
17. Temporary insolvency.
18. Unexpected large outlay just before Christmas or vacation.
19. Spot on new garment.
20. Scratch on new car or furnishing.
21. Losing electric power.
22. Receiving electric bill.
23. Ringing telephone.
24. Busy signal.
25. Receiving two or more identical gifts.
26. Children, sometimes.
27. Somebody else's pet that misbehaves.
28. Mental lapse.
29. Cigarette burns.
30. Health problems.
31. In-laws.
32. Toothache.
33. Car won't start.
34. Chain letters.
35. Misplacing something suddenly important.
36. Tax audit.
37. Bullies.
38. Loud, brash, pushy people.
39. Alarm sounding.
40. Malfunctioning appliances.
41. Junk mail.
42. Trodden toes.
43. Impertinent sales people.
44. Lousy food in restaurants.
45. Smoke blown in face.
46. Show canceled.
47. Pens run out of ink.
48. Calculator batteries run out.
49. Car breaks down.
50. Rain on your picnic.
51. Ants at your picnic.
52. Kitchen floor gets dirty.
53. Fuse blown.
54. Run out of food in house.
55. Shoes wear out.
56. Fashions change on you.
57. Neighbors gossip.
58. Winter comes.
59. Storms come.
60. Vending machine eats your money.
61. Show sells out.
62. Catch a cold.
63. Roast burns in oven.
64. "Wrong" party elected to office.
65. Paperboy throws paper in mud.
66. Dishes break.
67. Food spills.
68. Mosquito bites.
69. Other animal bites.
70. Spiders hatch in your house.
71. Mice invade house.
72. Break fingernail.
73. Coins fall in sewer.
74. Jewelry falls in drain.
75. Drain gets stopped up.
76. Mail strikes.
77. Transit strikes.
78. Run out of things when stores closed.
79. Baby born in middle of night.
80. Neighbor borrows cup of flour.
81. Phone rings while you're taking a bath.
82. Salesmen come to door.
83. Shoving in crowds.
84. Waiting for traffic lights.
85. Traffic jams.
86. Sit next to someone who smells bad.
87. Plant dies.
88. Person throws up on you.
89. You must remember relatives' birthdays.
90. Oven gets dirty.
91. Long-winded person calls when you're waiting for important call.
92. Ads on TV.
93. Snooty neighbor shows off things you can't afford.
94. You trip and fall.
95. You forget how to spell a word and have to look it up.
96. You forget someone's name.
97. Make arithmetic mistake on checking account.
98. Pencil breaks.
99. Cut yourself shaving.
100. Stepping in dog-poo.
101. Missing TV program.

102. Forgetting to buy necessity at food store.
103. Forgetting to meet someone.
104. Forgetting special occasion.
105. Zipper breaks.
106. Garbage bag breaks.
107. Run out of toilet paper.
108. Person sneezes on you.
109. Long-winded taxi driver.
110. Bookmark falls out.

---

## 325. Seven or more reasons for not being superstitious

1. Black cats make good pets.
2. 13 is a "baker's dozen"—bigger and better than 12.
3. Throwing salt over shoulder is a waste of money.
4. Knocking on wood gives splinters.
5. Sometimes it's hard to avoid ladders.
6. Vegetarians can't own rabbits feet.
7. Some sidewalks are too cracked to avoid stepping on cracks.
8. It's bad luck.
9. Don't know any superstitions.
10. My parents weren't superstitious.
11. My teachers weren't superstitious.
12. I don't believe in it.
13. I'm superstitious about being superstitious.
14. I never learned how.
15. There is a reason for everything which can be derived through logic and physical law.
16. Nothing unexplained ever happened to me.
17. Don't have time.
18. It's unprofessional.
19. It's not popular.
20. I don't do popular things.
21. But I am!
22. I can't afford it.
23. Because I'm educated.
24. None of my friends are.
25. My mommy won't let me.
26. I got enough trouble just making ends meet.
27. I broke a mirror and the seven years aren't up yet.
28. Can live on 13th floor.
29. Don't have to fear things unreasonably.
30. Subconscious won't cause superstitions to come to me.
31. Can walk on the cracks.
32. Freedom from ridicule.
33. Weren't raised superstitious.
34. Never heard any superstitions.
35. Hypnotized out of previous superstitions.
36. Saw superstitious people had trouble.
37. Reason rules in this person.
38. Am autistic.
39. Statistics show superstitions don't hold true.
40. You might miss out on something good.
41. Brain damage.

---

## 326. Eight or more consequences of being the first baby born in the new calendar year in the United States

1. Always being referred to as a New Year baby.
2. The parent wins prizes.
3. Parents may have hard time getting to hospital because of New Year's traffic.
4. Since birthday is on a holiday it may get overlooked.
5. For most jobs persons get New Year off as a legal holiday—so person wouldn't have to work on birthday.
6. May not enjoy birthday because are hung over from the night before.
7. When you get older and want to *forget* your birthday, it may be harder to do so. Every New Year you will be reminded of it.
8. A New Year's baby is just a few hours too old for parents to claim him/her as a tax exemption for the previous year.
9. Free publicity.
10. Lousy time for a birthday.
11. Hope the hospital staff were sober.
12. Stork shortage (all out whooping).
13. Parents get all of the prizes.
14. I'm cute and cuddly.
15. Everybody loves me.
16. The population grows one more.
17. My taxes will be higher.
18. Social Security will be broke before I retire.
19. Another mouth to feed.
20. The pediatrician has a new annuity.
21. The anesthesiologist has a fat fee.
22. The hospital has more work.
23. Children's stores will love my parents.
24. Dad will have to keep working.
25. Mom will have to go back to work soon.
26. Life goes on.
27. The economics of my family change.
28. I'll get a valentine in February.
29. I missed a Christmas present by six days.
30. Get name in paper.
31. Get free baby products.
32. Get name like Nova or Happy.
33. Get diapers for a year.
34. Get to be 5½ before starting school.
35. Get plaque indicating what millionth American you are.
36. Get congratulatory messages from politicians.
37. Get special tag in hospital.
38. Be compared with other first babies in other countries.
39. Get to tell all your friends.
40. Have trouble collecting birthday presents as distinguished from New Year's stuff.
41. Get free calendar.
42. First counted in census.
43. Butt of jokes.
44. Picture taken in "Baby New Years" garb.
45. Get extra attention from nurses.
46. Get to keep clippings from paper.
47. Mother gets bothered by newsmen.
48. Have people say "So you were born on New Year's, eh?"
49. Have horoscope cast publicly by local seer.
50. Be chased by a fanatic.
51. No trouble remembering birthdate.

---

## 327. Seven or more novel uses of crushed ice

1. Ice cubes for dolls.
2. In winter playground as slide.
3. To stick stamps without spilling.
4. A method to water plants without spilling anything—just add some ice to their pots.
5. Celebrate winter in July by making icy snowmen.
6. Buy pet penguins and give them ice to play with.
7. Buy pet polar bears and give them ice to play with.
8. To ski on.
9. Press into cubes.
10. Press into blocks.
11. Coat boilers.
12. Line bathtubs.
13. Cool coffee.
14. Cool air-conditioner compressers to save electricity.
15. Help sell ice crushers.
16. Make beer slushes.
17. Make chewy sandwiches.
18. Create your own hail showers.
19. Smother fires.
20. Make lakes.
21. Keep block ice in.
22. Destroy salt.
23. Cool lakes.
24. Surface irrigation.
25. Hide things in.
26. Fill pies.
27. Exchange energy faster.
28. Sculpture material in winter.
29. Mold for pouring wax in to make lacey wax sculpture.
30. Illustrate physics problem of melting ice affecting water level.
31. Use for snowballs in the summer.
32. Pack feverish people in it.
33. Put in plants before a trip to provide slow watering.
34. Put on steps of person you hate so he'll slip and fall.
35. Show to baby to illustrate "cold."
36. Put on face to shrink pores.
37. Stuff blanket with it in summertime.
38. Use to simulate Martian environment.
39. Put some in ring to wear in the cold as fake diamonds.
40. Put broken glass in it to hide broken glass.
41. Put in a sock to use for swollen bumps.
42. Put in mouth to chew ice if you've no teeth.
43. Use as winter landscape for dolls.
44. Use on ski slope when not enough snow.
45. Use as insulation material in arctic.
46. Use to show equatorial people what it is.
47. Lubricate arctic car.
48. Play marbles with it.
49. Use it in pea-shooter.
50. Use it as bullet that will be untraceable.
51. Pour it on angry person.
52. Fill sand box with it.
53. Preserve insects in it.
54. Ship it to Arabia.
55. Cool hands in it before touching hot thing.
56. Cool hands in it after touching hot thing.
57. Use as home for pet arctic worm.
58. Decorate Christmas tree with it.
59. Put on hall floor to slide on.

60. Drop it from airplanes to make rain.
61. Stuff it up nose to stop bleeding.
62. Drown things in it.
63. Put in container and use as flashing signal in sun.
64. Physics experiment to measure speed of sound through it.
65. Subject for a book.
66. Pretend to be it.
67. Test freezability of substances.
68. Film it melting.
69. Take pictures of it.
70. Paint pictures of it.
71. Drop pieces of it on person as a torture.
72. Fill humidifier with it for cold air in summer.

### 328. Nine or more reasons why European trains are profitable whereas most American trains are in the red

1. Americans are more car-conscious. Europeans have fewer cars and must use trains.
2. Americans like to "strike out on own" with a car, with trains one has to follow a schedule.
3. In Europe the major metropolitan areas are closer together so people find it easy to use the trains.
4. Europe has more youth hostels so kids travel on train and use youth hostels because it's a cheap way to travel.
5. Americans find flying quicker, easier, and more fashionable.
6. With a car one can visit national parks and scenic places with great ease.
7. American trains have been given bad press by airlines.
8. America has a better trucking system than Europe so companies send cargo on trucks rather than train.
9. Europeans would prefer to use their cars but the price of gas is much higher in Europe than America.
10. European trains run on time.
11. European trains run.
12. European train crews are courteous.
13. European trains are clean.
14. European train stations are clean.
15. European train stations are convenient.

16. European trains are convenient.
17. European trains are reasonably priced.
18. Europeans do not have as many transportation alternatives.
19. Europeans travel by train more.
20. Europeans are better businessmen.
21. European train companies are better managed.
22. European trains have three passenger classes.
23. Europeans still have trains.
24. European trains still carry people.
25. European trains are better subsidized.
26. Maintenance is better in Europe.
27. Americans ship goods by barge or truck.
28. More goods ride trains in Europe.
29. Europeans build things to last and take care of machines.
30. European trains leave at more convenient times.
31. Europeans have fewer airplanes so more is shipped by train.
32. Europeans don't have such strong unions.
33. More theft in America eats up profits.
34. European trains geared to passenger, American to freight.
35. European countries smaller, each looks after small bit of rail. American companies too big.
36. American companies only in the red officially, for tax purposes.
37. European companies more socialistic.
38. Europeans are better accountants.
39. European trains smaller, cheaper to run.
40. European trains more sophisticated, require fewer people to run them.
41. European trains have less frills.
42. European trains made of cheaper materials.
43. If European train trip not profitable, isn't made.
44. Farsightedness of European planners.
45. Fewer telephones, more transport in Europe.
46. European trains are older than American ones.
47. European trains were never attacked by Indians.
48. Red is a prohibited colour in

European accountancy books.
49. Roads are not so good in Europe.
50. European secretaries prefer their bosses to travel in train.
51. European governments are most concerned about economic results of trains.

### 329. Seven or more reasons for issuing a $3 bill

1. It offers something in between a $1 and $5 bill.
2. People have superstitions about $2 bills and don't like them.
3. They would be convenient to pay for $3 movies.
4. Anything new is exciting.
5. Neither the $1 nor $2 buy anything anymore.
6. So that "queerer than a $3 bill" will not offend anyone anymore.
7. So that you can change a $12 bill into 4 $3's or a $3 and a $9 bill.
8. Keeping the printing presses rolling.
9. Confuse tourists so they can be shortchanged easier.
10. Provide a collectors' item.
11. Sell additional proof sets.
12. Put in parking meters.
13. Replace the worthless greenback.
14. Give the people a *real* reason to write their Congressmen.
15. Divert America's computers from the binary standard.
16. Stop inflation.
17. Provide jobs.
18. Get Carter's face on a bill before he's dead.
19. Honor Adam Clayton Powell or Geo. Wash. Carver.
20. Destroy the gold system.
21. Support the World Bank.
22. So people can buy twenty postage stamps without getting change.
23. Easy token tip to cabbies, waitresses, etc.
24. Help the depressed paper, ink, and treasury industries.
25. Destroy the bank check industry.
26. Provide additional space (2/3) in mattresses.
27. Have bill with woman's picture on it.
28. Have bill with minority citizen's picture on it.
29. Show progress.
30. Give administration a positive act to point to when '80 elections come up.
31. To facilitate the raising of the

typical horserace bet to $3.
32. Because with inflation it's only worth $1 anyway.
33. To make it easier to purchase $3 items.
34. To make jobs for government designers.
35. To make jobs for government engravers.
36. To make the President under whose aegis this is done more famous.
37. To make it easier to have change for a $10 bill when you buy $7 worth.
38. Because with the new $1 coin you need a new bill under $5 to keep the same number of bills.
39. Stimulate the economy.
40. Provide opportunity for more counterfeiting.
41. Respond to demands for more overtime opportunities.
42. Give people "lucky number" money.
43. To be unique in the world.
44. Extra revenue for gov't by selling them to collectors.
45. Country changes to base 12 everything and needs $3, $6, $2, $4 bills.
46. To fulfill a prophecy.
47. As a joke.
48. Part of party platform of Anarchists, who are elected unexpectedly.
49. God wills it.
50. Voters demand it.
51. Printers made a mistake.

### 330. Eight or more reasons why only one woman is pictured on our national currency

1. Congress is chauvinistic.
2. Artists find women harder to draw than men.
3. We haven't enough types of money to picture everyone.
4. It cost too much to throw out the old currency plates and make new ones.
5. Women look better in blue than green.
6. Too many important women—it's hard to choose one or two over the rest.
7. Women are less conceited than men.
8. No women presidents.
9. Women won't approve any picture as looking good enough.
10. Women think etching makes them look fat.
11. Women think etching makes them look older.

12. Politicians can't agree on whose mother to honor first.
13. Why isn't apple pie pictured on our national currency?
14. Why aren't minority citizens pictured on our national currency?
15. Women don't want to be associated with "filthy lucre" or commercial enterprises.
16. Women don't look stern enough.
17. It's degrading when one considers what's happening to our currency.
18. That would inflate some woman!
19. There are no good platemakers left in the U.S.
20. Try one on a stamp and see if it sells.
21. Women bankers would be offended.
22. Women wouldn't spend the bill and depression would result.
23. What's "national currency" . . . a credit card?
24. A new denomination would have to be created.
25. This is an honor reserved for exceptional (?) past presidents.
26. Women weren't allowed to be presidents.
27. People thought women's place was in the home.
28. Pictures on currency date from before women's lib.
29. Men decided who was to be on currency.
30. Women on currency would encourage young girls to run for office, which wasn't liked.
31. Women hadn't done anything related to getting on $.
32. No one asked to have a woman on the currency.
33. Artists don't know how to draw women.
34. I'm in Canada—we *do* have women on our nat'l currency.
35. U.S.A. has had no queens.
36. The men pictured did more important things than any woman.
37. People wanted to keep women out of politics.
38. Coincidence.
39. Conspiracy of misogynists.
40. No pictures exist of women who were considered.
41. Americans need a father figure to guard their money.
42. No one thought of it.

---

**331. Seven or more reasons for not using a .22 long bullet as a tie clasp**

1. Your boss would fire you.
2. People might accuse one of being a warmonger.
3. The bullet may be needed for hunting.
4. Bullets are too expensive to waste.
5. Many people might consider it to be tacky and tasteless.
6. Not a member of the NRA (National Rifle Association).
7. They are dangerous until powder is removed.
8. It is dangerous to remove powder.
9. There are already too many kinds of tie clasps.
10. You are a woman.
11. Wouldn't wear it if I had one.
12. Why glorify a bullet?
13. It doesn't fit my personality.
14. Some people would be offended.
15. Some people might feel threatened.
16. I consider bullet jewelry in bad taste.
17. A .22 short is cheaper and serves the same purpose.
18. A gold replica weighs 1/2 oz. and is too expensive at today's gold price.
19. I'm not a straight shooter.
20. They are illegal.
21. It could explode if hit.
22. It could mark you as a violent man.
23. It could have been from a murder weapon.
24. A madman with an empty .22 gun could take it and shoot you with it.
25. It has no clip on it to hold your tie.
26. Your baby could choke on it.
27. Your boss would laugh at you.
28. A punk in the street would see it and hit you.
29. A smuggler could hide cocaine in it and you'd be caught.
30. It would make people remember you when you might want to be anonymous.
31. It could make you seem macho to a date who hates macho.
32. It could be the secret recognition of a secret society.
33. It could fall on your toe.
34. It could attract lightning.
35. It could give you lead poisoning.
36. It could fall on a midget with a cigar and explode on him.
37. It could leave a mark on your tie.
38. It could attract derision.
39. It could stop you from getting through the metal detector at airports.
40. It would fall off your tie.
41. You don't wear a tie.
42. You don't wear tie clasps.
43. You wear bow ties.
44. You vowed never to do it.
45. You are allergic to lead.
46. It's too heavy.
47. You don't have a .22 bullet.
48. You can't figure out how to make it clasp your tie.
49. You don't know ties should have clasps.
50. If it fell off near the scene of a crime you would be implicated.
51. You only use .44 caliber bullets.
52. You don't know what a bullet is.
53. You don't know what a tie clasp is.
54. You don't know what a tie is.

---

**332. Eight or more reasons for not running five or more miles per day**

1. I dislike running.
2. I've a bad heart.
3. I've got hay fever.
4. I get lost.
5. Tennis shoes wear out.
6. Warm-ups cost money.
7. I'm in a wheelchair.
8. I'm lame.
9. I swim for exercise.
10. I'm fat and I'm lazy.
11. I can't run that far.
12. Jogging is unhealthy.
13. Not enough room.
14. It's not important to me.
15. I'm bedridden.
16. Calisthenics are better for you.
17. My doctor told me not to.
18. My doctor didn't prescribe that.
19. It's too cold out.
20. I live on a small boat at sea.
21. I'm an astronaut in space.
22. I live underwater.
23. I'm a sprinter.
24. I run only red lights and stop signs.
25. I'm going to start next year.
26. I have to *walk* the dog.
27. Perversity.
28. Risk of arthritis.
29. Risk of mugging.
30. Risk of tiredness.
31. No time.
32. No legs.
33. No shoes.
34. Too lazy.
35. Waste of time.
36. No good place to run.
37. Too old.
38. No babysitter.
39. Your crowd doesn't do such things.
40. People stare at you.
41. You get overheated.
42. You have asthma.
43. You have fallen arches.
44. You will get fallen arches.
45. Your dog can't run that far.
46. You have no feet.
47. You live at the North Pole.
48. It will make your legs too muscular.
49. You are paralyzed.
50. Someone will pay you lots of money if you don't.
51. You lost a bet.
52. You promised you wouldn't.
53. Dogs will chase you.
54. Suspicious behavior attracts thought-police.
55. You don't want to inadvertently kill bugs by stepping on them.
56. Your head is permanently fixed facing sideways.
57. You'll ruin your clothes.
58. You'll get too sweaty.
59. You'll smell bad.
60. You are a snail.
61. A pedometer attached to a bomb is on you.
62. You are being held captive in a closet.
63. You are hypothyroid.
64. You live on an island 1 meter square.
65. You don't know how to run.
66. You made a bet you wouldn't.
67. You live in a bog.
68. The climate is too lousy.
69. Part of experiment on slab.
70. You're a baby.
71. Rather spend time with paraplegic fiancé.
72. You are too uncoordinated.
73. You hate your phys. ed. instructor.
74. Have to gain weight fast.

---

**333. Seven or more reasons why some combinations of letters are illegal on license plates**

1. Some combinations may already be in use—it would be confusing to have two cars with the same license plate.

2. The word may be obscene.
3. Some combination (like COQ) may be hard for cops to distinguish in the event of a chase.
4. Some letters have superstitious links.
5. Congress may have just wanted to pass a law.
6. The combination may have sexual connotations and upset little old ladies.
7. License plate makers get tired of making special plates for special requests.
8. They spell naughty words.
9. They might offend someone.
10. Puritan hang-up.
11. They could spell racial/nationality slurs.
12. The law is to preserve peace and the common good of society.
13. Some words incite emotions not congruous with intent of law.
14. Motor Vehicle Department doesn't want a lot of complaints.
15. Let's just avoid trouble.
16. Don't want to advertise illegal/sinful/harmful activities.
17. So people will forget those words.
18. Some combinations are against the public's welfare.
19. They lead to moral decay.
20. People have been paid off.
21. Offended people write politicians.
22. Offended people bomb offensive cars.
23. Offended people dislike attitude of offensive people.
24. The lawyers wanted more business.
25. The governor is trying for the conservative vote.
26. The dies for those combinations do not exist in the factory.
27. God willed it.
28. Each politician got to choose one forbidden combo.
29. Drivers will be distracted and cause collisions.
30. The words are illegal in other places too.
31. These combinations are morally wrong.
32. The lawmakers are social scientists running an experiment.
33. Politicians are afraid to legalize them.

---

### 334. Nine or more reasons for not having patents

1. Japanese don't honor ours.
2. Patents enable people to form monopolies.
3. Patents enable people to overcharge.
4. Patents enable people to quit trying to improve goods.
5. Patents are a lot of red tape.
6. Paying patent officers' salary means using taxes and taxes are high enough.
7. Takes too long for a new product to become marketable.
8. All inventions belong to all mankind.
9. All inventions belong to the state.
10. Patents are no longer enforceable.
11. Patents are a form of unfair competition/monopoly.
12. Patents prevent others from inventing the same thing "first" when they do it later on.
13. Patents only promote free enterprise for the owner.
14. It is too expensive and time consuming to obtain a patent.
15. No one is creating/inventing anymore.
16. Everything worthwhile is already patented.
17. They conflict with copyrights.
18. I never conceived anything patentable.
19. Patents are a bother.
20. Patents are a lot of legal hassle.
21. Most patents are ridiculous.
22. Patents are too broad and restrict free application, hence they deny adequate human advancement.
23. Companies can buy patent and keep in under wraps.
24. To eliminate patent laws.
25. To stop cases from tying up the courts.
26. To eliminate pride in inventions.
27. To make inventions less expensive.
28. To eliminate costly record-keeping.
29. To eliminate patent searches which cost time and money.
30. Patently obvious.
31. Don't believe in private property.
32. Nobody willing to check out patents.
33. To prevent future Einsteins from wasting time in patent offices.
34. There is nowhere to keep records of patents.
35. To prevent overbearingness of patent owners.
36. Governments have all collapsed rendering this stuff unimportant.
37. God is regarded as the source of all patentable novelties.
38. Cases of serendipity render patents unfair.
39. To stop the crime of patent infringement.
40. People suddenly forget how to write.

# DECEMBER

**Mental Calisthenic #12**
This exercise will take some doing! Consult an expert and learn how to "say" in both Braille and sign language, "I love you; be my friend." Share the communication with a blind person and a deaf person. Repeat the exercise with music and dance. That is, interpret the phrase with music and with body movements. Proceed with a Mental Jogging exercise.

## 335. Eight or more reasons for paying a speeding ticket

| Response | Score |
|---|---|
| 1. _____ | 1 |
| 2. _____ | 1 |
| 3. _____ | 1 |
| 4. _____ | 1 |
| 5. _____ | 1 |
| 6. _____ | 1 |
| 7. _____ | 1 |
| 8. _____ | 1 |
| **Bonus Responses** | |
| 9. _____ | 2 |
| 10. _____ | 2 |
| 11. _____ | 2 |
| 12. _____ | 2 |
| 13. _____ | 2 |
| 14. _____ | 2 |
| 15. _____ | 2 |
| 16. _____ | 2 |
| Total ☐ | |

## 336. Seven or more associations to the word "zyto"

| Response | Score |
|---|---|
| 1. _____ | 1 |
| 2. _____ | 1 |
| 3. _____ | 1 |
| 4. _____ | 1 |
| 5. _____ | 1 |
| 6. _____ | 1 |
| 7. _____ | 1 |
| **Bonus Responses** | |
| 8. _____ | 2 |
| 9. _____ | 2 |
| 10. _____ | 2 |
| 11. _____ | 2 |
| 12. _____ | 2 |
| 13. _____ | 2 |
| 14. _____ | 2 |
| 15. _____ | 2 |
| 16. _____ | 2 |
| Total ☐ | |

**337.** Eight or more reasons why some people continue to smoke in the non-smoking section of planes and trains

Response | Score
1. _____ 1
2. _____ 1
3. _____ 1
4. _____ 1
5. _____ 1
6. _____ 1
7. _____ 1
8. _____ 1

Bonus Responses
9. _____ 2
10. _____ 2
11. _____ 2
12. _____ 2
13. _____ 2
14. _____ 2
15. _____ 2
16. _____ 2

Total ☐

**338.** Eight or more reasons why it costs more to buy a train ticket after boarding than before boarding

Response | Score
1. _____ 1
2. _____ 1
3. _____ 1
4. _____ 1
5. _____ 1
6. _____ 1
7. _____ 1
8. _____ 1

Bonus Responses
9. _____ 2
10. _____ 2
11. _____ 2
12. _____ 2
13. _____ 2
14. _____ 2
15. _____ 2
16. _____ 2

Total ☐

**339.** Seven or more ways to increase an advertising budget

Response | Score
1. _____ 1
2. _____ 1
3. _____ 1
4. _____ 1
5. _____ 1
6. _____ 1
7. _____ 1

Bonus Responses
8. _____ 2
9. _____ 2
10. _____ 2
11. _____ 2
12. _____ 2
13. _____ 2
14. _____ 2
15. _____ 2
16. _____ 2

Total ☐

**340.** Eight or more reasons for discontinuing twenty-exposure film rolls

Response | Score
1. _____ 1
2. _____ 1
3. _____ 1
4. _____ 1
5. _____ 1
6. _____ 1
7. _____ 1
8. _____ 1

Bonus Responses
9. _____ 2
10. _____ 2
11. _____ 2
12. _____ 2
13. _____ 2
14. _____ 2
15. _____ 2
16. _____ 2

Total ☐

## 341. Seven or more reasons for not having a lock on your luggage

| Response | Score |
|---|---|
| 1. _____ | 1 |
| 2. _____ | 1 |
| 3. _____ | 1 |
| 4. _____ | 1 |
| 5. _____ | 1 |
| 6. _____ | 1 |
| 7. _____ | 1 |

Bonus Responses

| | Score |
|---|---|
| 8. _____ | 2 |
| 9. _____ | 2 |
| 10. _____ | 2 |
| 11. _____ | 2 |
| 12. _____ | 2 |
| 13. _____ | 2 |
| 14. _____ | 2 |
| 15. _____ | 2 |
| 16. _____ | 2 |

Total ☐

## 342. Seven or more reasons for never flying charter

| Response | Score |
|---|---|
| 1. _____ | 1 |
| 2. _____ | 1 |
| 3. _____ | 1 |
| 4. _____ | 1 |
| 5. _____ | 1 |
| 6. _____ | 1 |
| 7. _____ | 1 |

Bonus Responses

| | Score |
|---|---|
| 8. _____ | 2 |
| 9. _____ | 2 |
| 10. _____ | 2 |
| 11. _____ | 2 |
| 12. _____ | 2 |
| 13. _____ | 2 |
| 14. _____ | 2 |
| 15. _____ | 2 |
| 16. _____ | 2 |

Total ☐

## 343. Eight or more reasons why there are more holidays during the summer than during the winter

| Response | Score |
|---|---|
| 1. _____ | 1 |
| 2. _____ | 1 |
| 3. _____ | 1 |
| 4. _____ | 1 |
| 5. _____ | 1 |
| 6. _____ | 1 |
| 7. _____ | 1 |
| 8. _____ | 1 |

Bonus Responses

| | Score |
|---|---|
| 9. _____ | 2 |
| 10. _____ | 2 |
| 11. _____ | 2 |
| 12. _____ | 2 |
| 13. _____ | 2 |
| 14. _____ | 2 |
| 15. _____ | 2 |
| 16. _____ | 2 |

Total ☐

## 344. Six or more reasons for having 150 mm. cigarettes

| Response | Score |
|---|---|
| 1. _____ | 1 |
| 2. _____ | 1 |
| 3. _____ | 1 |
| 4. _____ | 1 |
| 5. _____ | 1 |
| 6. _____ | 1 |

Bonus Responses

| | Score |
|---|---|
| 7. _____ | 2 |
| 8. _____ | 2 |
| 9. _____ | 2 |
| 10. _____ | 2 |
| 11. _____ | 2 |
| 12. _____ | 2 |
| 13. _____ | 2 |
| 14. _____ | 2 |
| 15. _____ | 2 |
| 16. _____ | 2 |

Total ☐

## 345. Six or more reasons not to live in Iowa

| Response | | Score |
|---|---|---|
| 1. | _____ | 1 |
| 2. | _____ | 1 |
| 3. | _____ | 1 |
| 4. | _____ | 1 |
| 5. | _____ | 1 |
| 6. | _____ | 1 |

**Bonus Responses**

| | | |
|---|---|---|
| 7. | _____ | 2 |
| 8. | _____ | 2 |
| 9. | _____ | 2 |
| 10. | _____ | 2 |
| 11. | _____ | 2 |
| 12. | _____ | 2 |
| 13. | _____ | 2 |
| 14. | _____ | 2 |
| 15. | _____ | 2 |
| 16. | _____ | 2 |

Total ☐

## 346. Seven or more reasons not to live in New Jersey

| Response | | Score |
|---|---|---|
| 1. | _____ | 1 |
| 2. | _____ | 1 |
| 3. | _____ | 1 |
| 4. | _____ | 1 |
| 5. | _____ | 1 |
| 6. | _____ | 1 |
| 7. | _____ | 1 |

**Bonus Responses**

| | | |
|---|---|---|
| 8. | _____ | 2 |
| 9. | _____ | 2 |
| 10. | _____ | 2 |
| 11. | _____ | 2 |
| 12. | _____ | 2 |
| 13. | _____ | 2 |
| 14. | _____ | 2 |
| 15. | _____ | 2 |
| 16. | _____ | 2 |

Total ☐

## 347. Eight or more reasons for not having a Club Mediterranée resort in Newark, New Jersey

| Response | | Score |
|---|---|---|
| 1. | _____ | 1 |
| 2. | _____ | 1 |
| 3. | _____ | 1 |
| 4. | _____ | 1 |
| 5. | _____ | 1 |
| 6. | _____ | 1 |
| 7. | _____ | 1 |
| 8. | _____ | 1 |

**Bonus Responses**

| | | |
|---|---|---|
| 9. | _____ | 2 |
| 10. | _____ | 2 |
| 11. | _____ | 2 |
| 12. | _____ | 2 |
| 13. | _____ | 2 |
| 14. | _____ | 2 |
| 15. | _____ | 2 |
| 16. | _____ | 2 |

Total ☐

## 348. Seven or more rules of roulette if the zero and double zero paid ten to one

| Response | | Score |
|---|---|---|
| 1. | _____ | 1 |
| 2. | _____ | 1 |
| 3. | _____ | 1 |
| 4. | _____ | 1 |
| 5. | _____ | 1 |
| 6. | _____ | 1 |
| 7. | _____ | 1 |

**Bonus Responses**

| | | |
|---|---|---|
| 8. | _____ | 2 |
| 9. | _____ | 2 |
| 10. | _____ | 2 |
| 11. | _____ | 2 |
| 12. | _____ | 2 |
| 13. | _____ | 2 |
| 14. | _____ | 2 |
| 15. | _____ | 2 |
| 16. | _____ | 2 |

Total ☐

## 349. Six or more rules of poker if three of a kind beat a full house, straight, or flush

| Response | Score |
|---|---|
| 1. _____ | 1 |
| 2. _____ | 1 |
| 3. _____ | 1 |
| 4. _____ | 1 |
| 5. _____ | 1 |
| 6. _____ | 1 |

**Bonus Responses**

| | |
|---|---|
| 7. _____ | 2 |
| 8. _____ | 2 |
| 9. _____ | 2 |
| 10. _____ | 2 |
| 11. _____ | 2 |
| 12. _____ | 2 |
| 13. _____ | 2 |
| 14. _____ | 2 |
| 15. _____ | 2 |
| 16. _____ | 2 |

Total ☐

## 350. Six or more reasons for charging for compressed air at gas stations

| Response | Score |
|---|---|
| 1. _____ | 1 |
| 2. _____ | 1 |
| 3. _____ | 1 |
| 4. _____ | 1 |
| 5. _____ | 1 |
| 6. _____ | 1 |

**Bonus Responses**

| | |
|---|---|
| 7. _____ | 2 |
| 8. _____ | 2 |
| 9. _____ | 2 |
| 10. _____ | 2 |
| 11. _____ | 2 |
| 12. _____ | 2 |
| 13. _____ | 2 |
| 14. _____ | 2 |
| 15. _____ | 2 |
| 16. _____ | 2 |

Total ☐

## 351. Eight or more reasons for not having a large print edition of *The New York Times*

| Response | Score |
|---|---|
| 1. _____ | 1 |
| 2. _____ | 1 |
| 3. _____ | 1 |
| 4. _____ | 1 |
| 5. _____ | 1 |
| 6. _____ | 1 |
| 7. _____ | 1 |
| 8. _____ | 1 |

**Bonus Responses**

| | |
|---|---|
| 9. _____ | 2 |
| 10. _____ | 2 |
| 11. _____ | 2 |
| 12. _____ | 2 |
| 13. _____ | 2 |
| 14. _____ | 2 |
| 15. _____ | 2 |
| 16. _____ | 2 |

Total ☐

## 352. Nine or more reasons why the United States has more colleges and universities than any other country in the world

| Response | Score |
|---|---|
| 1. _____ | 1 |
| 2. _____ | 1 |
| 3. _____ | 1 |
| 4. _____ | 1 |
| 5. _____ | 1 |
| 6. _____ | 1 |
| 7. _____ | 1 |
| 8. _____ | 1 |
| 9. _____ | 1 |

**Bonus Responses**

| | |
|---|---|
| 10. _____ | 2 |
| 11. _____ | 2 |
| 12. _____ | 2 |
| 13. _____ | 2 |
| 14. _____ | 2 |
| 15. _____ | 2 |
| 16. _____ | 2 |

Total ☐

## 353. Six or more reasons why most foot doctors are Caucasians

| Response | Score |
|---|---|
| 1. | 1 |
| 2. | 1 |
| 3. | 1 |
| 4. | 1 |
| 5. | 1 |
| 6. | 1 |

Bonus Responses

| | |
|---|---|
| 7. | 2 |
| 8. | 2 |
| 9. | 2 |
| 10. | 2 |
| 11. | 2 |
| 12. | 2 |
| 13. | 2 |
| 14. | 2 |
| 15. | 2 |
| 16. | 2 |

Total ☐

## 354. Seven or more reasons for turning the pages of a book ten at a time

| Response | Score |
|---|---|
| 1. | 1 |
| 2. | 1 |
| 3. | 1 |
| 4. | 1 |
| 5. | 1 |
| 6. | 1 |
| 7. | 1 |

Bonus Responses

| | |
|---|---|
| 8. | 2 |
| 9. | 2 |
| 10. | 2 |
| 11. | 2 |
| 12. | 2 |
| 13. | 2 |
| 14. | 2 |
| 15. | 2 |
| 16. | 2 |

Total ☐

## 355. Eight or more reasons for not growing an elm tree in your house

| Response | Score |
|---|---|
| 1. | 1 |
| 2. | 1 |
| 3. | 1 |
| 4. | 1 |
| 5. | 1 |
| 6. | 1 |
| 7. | 1 |
| 8. | 1 |

Bonus Responses

| | |
|---|---|
| 9. | 2 |
| 10. | 2 |
| 11. | 2 |
| 12. | 2 |
| 13. | 2 |
| 14. | 2 |
| 15. | 2 |
| 16. | 2 |

Total ☐

## 356. Six or more reasons why oil companies advertise

| Response | Score |
|---|---|
| 1. | 1 |
| 2. | 1 |
| 3. | 1 |
| 4. | 1 |
| 5. | 1 |
| 6. | 1 |

Bonus Responses

| | |
|---|---|
| 7. | 2 |
| 8. | 2 |
| 9. | 2 |
| 10. | 2 |
| 11. | 2 |
| 12. | 2 |
| 13. | 2 |
| 14. | 2 |
| 15. | 2 |
| 16. | 2 |

Total ☐

## 357. Nine or more reasons for not whistling alone, at night, in a strange town, after 2:00 A.M.

| Response | Score |
|---|---|
| 1. _____ | 1 |
| 2. _____ | 1 |
| 3. _____ | 1 |
| 4. _____ | 1 |
| 5. _____ | 1 |
| 6. _____ | 1 |
| 7. _____ | 1 |
| 8. _____ | 1 |
| 9. _____ | 1 |

**Bonus Responses**

| | |
|---|---|
| 10. _____ | 2 |
| 11. _____ | 2 |
| 12. _____ | 2 |
| 13. _____ | 2 |
| 14. _____ | 2 |
| 15. _____ | 2 |
| 16. _____ | 2 |

Total ☐

## 358. Seven or more consequences of doing away with scales

| Response | Score |
|---|---|
| 1. _____ | 1 |
| 2. _____ | 1 |
| 3. _____ | 1 |
| 4. _____ | 1 |
| 5. _____ | 1 |
| 6. _____ | 1 |
| 7. _____ | 1 |

**Bonus Responses**

| | |
|---|---|
| 8. _____ | 2 |
| 9. _____ | 2 |
| 10. _____ | 2 |
| 11. _____ | 2 |
| 12. _____ | 2 |
| 13. _____ | 2 |
| 14. _____ | 2 |
| 15. _____ | 2 |
| 16. _____ | 2 |

Total ☐

## 359. Six or more reasons for driving a car in reverse at sixty miles per hour

| Response | Score |
|---|---|
| 1. _____ | 1 |
| 2. _____ | 1 |
| 3. _____ | 1 |
| 4. _____ | 1 |
| 5. _____ | 1 |
| 6. _____ | 1 |

**Bonus Responses**

| | |
|---|---|
| 7. _____ | 2 |
| 8. _____ | 2 |
| 9. _____ | 2 |
| 10. _____ | 2 |
| 11. _____ | 2 |
| 12. _____ | 2 |
| 13. _____ | 2 |
| 14. _____ | 2 |
| 15. _____ | 2 |
| 16. _____ | 2 |

Total ☐

## 360. Six or more reasons for not wearing name clothes

| Response | Score |
|---|---|
| 1. _____ | 1 |
| 2. _____ | 1 |
| 3. _____ | 1 |
| 4. _____ | 1 |
| 5. _____ | 1 |
| 6. _____ | 1 |

**Bonus Responses**

| | |
|---|---|
| 7. _____ | 2 |
| 8. _____ | 2 |
| 9. _____ | 2 |
| 10. _____ | 2 |
| 11. _____ | 2 |
| 12. _____ | 2 |
| 13. _____ | 2 |
| 14. _____ | 2 |
| 15. _____ | 2 |
| 16. _____ | 2 |

Total ☐

## 361. Nine or more reasons why some college students kill themselves

| Response | Score |
|---|---|
| 1. _____ | 1 |
| 2. _____ | 1 |
| 3. _____ | 1 |
| 4. _____ | 1 |
| 5. _____ | 1 |
| 6. _____ | 1 |
| 7. _____ | 1 |
| 8. _____ | 1 |
| 9. _____ | 1 |

Bonus Responses

| | |
|---|---|
| 10. _____ | 2 |
| 11. _____ | 2 |
| 12. _____ | 2 |
| 13. _____ | 2 |
| 14. _____ | 2 |
| 15. _____ | 2 |
| 16. _____ | 2 |

Total ☐

## 362. Eight or more reasons for adopting a baby even though he/she is sick and may die at an early age

| Response | Score |
|---|---|
| 1. _____ | 1 |
| 2. _____ | 1 |
| 3. _____ | 1 |
| 4. _____ | 1 |
| 5. _____ | 1 |
| 6. _____ | 1 |
| 7. _____ | 1 |
| 8. _____ | 1 |

Bonus Responses

| | |
|---|---|
| 9. _____ | 2 |
| 10. _____ | 2 |
| 11. _____ | 2 |
| 12. _____ | 2 |
| 13. _____ | 2 |
| 14. _____ | 2 |
| 15. _____ | 2 |
| 16. _____ | 2 |

Total ☐

## 363. Six or more reasons why Norman Mailer will never win the Nobel Prize for Literature

| Response | Score |
|---|---|
| 1. _____ | 1 |
| 2. _____ | 1 |
| 3. _____ | 1 |
| 4. _____ | 1 |
| 5. _____ | 1 |
| 6. _____ | 1 |

Bonus Responses

| | |
|---|---|
| 7. _____ | 2 |
| 8. _____ | 2 |
| 9. _____ | 2 |
| 10. _____ | 2 |
| 11. _____ | 2 |
| 12. _____ | 2 |
| 13. _____ | 2 |
| 14. _____ | 2 |
| 15. _____ | 2 |
| 16. _____ | 2 |

Total ☐

## 364. Seven or more reasons for not bringing a bathing suit to the beach

| Response | Score |
|---|---|
| 1. _____ | 1 |
| 2. _____ | 1 |
| 3. _____ | 1 |
| 4. _____ | 1 |
| 5. _____ | 1 |
| 6. _____ | 1 |
| 7. _____ | 1 |

Bonus Responses

| | |
|---|---|
| 8. _____ | 2 |
| 9. _____ | 2 |
| 10. _____ | 2 |
| 11. _____ | 2 |
| 12. _____ | 2 |
| 13. _____ | 2 |
| 14. _____ | 2 |
| 15. _____ | 2 |
| 16. _____ | 2 |

Total ☐

## 365. Eight or more reasons why some doctors charge more for the same services than other doctors

| | Response | Score |
|---|---|---|
| 1. | _____ | 1 |
| 2. | _____ | 1 |
| 3. | _____ | 1 |
| 4. | _____ | 1 |
| 5 | _____ | 1 |
| 6. | _____ | 1 |
| 7. | _____ | 1 |
| 8. | _____ | 1 |

### Bonus Responses

| | | Score |
|---|---|---|
| 9. | _____ | 2 |
| 10. | _____ | 2 |
| 11. | _____ | 2 |
| 12. | _____ | 2 |
| 13. | _____ | 2 |
| 14. | _____ | 2 |
| 15. | _____ | 2 |
| 16. | _____ | 2 |

Total ☐

# CONTRIBUTORS' SAMPLE RESPONSES

35. About to die and want to discharge debts.
36. About to die and want to relieve conscience.
37. Police are harassing you.
38. Don't want name on police computer.
39. Prove your electric car can reach these speeds.

---

### 335. Eight or more reasons for paying a speeding ticket

1. It's easier to pay than fight the courts.
2. If one hassles the arresting police officer all the cops may be out to get you from then on.
3. Setting good example for kids.
4. City may need the money.
5. Feeling noble about following the letter of the law.
6. Being rich so that one ticket doesn't matter.
7. Being a policeman yourself—it would look bad if you didn't pay the ticket.
8. Stay out of jail.
9. Avoid going to trial.
10. Save time.
11. Cop out on "lesser offense."
12. Avoid hassle.
13. Avoid penalty on top of fine.
14. Keep from being subject of a fugitive warrant.
15. Be a good citizen.
16. Stop worry.
17. Keep from feeling guilty.
18. 'Cause I was caught speeding.
19. I have little real choice.
20. Don't want to meet any more police.
21. It's the cheapest alternative.
22. So my family (neighbors, boss, etc.) won't know.
23. Believe in upholding the law by obedience.
24. Avoid loss of license.
25. Avoid criminal record.
26. Want experience.
27. Need to get rid of some money.
28. Want to meet a cute policeman.
29. Want to feel guilty.
30. To be nice to person who was speeding by paying his ticket for him.
31. Prove to people that you were speeding.
32. Get name in paper.
33. You're on parole and one slip means back in the hoosegow.
34. You're loaded with phony money and want to get rid of it.

---

### 336. Seven or more associations to the word "zyto"

1. "Heigh ho" (as in "Silver, away!").
2. Creature from another world.
3. A new toy.
4. Another company making repro machines.
5. A patent medicine.
6. Another "do everything" drug.
7. Zip Zyto, a new movie star.
8. One more hard rock group.
9. Super glue!
10. Du Pont's latest invention.
11. Appropriate name for my household robot.
12. A new enzyme.
13. Brought to you by the wonderful new science of genetics.
14. A misspelled Italian first name.
15. Ancient Greek alphabet.
16. Measure of national debt in year 2000 meaning one million dectillions and short for zytillion.
17. Greek for "life."
18. Zoo you to(o).
19. Misspelling.
20. Zygotes tour.
21. Otyz spelled backwards.
22. Tozy spelled inside out.
23. Zircons, yellow, to order.
24. 26252015.
25. Neato.
26. Frito.
27. Poteeto.
28. Association for Protection of Zyto.
29. Otis elevators.
30. Ozymandias, king of kings.
31. Oats.
32. Cornelia Otyz Skinner.
33. Lou "Zy To" Groza, football player.
34. "You go in snow or we pay Zy to W."
35. Bite-o.
36. Zounds! You too!
37. Toyz spelled inside out.

---

### 337. Eight or more reasons why some people continue to smoke in the no-smoking section of planes and trains

1. Blindness—weren't aware there were signs.
2. Being an anti-conformist.
3. Being a tobacco farmer who is trying to convince ex-smokers to smoke again.
4. They can't read.
5. They don't care.
6. No one else seems to mind.
7. No one does anything to stop them.
8. Some people are both smokers and rebellious.
9. No room available in smoking section.
10. They just have to have another smoke *now*.
11. They have no respect for their non-smoking fellows.
12. It's a habit and smokers don't think about doing it.
13. Smokers continue to ride trains and planes.
14. People continue to smoke.
15. Smokers don't realize that some people can't stand smoke.
16. Smokers can't realize that some people don't like smoke.
17. Smokers are thoughtless.
18. Non-smoking sections are too large.
19. It's inconvenient to move from the non-smoking section to smoke.
20. Some people don't smoke but they travel with smokers.
21. Addicted to cigarettes.
22. Like to flout authority.
23. Nervous about getting there.
24. Figure no one will stop them.
25. Like to annoy others.
26. Think rule is stupid.
27. Haven't read the sign.
28. Everyone else is doing it.
29. Nowhere to put out cigarettes.
30. Do it on a bet.
31. Do it on a dare.
32. Do it for assertiveness training.
33. To keep mosquitoes away.
34. So as not to catch TB from other passengers.
35. Civil disobedience protesting law.
36. Think law applies only to tobacco and they're smoking pot.
37. Have to get rid of cigarettes by end of trip and this is only way they know.
38. Think they are beyond the law.
39. Want to start a fight.
40. Want to start a fire.
41. Want to look tough.
42. Want to look sophisticated.
43. Want to fill compartment with smoke to conceal their actions.
44. For a movie.
45. For a psychology experiment.
46. Compulsive.
47. For a sociology experiment.
48. To experience being arrested.
49. On principle.
50. Unaware of prohibition.
51. Don't want people mooching their cigarettes.
52. To test the law.
53. As a signal to secret agent.
54. Need to be different.
55. To burn secret message.
56. Smoking section is filled.
57. Bring on fatal asthma attack in rich relative.
58. Meet cute policeman.
59. Get the attention of passenger smoker wants to meet.
60. Conceal face in cloud of smoke.

---

### 338. Eight or more reasons why it costs more to buy a train ticket after boarding than before boarding

1. High demand with a low supply.
2. To discourage late arrivals.
3. To compensate for the extra bother it causes conductors.
4. Trains are going bankrupt so owners want as much money as possible.
5. Late arrivals may cause the train to leave late—upsets the schedule.
6. Maybe the conductor hates passengers and would rather be on a cargo train. He punishes latecomers out of vindictiveness.
7. Maybe the ticket seller is an embezzler and pockets the difference.
8. There is no discount.
9. Conductors don't want to be bothered.
10. Railroads are trying to teach people to plan ahead.
11. You are now facing a sole source situation (no competition).
12. You are captive and must pay or be put off between trains.
13. To penalize you for not

using the ticket agent.
14. Company rules.
15. Union rules.
16. ICC rules.
17. Because it's not illegal.
18. Trade insult for inconvenience.
19. Fewer tickets kept on board.
20. Nowhere to store money on board—discourage people from doing it.
21. Have to pay trainmen for something outside his regular job—extra work caused.
22. Harder to account for this money—extra work caused.
23. No cash register on board.
24. You're stuck once you're on.
25. You can't switch to competing train.
26. Conductor keeps some for himself.
27. Train is run by Mafia.
28. It's a law.
29. Foreign exchange higher on train.
30. Inflation.
31. You can't exchange it once on board.
32. You're buying a sure trip that can't be cancelled.
33. Custom.
34. God wills it.
35. Chance.
36. You can't be bumped due to overbooking.
37. Not so convenient for train company.
38. Harder to keep records on train.
39. Train can't add more cars if needed at this point.

## 339. Seven or more ways to increase an advertising budget

1. Cut packaging costs and spend the savings on ads.
2. Don't buy prime time on TV.
3. Charge more for product and use difference for ads.
4. Pay employees less and use difference for ads.
5. Cheat on IRS return and use difference for ads.
6. Rob a bank and use the money for ads.
7. Sue people—news coverage is *free* publicity.
8. Wish on drumsticks, falling stars, and new moons for more money for the budget.
9. Lobby for more money.
10. Convince management that more advertising will increase profits.
11. Convince management that more advertising will increase sales.

12. Convince management that more advertising will increase company image.
13. Subliminal messages.
14. Convince management that more advertising will capture a new market.
15. Convince management that more advertising will reduce inventory.
16. Convince management that more advertising will improve productivity.
17. Convince management that more advertising will lead to expansion of plant.
18. Produce better return on net assets (or investment).
19. Show effective use of past and present budget and paint rosy picture of what else can be done with more (which management wants).
20. Introduce new products with great potential.
21. Penetrate new market segments which have great potential.
22. Get more clients to kick in.
23. Improve results (bang for the buck) this year—get more next year.
24. Prove more money in advertising will produce more profit.
25. Boss's son in charge of advertising.
26. Pay off those who vote for more $ in advertising.
27. Better ads.
28. Computer guy gives more $ to advertising by mistake.
29. Put your personal money into it.
30. Take up collection for it.
31. Become person who allocates the money and do it.
32. Buy the company and do it.
33. Make sure that only ad men can be on the board.
34. Turn company into an ad company only.
35. Expand company in general.
36. Phony reports on efficacy of ads.
37. Hire more ad men.
38. Hire super-duper ad whiz who commands huge salary.
39. Inflation increases it automatically.
40. Hypnotize budget writers.
41. Advertise the department itself.
42. Make competition increase *his* ad budget.
43. Develop new product that needs ad.
44. Make law requiring greater percentage spent on ad.
45. Increased costs.
46. Tie budget to cost of living rate.

47. Company that believes in more ad $ buys your company.
48. New boss who believes in more ad $ buys your company.

## 340. Eight or more reasons for discontinuing twenty-exposure film rolls

1. Twenty-exposure film rolls are a bargain for the buyer, but the company makes more on twelve-exposure ones.
2. Small rolls are less likely to jam camera.
3. Small rolls are easier and quicker to develop.
4. Small rolls are preferred by customers because it's easier to quickly fill a small roll (few pictures to take).
5. Chemicals are becoming so expensive people are taking fewer pictures and want smaller rolls.
6. Maybe the president of the company has a phobia about the number 20.
7. Maybe the board got bored and just felt like changing something.
8. Maybe they are trying to discourage still pictures so people buy the more expensive movie camera.
9. They don't sell.
10. They don't fit new cameras.
11. They get too expensive.
12. They are inconvenient to produce.
13. New invention makes film rolls obsolete.
14. Market glutted with new twenty-eight-exposure film rolls.
15. Cameras are outlawed.
16. The world is destroyed.
17. New invention eclipses cameras and film as we know it.
18. Raw material shortages or non-availability.
19. It's no longer economically feasible.
20. Competition almost all undersell Kodak.
21. Government/legal injunction.
22. It's unprofitable.
23. It's dangerous.
24. OSHA shuts production down.
25. Smaller rolls mean more frequent trips to film store for extra purchases.
26. They go metric and only do ten- or one hundred-rolls.

27. Studies indicate twenty-film rolls go bad in cameras.
28. Manufacturer goes out of business.
29. The entire country is destroyed by nuclear explosions.
30. A saboteur poisons many twenty-film rolls and customers refuse to buy them after that so manufacturer stops making them.
31. Manufacturer makes too much money on them and is advised by accountants to stop for tax purposes.
32. Employees refuse to make them.
33. Dictator takes over the country and forbids film on religious grounds.
34. Holograms become so cheap, bottom falls out of film market.
35. Country goes to war and twenty-film rolls are declared wasteful.

## 341. Seven or more reasons for not having a lock on your luggage

1. You don't like your clothes.
2. Your luggage is insured, and its contents, too.
3. It's empty.
4. You're not going anywhere.
5. Your sister borrowed it.
6. There's just a Bible inside.
7. You forgot to bring it.
8. You lost your key.
9. You don't own anything worth stealing.
10. The way you packed it, no one could undo the latches anyway.
11. It's in the junk.
12. The latches are booby trapped.
13. You have a security phobia.
14. You only keep dirty socks in it.
15. Adding a lock would make it too heavy.
16. You don't like carrying keys around.
17. You can't remember combinations.
18. It looks infested, no one would take it.
19. It's a hand-me-down anyway.
20. You only use it to hide Christmas presents in before Christmas.
21. You want to look poor.
22. You're shipping yourself to Australia in it.

23. You don't want your kid to lock himself in it.
24. It was in the attic when your house burned down.
25. It's small enough to keep with you everywhere.
26. It'll probably get lost in transit anyway.
27. You don't like locks.
28. The glare of reflected light might attract an assassin's bullet and provide a point of aim.
29. Dogs might be attracted by its reflected light and be tempted to pee on it.
30. Without locks there is a more stable surface to rest things on.
31. To encourage thieves to steal it, so I can make a claim for a new, better set.
32. To confuse potential thieves and mystify them, arousing their suspicions.
33. It won't snag the nylons of the baggage handlers.
34. It won't scratch the steps when it is kicked down them by baggage handlers.
35. Luggage would weigh less and be cheaper to ship.
36. It would cut down on manufacturing cost (and purchase price?).
37. Lockless luggage is "sleeker"; has more chic and visual appeal.
38. To confound everyone and make them wonder why it has no lock.
39. To ease the shortage of metal.
40. The luggage is a "farewell" present, and I'm having it buried with me.
41. It would fit better with my colour scheme.
42. My mother-in-law is nosey; there's a bomb in the luggage and I never did like her anyway.
43. A flat suitcase top may be sat on without the painful protrusion of a lock.
44. A flat, unadorned suitcase top would be a splendid surface to use to measure (a) flying angles of UFO's; and (b) shell trajectories.
45. It can be used as an emergency writing surface.
46. Nervous people with suitcase fetishes can fondle and rub the top with less difficulty.
47. To avoid the inconvenience resulting from the loss of the key.
48. It would be one less thing that could break.
49. There is a greater chance of the *exciting* experience of having a suitcase open while one is running to catch a train/plane/bus.
50. It is faster to open—save time during baggage search.
51. There would be one less key on my key chain, which is too heavy.
52. Suitcase would be easier to clean, with fewer things to catch dust.
53. It would eliminate a hiding place for spiders.
54. Reduce the possibility of freezing fingers on cold metal parts.
55. If I fall into my suitcase, I can get out.

## 342. Seven or more reasons for never flying charter

1. You hate airplanes.
2. You hate groups of people.
3. You don't get free cocktails.
4. You don't like sitting in the back of the plane.
5. You work for Amtrak.
6. You can't afford it.
7. The stewardesses aren't sexy.
8. I like vacationing in out-of-the-way places not served by charter flights (e.g. South Georgia Islands, Aldabra).
9. I'm a senior airline executive and get free flights.
10. I have my own executive jet and/or Cessna 4-seater.
11. I have my own refurbished submarine.
12. I have my own sailplane.
13. I have my own hot-air balloon.
14. There ain't no one going to get me in one of them planes (fear of flying)!
15. I'm doing 25-75 years in San Quentin pen.
16. I'm a member of the USAF and they don't fly charter.
17. I'm given to keeping up appearances and I wouldn't be caught dead with the rabble in a charter flight.
18. I'm impulsive and usually arrange things less than twenty-four hours in advance.
19. The local welfare board would never make the extra allowance.
20. Poverty.
21. I'm a veteran of the Boer War and too old to travel.
22. They won't let me out of the isolation ward with this case of bubonic plague.
23. The food is better on regular flights.
24. I get a thrill gambling on the risk of getting bumped.
25. I'm seven feet tall and need the extra room on regular flights to stretch out.
26. I don't like leaving at two in the morning.

## 343. Eight or more reasons why there are more holidays during the summer than during the winter

1. Because they don't like snow.
2. They're allergic to frost.
3. I prefer them during the summer.
4. You can enjoy them more during the summer.
5. Christmas is big enough to make up for the loss.
6. Summer holidays are easier to calibrate.
7. If we had a lot of other holidays, the Christmas spirit wouldn't last long enough.
8. We can spend more holidays on the beach.
9. The sun attracts holidays.
10. They make vacations last an extra weekend, hence longer campouts and vacations.
11. Summer allows more holiday activities.
12. Winter cools our holiday spirits down.
13. We can't get snowed in on a holiday.
14. Everyone's in a partying mood.
15. People are more susceptible to enjoyment during the summer.
16. Santa Claus bought up exclusive rights to winter.
17. Summer lasts longer.
18. Winter doesn't have time for holidays.
19. Winter **doesn't** want us to be **happy.**
20. I'd **rather** celebrate during the summer and hibernate all winter anyway.
21. The summer heat drives men to revolutions and uprisings, which are commemorated by holidays.
22. The bureaucrats, who create many of the holidays, make more of them in the summer to take advantage of longer days.
23. Warmer days.
24. School summer recess.
25. The insidious "Golf lobby":

Have you ever tried playing the game in three feet of snow? They couldn't either, and have pressed for summer holidays ever since.
26. People get more miles per gallon of gas in the summer than in the winter.
27. Are there *really* more holidays in summer than in winter? I doubt it. Winter is a long "holiday" for farmers and seasonal workers (fishermen, construction workers, bees, baseball players).
28. Holidays proliferate in summer when man's hormones and desires rise in hot blood and feelings of lassitude abound.
29. Holidays mate in the early spring and give birth in early summer. They are killed off in great numbers by frost. Therefore, the population of holidays is highest in summer.
30. Holidays hibernate during the winter. A few get hungry and emerge, looking for food, but generally they are scarce during the winter.
31. Holidays shrivel away to nothing in the cold.
32. Holidays are white, and cannot be seen against the snow.

## 344. Six or more reasons for having 150 mm. cigarettes

1. I prefer Mm's to tobacco 150 to 1.
2. You can't smoke as many.
3. They cost more.
4. They last longer.
5. They look sexy sticking out of your pocket.
6. You can watch them burn while smoking them.
7. The ashes won't fall on your hand.
8. They're easier to light.
9. They smoke just like short ones.
10. You can't singe your eyebrows lighting them.
11. They don't fall out of ashtrays as easily.
12. They balance in your fingers better.
13. They're easier to Bogart.
14. They fill a pocket better.
15. They're part of your image.
16. That's all you could burn.
17. When you roll your own you take 'em as they come.
18. You're trying to burn the person you're talking to.

209

19. You'd pay less tax for more tobacco.
20. They have longer filters.
21. To increase the opportunities for American and Canadian doctors to treat (a) high blood pressure, (b) lung cancer, (c) emphysema, (d) rigor mortis.
22. Musicians can cut them in half and finally have an economical cigarette when they "take five." The regular cigarettes are too long for short breaks, and musicians stub out long butts.
23. They would be just long enough to paint miniatures on.
24. Mendicants and other assorted derelicts will have longer butts to work with, and live a little longer before contracting cancer. Since butts concentrate carcinogens, but longer butts will have a lower overall concentration of carcinogens.
25. Longer cigarettes will allow a man to scratch more inaccessible places.
26. Longer cigarettes will allow a man to do a deeper job cleaning his ears.
27. Lacquered, they would make good emergency (a) chopsticks, (b) drinking straws, (c) storage compartments, (d) nit pickers.
28. A longer cigarette will make a longer bomb fuse. (See any demolition text for the "cigarette fuse" trick.)
29. One could smoke in the shower, with the cigarette protruding.
30. A boon to procrastinators; "As soon as I finish this cigarette I'll . . ."
31. Less risk of setting hair on fire while lighting a cigarette.
32. Advertisers would have the opportunity for producing humorous commercials.
33. One could chain smoke with fewer matches.
34. One would get less smoke in the eyes.
35. The larger cigarette pack would give more room for notes, diagrams, maps, and doodles.
36. Since they last longer, one would smoke fewer and be able to cut down on the number smoked (and brag about it), without going into nicotine withdrawal.
37. For those difficult waiting periods, too long for one

regular cigarette, but too short for two.
38. If one smokes as much of a long cigarette as of a regular cigarette, a longer butt is left. The butt filters out more of the tar and other carcinogens.
39. I'm a torturer for the Mafia. I can inflict more burns per cigarette.

## 345. Six or more reasons not to live in Iowa

1. It's too far away from home.
2. You can't go Coho fishing.
3. It has no ocean frontage.
4. I once knew a girl from Iowa and . . .
5. My suitcase says Maine or bust.
6. I don't know where it is.
7. My mother says I can't run away this week.
8. I don't like farmers.
9. I don't like living in the boondocks.
10. I have hay fever.
11. I'd miss my mother.
12. My girlfriend wouldn't come with me.
13. Iowa is much too close to Kansas City, and Aunt Sally lives there!!
14. Iowa would be fatal to anyone with an allergy to corn.
15. Iowa would be very dangerous for anyone with "progressive political persuasions."
16. I've got a bad case of agoraphobia (and wide open spaces . . . gyahhhh!).
17. Iowa is too close to the Effigy Mounds and my haunting ancestors.
18. I would never live in the state of Herbert Hoover's birthplace.
19. Iowa is too close to Nebraska.
20. I have a penchant for peripheries and Iowa is much *too* central.
21. Iowa is outré.
22. The Omaha, Neb., to Rockford, Ill., road is too greasy, and you can never stop in time; you slide right through Iowa.
23. I'm an avid skier. Iowa is too flat and Vail, Colorado, is too far away.
24. I have a morbid terror of grasshoppers, and Iowa is over-endowed.
25. I do not like the tornados that regularly roll up the Mississippi River valley.

26. The winters are too cold.
27. Have you ever tried to find a Kosher butcher in Iowa? Or meet a nice Jewish girl in Des Moines?
28. I'm a surfer; there's no surfing in Iowa.
29. The outlines (shape) of the state are irregular and hard to draw.
30. There are no caravanseries in Iowa. Where is a Tuareg warrior to water his camel?
31. There are no tantric lamaseries in Iowa. I am an orthodox tantric lama.

## 346. Seven or more reasons not to live in New Jersey

1. I grew up in New Jersey.
2. I don't like the accent.
3. It's too close to New York.
4. I hate subways.
5. I hate commuting to work.
6. It's too small.
7. It's too far East.
8. They have a good vice squad.
9. They don't allow pets.
10. I'm allergic to Mafia garbage collectors.
11. New Jersey beaches are infested with sharks.
12. New Jersey is too wet and cold in the winter.
13. There is this difficulty with the language. I speak only English.
14. Gambling casinos make me broke or break out in hives.
15. New Jersey is too far away from little old granny in Kenosha.
16. On the whole, I'd rather be in Philadelphia.
17. New Jersey is fine, but Jersey (Channel Islands) is oneupmanship, and has lower taxes.
18. Would *you* like to live in a new cow?
19. My right-hand-drive Phoenix Mini is not made for New Jersey roads.
20. It's a little too far to commute daily to Kuala Lumpur, where I hold an executive position. (I'm afraid of flying and there are no direct trains.)
21. I'm a veteran of Mao Tse-tung's eighth route army and U.S. immigration won't let me into the country.
22. There is an outstanding warrant on me for defalcation ($30,000,000) and I am enjoying the weather

and extradition immunity in Recife, Brasil.
23. They buried me last month in Forest Lawn and travel arrangements would be difficult and expensive.
24. You call that living?

## 347. Eight or more reasons for not having a Club Méditerranée resort in Newark, New Jersey

1. The climate is not conducive.
2. The original Club Méditerranée would sue.
3. My parents wouldn't approve.
4. I don't have the start-up capital.
5. Newark wouldn't approve.
6. It'd be more challenge to have one in Salt Lake City.
7. The Club Africaans might complain.
8. Newark is dry.
9. Newark is not my favorite spot.
10. Newark has enough clubs.
11. The chamber of commerce doesn't allow clubs.
12. The licenses cost too much.
13. New Jersey has a good vice squad.
14. Newark is too small.
15. There are too many clocks in Newark (Club resorts have no clocks).
16. The town has too many diversions and potential activities of which the club doesn't get a percentage.
17. Much of Newark accepts Master Charge, Bankamericard, and Visa, of which the club gets no piece of the action.
18. The Club brass have family in Wilkes-Barre, Pa., and they could not justify building there. If they built in Newark without building in Wilkes-Barre, the family would ask embarrassing questions.
19. What's a "Club Méditerranée"?
20. No one speaks French (or English) in Newark.
21. The Mob already holds all the concessions and the Club is not welcome.
22. It is prohibitive to get Vichy and Perrier water through the taps.
23. The Club is not happy with Newark's anti-bidet ordinances.

24. Newark, N.J., does not have the imprimatur of the Pope.

## 348. Seven or more rules of roulette if the zero and double zero paid ten to one

1. Zero and double zero will pay ten to one.
2. Maximum $150 bids on 0 and 00.
3. You can only bid 0 or 00 four times in a row.
4. Minimum bids on all other numbers $5.00.
5. All other numbers will pay five to one.
6. The house can refuse bets.
7. No one can play wearing tennis shoes.
8. No drinking and betting at the same time.
9. You must take an oath of celibacy to play.
10. Payment for a zero or double zero is to be made in Monopoly money.
11. Pay-offs are made only when zero or double zero happens two times in a row.
12. Only one such bet per customer per hour allowed.
13. The zero and double zero in the wheel have a convex bottom instead of the usual concave slot.
14. The roulette ball is square and the zero and double zero slots have hemispherical depressions.
15. The zero and double-zero slots are coated with Teflon and are one-third as deep as the other slots.
16. Bets on zero and double zero are taken only on Sundays (when the casino is closed).
17. Payment of zero and double-zero bets will be made in Imperial Czarist bonds or Confederate dollars.
18. The casino is declared a charitable institution and is financed by the government.
19. Odds paid on all other bets (except even money bets) are reduced. Odds on "en plein" (straight) for example, are reduced from 37-1 to 30-1.
20. No change. Since the odds of 0 to 00 are 19-1 (38 ÷ 2), and it only pays 10-1, the casino should still come out ahead, although their profit will be reduced from 5.26% of all bets.

## 349. Six or more new rules of poker if three of a kind beat a full house, straight, or flush

1. Two of a kind beats three of a kind.
2. Full house beats straight or flush.
3. Straight beats royal flush.
4. Flush (low) beats royal flush.
5. No wild cards on Thursdays.
6. You can draw twice.
7. No betting after 5:00 P.M. Tuesday-Thursday.
8. No betting on Sunday.
9. One of a kind beats two of a kind.
10. Deuces are high.
11. Deuces are low.
12. One deck of blackjack will be dealt after every two hands where a flush is played and loses.
13. No drinking while non-betting hours are in force.
14. Stripped decks will be allowed.
15. Remove all hearts from the deck.
16. Introduce two new ranks, namely earls and viscounts.
17. No wild card may be used to form a threesome.
18. Two pairs beat a trio.
19. No raise betting for a trio.
20. No special rules, because trios would become common and straights, flushes, and four of a kind would become insignificant. Players would collect trios and bet accordingly and the odds would adjust themselves accordingly.
21. None of a kind beats a trio.
22. Four cards in a suit would constitute a flush, and four cards in sequence, a straight.

## 350. Six or more reasons for charging for compressed air at gas stations

1. It would keep little birds from playing with the hoses.
2. To bring in extra profit.
3. To keep people from buying air.
4. To keep kids from filling up their tires there.
5. To keep kids from filling up their balloons there.
6. To keep kids from filling up their footballs there.
7. To keep people from filling their tires there.
8. Because the compressors are expensive.
9. Because money's cheap.
10. Because you feel like it.
11. To defer the cost of hiring help.
12. To get rich.
13. To pay for the wife's beer.
14. To build bad P.R.
15. Nothing else in life is free, including toilets, so why should compressed air be free?
16. Children will get exercise using bicycle pumps.
17. People will use compressed air only when necessary, and save the energy required for compressing.
18. Bicycle-pump makers will ge more business.
19. Payment would enable gas stations to pay an attendant to see that tire inflation is properly done.
20. To reduce the abuse of compressed air.
21. Politicians have been noticed filling up before debates (they have to get all that hot air somewhere), but should garages bear the cost?
22. To discourage little urchins from overfilling their tricycle tires.
23. It's all a big plot to discourage people keeping their tires full, thus causing tires to wear out more quickly and increasing tire sales.
24. Auto body shops will profit from increased accidents caused by underinflated tires.
25. Morticians will profit from increased accidents caused by underinflated tires.
26. Garage price competition has forced owners to introduce perfumed and coloured air and the price has become too high.
27. The cost will discourage potato chip jobbers from inflating their packages.
28. The cost will discourage people using the air hoses to clean out their sinuses, or
29. To dust books in bookmobiles, or
30. To dislodge earwax, or
31. To unstick magazine pages.

## 351. Eight or more reasons for not having a large print edition of the *New York Times*

1. I can't read.
2. I don't like the *New York Times.*
3. I'm not blind.
4. I don't read the paper.
5. I'm a small person.
6. I'm nearsighted.
7. It costs more.
8. It's too bulky.
9. My wife prefers smaller print.
10. I can read smaller print faster.
11. Small print is sexier.
12. I can't afford a paper.
13. It doesn't come to home delivery customers.
14. The mailman always reads it first.
15. Postage is too high in Kalamazoo.
16. My neighbor gets it.
17. It's too tabloidish.
18. I don't want to.
19. The letters are too big.
20. To save paper and ink.
21. Rolled up, it would make a good baseball and the ball manufacturers would be upset.
22. Delivery boys (and girls) and readers would get hernias from the extra weight.
23. Those with poor vision should be protected from the *New York Times.*
24. Rolled up, it would make even more yule logs, and wood suppliers would be upset.
25. It would be so large as to be impossible to read on the commuter train.
26. No large type would be left to print headlines for the regular edition.
27. Hitting a dog with the rolled-up paper would require a lot of strength, and could result in a call from the SPCA.
28. There would be even more litter, due to the larger size of the paper, and N.Y. would be buried in it.
29. The wind would catch a larger paper and carry it away.
30. Larger paper could be used more easily for wallpaper and the wallpaper makers are nervous.
31. Can you imagine what a large print weekend *N.Y. Times* would weigh? (a) It would kill you if it fell on

you. (b) Women over eighty wouldn't be able to lift it. (c) News vendors wouldn't have room for any other papers or magazines.

32. It would be easier for someone to read it over your shoulder on the bus, which is already annoying.

---

**352. Nine or more reasons why the United States has more colleges and universities than any other country in the world**

1. We have more students.
2. We have more teachers.
3. We are a bigger country than most.
4. We stress literacy.
5. It's a good way to spend a couple of years.
6. You need it to get a job.
7. We all enjoy learning in the U.S.
8. The nation stresses education.
9. We like college sports.
10. Colleges provide an outlet for spending tax dollars.
11. Students need something to do.
12. God planned it that way.
13. We are more advanced than most countries.
14. Technology depends upon college training, and we are the most technologically advanced country.
15. People enjoy giving money to build colleges.
16. Donating wings to colleges is good tax relief.
17. We are richer people.
18. We enjoy the tax burden.
19. We like bragging about this or that school that we went to.
20. We like the socializing colleges provide.
21. We need some place for our young athletes to compete on a large scale.
22. We need someplace to use all of our books.
23. College is big business—it makes sense.
24. Colleges build communities.
25. The U.S. has high standards for most jobs. I.e., you need an LLB to fill out your tax return, and a PhD to blow your nose. (Seriously, USAF will not let a man fly a plane without a bachelor's degree.)
26. Educational equality is entrenched and everyone can go to university.
27. They have so many schools to employ an oversupply of Ph.D. instructors.
28. The schools keep young people out of the job market.
29. The schools keep young people off the streets.
30. Obviously, because they're known by other names in foreign countries. There are no "colleges" or "universities" in Germany; they are "Universitäten," etc.
31. Americans must go to college in order to acquire the social graces and knowledge that high schools in Europe provide.
32. U.S. colleges provide an excuse for parents to get overgrown adolescents out of the house and out of town. In Europe, children of this age go to work.
33. Where else can an adult American male learn the essential skills of bridge, hearts, and poker?
34. These skills provide a supermarket for American females to appraise and capture prospective husbands.
35. Colleges are a U.S. government excuse to spread tax largesse in depressed areas, such as Lower Squeedunk Ohio U.
36. Colleges were a useful device to allow those of wealthier backgrounds to avoid Selective Service during the Vietnam War.
37. Colleges in the U.S. provide a remedial service. They teach people how to read, write, and "cipher," and give them a little *world* geography and history, knowledge the public schools have not provided.

---

**353. Six or more reasons why most foot doctors are Caucasians**

1. Caucasians are sadists.
2. Caucasians are masochists.
3. Foot doctors need love, too.
4. Would you trust a foot doctor who couldn't speak English?
5. Examination boards are prejudiced.
6. Caucasians have a lot of foot fetishes.
7. Caucasians prefer that position in life.
8. Foot doctors have more fun.
9. Because most Caucasians are neurotics who frequent foot doctors.
10. Foot doctor school's easy.
11. No one else wants to be a foot doctor.
12. No one else can afford foot doctor school.
13. Everybody loves a foot doctor, so . . .
14. Caucasians like to start at the bottom.
15. There's plenty of room to work your way up.
16. The jogging craze in the U.S. has increased the need for North American chiropodists.
17. Caucasians are relatively tall, spend much of their time looking down, and are more aware of feet.
18. The disgusting morals of Caucasians caused an exodus of uro-genital specialists to other specialties. Many chose feet.
19. Orientals find feet erotic, and shy away from the specialty.
20. Feet smell like cheese. Caucasians are cheese-eaters, but Orientals generally don't like cheese.
21. Caucasian society dictates covered feet (shoes) and the allure of disrobed toes is very strong for medical students.
22. Since the Vietnam war many Orientals have no feet. Therefore there are fewer customers and less need for Vietnamese chiropodists.
23. Orientals have a custom of removing their shoes when indoors. Unconfined by shoes, their feet are healthier.

---

**354. Seven or more reasons for turning the pages of a book ten at a time**

1. You're breaking in the book.
2. You're an Evelyn Wood graduate.
3. You don't like the book.
4. You can't wait to get to the end.
5. You lost your glasses.
6. The book's upside down anyway.
7. Someone said it was a cure for baldness.
8. You can't read.
9. The pages are thin.
10. The plot hasn't thickened yet.
11. Your wife wants you to come to bed.
12. It's less boring.
13. I can get to the end of the book more quickly.
14. I have arthritis and I'm very clumsy.
15. I'm Superman; I have myopic X-ray vision and can read ten pages at a time.
16. It's more challenging to follow the plot.
17. I have a defective book which is printed only on every tenth page.
18. The heavier bundle of pages gives my fingers more exercise.
19. There is less wear and tear on the book.
20. It discourages others from reading over my shoulder on the bus.
21. Due to St. Vitus dance, I lack the fine muscle control to turn pages slowly.
22. I took a speed reading course and got carried away.
23. I drink twenty-five cups of coffee a day and I'm *very* impatient.
24. I don't read, I only look at the pictures.
25. I'm a quadraplegic and turn pages with my teeth. It's too difficult to turn pages singly.
26. I only read one book and I know how it goes.
27. I get my books from the public library and only read pages with the Carnegie stamp on them.
28. This particular book has ten interleaved stories.
29. I'm a member of Mensa. I don't need to read all the pages.
30. I have a vivid imagination and like to make up the interstices in the plot.
31. Someone stapled the pages together.

---

**355. Eight or more reasons for not growing an elm tree in your house**

1. My house isn't tall enough.
2. I don't have a big enough pot.
3. My mother wouldn't like it.
4. It wouldn't get enough sun.
5. I couldn't afford to water it.
6. The fertilizer is too messy.
7. I can't afford a gardener.
8. It would get too tall to trim.
9. The squirrels would drive me nuts.
10. Because I already have a mimosa tree growing in my dining room.
11. My potted ferns would get jealous.

12. It's not covered on my insurance.
13. Because most of my furniture is oak.
14. Because I don't own a house.
15. Because I don't own an elm tree.
16. The city would declare my house a park.
17. It would die of Dutch Elm disease and have to be removed.
18. There is a dearth of large trees due to Dutch Elm disease.
19. The local vigilance committee insists on using our tree for periodic necktie parties, which offends my sensibilities.
20. Its roots would invade the pipes and clog the bathtub drain.
21. It would attract birds, which make a terrible racket and wake me up unreasonably early in the morning, like 10:00 A.M.
22. Bird droppings are hard to clean off the floor.
23. It would cut out the light from the windows and shade our houseplants.
24. Sweeping up fallen blossoms (spring) and leaves (fall) would be a nuisance.
25. I would have to cut a hole in the roof to accommodate it.
26. It would encourage fox-bats, which tend to leap on dinner guests.
27. It would clash with the decor.
28. The cleaning lady would refuse to dust it.
29. I would have to remove the saquaro cactus to make room.
30. It would attract the hordes of local elm worshippers.
31. The Dutch Elm beetles would get into the closet.
32. I prefer oaks.
33. Elms make rather poor Christmas trees.
34. The alcoholic fumes that pervade my residence would be lethal to it.
35. Amorous tomcats would be attracted to sing in its branches.
36. I'm allergic to tree pollen.
37. Birds would be attracted to build nests and raise baby birds, which could be killed by my cats, which I would find emotionally upsetting.
38. I'm a hard-shell, born-again Anabaptist. Tree worship is a no-no.
39. Fido would get carried away marking out his territory and

pee on it.
40. The roots will strangle my gardenias.
41. It would attract hang-gliders, who launch themselves from high places.
42. Clause 21(1)(c) of my lease is an anti-elm provision.
43. I would have to increase the light level, which would be incompatible with my mushroom culture.
44. Mrs. Jones down the street already has one. Am negotiating for the installation of a 300-ft. mahogany.
45. The woodpeckers would damage it.
46. It would encourage gophers to dig up the Astroturf.
47. It would attract vultures to sit in the top branches, which would make me nervous.

---

356. Six or more reasons why oil companies advertise

1. To get customers.
2. To repel customers.
3. To spend excess dollars.
4. To make up for the oil spills (P.R.).
5. To support our local stations.
6. To support our local programs.
7. To give us a break from the programs.
8. To build good P.R. with the other advertisers.
9. To put a decent show on T.V. for sixty seconds.
10. To justify their existence.
11. To tell us who they are.
12. To get people to use their credit cards.
13. Oil people, like their product, are unctuous. They need an outlet.
14. They have to spend their profits on something.
15. All oil products, regardless of brand, are the same. Advertising is the only way to get people to buy one brand over another.
16. Oil people are insecure and want to be loved.
17. Advertisements provide employment for advertising executives and second-rate actors.
18. Company executives get their pictures on T.V. and in magazines.
19. Advertising is part of the great American way of life.
20. Oil company executives get a

sadistic pleasure out of inflicting their nauseating ads on the public.
21. To convince people to use more oil so oil companies can earn more money so they can afford to explore for more oil.
22. It's the most effective way to convince Americans of a non-existent oil crisis.
23. If they did not produce incessant ads, the public might come to their senses and turn to coal, solar energy, wind and wave power, and OTEC (ocean thermal energy conversion).
24. Advertising forestalls the public's move from oil to graphite for lubrication.

---

357. Nine or more reasons for not whistling alone, at night, in a strange town, after 2:00 A.M.

1. You don't like attention.
2. You don't like to.
3. You don't know any songs to whistle.
4. You like to sing better.
5. There's an ordinance against it.
6. You have your radio on.
7. Your bodyguard doesn't like it.
8. You're a police officer on secret assignment.
9. You're a detective.
10. You can't whistle.
11. You don't have a teakettle.
12. Your mom wasn't Whistler's mother.
13. You can't whistle and chew gum at the same time.
14. You're too scared.
15. There aren't any pretty girls around.
16. It would disturb sleeping neighbours.
17. It might attract the attention of feral dogs.
18. People might think that you were a bird announcing morning and get out of bed.
19. There is probably a city by-law against it.
20. It's bad luck to whistle alone at night in a strange town after 2:00 A.M.
21. People might think it was a police whistle.
22. In the empty streets (after 2:00 A.M.) there is more echo and a greater chance of resonance causing structural damage to buildings.

23. It would announce your presence to muggers.
24. I would end up with chapped lips.
25. It's hard for me to walk, navigate, get my bearings, AND whistle at the same time.
26. My skirt is so tight that if I whistled the buttons would pop off.
27. I might be whistling in the wrong dialect and offend the natives.
28. I couldn't play my trombone alone after 2:00 A.M. in a strange town if I were whistling.

---

358. Seven or more consequences of doing away with scales

1. Smooth skin.
2. Not being able to weigh your urine specimens.
3. Nobody would be fat.
4. Nobody would be underweight.
5. Fish couldn't swim.
6. Eels wouldn't be slippery.
7. Trucks couldn't be weighed.
8. People would get fat quicker.
9. Borg and other manufacturers would go out of business.
10. We would buy meat and other things by volume measured by the displacement principle discovered by Archimedes.
11. Overweight people would be less neurotic about their weight.
12. And Weight Watchers International would go broke.
13. Chemistry would become very difficult.
14. Expressions such as "a ton of bricks" and "an ounce of prevention is worth a pound of cure" would become obsolete.
15. Pennies, once used to pay scales, would become worthless.
16. The blindfolded figure, symbolizing Justice, would have to hold something other than a set of scales, such as a set of measuring cups.
17. Snakes would have a hard time crawling without scales.
18. Fish would have bony plates and thus would not be kosher.
19. Young piano players would

not have scales to play, and would be relieved.

20. Alligators and crocodiles would have fur or feathers.
21. We wouldn't know what distances were represented on maps.
22. Birds would have smooth legs.
23. Butterflies and moths would get caught in spider webs more often. Now, the scales on their wings stick to the webs, but come off the wings, allowing the insects to escape.

### 359. Six or more reasons for driving a car in reverse at sixty miles per hour

1. To get killed.
2. To run over your mugger.
3. To run over your mother-in-law.
4. To get where you're going.
5. To get the carbon out of your engine.
6. To rearrange the back end of your car.
7. To spoil your driving record.
8. To rearrange the shrubbery.
9. To scare your passengers.
10. To discourage hitchhikers.
11. To get lost.
12. You're just learning how to drive.
13. You have a long driveway.
14. Your car won't go forward.
15. You're late.
16. To get a ticket.
17. You took a dare.
18. You're a masochist.
19. You like danger.
20. You want to buy a new car.
21. It would be very exciting.
22. It would give exercise to the reverse gear.
23. You can see where you've been.
24. You can watch to see if you're being followed.
25. It would confuse pursuers.
26. There would be no chance of the hood flying open and blocking vision.
27. As an exercise in creativity.
28. There would be no chance of stripping the gears, since there's only one reverse gear.
29. To improve one's ability to drive in reverse.
30. To attempt to go backwards in time.
31. As a fraternity initiation exercise.
32. I'm a stunt driver, in a remake of W. C. Fields' *The*

*Bank Dick.* (There's an involved car chase in it.)
33. I've just had a neck vertebra fusion and the surgeon goofed and got my head on backwards.
34. I have a preference for looking over my shoulder.
35. My front windshield was stolen and I don't like the draft.
36. You were stuck with front wheel drive, you're a stubborn traditionalist and insist on having the powered wheels in the rear.
37. I'm a reactionary; I like to go backwards.

### 360. Six or more reasons for not wearing name clothes

1. They get dirty.
2. They lack class.
3. Nobody wears them anymore.
4. Your mother doesn't make you wear them anymore.
5. They look corny.
6. Your friends make fun of them.
7. Your dog chewed all of them up.
8. You're a nudist.
9. You never bought any.
10. They're expensive.
11. I'm not the kind of person who wears trendy things.
12. Makers of name clothes don't work in black leather and rivets.
13. I can't get name clothes in my size—I'm five feet tall and weigh 300 lbs.
14. Reverse snobbery—I only wear tacky things from Woolco.
15. I wouldn't give those designers my hard-earned dollars.
16. Some of those name brands are identified by initials. Could you imagine the havoc that would be created if Mr. Gucci or Pucci claimed that all the garments with their initials were "obviously" their personal property. Their wardrobes would become huge.
17. Most of the prestige chaps are non-American and any royalties paid mean money leaving the country, which is disloyal and plays hob with the balance of payments.
18. All my clothes are custom made, with my own name embroidered on them.

### 361. Nine or more reasons why some college students kill themselves

1. It's an easy way to get an A in "Fear of Dying" class.
2. It's the latest fad.
3. They don't like flunking out.
4. It's fun.
5. Their friends all did it.
6. They enjoy pain.
7. Their girlfriends told them to.
8. They didn't want to go home for vacation.
9. They had a physics test coming up.
10. They got caught sleeping in calculus class.
11. They lost the big game.
12. They can't afford to stay in school.
13. They got put on academic probation.
14. Eye fatigue.
15. They lost their lunch money.
16. Their heart-throb turned them down.
17. They got evicted.
18. As a Social Science 200 exercise.
19. To avoid having to write exams.
20. They are lonesome away from home.
21. Shame of low grades.
22. As an economy measure.
23. They are under the influence of drugs.
24. Mental illness.
25. They have a terminal illness and don't want to suffer.
26. To avoid facing an uncertain future.
27. To be the center of attention.
28. In imitation of other well-publicized suicides.
29. As a result of a false suicide attempt that unintentionally succeeds.
30. As a result of academic and social stress.
31. Out of experimental curiosity—to see what it feels like.
32. Out of religious fervor—to see God.
33. For revenge—to cause someone pain and sorrow.
34. To remove oneself as an obstacle in someone else's life.
35. As an artistic, creative exercise.
36. As a personal solution to the energy crisis.
37. To break bad habits, such as nail biting, smoking.
38. To verify the tenets of Christianity.
39. To learn of one's next reincarnation.

### 362. Eight or more reasons for adopting a baby even though he/she is sick and may die at an early age

1. Money for the casket would be considerably lower.
2. Won't have the expense of college.
3. You wouldn't have to put up with him/her when he/she goes through the teen years.
4. It's cheaper than raising a kid.
5. They might not die after all.
6. You can give them more love.
7. It gives you a chance to buy "sick" games.
8. It gives the kid a respectable place to die.
9. It gives you a chance to cry.
10. No one else will.
11. It's easier than starting your own family.
12. You at least know what you're getting.
13. You don't have to worry about teaching him how to cross streets.
14. You are expecting a food shortage.
15. You have leftover diapers from the last one.
16. So it's the last time he/she may be more happy.
17. To qualify for an inheritance which specifies that one have a child.
18. To give it a religious upbringing so it will get into heaven when it dies.
19. To bring some happiness, however short-lived, into one's own life, which may outweigh later sorrow.
20. To gain sympathy.
21. As a temporary source of income in the child porno trade.
22. I'm a pathologist, and wish to observe first hand and write up the symptoms for my next medical research paper.
23. You can smuggle cocaine in the child's diaper when going through Customs. They're suspicious about a fat diaper on a doll or your girl friend.

## 363. Six or more reasons why Norman Mailer will never win the Nobel Prize for Literature

1. He's a lousy writer.
2. They never decided to give it to him.
3. He doesn't want it.
4. He will.
5. It's only given to Americans as a last resort.
6. His mother told them not to.
7. It's been discontinued.
8. Norman Mailer does not have the necessary (a) sex appeal, (b) political background, (c) proper biography, (d) wardrobe required of a Nobel Literature winner.
9. The Jewish quota has been filled. Isaac Bashevis Singer won this year's prize, and it'll be several years before the quota will allow another Jewish winner.
10. Mr. Mailer does not fly nor venture on the ocean so he could not collect the prize in Stockholm.
11. The prize has now been given to a surfeit of English-language writers, and it is now time for Urdu, Tagalog, prehistoric Samoan, and Malay.
12. Mr. Mailer does not write literature.
13. Mr. Mailer's work has been placed in the scatological class.
14. Sweden has just been acquired by His Extreme Highness of Kuwait, Prince Abdul Ibn Falwed, and he is more partial to several dozen Arabic writers.
15. Mr. Mailer's writing has defied all previous attempts by cryptanalysts to derive sense from it. His manuscripts are now being correlated with the Voynich manuscript in a last desperate attempt at decipherment.
16. Mr. Mailer's works are banned in Sweden (notwithstanding their notoriously lax moral strictures and standards) and thus they cannot review his work for the prize.
17. Mr. Mailer's family is heavily represented in the Nobel Literature Judging Panel (you didn't know he was originally Swedish, did you?)

and they could not award it to their "cousin"; it would look like conflict of interest.
18. Norfigstra orkufney maklesh gom, nordifu maggah Mailer Megwubungu.
19. Mr. Mailer is alive and hiding in Rio de Janiero and wanted for selling adulterated Kum Quats in Washington, D.C. The prize cannot be awarded to fugitives, can it!? That would create a bad example for our young people.
20. After Mr. Mailer was awarded the more prestigious Cornelius Mugwump Meritorious Medal and Prize for Literature, the Nobel Prize would pale by comparison, and would be lost in the caliginous penumbra of the Mugwump Award.
21. Mr. Mailer's writings are mere adumbrations and not sufficiently full descriptive narratives. In effect, his writing is too sketchy and only a few idiot savants seem to derive any coherence from them. We cannot condone that!

## 364. Seven or more reasons for not bringing a bathing suit to the beach

1. To get an even tan.
2. They are too warm.
3. Too heavy to carry. Could cause exhaustion.
4. Nobody else wears one.
5. It will get wet.
6. You don't own one.
7. Your mother won't let you.
8. Your girlfriend stole it.
9. The sun isn't out today.
10. It's winter.
11. You'd rather wear it than bring it.
12. You have impeccable taste in underwear.
13. It's a nude beach.
14. I don't want white strap marks across my back and two white breasts on a gorgeous brown background.
15. I'm dying to get a gorgeous tan, age my skin, and look like a wrinkled, played-out walrus at age forty.
16. Bathing suits are lewd, revealing, and sinful! People should be fully clothed at the beach.
17. The beach is at Rejkyavik, Iceland, and it's c-c-cold!
18. Nudity will allow all the

participants to superficially identify the other sex.
19. Bare skin shows up better in aerial photographs and will make MIG 25 reconnaissance jet pilots horny. They might even defect.
20. Why have useless accoutrements on and delay the inevitable seduction.
21. The latest bathing suit is an invisible one, manufactured by the man who patented pet rocks. Don't laugh; he's charging $75 for each one.
22. There is less chance of getting ants, fleas, and chiggers in your bathing suit if you aren't wearing one.
23. No suit reduces friction and drag, so you can swim faster.
24. Bathing suits cost money.
25. I'm planning to commit suicide by drowning, and nudity will give the lifeguard less to hold on to.
26. My chain-mail bathing suit might rust, drag me down, etc.
27. All my bathing suits are embroidered with obsolete political slogans and I'm embarrassed to wear them. How would you feel if you had "Nixon's the One" on your chest?
28. I weigh 600 lbs. and if I shed my clothes at the beach I might be mistaken for a walrus and harpooned.
29. Beach #5052 (my favorite watering spot) won't allow anyone on the beach without a shirt and tie.
30. A bathing suit is too revealing. They'll see my needle tracks (I shoot up milk intravenously for a high).

## 365. Eight or more reasons why some doctors charge more for the same services than other doctors

1. They have richer patients.
2. They're cheaper for other stuff.
3. As a deterrent to coming back.
4. To give you a bigger tax deduction.
5. To make you feel like you're getting more.
6. So they can pay a larger office staff.
7. So they can justify making you wait longer.

8. To make their diagnosis more accurate.
9. They drew different numbers out of their hats.
10. They have different numbers of mouths to feed.
11. Some are employed by clinics and subsidized or standardized.
12. They are masochists.
13. They don't want to be accused of price fixing.
14. Dr. A charges more, but promises that you will survive.
15. Dr. A will throw in extras, such as anaesthesia, sterilized equipment, and bedside care.
16. Dr. A practices in a high-priced area, with high overhead, and you will have to pay for this.
17. Prestige doctors cost more. If you want to keep up with the Joneses, you pay.
18. Dr. A, a recent graduate, owes $90,000 for school fees, has just bought a $4¼ million home and a $50,000 mundomugor model Cadillac. The bank has warned him that he'll have to raise his fees or they'll foreclose and repossess his wife, stethoscope, and ears.
19. Some doctors claim the "literacy bonus." If you want a doctor who can also read, you pay extra. If you want one who can also write, you pay even more.
20. That depends on whether you see (a) naturopath, (b) chiropractor, (c) homeopath, (d) voodoo hungan, (e) Shona witchdoctor, (f) Marabout Ziffra, (g) general practitioner, or (h) specialist. Their rates differ, you know.
21. You'll have to pay more for a specialist with rare skill. You really pay through the nose for a bilateral introlinial oxillectomy.
22. Licensed doctors charge more than de-licensed malpractitioners.
23. When you get green stamps from your physician, you can rest assured that the cost of those stamps is reflected in his fees.
24. Many doctors golf on Wednesday and do *not* make up that day during the rest of the week, so they charge more. You never thought that you had something in common with a nine iron, did you?! Well, you do.
25. Some doctors have higher

malpractice insurance premiums to pay. (Your doctor may chronically forget his surgical instruments inside his patients.)

26. It may depend on what country your doctor practices in. You may get a cheaper doctor if you save your medical work for your holiday in Colombo, Sri Lanka. (But don't complain when your physician prescribes cow dung poultice for your ingrown toenail.)

# SELECTED RESOURCES

Adams, J. C. "The Relative Effects of Various Testing Atmospheres on Spontaneous Flexibility: a Factor of Divergent Thinking." *Journal of Creative Behavior* 2 (1968): 187–194.

———. "The Psychology of Imagination." *Scientific American* 199 (1958): 151–66.

———. "Originality in Relation to Personality and Intellect." *Journal of Personality* 23 (1957): 730–42.

Barron, F. *Creativity and Psychological Health.* New York: Van Nostrand, 1963.

Belcher, T. L. "Effect of Different Test Situations on Creativity Scores." *Psychological Reports* 36 (1975): 511–14.

Beloff, J. "Creative Thinking in Art and Science." *British Journal of Aesthetics* 10 (1970): 58–70.

Biller, H. B., Singer, D. L., & Fullerton, M. "Sex-Role Development and Creative Potential in Kindergarten-Age Boys." *Developmental Psychology* 1 (1969): 291–96.

Boersma, F. J., & O'Bryan, K. "An Investigation of the Relationship Between Creativity and Intelligence Under Two Conditions of Testing." *Journal of Personality* 36 (1968): 341–48.

Bogen, Joseph E. "The Other Side of the Brain." In Ornstein, R. E., Ed., *The Nature of Human Consciousness.* New York: The Viking Press, 1974.

Burhenne, D. P., Kaschak, E., & Schwebel, A. I. "The Effect of Altering the Administration Procedure on Four WAIS Subtests." *Educational and Psychological Measurement* 33 (1973): 663–68.

Burt, C. L., & Williams, E. L. "The Influence of Motivation on the Results of Intelligence Tests." *British Journal of Statistical Psychology* 15 (1962): 129–36.

Busse, T. V., Blum, P., & Gutride, M. "Testing Conditions and the Measurement of Creative Abilities in Lower-class Preschool Children." *Multivariate Behavioral Research* 7 (1972): 287–98.

Butcher, H. J. *Human Intelligence: Its Nature and Assessment.* London: Methuen, 1968.

Campbell, J. *The Masks of God: Primitive Mythology,* New York: The Viking Press, 1959.

Cashdan, S., & Welsh, G. S. "Personality Correlates of Creative Potential in Talented High School Students." *Journal of Personality* 14 (1966): 445–55.

Channon, C. E. "The Effect of Regime on Divergent Thinking Scores." *British Journal of Educational Psychology* 44 (1974): 89–91.

Chomsky, N. *Syntactic Structures.* The Hague: Mouton, 1966.

Christensen, P. R., Guilford, J. P., & Wilson, R. C. "Relations of Creative Response to Working Time and Instructions." *Journal of Experimental Psychology* 53 (1957): 82–88.

Clark, C. H. *Brainstorming.* New York: Doubleday, 1958.

Crockenburg, S. B. "Creativity Tests: a Boon or Boondoggle for Education?" *Review of Educational Research* 42 (1972): 27–45.

Cropley, A.J. "A Five-year Longitudinal Study of the Validity of Creativity Tests." *Developmental Psychology* 6 (1972): 119–24.

———. "The Relatedness of Divergent and Convergent Thinking." *Alberta Journal of Educational Research* 11 (1965): 176–81.

———, & Maslany, G. W. "Reliability and Factorial Validity of the Wallach-Kogan Creativity Tests." *British Journal of Psychology* 60 (1969): 395–98.

Crutchfield, R. S. "Conformity and Creative Thinking." In Gruber, H. E., Terrell, G., & Wertheimer, M., Eds., *Contemporary Approaches to Creative Thinking.* New York: Atherton Press, 1962.

Dallas, M., and Gaier, E. L. "Identification of Creativity: the Individual." *Psychological Bulletin* 73 (1970): 55–73.

Dansky, J. L., & Silverman, I. W. "Effects of Play on Associative Fluency in Preschool-aged Children." *Developmental Psychology* 9 (1973): 38–43.

DeBono, E. *Lateral Thinking.* New York: Harper & Row, Colophon Edition, 1973.

Dentler, R. A., & Mackler, B. "Originality: Some Social and Personal Determinants." *Behavioral Science* 9 (1964): 1–7.

Drawl, R. L. "The Influence of Psychological Stress upon Creative Thinking." *Polish Psychological Bulletin* 4 (1973): 125–29.

Elkind, D., Deblinger, J., & Adler, D. "Motivation and Creativity: the Context Effect." *American Educational Research Journal* 7 (1970): 351–57.

Ellenberger, H. *The Discovery of the Unconscious*. New York: Basic Books, 1970.

Flach, F. F. *The Creative Process in Psychiatry*. Monograph in Creativity in Psychiatry series 1 (1975).

Frenkel-Brunswik, E. "Intolerance of Ambiguity as an Emotional and Perceptual Personality Variable." In Bruner, J. S., & Krech, D., Eds., *Perception and Personality*. Durham: Duke University Press, 1949.

Garfield, P. *Creative Dreaming*. New York: Simon and Schuster, 1974.

Gerard, R. W. "The Biological Basis of Imagination." In Ghiselin, B., Ed., *The Creative Process*. Berkeley: University of California Press, 1952.

Golann, S. E. "The Creativity Motive." *Journal of Personality* 30 (1962): 538–600.

———. "The Psychological Study of Creativity." *Psychological Bulletin* 60 (1963): 548–65.

Gordon, W. J. *The Metamorphical Way*. Cambridge, Mass.: Porpoise Books, 1971.

———. *Synectics*. New York: Harper & Row, 1961.

Guiford, J. P. *The Nature of Human Intelligence*. New York: McGraw-Hill, 1967.

———. "Some Misconceptions Regarding Measurement of Creative Talent." *Journal of Creative Behavior* 5 (1971): 77–93.

———. "Three Faces of Intellect." *American Psychologist* 14 (1959): 469–79.

Hadley, D. J. "Experimental Relationship Between Creativity and Anxiety." *Journal of Creative Behavior* 1 (1967): 215–16.

Halpin, G. "The Effect of Motivation on Creative Thinking Abilities." *Journal of Creative Behavior* 7 (1973): 51–53.

Hammaker, M. K., Shafto, M., & Trabasso, T. "Judging Creativity: a Method for Assessing How and by What Criteria It Is Done." *Journal of Educational Psychology* 6" (1975): 478–83

Hargreaves, D. J. "Situational Influences on Divergent Thinking." *British Journal of Educational Psychology* 44 (1974): 84–88.

Harrington, D. M. "Effects of Explicit Instructions to 'Be Creative' on the Psychological Meaning of Divergent Thinking Test Scores." *Journal of Personality* 43 (1975): 434–54.

Harris, R. A. "Creativity in Marketing." In Smith, P., Ed., *Creativity*. New York: Hastings House, 1959.

Karagulla, S. *Breakthrough to Creativity*. Los Angeles: DeVorss, 1967.

Koestler, A. *The Act of Creation*. New York: Macmillan, 1964.

Kogan, N., & Morgan, F. T. "Task and Motivational Influences on the Assessment of Creative and Intellective Ability in Children." *Genetic Psychology Monographs* 80 (1969): 91–127.

Krop, H. D., Alegre, C. E., & Williams, C. D. "Effect of Induced Stress on Convergent and Divergent Thinking." *Psychological Reports* 24 (1969): 895–98.

Land, G., *Grow or Die*. New York: Random House, 1973.

Lee, H. B. "On the Esthetic States of the Mind." *Psychiatry* 10 (1947): 81–306.

Leith, G. "The Relationship Between Intelligence, Personality, and Creativity Under Two Conditions of Stress." *British Journal of Educational Psychology* 42 (1972): 240–47.

Levey, H. B. "A Theory Concerning Free Creation in the Inventive Arts." *Psychiatry* 3 (1940): 229–93.

Levy, H. "Originality as Role-Defined Behavior." *Journal of Personality and Social Psychology* (1968): 72–78.

Lieberman, J. N. "Playfulness and Divergent Thinking: an Investigation of Their Relationship at the Kindergarten Level." *Journal of Genetic Psychology* 107 (1965): 219–24.

Lorenz, K. *Evolution and Modification of Behavior*. Chicago: University of Chicago Press, 1965.

MacKinnon, D. W. "The Nature and Nurture of Creative Talent." *American Psychologist* 17 (1962): 484–95.

———. "Personality and the Realization of Creative Potential." *American Psychologist* 20 (1965): 273–81.

Maddi, S. R. "Motivational Aspects of Creativity." *Journal of Personality* 33 (1965): 330–47.

Maier, N., & Solem, A. "Improving Solutions by Turning Choice Situations into Problems." *Personnel Psychology* 15:2 (1962): 151–57.

Maltzman, I. "On Training of Originality." *Psychological Review* 67 (1960): 229–42.

Manske, M. E., & Davis, G. A. "Effects of Single Instructional Biases upon Performance in the Unusual Uses Test." *Journal of General Psychology* 79 (1968): 25–33.

Maslow, A. "Creativity in Self-Actualizing People." In Anderson, H., Ed., *Creativity and Its Cultivation*. New York: Harper & Row, 1959.

Matthews, J. "The Psychology of Creative Thinking Groups." In Parnes, S., & Harding, H., Eds., *A Source Book for Creative Thinking*. New York: Charles Scribner's, 1962.

McCully, R. S. "Archetypal Energy and the Creative Image." *Journal of Analytical Psychology* 20:2 (1975).

Meadows, A., & Parnes, S. J. "Evaluation of Training in Creative Problem Solving." *Journal of Applied Psychology* 43 (1959): 189–94.

Mednick, M. T. "Research Creativity in Psychology Graduate Students." *Journal of Consulting Psychology* 27 (1963): 265–66.

———, Mednick, S. A., & Jung, C. C. "Continual Association as a Function of Level of Creativity and Type of Verbal Stimulus." *Journal of Abnormal Social Psychology* 69 (1964): 511–15.

Mednick, S. A. "The Association Basis of the Creative Process." *Psychological Review* 69 (1962): 220–32.

Newmann, E. *Art and the Creative Unconscious.* New York: Pantheon, 1959.

Ornstein, R. E., Ed. *The Psychology of Consciousness.* New York: The Viking Press, 1973.

Osborn, A. F. *Applied Imagination.* New York: Charles Scribner's, 1963.

Parnes, S. J. *Creative Behavior Guidebook.* New York: Charles Scribner's, 1967.

———. *Creativity: Unlocking Human Potential.* Buffalo: D.O.K., 1972, 1975.

———, and Harding, H., Eds. *A Source Book for Creative Thinking.* New York: Charles Scribner's, 1962.

———, and Meadow, A. "Effects of 'Brainstorming' Instructions on Creative Problem-Solving by Trained and Untrained Subjects." *Journal of Educational Psychology* 50 (1959): 171–76.

———, and Noller, R. *Toward Super-Sanity: Channeled Freedom.* Buffalo: D.O.K., 1973.

Piers, E. V., & Kirchow, E. "Productivity and Uniqueness in Continued Word Association as a Function of Subject Creativity and Stimulus Properties. *Journal of Personality* 39 (1971): 264–76.

———, & Morgan, F. T. "Effects of Free Association on Children's Ideational Fluency." *Journal of Personality* 41 (1973): 42–49.

Pines, M. "We Are Left-Brained or Right-Brained." *The New York Times Magazine,* September 9, 1973.

Prince, G. M. *The Practice of Creativity.* New York: Harper & Row, 1970.

Quereshi, M. Y. "Mental Test Performance as a Function of Payoff Conditions, Item Difficulty, and Degree of Speeding." *Journal of Applied Psychology* 44 (1960): 65–77.

Reichenbach, H. *Experience and Prediction.* Chicago: University of Chicago Press, 1938.

Rogers, C. R. "Toward a Theory of Creativity." In Anderson, H. H., Ed., *Creativity and Its Cultivation.* New York: Harper, 1959.

Rosner, S., & Abt, L. E., Eds. *The Creative Experience.* New York: Grossman, 1970.

Rugg, H. *Imagination.* New York: Harper & Row, 1963.

Sachs, H. *The Creative Unconscious,* Cambridge, Mass.: Sci-Art, 1951.

Shaffer, R. D. "Cerebral Lateralization: the Dichotomy of Consciousness." *International Journal of Symbology* 5 (1974): 7–13.

Speller, K. G., & Schumacher, G. M. "Age and Set in Creative Test Performance." *Psychological Reports* 36 (1975): 447–50.

Stein, M. I. "Creativity and Culture." In Mooney, R. L., & Razik, T. A., Eds., *Explorations in Creativity.* New York: Harper & Row, 1967.

———. *Stimulating Creativity:* Vol. 1, *Individual Procedures;* Vol. 2, *Group Procedures.* New York: Academic Press, 1974, 1975.

———. "A Transactional Approach to Creativity." In Taylor, C. W., & Barron, F., Eds., *Scientific Creativity: Its Recognition and Development.* New York: Wiley, 1963.

Storr, A. *The Dynamics of Creation.* New York: Atheneum, 1972.

Suedfeld, P., & Vernon, J. "Stress and Verbal Originality in Sensory Deprivation." *Psychological Record* 15 (1965): 567–70.

Synectics, Inc. *Making It Strange.* New York: Harper & Row Author's Manual, 1968.

Taft, R. "Creativity: Hot and Cold." *Journal of Personality* 39 (1971): 345–61.

——— & Rossiter, J. R. "The Remote Associates Test: Divergent or Convergent Thinking?" *Psychological Reports* 19 (1966): 1313–14.

Taylor, I. A. "The Nature of the Creative Process." In Smith, P., Ed., *Creativity.* New York: Hastings House, 1959.

Torrance, E. P. & Staff. *Role of Evaluation in Creative Thinking.* Revised summary report, U.S. Office of Education, Department of Health, Education, and Welfare, Cooperative Research Project No. 725. Minneapolis: Bureau of Educational Research, University of Minnesota, 1964.

Van Mondfrans, A. P., Feldhusen, J. F., Treffinger, D. J., & Ferris, D. R. "The Effects of Instructions and Response Time on Divergent Thinking Test Scores." *Psychology in the Schools* 8 (1971): 65–71.

Vernon, P. E. "A Cross-Cultural Study of Creativity Tests with 11-Year-Old Boys." *New Research in Education* 1 (1966): 135–46.

———. "Effects of Administration and Scoring on Divergent Thinking Tests." *British Journal of Educational Psychology* 41 (1971): 245–57.

Waite, R. R., Sarason, S. B., Lighthall, F. F., & Davidson, K. S. "A Study of Anxiety and Learning in Children." *Journal of Abnormal and Social Psychology* 57 (1958): 267–70.

Wallach, M. A. *The Intelligence/Creativity Distinction.* Morristown, N.J.: General Learning Press, 1971.

———, & Kogan, N. *Modes of Thinking in Young Children.* New York: Holt, Rinehart & Winston, 1965.

———, & Wing, C. *The Talented Student.* New York: Holt, Rinehart & Winston, 1969.

Wallas, G.: *The Art of Thought.* New York: Harcourt Brace, 1926.

Ward, W. C. "Creativity in Young Children." *Child Development* 39 (1968): 737–54.

———. "Rate and Uniqueness in Children's Creative Responding." *Child Development* 40 (1969): 869–78.

———, Kogan, N., & Pankove, E. "Incentive Effects in Children's Creativity." *Child Development* 43 (1972): 669–76.

219

Warren, G. H., & Luria, Z. "Evaluational Set and Creativity." *Perceptual and Motor Skills* 34 (1972): 436–38.

Williams, T. M., & Fleming, J. W. "A Methodological Study of the Relationship Between Associative Fluency and Intelligence." *Developmental Psychology* 1 (1969): 155–62.

Wertheimer, M. *Productive Thinking.* New York: Harper & Row, 1945.

Wheeler, J. A. "The Universe as Home for Man." *American Scientist* 62:6 (1974): 683–91.

Whiting, C. S. *Creative Thinking.* New York: Rheinhold, 1958.

Wild, C. "Creative and Adaptive Regression." *Journal of Personality and Social Psychology* 2 (1965): 161–69.

Wodtke, K. H. "Some Data on the Reliability and Validity of Creativity Tests at the Elementary School Level." *Educational and Psychological Measurement* 24 (1964): 399–408.

Worthen, B. R., & Clark, P. M. "Toward an Improved Measure of Remote Associational Ability." *Journal of Educational Measurement* 8 (1971): 113–23.

Yamamoto, K. "Effects of Restriction of Range and Test Unreliability on Correlation Between Measures and Creative Thinking." *British Journal of Educational Psychology* 35 (1965): 300–5.

———, & Dizney, H. F. "Effects of Three Sets of Test Instructions on Scores of an Intelligence Scale." *Educational and Psychological Measurement* 25 (1965): 87–94.

# CONTRIBUTORS

Judd Adams
Hartford, Connecticut

M.N. Andrews, Jr.
Homewood, Alabama

Victor Armbrust
Oakland, California

Iris Bass
New York, New York

James L. Baustert
Minneapolis, Minnesota

Richard Blumenthal
Fullerton, California

Mark Burger
Rochester, New York

Antonio Caseo
Zaragoya, Spain

Louisette Castonquay
Detroit, Maine

Karen Chiappinelli
Edison, New Jersey

Pamela Coffield
Columbus, Georgia

Douglas F. Cowen
Edison, New Jersey

Edward R. Cowen
Edison, New Jersey

Larry Crain
Fairway, Kansas

Thomas F. Costello
Rockville, Connecticut

Sheldon Crook
Glendale, Arizona

Norman Daitzman
Havertown, Pennsylvania

Allegra D'Adamo
New York, New York

Hilarie Davis
Rochester, New York

Roy Davis
Monticello, Illinois

Lois P. Dyer
Towson, Maryland

Babette Eddleston
Santa Monica, California

Thomas A. Farrier
Ft. Rucker, Alabama

Nancy Finman
Edison, New Jersey

Amy Franklin
Chadron, Nevada

Patricia Groom
Gravesend, Kent, England

Tim Healey
Barnsley, South Yorkshire,
England

J.H. Hendriks
Wellington, New Zealand

Howard R. Hollander
Roy, Utah

Stewart Quentin Holmes
London, England

Lida Allen Karp
Willandale, Ontario, Canada

Pam Keller
Boonton, New Jersey

Lt. Comdr. Walter H. Kopp
FPO, New York

Lis Anne Lazich
Wallingford, Pennsylvania

Eric P. Lofgren
Edgewater, New Jersey

Michael Long
Lewisville, Texas

Colin C. MacRae, Jr.
Mobile, Alabama

Frances Mairey
Southampton, England

David Carl Martin
Three Oaks, Michigan

Peter C. McGeeney
Bellshell, Lanarnshire, Scotland

Patricia Miller
Chicago, Illinois

Richard J. Murphy
Long Beach, California

Michelle Napoli
Edison, New Jersey

Martha I. Nicholas
Billings, Montana

John Nye
Tunbridge Wells, Kent, England

A.N. Pabari
Dar-es-Salaam, Tanzania

Vinod B. Patel
Matamata, New Zealand

Wilfred T. Pidduck, Jr.
Lachine, Quebec, Canada

Mary Quirke
Twickenham, Middlesex, England

Peter D. Ransome
Cambridge, England

Mitchell Ratner
Edison, New Jersey

Mary Rawlins
Bartlesville, Oklahoma

R.N. Reynolds
Gonubie, South Africa

Joshua D. Rosenblum
Edison, New Jersey

Andrew P. Ruddle
Twickenham, Middlesex, England

Jack David Seidel
Dallas, Texas

Ken Sinnott
Edison, New Jersey

Marian L. Shatto
Lititz, Pennsylvania

Raven Smith
Phillipsville, California

Bruce Steinhorn
Edison, New Jersey

Edwin Sterberc
San Jose, California

Mark Stitham
South Portland, Maine

Daryl M. Stotland
Ottawa, Ontario

Patricia A. Stotland
Ottawa, Ontario

Sandra Tomezik
Hazlet, New Jersey

Mark Torres
Edison, New Jersey

R. Laurraine Tutihasi
Webster, New York

Arnold Vagts
Santa Ana, California

J.A. Jorge J. Viaña Santa Cruz
Buenos Aires, Argentina

Jackie Ann Zurcher
Wilmot, Ohio

## ABOUT THE AUTHOR

Reid J. Daitzman was raised in Philadelphia and attended Rutgers University. He received a BA in psychology in 1969 and a PhD from the University of Delaware in 1975. After spending two years on the medical faculty at the University of Virginia, he settled in Stamford, Connecticut, where he is a consultant and psychologist in independent practice. He is the author of numerous professional papers and five books. Dr. Daitzman's dissertation was awarded the American Psychological Association Social Issues Dissertation Award for the outstanding dissertation combining scientific excellence and social relevance. In addition to his writings and practice he is the inventor of seven adult strategy board games.